A chronicle
under life presi 7/18

AND CROCODILES ARE HUNGRY AT NIGHT

a memoir by
Jack Mapanje

ayebia

An Adinkra symbol meaning
Ntesie matemasie
A symbol of knowledge and wisdom

Ayebia Clarke Publishing Limited gratefully acknowledges Arts Council SE Funding

First published in the UK in 2011by
Ayebia Clarke Publishing Limited
7 Syringa Walk
Banbury
Oxfordshire
OX16 1FR
UK
www.ayebia.co.uk

ISBN 978-0-9562401-7-0

Distributed outside Africa, Europe and the UK and exclusively in the USA by
Lynne Rienner Publishers, Inc.
1800 30th Street, Ste. 314
Boulder, CO 80301
USA
www.rienner.com

Distributed in Africa, Europe and the UK by *TURNAROUND* Publisher Services at
www.turnaround-uk.com

Co-published and distributed in Ghana with the Centre for Intellectual Renewal
56 Ringway Estate, Osu, Accra, Ghana
www.cir.com

British Library Cataloguing-in-Publication Data
Cover Design: Amanda Carroll / www.millipedia.co.uk
Illustration: Shutterstock
Photographs of Jack Mapanje © David Clarke at Ayebia Clarke Publishing Ltd.
Typeset by FiSH Books, Enfield, Middlesex, UK
Printed and bound by CPI Group (UK) Ltd, Croydon, CR0 4YY

Available from www.ayebia.co.uk or email info@ayebia.co.uk
Distributed in Africa, Europe, UK by *TURNAROUND* at www.turnaround-uk.com
Distributed in Southern Africa by Book Promotions (PTY) Cape Town, South Africa
For Enquiries: enquiries@bookpro.co.za or For Orders contact: orders@bookpro.co.za

The Publisher wishes to acknowledge the support of Arts Council SE Funding

Contents

Dedication

To the cellmates with whom I suffered at Mikuyu prison; to the brave young man from Chancellor College, University of Malawi, who said he had written a play called *The Trial of Jack Mapanje*, depicting the trial I never had; to other Malawian youths who are desperate to know the past, which Banda's minions have subtly erased from the nation's memory or people's consciousness; I hope the events I have selected will satisfy the spirit of your inquisitive minds.

I dedicate this narrative to the unflinching resilience, solidarity, love, support and infectious humour of Mercy, my wife and Judith, Lunda and Likambale, our children. I cannot adequately thank Landeg White, David Kerr and Fr Pat O'Malley for staking their energy, time and honour in the campaign that eventually liberated not just me but Malawi from the claws of Banda and his cabal – this narrative does not even begin to do justice to the immeasurable humanity, camaraderie and devotion of the many friends, compatriots, colleagues, strangers and linguistics, literature and human rights organisations they involved in the struggle for my release including PEN International, Amnesty International, Africa Watch, Human Rights Watch and others.

Acknowledgements

This memoir has gone through agonising metamorphoses at the various educational institutions where I taught or stayed as a writer in residence. I would like to acknowledge gratefully the time and space that colleagues and students offered me at the African Studies Centre of the University of Leiden, the Netherlands; the School of English, University of Leeds; the Faculty of Humanities, University College Cork, the Republic of Ireland; and the School of English, Newcastle University. The charm of the director, Robert Woof, and his staff at Dove Cottage, The Wordsworth Trust, Grasmere, Cumbria was inspirational.

I would also like to thank the editors of the *Times Literary Supplement*, *Stand Magazine*, *Index-on-Censorship Magazine*, *Sable Literature Magazine*, *Light Transports -Commutes*, Route Press and the bulletin of International PEN Writers in Prison Committee, Bellagio, Italy, where excerpts of this memoir first appeared.

For small grants that facilitated my research I am indebted to the Arts Council of England, Yorkshire and the British Academy, London. For enabling me to complete the write-up with peace of mind, grateful thanks to Eileen Gunn and her committee at the Royal Literary Fund, London; Paula Johnson and her committee at the Society of Authors, London; and the Faculty of Arts at York St John University. Many thanks to John Short, Patrick Culbertson and Steve Dearden for their incisive comments on the original manuscript of this memoir; and a special hug to my publishers David and Nana Ayebia Clarke MBE, the cover designer Amanda Carroll and the editors Penny Ormerod and Bruce Clarke for their unwavering support and commitment to this book. The responsibility for any shortcomings is mine.

Foreword

I have known Jack Mapanje for nearly forty years. He was a lecturer when I was a student at Chancellor College, the University of Malawi. I remember him fondly for his warmth, wit, charm, and that endearing smile of his; for his sharp intellect, for that incisive, exquisite poetic voice the world has come to know and admire since he published his first collection of poetry, *Of Chameleons and Gods*, in 1981. He was our inspiration, our role model for the engaged life of the mind, for a principled way of living, for the simple dignity of being a conscious and critical citizen under a ruthless, banal dictatorship. His humane and democratic passions and commitments were guided by the fact that he loved his nation so deeply. For that he paid a high price: detention without trial for 3 years, 7 months, 16 days and more than 12 hours.

Of course, he was never told why he was detained and was never tried. He was just picked up one day while having lunch with a friend and tossed into prison, left there to rot for years and then released unceremoniously without explanation, without apology, let alone compensation. This powerful, engrossing and beautifully written memoir of his arrest and prison life offers us an unsettling and searing indictment of the depraved Banda dictatorship, its unimaginable wastage of the lives and possibilities of its people, and its monstrous moral and political bankruptcy. Banda's Malawi, like so many postcolonial African dictatorships, aborted the nationalist dreams of independence for democracy and development. It was a land of pervasive fear and insecurity, where stupefying terror and silence reigned, where everyone suspected everyone else, where people policed each other, which allowed them the perverse pathologies and pleasures of settling their real and imagined differences and jealousies by spying on each other.

In this memoir we see the depravity of this grotesque dictatorship in all its brutality and pettiness. The detainees are kept in unimaginable squalor and deprived of the most elementary human rights enshrined in international law. They are huddled together in filthy, congested cells, fed unhealthy gruel, denied medical care and subjected to routine humiliating searches. The purpose of all this calculated cruelty is to break their dignity and spirits, to dehumanise them. As I read the memoir, my blood boiled in anger and deep sadness at the depths my country sank to in its political decadence and debilitation. At the turn of the 1980s, I interviewed several former detainees when I was writing my novel, *Smouldering Charcoal*, a third of which is set in a detention camp, but Mapanje brings the grim realities of prison to life with the poignancy and power that only a fine poet and writer can.

The memoir is a tribute to the endurance of the human spirit, to the indomitable courage of Mapanje and his fellow detainees, who – in their fortitude, creativity and solidarity – continuously subverted the regime's fantasies of omniscient power and the terrorising technologies of prison surveillance. One marvels at their efforts to retain dignity out of their relentless brutalisation, to maintain surreptitious contacts with the outside world, to create order out of the involuntary turmoil of their lives. One admires their refusal to become dehumanised and depoliticised, their unflinching conviction in their innocence and hope in their eventual freedom. One reads with profound awe for these men as they tell each other redemptive stories, try to keep their surroundings habitable, prepare and share food, tend to plants and cherish the colourful sights of butterflies, dragonflies, bumblebees, moths and flying geese. Mapanje waxes lyrical as he peeps at the blue skies and catches glimpses of the extraordinary ordinariness of the outside world.

The memoir is a moving celebration of the complexity of the human condition even under the most harrowing of circumstances. We see prison guards and officials some who are cruel, cynical and others who are caring. We encounter prisoners who are courageous, selfless, boisterous and opinionated. We are shown moments of cohesion and conviviality as well as discord and despair. There are all those touching, brief intimacies of reunion with family, of the restorative connectedness to loved ones, followed by agonising stretches of loneliness and longing. The reader is captivated by the periodic and increasingly subversive intrusions of the outside world into the suffocating and cloistered world of the prison as the international campaign for Mapanje's release gathers momentum and the political landscape of Southern Africa shakes and shifts with the momentous release of Nelson Mandela and the implosion of apartheid, a regime to which Banda's feckless dictatorship was shamefully allied.

The memoir unveils Mapanje's personal and professional lives compellingly and lucidly as he reflects on what may have led to his detention without trial. He marshals memories of his youth growing up in rural Malawi, followed by his life as an undergraduate student at the country's then only university and later as a graduate student at the University of London, his rise to fame as an internationally renowned poet, and as a highly respected linguist in Southern Africa. I was struck by his courage in naming names of those who may have connived in his arrest, most of them colleagues at the University of Malawi. This is a sad testimony to the complicity of intellectuals in the construction and reproduction of tyranny in our societies.

As the story of his life unfolds, his deep humility, wiry humour and endearing humanity shine through making his detention without trial all the more inexplicable and inexcusable. The narrative derives its distinctive narrative force from the interspersion of poetry he wrote in prison. Learning of the events that inspired some of the poems enriches the reader's understanding of his prison poetry collection, *The Chattering Wagtails of Mikuyu Prison*. The reader shares with Mapanje his stunned joy when he is finally released, but the sense of bewilderment, even bitterness at all those wasted years, the lost opportunities, lingers and the trepidation about the future lurks in the background.

Mapanje's release was facilitated by the international campaign, which he records brilliantly, underscoring the power of transnational solidarity in human rights campaigns. He quotes Ngũgĩ wa Thiong'o, who once wrote about his own experience as a political detainee: "As a person who has been in detention myself and whose final release was as a result of international pressure, I know how important even the smallest one-line letter of appeal can be". Mapanje writes in astonishment as he comes to learn of the scale of the campaign led by Ngũgĩ wa Thiong'o, Wole Soyinka and several other prominent African writers, as well as British, American and Canadian writers, scholars and human rights organisations for his release.

The book could not be published at a better time. Mapanje's release presaged the rise of the democratic movement in Malawi, the intensification of the struggles for the "second independence", which led to the collapse of the Banda dictatorship in 1994. But, as with the first independence arising out of the nationalist struggles against colonialism, Africa's wily dictators wearing ill-fitting democratic garbs have learned to manoeuvre democratic politics to their advantage. In Malawi, as in many countries touched by the winds of democratic change in the 1990s, democracy has yet to establish firm roots. Indeed, it seems to be taking a retreat.

One could argue that from 1994, Malawi's new democracy amounted to little more than the recycling of factions of the same bankrupt political class and since then elections have increasingly been marred by harassment and intimidation of the opposition, violence, vote-rigging and human rights abuses, not to mention third-term campaigns. President Bakili Muluzi, who succeeded President Hastings Banda, unsuccessfully sought to stay beyond the constitutional limit of two terms. When that failed he selected a relative to succeed him, current President Bingu wa Mutharika, who is shamelessly trying to ensure succession by his brother.

Mapanje's book is a stark warning against the madness and horrendous human costs of dictatorships. It should be read by every freedom-loving African and friends of Africa and the proponents of freedom everywhere, committed to the enduring and inseparable triple dreams of *uhuru* – democracy, development and self-determination.

Paul Tiyambe Zeleza
Los Angeles, April 20, 2011.

Book One
The Hell-Hole

1

Crocodiles

25 September 1987, Friday. Payday. When payday falls on a Friday, do not venture out, claims one Zomba township saying. The lean crocodiles that protect the life president of Malawi, Dr Hastings Kamuzu Banda, and the vicious snakes of his inner circle, will be prowling about the dry land, looking to crack the brittle bones of their presumed political enemies. I dismiss this as another of the simplistic clichés that characterise and sustain our despotic times. I pride myself that I am neither gullible nor am I my president's or his cabal's political enemy. So quite oblivious of these and other fears, I grab my car keys, say goodbye to my fragile mother, and first head for Zomba market, where I owe a woman her dues for the vegetables and fruit I borrow from her stall every month; then for my office, to consult colleagues about the kind of reception we should offer the new lecturer who has joined the English department from Australia. With hope for another bright day, I embrace the cool fresh air outside my university house, which stands firmly under the belly of the massive Zomba plateau. Sprawling in the distance before me are Chirunga campus, the police headquarters, St Mary's township, and beyond that the slums of Three Miles village with their huts flung like abandoned turtles in the hills that lead to Blantyre, Malawi's commercial capital city.

Your favourite route along the chipped, narrow and winding tarmac is covered in the morning mist, which should lift when the sun is above the head. Forget the bumps and potholes. Zomba town council will never sort those out, whatever tax you pay. Let the silver brooks, streams, torrents gurgle, slither and cascade past gullies, rocks and woods, snaking down to become Mulungusi, Mponda, Bwaila, Likangala rivers and the bridges, some of which you will cross later. Zomba plateau itself feels reassuringly solid as you manoeuvre around the potholes, noting the special places lodged permanently in memory: ESCOM offices, the Post Office, the Parliament Buildings, The Government Hostel, the Malawi Examinations and Testing Board building, the Top Hospital, the vice-chancellor's house, the State House, Zomba Gymkhana Club and the famous Kandodo superstore. Note the 'veranda market' at Kandodo, crowded with vendors and others shouting competitive prices for their fresh pineapples, paw-paws, bananas and basketfuls of strawberries. Note the sellers of palm-leaf hats, mats, batiks and wooden carvings, harassing prospective university customers from every angle – it's Friday and payday!

Purple and red flowers from jacaranda and flamboyant trees respectively carpet the avenues of the town as they have done from time out of mind. Muslims in white robes are shuffling towards the town's imposing mosque, responding to the *muezzin* who must have already summoned worshippers to Friday prayers. The streets are plagued with their everlasting, sometimes aggressive beggars – the town and its market hustle and bustle, with colourful people buying and selling their wares. It's a typical Friday on a typical university payday in a typical university town. Park your car near the market's main gate and walk in. But your fruit-and-vegetables woman has not come today. Says the neighbour next to her stall: "You might have to come back later in the day or week." She suggests, "I'll tell her you've been and will come again later, unless you want to leave with me whatever you owe her," she says grinning cheekily at you. Nothing untoward at the office either. The new member of staff is happy with his university house and the office he has been offered. You are secretly pleased that you have a fellow linguist with whom you can share your course in pragmatics. The dates for departmental meetings and the rest of the 'administrivia' – as poet and colleague Steve Chimombo calls them – required under the bureaucracy of the one and only president for life are duly done. God's in his heaven, all's fine with the world below – the devil is temporarily locked up in Hades and daren't disturb the life president's cornerstones of unity, loyalty, discipline and obedience upon which this country, the so-called warm heart of Africa, was founded.

The phone at my desk rings. I jump for the receiver. It's Judith at the other end of the line. "Dad," she says, "Lunda, Lika and I are back from the lake, safe and sound; uncle's family in Mangochi are sending their love; they want us to visit them again; your home district is hot but fine; we've brought your favourite fish; lunch will be ready soon; but we'll wait for you so we can tell you all about it." She stops. I tell her I won't take long; I will only make a whistle-stop at the bank – thinking of water and electricity bills, which must be paid before the salary runs out. But outside the Commercial Bank of Malawi a colleague and fellow writer, Anthony Nazombe, has another proposition: "It's payday; a treat; fish and chips; at Zomba Gymkhana Club; on me," he says cheerfully. I invite him home instead, where lunch will be ready and the children will be waiting for me. Anthony suggests that we get to the children later and declares: "I too would like to fry fresh *chambo* tonight; I am sure godson Lika has brought one *tilapia* from the lake for me," he concludes. I feel reluctantly persuaded, though I know Lunda will be disappointed if we are late for lunch.

The bar overlooking the ex-colonial cricket pitch at Zomba Gymkhana Club is almost deserted when we arrive – nobody plays cricket here anymore, occasional football and athletic competitions for schools, yes. Apart from the barman and a soldier perched on a stool near the counter, we are the only customers present. We wash down the delicacies with our tipples, gags and other habits, some acquired in our student days in Sheffield and London respectively. Then Anthony makes a discovery: "Do you see what I see? Queen Victoria missing from the bar shelf!" We laugh and laugh with full hearts. For many years the papier-mâché monarch has reigned over lesser relics of the British Empire – golf, tennis, squash, snooker, darts and football trophies – to which prison the blooming woman has been sent, when and why, we cannot tell. But a ruder voice cuts through our musings and laughter. "Anyone here by the name of Mapanje?" the fellow asks earnestly. "Dr Jack Mapanje?" he repeats. Anthony and I look at each other in silence. Trouble? Someone selling curios and carvings outside the club, and trying to entice university customers? It's payday. Could be anything. The enquirer, wearing a dark blue blazer and formidable black boots, walks away ponderously like a tired mask dancer, disappointed. He returns after a few minutes, to put the question directly to us a second and third time, his tone getting more sarcastic each time.

"Supposing I was?" I answer back irritated by his arrogance.

"There's a gentleman in the golfers' bar next door who would like to see you," he replies, with an air of hastily gathered authority.

Since the British surrendered Nyasaland Protectorate to us after the struggle for independence, this club has been well patronised by the locals, mostly from the university, the army and the police; bars are intact, set aside for golf, tennis, cricket, football, darts, snooker players and others to relax after their games or after work. But who wants to see me? And why doesn't he just come straight to me instead of going through this fellow? Isn't it the monkey that goes to the mountain, not the other way around? As I recall the famous maxim. And why the golfers' bar when I do not play golf myself? Anthony and I reluctantly stand up and walk towards the bar next door – where ha! My heart sinks into my boots, and begins to thump. It's the eastern division commissioner of police! Everyone recognises him, very few know his name, no-one wants to find out; but there he is spruced up in full commissioner regalia, perched on one of the tall stools, his polished cane under his left arm, his cap still on, his perfectly ironed khaki uniform looking impeccable, his front buttons polished clean – altogether standing as if he was about to order a drink. What's he doing in his awesome outfit in the deserted golfers' bar? The whiff of stale beer that hits my nose offers no answer. The dartboard on the wall is shut; the empty chairs are heaped one on top of another; the room, which is typified by a calm and cheerful atmosphere, looks cowed – was there another chair-throwing fight among the lads last night? What does the commissioner want me for? What wrong have I done him or anybody? These and other thoughts racing through my quizzical mind are suddenly interrupted:

"Are you, Dr Jack Mapanje?" the commissioner asks authoritatively.

"Yes," I answer boldly, refusing to be subdued.

With the cane under his arm he points to the door where we must all troop out. Pointing with a stick where people should go is rude, isn't it? I ask myself. Anthony stops at the gate and watches me follow the commissioner alone. As he begins to sprint homeward, I stumble over the broken bricks that segment each car parking area in the dusty car park. I almost fall where the police vehicle is standing next to my car.

"You are Dr Jack Mapanje, head of the English department, Chancellor College, University of Malawi?" the commissioner asks again, his tone suggesting this is not a question but a statement of fact.

"I am," I reply firmly.

"We've been directed by his excellency, the life president, the Ngwazi Dr H. Kamuzu Banda, to arrest you."

"But I do not know his excellency the life president...what I mean is...I know his excellency the life president is his excellency the life president of this country and the chancellor of the university where I teach...but I do not remember doing him any wrong that would deserve..."

"Is that so?" He cuts in very dryly. "We'll give you permission to tell your story when the 'higher authorities' see you later." His tone is contemptuous. "Have you brought the handcuffs?" He barks at one of his minions. The fellow in the dark blue blazer comes forward and first shrugs his shoulders at his boss in respect, then he says: "Yeesaa!" "Show him," comes out the order. Suddenly more than four officers in plain clothes, who must have been waiting in the vehicle for this moment, jump down and surround me. I feel the cuffs bite my wrists. One fellow dips his barbarian hands into my trouser pockets to fish out my car keys. I am manhandled into the back of their vehicle and rescue my spectacles in time as the vehicle accelerates at break-neck speed out of the car park towards Kandodo superstore. The wheels squeal to a sudden halt opposite the store; we turn left into Kamuzu Highway, where I see Anthony sprinting down the road towards Mponda Bridge, over which we madly accelerate, and turn right into Chancellor College Road. The speed with which we cover the mile-long distance is reminiscent of the 1959 State of Emergency, during our struggle for independence, when British colonial jeeps seemed to have a spiteful and threatening personality of their own. And, as if we were avoiding a head-on collision, the vehicle squeaks hard and loud as we stop at Chancellor College car park.

The officers' precision as they jump out, flank me, left and right and frog-march me towards the college reception, is remarkable. The shackles begin to blister my wrists. My knees wobble. I stumble past the college reception to the full view of frightened and embarrassed colleagues, administrative and support staff. When blood begins to flow as the cuffs cut into my raw flesh I remember where we believed such 'cutting-edge' handcuffs came from: Sheffield in the UK, the apartheid regime in South Africa or Israel; but that's neither here nor there, now. I remember a robber who was apprehended in our village once. The whole village confronted him, shouting, spitting and hissing, their eyes popping out, their faces blacker with anger than I had ever known them. I can imagine what he must have felt, though I am neither a robber nor have I wronged my country, my president, my university or anybody, to my knowledge. The commissioner is given the bunch of keys that one of his underlings took from my pocket; he tries one key after another to open the door to my office until he finds the right one. He enters the office, sits at my desk and begins ferociously slamming the drawers open and shut, open and shut, looking for goodness knows what. I let myself sit in the visitor's chair facing the commissioner as he flicks through the contents of the drawers he is slamming shut. His sycophants have inhabited the four corners of the little office, which is full of books – on the table, on the floor, on the chairs, everywhere, some criss-crossed and heaped on the shelves, others strewn on the floor. There is a heap of planks in the corner, too, with which the college maintenance department had been planning to build shelves for the books to ease storage. The reckless mix of the books and planks infuriates the commissioner:

"What kind of an office is this?" He spits out angrily. "How could anyone possibly work in this mess, this confusion?"

Then, changing his tone, he announces more to himself than to his junior officers:

"And I was going on leave today, you know. Is this what I have to see to first, before taking my leave? Why? What kind of a country is this?"

His officers refuse to be drawn in to their master's observations about the kind of country this is or the leave he should have begun; they merely glare at the books as if they were personal enemies. In this country ignorance may not be bliss, but can often be safer than knowledge. I wonder what these fellows are looking for; are these books connected to my arrest? The department was instrumental in trying to solve a crisis over the shortage of student textbooks in literature. In their boundless wisdom, the International Monetary Fund (IMF) pushing their structural adjustment programmes to Third World countries had directed that Banda's government should impose fees on university students as one precondition for bailing out the country's economy. The Chancellor College principal Zimani Kadzamira and university registrar Robert Mbaya called for an academic college staff meeting to discuss the implications of the directives for students. Most lecturers objected to the IMF's belated form of economic re-colonisation and urged the university not to accept the imposition of the fees, particularly for the poor students, who tended to be the brightest. We argued that the introduction of fees would disadvantage many students; that meritocracy which we bragged about, as being fundamental to our educational system would disappear; and that education in general would become the preserve of the rich. Even if some students could scrape together the fees with help from their poor parents or benefactors, they would be crippled by having to buy the literature texts they could not do without. We lost the argument. Predictably. Instead we established a fund to which all academic staff pledged to contribute a certain sum every month – the amount was to be deducted from our salaries at source by the university's finance officer. Some colleagues, who would have gladly wanted the literature section of the English department to close because they believed it was the most disloyal to Banda's government, found good support in the IMF directives, which had one far-reaching implication for us – the literature section of the department would be reduced considerably and probably eventually close, leaving literature colleagues without employment – a situation we could not stomach.

As I had just been invited to the Second Stockholm Conference of African Writers in Uppsala, Sweden, I decided to seek donations of textbooks for our students. The department listed the titles of the literature texts we used in our courses, and I used the few days in transit in the UK to look for donors. I persuaded Liz Moloney of the British Council in London and Rosalind Richards of the Ntchima Trust in York, who generously bought the books we needed. These are the books that the commissioner and his dogsbodies are trampling on without restraint. We now have twenty-five copies of each text, and for the next fifteen years we will offer students five literature courses without their having to buy the texts they require. The students will simply borrow them from the office shelves, and with staff supervision, return them at the end of each course, for use by other students the following year. If they wear out, the bookbinding section of the university library has promised to bind them for us. These books were due to be officially presented to the department by representatives of the British Council and the Ntchima Trust. With me now arrested that programme will have to be deferred. Colleagues from other departments who were envious of our small achievement will probably be happy that my arrest will overshadow what we have accomplished for students. But the question still remains: Why are they arresting me now? Is this the kind of treachery that's punishable by arrest? The commissioner's frantic opening and shutting of the drawers provides no clue. And yet I must do something, despite my shackled hands. I must alert Lyscar Chisale, the department's secretary, next door and tell her what's happening. I must ensure that she sees the cuffs and tells my wife later about what's happened. I chuckle and shout her name. She knocks on the door, opens it and asks:

"You called, sir?"

The commissioner and his gofers stop their search to watch what game I intend to play.

"Yes," I reply, and pointing at my visitors with both hands so she can see without ambiguity that I have been chained, I instruct her: "In case these gentlemen want to search the files of staff members, could you please co-operate? Give them my file to examine too."

"Yes, sir", she answers, closing the door calmly, patently subdued. I hear her ringing a friend and speaking in chiBemba, a Zambian language which only a few Malawians in the university understand. I do not know to whom she is telling my story or what to infer from this, but I know that she will eventually tell my wife about the chains she has seen. After about an hour of their searching my office, I am told that two officers will continue here, while the commissioner and the rest of his crew dash for my house. I find myself, still handcuffed, being pushed down the stairs, past frightened colleagues, administrators and support staff, into the police vehicle waiting at the college car park. The mad race starts up again, their vehicle crossing Mulungusi brook, trundling up the hill, turning right, and then second left, heading for my house on 11 Mulungusi Avenue.

2
Mother

Mother, nearly eighty, sitting on the veranda, is weaving when we arrive. At the sight of her son in cuffs, led by the plain-clothes policemen and their overdressed commissioner, she drops her palm leaf mat in horror, cries out to her grandchildren playing in their bedroom to come out and see daddy; but her voice trails and dries out. She is shocked to see me being roughed up and pushed past the dining room. I am mortified when I see the lunch I was supposed to have had with my children still untouched on the table. Mother tries to stand up but collapses beside her wooden Zimmer frame, chin in hand, tears rolling down her lined face, and despairing, she mutters to herself:

"I've never seen any of my children or relatives treated in this humiliating manner before, even during the colonial times."

The commissioner and his thugs crash into the living room instead, pulling down my books from the shelves, and piling in one mess in the corner the newspapers I had kept neatly on the shelf. They go for the hi-fi where the albums spin on the living room floor like my childhood tops. Having heard the noise from the tumbling of books and records, Mother's grandchildren – aged eleven, ten and five-and-a-half – are on the scene. They tremble when they see their dad in cuffs. They simply cannot understand what's happening. Who could? Not even I.

Their mother, Mercy, is on a community nursing course in Lilongwe, the capital city, about two hundred miles from here. They mill nervously around their granny, confused, not knowing what to do or say; tears begin running down their cheeks when

12

they see my shackled hands. After hurling everything on the floor, the officers push me into the children's bedroom, where they disperse their toys and rip out their pillows and mattresses – God knows what they are looking for. It's an orgy of destruction that they create, panting noisily as if they were killing an animal. They drag me to the toilet, flush it, open the cistern, watch it fill up with water, and flush it again. They are obviously looking for something. A gun? Would I be so stupid as to hide it here? I howl my protest when they push their way into Mother's bedroom. It's taboo of the highest order to enter another person's mother's bedroom, let alone search it, but they trash the taboo with a kind of demonic glee. We return to the living room where they face Mother's anger:

"Why are you people scattering this peaceful house so? What wrong has my son done? Leave him alone. Take me and kill me instead, you insensitive men!"

Lika joins Mother: "Don't touch that toy police van my dad brought me from Harare; look at them; the animals!"

"Shut up you two! Do you want to be arrested too?" The officers threaten them. Mother challenges them:

"Why don't you do that? Why don't you arrest me and kill me? I am already dead anyway!"

They push me into our bedroom where they create more havoc.

"That's my academic work; please do not touch it!" I hear myself declaring without paying due regard to what these fellows are capable of doing. One of them gives me bloodshot eyes. I ignore him and recall that I was going to use the photocopies of the essays, articles and draft chapters in the publication of a textbook on Bantu languages – a project I had been working on for some time. As originator and chairperson of the Linguistics Association for SADCC Universities, LASU – an association for the nine universities of Africa south of the Sahara minus the universities in apartheid South Africa, I was writing a leading article on the interpretation of tense and aspect in Bantu languages for the anthology whose central essay was tracing 'The

Ghost of Temporal Distance: The Relevance – Theoretic Approach'. I remember arguing in it that in actual speech some morphological markers of past, present and future time in Bantu languages often rendered vacuous the time they encoded; that is, the one-to-one correspondence between the marker and the time they marked was often violated in actual use or speech. I feel heartbroken when I watch how these fools throw into one heap such precious research. The book itself was going to be published by SADCC university press, which was another two million US dollar project originally proposed by Emmanuel Ngara of Zimbabwe University and myself. Essentially, LASU was going to establish the press in order to alleviate the problem of expensive textbooks for the universities of the region. And NORAD and SAREC, the research sections of the Norwegian and Sweden governments respectively, had made early indication that they would finance the project if Ngara and I directed it. But my being involved in such regional projects might have displeased some 'higher authority', which is probably why I am being arrested today – here the authorities resent our involvement in regional projects because they draw local attention away from them.

My heart almost stops when one fellow finds some pamphlets I had brought back from the Second Stockholm Conference of African Writers in 1985. These link the Tanzanian government's socialist programme with the struggle against apartheid in South Africa by the African National Congress (ANC). Life president Banda has declared publicly that any enemy of the South African apartheid regime is his enemy – notwithstanding the official policy of the Organisation of African Unity (OAU) to the contrary. It would be a bitter pill to swallow if I were jailed or killed for opposing apartheid so far away from South Africa. Fortunately, either the significance of the pamphlets is not recognised or they simply ignore the ANC bumf, adding it to the general rubbish heap they have created at the door. I breathe a sigh of relief. But my fear returns when I recall the paper 'Censoring the African Poem: personal reflections' that I presented orally at the Stockholm Conference. In it I had discussed the problems of censorship in

14

Malawi and quoted the Polish novelist Tadeusz Konwicki to the effect that censorship forced the writer to use symbols and metaphors that raised the general standard of one's writing. I had cherished the thought that Banda's censorship board might have improved the level of my poems – not the kind of tale dictators and their henchpeople find funny. But the paper could spell danger if they found it in the office files, though I doubt Lyscar would expose it to these fellows so easily. I also remember my book of poems *Of Chameleons and Gods*, officially 'withdrawn from public circulation' by the censorship board in June 1985. But they won't find a copy of that here. The only copy I have is buried in the confusion of books at the office.

From our bedroom their vandal haul is two passports – my wife's and mine – and a novel, *Detainee*, by Legson Kayira, which is banned because the author is exiled in London and is considered one of Banda's political opponents. As these characters tear up our pillows and mattresses looking for whatever, I begin to get worried, very worried. I begin to think about what I should do and discover I cannot do very much. But I can think; they cannot stop that! In case they drag me to one of their corrupt courts, I need to prepare and rehearse my defence, I tell myself. As indicated by our passports, I hope to claim, my wife and I have never visited communist or socialist countries in Africa or abroad. I kept the banned novel in our bedroom in order to protect the public from the author's rebel ideas. I was taking it to the National Archives, where all banned books have to be surrendered by heads of departments of all institutions in this country. But though I believe that there is no harm in preparing for such a defence, I fear that it won't wash with our stubborn authorities.

After about an hour of searching inside and outside my house they drag me with them to see the higher authorities at the southern region police headquarters in Blantyre. Before we set off Anthony Nazombe arrives with Steve Chimombo, the previous head of the English department. Anthony must have broken the national sprint record to have found Steve and got to my house in time. I break away from my captors, dash to my colleagues, still chained, and before the officers stop me, I tell them I am being taken to the police headquarters in Blantyre, and beg them to welcome the new lecturer from Australia with open arms, and to do nothing rash that might make it difficult for students to continue with their education; they should do nothing that might force the authorities to sack them from their jobs. It's all a silly mistake; everything would be back to normal; I would be vindicated; I am not the first academic to be arrested anyway, I claim. Just then Fr Pat O'Malley of St. Patrick's Irish Missionaries, the Republic of Ireland, a colleague in the department and a close family friend, arrives. We are already deeply indebted to him for his kind visits in the absence of my wife. I bid him hello and goodbye unambiguously displaying my cuffed hands to him. And though I do not know it then, I will owe much, much more to him in the future – perhaps even my life.

So, I lift my shackled hands in a pathetic farewell to my weeping children, my sobbing Mother and my scared and embarrassed colleagues. We depart, stopping in town at Oilcom Petrol Station to fill up and pick up a young fellow whose English accent is South African – he must be one of the agents they use to find out about what we do and say across our country's borders. After covering about thirty miles at break-neck speed, the vehicle squeaks to a sudden halt at Mbulumbuzi market, near Chiradzulu Mountain. We were about to kill a dozen goats crossing the road. When the mad speed resumes, I begin to ask myself: What crime have I committed? Are they really taking me to the southern region police headquarters to see the higher authorities? Or are we going to the dingy offices of the Malawi Congress Party headquarters, where Banda's presumed political opponents are interrogated and tortured to death? Is this how politicians Aaron Gadama, Dick Matenje, David Chiwanga and Twaibu Sangala were taken? Is this how they met their death? Have I really become Banda's political opponent? What kind of death will I suffer today? And why? We drive past Limbe Catholic Cathedral on the right, join the road that links Limbe township to Blantyre township, drive through the Independence Arch, the football stadium on the right, the High Court on the left, followed by the Malawi Broadcasting Corporation, until we finally arrive at the southern region police headquarters, which is wedged between the radio station and the Polytechnic of the University of Malawi.

3

Waiting for Death

The security officers made me run up the stairs to the second floor of this building still manacled. And pushing me into this dismal windowless waiting room that stinks of stale tobacco, they have made off to their offices, leaving me panting, sweating and gutted. At least they have removed the cuffs, though whether I have come here to be interrogated, murdered or both, I have no idea. All I hear around me are doors banging, boots knocking, laughter cracking and cries of frightened souls probably being tortured to death in distant rooms. Or am I dreaming about them? Is it a tape recording of these that I hear? Whatever it is, the eerie atmosphere created by the noises in the rooms above, below and around me would rupture any calm mind. The truth is I am scared. And I can't think straight. I hear a continuous sharp shrill of cicadas and crickets in my head. My heart is thumping fast too. I cannot concentrate. The awe-inspiring and mind-fracturing laughter of hyenas that I once heard when I walked past village graveyards at night was nothing compared to this. Is this what happens when one is abducted for political reasons and awaits torture, imprisonment or death? And what crime could I have committed to deserve this? The blisters around my wrists continue to weep, the skin to break at mere touch.

When I dig deeper in memory for the crimes I could have committed against my country, my president, my university or anyone in authority for me to be arrested, I find I might have committed what can only be called 'amorphous' crimes. These are speculative stories culled from a complex web of spies, agents and

18

informers of president Banda and his cohort, claiming that I am a potential 'dissident' or their political opponent. It suddenly dawns on me at this point that I might be in the security headquarters whose rooms we used to call 'Banda's abattoirs'! I am probably waiting to be 'accidentalised'; that is, to be turned into an accident! Besides, I am alone. This is dangerous. I must find something better to occupy my mind. And soon. Before I crack up. Rubbing my hands silly won't help. The newspapers and magazines on their wobbly stool are dated. I won't touch them again. Too dusty. What's the use of reading on 25 September 1987 about the resignation of US president Nixon as reported in *Time* magazine of many years ago? Anyway, nobody abducted, driven more than forty-two miles at break-neck speed, expecting to be interrogated, would be in the mood to read anything. This is torture. My captors are probably watching every twitch I am making by remote control – the buggers!

Today the public houses will be full of stale jokes: another one bites the dust; another has met his 'orality justice' of our 'orality politics'; and many others. The truth, of course, is that Banda, his coterie and their security officers have been destroying whatever written traditions the British might have left behind. They've been creating a kind of oral culture where documentary evidence for the crimes that their death squads commit against innocent people are carefully erased from files and memory. So that when they are brought to book in the distant future – should political changes happen with the grace of God – there should be no concrete evidence to incriminate them for their wrongs. Banda and his cabal have become *the law, the judge and the jury* in this country. That's a fact. And when people are arrested, imprisoned, murdered, exiled or deported for security reasons in this country, it is not Banda's despotic politics that are at fault; it is not the fault of the clique that disperses his authority; it is the fault of the victims themselves. Those exercising power under Banda's patronage do not see themselves as possible agents of social and political change for the betterment of ordinary people's lives; they do not consider it their duty to explain their actions to their subjects; they are not accountable to anyone; only they know what is best for us, for the university or for the institution where we work, or for the country. In the political arenas our leaders audaciously declare that whoever is arrested must know the reasons for his arrest; the security officers could not have apprehended them for nothing; there is no smoke without fire. That's the kind of justice we suffer everyday. Today I will be lucky if the officers take me to their corrupt traditional courts to try and charge me with whatever offence they will invent.

Do not ask me where we got this kind of arrogance. We could not have inherited it from our ancestors. We could not have got it from the British who colonised us. No. This horror that we endure is of Banda's own creation, obviously encouraged by his vicious faction, currently the Kadzamira-Tembo family. Our problems started after the cabinet crisis, which happened only weeks after we attained independence from Britain. The then Prime Minister, Hastings Kamuzu Banda, developed the habit of calling his cabinet colleagues 'my boys' in parliament, on political platforms, everywhere. He disagreed with his minister of foreign affairs, Kanyama Chiume, who wanted to open diplomatic relations with Communist China and the USSR after achieving our self-rule and independence. Banda wanted to introduce fees for hospital treatment – the famous tickey charges (threepenny charges), of which his cabinet colleagues did not approve. He wanted his cabinet colleagues to report to him how they ran their ministries; and above all, he adopted the very 'divide and rule' philosophy that the British had used to rule Nyasaland Protectorate. All in all, he wanted to continue to act as he had done during our struggle for liberation from the British. He avoided serious discussion or debate on these and other important matters, which culminated in his sacking six of his dissenting cabinet ministers, causing what has become known as the 'cabinet crisis'. Now even the lawyers, who are supposed to defend whoever is presumed to be a political opponent, have been rendered impotent. They prefer to cry foul from the safety of their homes, helplessly wondering when our ugly politics would change. For instance, no lawyer will defend me against this abduction; he simply will not dare; if he tried he would be accused of conspiring with the president's political opponents and sent where I will eventually end up after this.

Even worse my employers will not inform my family about my abduction. When the Special Branch searched my office, principal Zimani Kadzamira conveniently disappeared from his office. He will not tell my wife what his sister at the state house has told him about my abduction. Should he find it necessary to explain himself to my colleagues, the clichés he will use are predictable: this is a political matter; no principal can do anything about it; I hear he wrote rude poems about the higher authorities; I gather his teaching was subversive; I understand he boasted about having overseas contacts; he wanted to take over my job as principal; the police say he was another brat who bit the finger that fed him; he was boasting about travelling too freely across the country's borders, where he told tales that tarnished the image of the country to outsiders; he was washing his country's linen in public; he was a traitor – the list is endless.

Should I be lucky enough to end up in prison today, the regime there will probably add more lies to the above repertoire: You have been brought into prison for your own protection; too many people were jealous of your achievements et cetera, et cetera, et cetera. Essentially all the rubbish we imagined or heard about from political prisoners who had been released will be confirmed. No-one will produce any shred of evidence against me; no-one will see my detention, imprisonment or death as tarnishing Banda's, his coterie's or the country's image. But tried and charged I will be in the public houses and in people's homes. Again and again, I will be accused of being principally rude to authority, which is punishable by arrest, detention, imprisonment, exile, death; or, if you are a foreigner, deportation. What is maddening and intolerable in all this, of course, is the notion of 'being rude to authority' itself. For no law has been passed to define what constitutes rudeness to authority and what does not; what constitutes a rude poem, story, play, event or joke to authority and what does not. Nor are there any guidelines as to how such rudeness might be punished. That's the kind of 'orality politics' and 'orality justice' this nation suffers in silence everyday.

But I will concede I am not without blemish. I am not a perfect citizen. I have always detested Banda's foreign policies, particularly when he ignores the wisdom of national and international law and disregards, for example, what the Organisation of African Unity (OAU) says about how independent African countries might fight apartheid in South Africa – why independent African countries must support the ANC and other anti-apartheid movements. By being the first independent African leader defiantly to open diplomatic relations with the apartheid regime, Banda has made not just himself, but Malawi and its people a laughing stock on the African continent. We have become traitors to the African struggle against colonialism and racism. I detest Banda's domestic policies too; his human rights record is appalling; I particularly hate how he and his cabal get us arrested without reason; I loathe it when they exploit the trust, ignorance, illiteracy and naïveté of the ordinary people in villages and towns. Above all, I hate how these so-called higher authorities want us to convict ourselves for the crimes we have not committed; I do not like it when they want us to speculate which event, friend, enemy, informer reported us to them.

I've never declared these views to anyone before; it's this stupid tobacco-stinking waiting room that has brought them out. Take now. Why doesn't someone tell me what or who I am waiting for? Or how long I will sit in this stench? The commissioner's cap has been peeping in and out at intervals since they dumped me here. Why doesn't he say what he wants? Will he imprison me? Is he going to murder me? Has he been peeping in and out to check if I haven't run away? Where does one run to from these concrete walls? And why is this dirty orange chair squeaking like a dying duck? Shit!

4
Interrogation

The door opens violently. The commissioner's cap peeps for the umpteenth time; but this time the voice behind the cap intones: "Follow me." My heart jumps, thumping faster and faster. This is it, I think: death. I stand up with difficulty: the cramps. I feel hot; begin shivering with fear; my throat dry. I wonder how long I have been sitting in their stuffy room brooding on what kind of death I am fated to suffer, and why. He pushes me into a corridor and hurriedly ushers me into a large bare room. I am told to sit down on a chair at the edge of an oval-shaped mahogany table, which is flanked by eight or so fearful-looking commissioners of police. Their inspector general is at the head. The doubled-chinned commissioners, silver-pipped and silver-buttoned, the black leather straps of their Sam Brownes slung menacingly across their fat bellies, take off their caps. And placing them gently on the table, they cast their fearsome eyes on me at once. I feel totally subdued and begin gritting my teeth, nervously. "This is the moment, Lord," I pray. "Please give me the strength to manage this overwhelming court – notwithstanding the provision of no defence lawyers. And, Lord, I have prepared my case the best I could; it's your turn now." The inspector general calls the meeting to order and what I take to be my interrogation and court begins:

"Dr Mapanje, welcome. And gentlemen, thank you for making time to come at short notice. Dr Mapanje, I am inspector general Elliot Mbedza and the chairman of this country's security council. At 11.00 a.m. this morning I was summoned by his excellency the life president Ngwazi Dr H Kamuzu Banda to update him on the country's security – I perform such duties every Friday. But after our deliberations today, his excellency (the H.E.) has directed me to arrest you and imprison you, Dr Mapanje. He did not tell me why; I did not ask him why; and since it is a directive from above, I must tell you we are not going to investigate your case. It would be questioning the wisdom of the H.E., the highest authority in the land. I invited these commissioners from their posts all over the country, therefore, to find out if there is anything in our files about you. There is nothing. I repeat, Dr Mapanje, these commissioners say you are not in our books. So, before we take you to prison according to the wishes of his excellency, we thought we should ask you just three questions. Who are you? Why do you think we should detain and imprison you? What have you done to each other in the university to warrant imprisonment?

Stunned. Loaded questions. Speechless. I don't believe what I have just heard. I have read about the brutal interrogations of the security officers in apartheid South Africa. I have heard about the barbarism of Ian Smith's hit squads during the Unilateral Declaration of Independence (UDI) in what was Southern Rhodesia. I have seen documentaries of the ferocity of Idi Amin's firing squads in Uganda. There have been other African forms of terror. My interrogation is another thing; it shatters by its apparent simplicity. And according to my country's 'orality politics' whatever answer or defence I might provide will be used against me; I will be implicated in some crime or other. Therefore, I must not answer. And anyway, if the police are not going to investigate my case, why should I bother to co-operate? Banda's ubiquitous image, watching these proceedings from the frame above the I.G.'s chair, mocks, but I let him hang in there.

Yet I am not deaf. The inspector general has asked me three questions: Who am I? Why should they imprison me? What have we done to each other in the university to justify imprisonment? And rubbing my sweating hands as I am doing is not the answer. The questions suggest that these authorities do not know what I have done; whoever reported me to the president did not go through them; this implies that I am not Banda's political enemy; therefore, I could only have wronged his Kadzamira-Tembo coterie. For, according to this country's power structure and in the context of the university, the options as to who might have reported me to Banda, without going through these police chiefs, must whittle down to two: the chairman of the university council John Tembo, or his nephew and Chancellor College principal Zimani Kadzamira, or both. Only these 'higher authorities' take pride in having direct access to Banda, largely because Cecilia and Mary Kadzamira are Banda's permanent companion and private secretary respectively at Sanjika Palace in Blantyre or the State Houses in Zomba or Lilongwe.

These are the people that everyone fears, often more than Banda himself, and are believed to be behind the president's autocratic power. Other members of Banda's lieutenants include the secretary to the president and cabinet and head of the civil service (SPC), currently Sam Kakhobwe; the defence chief and army general, Mervin Khanga; the head of Malawi young pioneer paramilitary movement, Dr McAlpine Mlotha; and the police inspector general himself. Yet indeed, who am I? I have never asked myself the question. What can anybody be where everybody must play Mr Nobody? You are not supposed to be anybody in this country. It's dangerous. It challenges Banda's authority and the authority of his cabal. I now realise that I have been too naïve, too foolish, too blind; for college cleaners, messengers, drivers, colleagues and others warned me again and again, particularly from the time I became head of the English department, to watch the colleagues who reported the subversive activities of supposed rebel lecturers to the principal or directly to his uncle. Of course, I did not believe these stories. I dismissed them for what they were – rumours – though today in the presence of these commissioners, I wonder if I might not have been foolish to ignore them. The silence that ensues, as I think these thoughts, is so embarrassing that inspector general Mbedza decides to intervene:

"So, tell us, Dr Mapanje, which schools, colleges and universities were you educated at? Which countries have you recently visited? And, generally, what do you do in the university?"

That's better, I tell myself, and produce a list of educational institutions where I went, with the qualifications I got from each of them: Kadango Junior Primary School, Mangochi district; Chikwawa Catholic Primary School; Zomba Catholic Secondary School; Soche Hill College; Chichiri campus of the University of Malawi; University of London Institute of Education and University College London. I then add:

"I have just returned from the University of Zimbabwe where the Linguistics Association for Southern African Development Co-ordinating Conference (SADCC) universities, (LASU), of which I am chairperson, held a very successful regional conference."

But neither the I.G. nor his commissioners seem keen to find out what happened there. Mbedza merely cuts in:

"Gentlemen, could you please ensure that Dr Mapanje is kept in a prison where the cockroaches are controlled, until such time that his excellency decides to have him released?"

This said in a tone that is totally without irony. The chief commissioners chorus their approval as they noisily push back their chairs under the table each putting on his fearful cap – my interrogation is done! On the wall, the father and founder of the Malawi nation – our very own Papa Doc, the Ngwazi Dr H. Kamuzu Banda gazes intently on. I feel duped that the chapter of my brutal arrest and search should end so tamely, with all the appearance of a departmental meeting at the university. Without attracting anybody's attention, I wipe away the blood that trickled from my wrist to the table I was leaning on and tell myself: you are going to jail; you have been left alive; can you believe that? But a tap on my shoulder. And my heart jumps. One of the commissioners says I should follow him. I rise with difficulty. My knees stiff. His office has a smaller replica of the oval-shaped mahogany table I had just been 'sentenced' at. Banda's ubiquitous portrait on the

26

wall still glares ominously at me, but this commissioner is in a hurry, there's no time for us to sit down:

"Dr Mapanje, I'm McWilliam Lunguzi," he announces. "I am the head of security and intelligence services (SIS) in this country. I report directly to him," he says, pointing at the president's portrait on the wall, and continues: "I thought we should have a brief chat before they take you to prison. By the way, what religion do you belong to? Which church do you go to pray?"

A very unexpected question indeed; what's he up to now?

"Roman Catholic", I answer.

"So am I," he says, "though not a very good one, I'm afraid; but once a Catholic always a Catholic," he concludes. Then back to the business at hand. "So, tell me, Dr Mapanje, what happened at the university? I want to present your case to the H.E. in the best possible light. Hold nothing back as you might have done before the other commissioners just now – understandably so – however important the names you withheld in the other office might be, it'll be safe with me, trust me, I'm a fellow Catholic, remember?"

"Look," I say sickened by his hypocrisy but frightened by his power, "I did not talk to any of his excellency's political opponents in Zimbabwe. The LASU conference at Harare campus of the university was organised by our executive committee and funded principally by Norwegian and Swedish governments respectively. Zimbabwe's Minister for Higher Education, Dr Dzingai Mutumbuka, officially opened the conference. His address was preceded by words of encouragement and wisdom from Professor Walter Kamba, the vice-chancellor. Both officials urged us to take seriously the regional language and linguistics research projects we were going to be engaged in; they particularly wanted our organisation to engage in projects that would be relevant to education in the schools and colleges of the region; they emphasised the need for the translation of world classics in literature into African languages. Our Malawi lecturers presented papers that became superb reference points for the rest of the conference – they did the university and Malawi proud. You could check this information with my principal, who has an official record of my academic career and to whom I have already given a verbal report of the conference. As for the story of my political activities, your dutiful staff must know that I am not a member of any dissident political organisation fighting this government from within or outside the country... "

I pause upon discovering that the fellow's attention is elsewhere. Banda's portrait on the wall still glares at my daring. My armpits are sweating copiously. I've pushed myself too hard. But I don't want anyone probing further matters that are, in all honesty, irrelevant. The fellow simply declares:

"I'll do everything in my power to get you out of this. Meanwhile, you had better say three Hail Marys everyday so that the H.E. does not forget about you in prison."

This is cold comfort for the country's newest political prey.

5
Detour

My way to prison begins on a mundane note. The eastern division commissioner of police who arrested me this afternoon is hungry. We must, therefore, stop for dinner at his friend's house before they drop me off at my destination. "You must be hungry too by now," he tells me, "and there might not be any food when we arrive where we are going." I detest the casualness with which he treats me. He arrested me at 1.35 p.m. – it's now about 8.35 p.m.; in that time he searched my office and my house where he treated me, Mother and my children like dirt; how dare he handle me like I am suddenly human! The officers squashing me at the back of their vehicle provide no justification. I am still fuming and confused about the implications of my interrogation. I don't believe they are taking me to prison either. What wrong have I done to John Tembo, Zimnani Kadzamira or the Kadzamira sisters at Banda's palace? I don't even know these people. Apart from Zimani in the university, I have had no dealings with them. Nor do I believe that we are going for dinner wherever we are going. I keep telling myself: they should have killed me; I would probably have been at peace with myself by now. Perhaps I'd have met the politicians I loved: Henry Masauko Chipembere and Dunduzu Kaluli Chisiza or the last batch of dissidents that Banda and his ruthless coven 'accidentalised' four years ago – Aaron Gadama, Dick Matenje, David Chiwanga and Twaibu Sangala. We'd have been chatting about Banda's methods of exclusion of his presumed political opponents. I'd have suggested that we organise a welcome feast for Banda when his turn to join us came. I would have mobilised all his victims and put on a play to remind him how he had eliminated us, one by one. I am sure he would have loved the play. Why did they not kill me? Yet perhaps it's just a matter of time. Perhaps these fellows are going to kill me eventually. And why are my knees knocking one against the other? What do these men, one on my left and the other on my right feel, when they see me juddering between them so? What a profession! Would I enjoy squashing the political prisoners I arrested for nothing, year in year out? I suppose they have no choice; they have to do what they have to do to survive.

We head for Limbe township, past the Independence Arch, branch into Zomba Road, past what used to be called the International Hotel on the left; the Majestic Cinema, Lever Brothers Co. and Grain and Milling Co. buildings on the right. And before reaching Limbe Catholic Cathedral on the left, we veer to the right, past Mpingwe Cricket Club to the left, and left again just before the Shire Highlands Hotel. It's dark but I know where we are. When I visited my cousin's relatives after their return from diplomatic service in London, I used to take these jacaranda avenues to join the road further on. The purpling jacarandas looked beautiful during the day, but in this pallid moonlight even colourful jacarandas are bound to look miserable. Our vehicle stops on the left side of the avenue beside a house with a high brick wall and an iron gate. Four powerful beams immediately light up, blinding us totally; the gate opens; our vehicle enters; a mansion appears. Hounds run towards us, barking wildly at our intrusion. My heart is already thumping. I fear dogs. I particularly loathe these. They are huge and scary. We must all get out. I hesitate. The men between whom I am crushed push me out. The hounds continue to bark menacingly; uniformed security guards show up; they try to stop the hounds harming us. In the midst of the confusion a whiff of sweet fragrant night jasmine at the iron-gate warms my cold nose, but I am too frightened to appreciate the full effect of its fragrance. The floodlights around the house seem to follow whatever direction we approach the mansion – I have never felt so exposed, so dazzled into submission, in all my life. I begin to puzzle about the fortress we are approaching: Whose is it? What do they use it for? Are we really coming for dinner here?

Couldn't this be the gateway to the torture chambers I've heard about, where, after confessing their lies, in the hope that they would be left alone or freed, Banda's presumed political enemies were beaten, tortured, bundled into sacks, and driven to the Lower Shire Valley to become meat for the hungry crocodiles there? Why is sweat pouring under my arms again? Is it the barking hounds? I mustn't fear them; I mustn't walk like a drunk; these hounds are trained to detect nervous people; I will not be nervous!

A huge Indian woman and a rather feckless Indian man give the commissioner a loud welcome to their mansion. We are ushered into a large living room and asked to feel at home on the sofa. The hounds continue to bark their blood-curdling welcome outside. The smiles between the commissioner and his friends seem plastic, the meeting contrived; I am probably wrong; for after her carefully orchestrated hand-clapping greeting, the lady gestures to her servants for the table to be ready for dinner. I feel a sharp tingle of discomfiture. All along I have held the view, perhaps naively, that no serious relationship, beyond the commercial, could be cultivated between the Asian community and the locals in this country – Banda's politics have not allowed it to bloom naturally. Today, haven't I walked into the residence of Malawian Asians who seem to be the commissioner's true friends? The warmth and ease that slowly emanates between them seems so natural that I cannot help feeling suspicious. And watch as the blatant lies I feared would soon pour out. The commissioner's servile juniors are introduced as his friends. I am his colleague being given a lift to the life president's famous university in Zomba where I will eventually be dropped off. First grade for his play on words – everyone knows that prisons are called universities; the ambiguity is therefore intended. And note the other lie:

"Mr Commissioner, in my capacity as your sister-in-law, I must protest; you promised to arrive at 7 p.m. when my dinner was still steaming and smelling delicious; it's about 9 p.m. now; by arriving this late, did you intend to put my cooking to shame in the presence of your university colleagues?"

Before the commissioner defends himself, however, the lady of the mansion already understands how busy his excellency's commissioners can be. Ours is, therefore, absolved of his crime before he opens his mouth. The lie sickens its way to the table where I am forced to move, past the rice and hot chicken curry – all of which would have been otherwise very tasty. She interrupts my thoughts again:

"And you, professor, why are you so quiet? Why don't you take more rice or *nsima** and more chicken curry? Do you want my sister at the university to cook for you in the middle of the night? Don't tell us she'll be jealous when she hears you've eaten my food! She won't be. It'll be too late for her to cook when you arrive. Please, take more chicken!"

Perhaps the poor woman has not been told that I am a prisoner in her house. She does not seem to detect that I am frozen stiff with fear. Nor can she see the weeping blisters on my wrists. If she has been told who I am, she is putting on a brilliant show. I know her food is delicious, but I am watching every move the commissioner and his cronies are making to ensure that they do not drop poison in my plate. These fellows are reputed for dropping bits of poison lodged in their fingernails into the plates of the people they pass their food to – if you are easy to poison in his excellency's warm heart of Africa, you'll disappear before your time. I soon discover that my speculations about our hosts are wrong. The commissioner's friends expose chiSena tonal patterns in their speech; therefore, they must come originally from Mozambique. This conjures up another thought. Might I be treading in that highly volatile chamber of *mandrax* or the local leaf, *chamba*, referred to in the drug culture as 'Malawi Gold'? Is this the *chamba* and *mandrax* territory secretly referred to as 'RENAMO' – named after the bandit political movement fighting the government of neighbouring Mozambique? Might not the lady's speech in the

---

* Hard porridge from maize flour, maize meal.

32

Sena dialect of Malawi's national language, and her inexplicable genuflections, bows and counter-bows in apparent politeness, be another cover for something more sinister? With the trivia of conversation going on at the table and the hot chilli sauce in my chicken curry and rice, with more than eight hours in police custody, I am only too happy to break the taboo and ask for the toilet – the lady of the mansion points me in the right direction.

When we hit the road again, the next drama is at Njuli Trading Centre beside Chiradzulu Mountain, where our vehicle suddenly begins to sway dangerously from left to right and back again, as if the tyre had exploded and the driver was struggling to control the vehicle. The commissioner in the front seat is shouting at someone that we soon realise is a drunken driver. The fellow is arrested instantly; his vehicle impounded and driven by one of the commissioner's lackeys until we reach Namadzi police station, where it is temporarily kept. When I hear the commissioner declaring that he hates to see drunks on his excellency's roads, I wish to laugh but my spine is too cold, the legs and feet too numb to respond. For a moment I thought the swaying of the vehicle and the commissioner's shouting was their excuse for causing an accident where I was going to be fated to die. But I tell myself to calm down, hang on and think about the road accidents I have known – one of which immediately comes to mind.

We were returning to the Government Hostel from Matawale Night Club. I was dropping off Professor Lewis Nkosi with David Kerr, the former a friend and external examiner in the English department from the University of Zambia, the latter my teacher and colleague in Chancellor College. We were getting excited, reminding ourselves of the meetings we used to have in west London pubs: Marlborough Arms, off Gower Street and the University Tavern on Store Street. We had been talking about Banda's contradictory politics on apartheid in South Africa; that is, how the African National Congress (ANC) often threatened Banda's Malawi Congress Party (MCP) secretary general and administrative secretary, Albert Muwalo, and forced him to give them MCP vehicles to transport ANC soldiers across the borders of

Mozambique and Malawi into Tanzania, despite Banda's official association with the apartheid regime. We were laughing about this when an on-coming police vehicle speeding down the steep road from the Government Hostel gave us the floodlights. I dipped my lights immediately, but the on-coming driver did not, and was directly in front of us. I panicked, swung to the left to avoid a head-on collision, and into the ditch I went, then into a tree trunk crash! The three of us were fine, the car was not; and was I terrified! The following morning I had to retrieve my car from the police and take it to Kamoto's Home Garage near Matawale Night Club. I felt mortified and guilty that I might have caused the death of two distinguished academics that night – and that's the car I left at the Gymkhana Club when I was arrested this afternoon. I hope the police do not chuck it behind their station garage, where vehicles for presumed political dissidents rust to extinction, while their owners languish in prisons.

How Lewis Nkosi, that robust South African exiled writer, literary critic, and tireless fighter against apartheid, became our external examiner for three years in the university of an indepent African country that boasted cosy diplomatic relations with the apartheid regime was a miracle. David and his wife Mary Nyandovi-Kerr, with whom Nkosi had worked at the University of Zambia, must have influenced his decision to visit. The previous heads of the English department must also have tactfully put the academic case beyond the bounds of John Tembo and Banda's security officers who were often remarkably short-sighted, particularly on matters such as external examining, which were often beyond their comprehension. As these thoughts flick through my mind, our vehicle slows down to a halt at Zomba Inn; turns right, past Matawale Night Club on the right, Kamoto's Home Garage on the left, and speeds towards Zomba aerodrome and the army's 'Turf Club', where I remember playing darts with Anthony Nazombe and assistant university registrar Sebastian Musa only the day before. When we turn into the dusty, secluded road towards Mikuyu maximum detention prison, my heart sinks.

6

Hell-Hole

It's well after midnight when the gates of Mikuyu prison finally swing open. After more than ten hours in police custody, I am exhausted. My legs and feet feel sedated as I am led up a dingy staircase to a small, ill-lit office. The president's portrait on the wall still watches us as his eastern division commissioner of police enters my name, time of arrival and his signature in the prison's gate book. He orders the officer-in-charge of prison to keep me in a 'well-sheltered' place – no mention of inspector general Mbedza's directive for me not to share a cell with creepy-crawlies. I was suspicious of this fellow's honesty from the time I saw him, and now when he says he'll see me soon, I do not believe him. Officer-in-charge Sitima – I was to discover his name the following day – says he too has to go; he's leaving me in the able hands of the night shift commander and his guards, who will look after me. The prison rituals begin again: my name, place of work, where and when I was arrested. The commander will offer me blankets and I will change into uniforms he calls the *foya*. He opens a cupboard and takes out blanket rags and the *foya* – loose, dirty, oversize pyjama-like shirt and shorts without pockets – and throws them at me. They land on my lap and smell rancid; clearly they were never washed after use and whoever used them must have suffered from the scabies or some other pus and blood-weeping disease. I almost throw up at the stink of the starch-stiff black-red spotted *foya*; the material is of the cheap cream-white cloth sold in Malawi villages for use as shrouds – an uncomfortable portent. Then the commander pugnaciously pulls

35

down my trousers – the start of total dehumanising stripping – my shirt, shoes, socks and underwear are stuffed into a dirty creamy bag that already holds my sweater. They'll be kept there, I'm told, until my release. I don't know when that will be, but I can see I am as naked as Adam, and suddenly begin shivering. He runs his coarse hands over my naked body as if to confirm what else I might be hiding under the skin. I weep inwardly with angry impotence. Finally, he removes my glasses but I grab those back, I cannot see without them, I tell him. There's a kind of see-sawing that goes on until I eventually give up, and decide to fight for them the following day.

"These rules must be followed in order to protect you," the commander declares.

"Protect me from myself?" I ask, utterly incensed.

"We know what we are doing," one of his guards shouts, "we've seen political prisoners kill themselves with their own spectacles here!"

That's a shameless lie, I think to myself, even he must know that – despicable fool! Then the final humiliation – the guards rough me up, bend me over so that the commander can search my bottom:

"But I am not a drug dealer for you to do this."
"That's what they all say," he hits back.

I cannot believe this is happening to me in my own country. And I have not committed any crime. I feel totally humiliated and deprived of any remnants of dignity. I soon notice that I am actually naked and still shivering uncontrollably. The muscles begin to twitch; a rash has already broken out all over my body, as if I were about to suffer the fits of long-maturing malaria.

"Those will keep you warm," the night shift commander says, pointing at the *foya* on my lap. His guards know that I will not willingly wear their *foya*. One of them sees through my resistance, takes the *foya* and forces the narrow neck of the sleeveless shirt over my head while the other grabs my trembling cold legs and pushes them into the over-sized shorts, one by one, as if he were dressing up a difficult child. Well, I suppose I am a kind of child; prisons always make us children, don't they say? The pocketless *foya* feels stiff, coarse and scratches uncomfortably against my delicate skin:

"These precautions are being taken for your own safety," the commander repeats by way of a crazy shield of his inhumane treatment. I look away in disbelief, wondering how many times I have heard the lie about precautions being taken for our safety. He continues:

"We got these prison rules from the British."

"Who stopped you throwing away the bad rules, keeping only the good ones at independence? Why do you always like to blame others for the evil you do?" I find myself rather foolishly muttering through chattering teeth. Oddly enough, he doesn't seem offended, but simply says:

"Prisoners have smuggled stranger things into this prison before: guns, knives, razor blades and other dangerous objects." Then he suddenly changes the subject:

"Do you remember the Zomba-born Chemistry professor at Chancellor College – he's probably a friend of yours?"

"Yes."

"Well, I used to beat him in class at the primary school."

"So?"

"Well, I just thought you might like to know; nobody expected him to become a professor!"

"And you eventually landed upon this?"

"No school fees to continue, I am afraid," he says.

"Shame," I answer, rather surprised that he should suddenly seem human.

We must return down the dingy staircase, through the office block gates, into the yard outside. I do not know where we are going. It's a clear night. The shimmering stars are at their brightest above my head. A lone dog barks loudly somewhere in the prison's compound and whines at great length. I close my eyes. A picture of this year's celebrations of our independence anniversary flashes past. Zomba district has four prisons that are always crammed with prisoners, political and criminal – Mikuyu, Zomba Central, Domasi and Mpyupyu. The first two are the most notorious. Before each anniversary celebration, prisoners selected from these prisons and wearing dirty *foya* like the one I am now wearing, form a line twenty yards apart on both sides of Kamuzu Highway, and the other main roads and avenues in town. They dig holes with mattocks and plant poles carrying national flags to cheer the president, who loves to be driven in his 'royal' cavalcade between the rows of the fluttering flags as the people shout, "The lion, the lion," accompanied by hand clapping and praise-song chanting. The question is: Will I dig those holes wearing these stinking *foyas*, as the father of the nation takes the salute at our independence anniversary celebrations on 6 July next year? How will I take the humiliation? The sand and grit bruising the bare soft skin under my feet bring me back to other fears. Won't I get the horrid jiggers from walking barefoot in the filth of this prison? The bright moonlight and shining stars in the clear sky provide no hint. The commander easily sorts out one key from his noisy bunch to open the main gate. I see birds flying out and coming back to settle on the wire mesh above the courtyard. He breaks the brief silence again:

> "This is the New Building Wing – it's also called the VIP section of Mikuyu prison – where we keep his excellency's VIP political prisoners like you!"

I am disgusted, not flattered. We are standing in a courtyard before a row of four doors. He finds the right key, and the padlock to the first door on our right gives way. He barges straight in, knocking over what sounds like a bucket, then quickly returns, cursing the sharp buzzing of the night flies and singing mosquitoes. He had forgotten to switch on the naked electric bulb that hangs dangerously in the cell. He pushes me in, bangs the door, bolts it and locks it from outside. A pungent sting of stale urine hits my nose as the heavy boots crunch their way into the distant night. This is it then, I declare, trying to recollect myself. My country's senior lecturer and head of the English department; twelve academic members of staff; two secretaries; a messenger; more than five hundred students taking English each year; the chairman of the Linguistics association for the nine universities of Africa south of the Sahara. Arrested. Not tried. Not charged. No defence. Stripped naked to the bone. Made to wear putrid pocketless *foyas*. Then dumped in this stench, three paces by three. Hey, Mister, pinch yourself. Is this really you? Has it really come to this? Who did you think you were? Is this what you really are – another Mr Nobody? And do you want to cry? Or would you rather laugh this off? Probably not worth either. Thank the God of your ancestors they left you alive. It could have been worse. But seriously, what wrong have I done anybody? What wrong have my wife and children done to deserve a family without a dad? What wrong has my frail Mother done? Where are these gentle people now? What kind of sleep have they had? Are they still crying for their dad? Will they sleep at all from now on? And why, Lord, why did you allow this to happen? My family will be thrown out of the university house tomorrow; the children will be expelled from school; my wife will not be allowed to finish her course on community nursing; she will probably be dismissed from her job – all because of me – rebel husband, rebel son, rebel dad, rebel whatever; but people, what is rebel about me? And did I hear mosquitoes singing for company? God, the stench is unbearable! Tattered blanket rags; cold, dusty cement floor; incomprehensible graffiti on filthy walls. But listen, someone is scratching your wall. Where? Place your ear against the wall and listen. Tap, tap, tap. Hear that? My heart thumps faster and faster. Tap, tap, tap! Oh, I know. Somebody in the next cell's tapping for attention. I didn't realise there would be anybody there at this hour. It was so quiet. Where did I first read about this kind of communication?

"Yes!" I respond.

"My name is Alex Mataka. I'm in the cell next to you. Where have you come from?"

"English department, Chancellor College, University of Malawi".

"Welcome to Mikuyu. There are many of us here, from all over the country as well as outside. Relax. See you tomorrow. Good night".

"Good night".

I hear another tap on the distant wall of his cell and him relaying the news of my arrival to his mates. It must have gone past one in the morning. Do people ever sleep here? But I feel a sudden warmth after the tapping, despite the suffocating stench of urine from the bucket that the commander knocked over. A cold shiver runs up my spine as I step onto the slimy floor – probably the urine of the man whose *foya* I'm wearing. The scruffy blanket rags smell of rottenness. And look at the cockroaches crawling all over the wire gauze ceiling above and watching me watching them! Bloody hell! Who said I should be put in a prison that had no cockroaches? I imagine the scorpions, maggots, ticks and fleas that will be pouring out of every crack in the wall and on the caked cement floor, becoming my new mates! Sleep will be hard to come by tonight – swarms of mosquitoes in the corner chorus their 'amen'.

Book Two
Hold Them Tight

7
Breakfast

26 September 1987, Saturday. I sit up with a start. I did not hear any bell ring or anyone shout my name, but I know there is someone outside my door, I can hear him fiddling with the padlock trying to open it. I recall with a terrible shock where I am. Prison. I must have nodded off. Light still blaring into my eyes. Graffiti on the walls difficult to decipher. Mosquitoes bloated with my blood on the wall. I cannot see properly. Why did they take away my glasses? The bucket in the corner stinks worse than rotten eggs. Spinning head. Splitting too. Eyes feeling as if someone has thrown pepper in them. What in heaven's name am I doing here? The door is flung very wide open. The cell chokes with a dozen prison guards, carrying truncheons and shouting their heads off – I wonder why they were so quiet before the door opened. An officer with a polished cane under his arm leads the rowdy lot. He waves his cane desperately in the air, calling for silence. I recognise only the commander from the early hours of the morning and wonder with a repulsive confusion if I am to be bludgeoned to death here and now. Frankly, I hardly care as I half-hear snippets of their running commentary on their new arrival – me.

"Look at the bloodshot eyes of our new VIP rebel!" One of them shouts. Hysterical laughter breaks out as the mockery ripples around the crammed little room, three paces by three. Another declares: "*Takaonani kachigawenga kache mchim-wene**!" More frenzy ensues. Yet another asks: "Could this little

---

* Brother, look at the despicable little rebel before us!

43

buffoon overthrow anybody's government, let alone the life president's?" "That'll be the day!" his friend answers.

"Why do these higher authorities waste our time making us look after such an ungrateful swine?"

"Very true," another agrees. "Why don't they sort them out before they come here, so we just have the business of burying them?"

They wouldn't even have to bury me if they threw me into the chemical basins, which their young pioneer bases are reputed to have. I'd merely dissolve into total extinction like so many before me. Yet, I continue to think to myself, these guards, their breath heavy with the smell of traditionally distilled *kachasu* and cheap commercial brew, *chibuku,* are, in a kind of way, victims too of the present reign of terror. Shrugging his shoulders in respect first, the night shift commander announces my presence:

"'ttention *Bwana*, this is the rebel that the Special Branch brought in last night, saah!" My heart still plummets at the local word, *kachigawenga* – despicable little rebel – that was uttered with the contempt reserved for an assassin. It's something of a surprise, therefore, when the officer calmly asks how I slept. I produce the blandest of replies, for which I am sharply rebuked by a truncheon poking at my ribs:

"Eh, this is the University of Mikuyu, not the University of Malawi; when people in authority ask you questions here, you must answer politely, clearly and promptly – you hear?"

With hyena-like hysterics the gang marches out of my cell into the next cell, leaving me devastated, but glad that they did not use their truncheons on me. One guard shouts at the fellow next door:

"Alex, we've brought you a special yes-yes friend!"

More raucous laughter ensues as the gang rushes out, aggressively banging and bolting the courtyard gate. I hear their boots crunching towards the office block where they came from, as an uninvited visitor walks into my cell, stretches his hand and says:

"Good morning, professor. Alex Mataka is my name. I tapped on your wall last night."

"Good morning, Alex. Call me Jack, please, and I'm not professor yet – and will probably never be now, with this!" I declare, pointing at the prison walls surrounding us.

"I know, professor," Alex answers, "it is jealousies, jealousies and jealousies that bring us here. Same story every time. Everywhere. I'll call you Doc then. Is that all right? I gather everyone who teaches at the university has one of the degrees by which we call them Doc, don't they?"

"Yes, but I'd be happier if you called me Jack."

"No, no, no, Jack's the least I will call you. What Banda, his ruthless coven and their henchpeople want is to strip us of everything that matters: erase our names, our titles, our lives and us from history. We can't let that happen. Me, Alex; you, Doc; OK?"

Alex is about four foot ten and in his late thirties. He is thin, speaks English fluently, speaks French too, he says; his Portuguese is native as he was born, raised and educated in the ex-Portuguese colony of Mozambique. He speaks the Dedza district dialect of the Malawian national language as if he was born there. His crime is unusual. He was working for the Mozambique embassy in Lilongwe and was arrested at Kamuzu international airport on his return from a mission in communist China. I do not know whether to believe his story or not; but he is now one of the old 'lags' in Mikuyu, so he says, despite protestations from his embassy to Banda's government. He says: "Doc, welcome home. As your cell was left open we can spend all day in the courtyard together."

I have an effective mentor with whom to do my time. But first he must give me a quick, guided tour, pointing out the layout of our 'home' as he insists on calling it. He continues: "If there's anything that other prisoners admire about this section, it's the shower that we can have any time we like when the prison is not closed. The two pipes standing against the wall in the corner are a combined latrine/shower," he says, "we 'slop out' our night

45

buckets in the pit latrine there, and have a shower when we feel like it." He shows me how the water is turned on for it to come out at all. Tour over, he dives into my cell and reappears with my ablution bucket. He turns on the knob on the tap and the water shoots straight into the bucket making a rattling noise. He traps this water, swills it round, throws it down the latrine and starts again, repeating the operation until the bucket is as clean as it could possibly be for him. He walks to the far corner of the courtyard and turns the bucket upside down to dry.

"We'll take it back to your cell later," he tells me. Then he stands astride the latrine, opens the tap again, fills his cupped hands with water from the tap and rubs them clean. Next he washes his face, making sure that every drop of water lands in the middle of the latrine basin below. He uses his right hand index finger to brush his teeth, fills his mouth with the cupped water and spits the dirty water into the latrine. He repeats the operation until he is satisfied that his teeth feel clean and his mouth fresh. Finally, he reduces the flow of the water and with his mouth wide open, allows the tap water to fall directly into his mouth; then gulping down this 'uncontaminated' water he invites me: "Your turn, Doc, wash your face and brush your teeth; breakfast's on its way".

We are back to the beginnings of time, I think, but notice that Alex seriously wants me to follow suit. I remember washing my face and brushing my teeth in this manner when we crossed rivers going to school in our village when I was young. I take Alex on, though it takes me several days to work up a thirst for the 'uncontaminated' water – he has established my routine for the rest of my time. Then stories about the VIP section of the prison begin: Malawi's first Queen's Counsel, Orton Ching'oli Chirwa, stayed in this cell. Aleke Banda, the first secretary general of the MCP was transferred from this cell to Mpyupyu prison less than ten miles away. Apparently he was found to be in possession of a small powerful transistor radio, which he used to tune in to world radio stations in his cell after lock-up. The other side of this wing also has four cells like here; the notorious secretary general and administrative secretary of the MCP, Albert Muwalo, went blind in one of them before they hanged him at Zomba Central prison for alleged treason. Aaron Gadama, Dick Matenje, David Chiwanga and Twaibu Sangala stayed here one night that fateful day in May 1983. The following day Special Branch officers told them Banda had forgiven them. They were being released. Together they knelt down and thanked God and the Special Branch who had come to release them. Little did they realise that they were going, not to be released, but clubbed to death, allegedly on instructions from Banda and his official hostess, the Mama. I am confounded by these stories and the new information about the death of what we nicknamed 'the famous gang of four'. We hear the noise of the bunch of keys outside our gate as Alex announces: "Breakfast's coming". The gate is thrown wide open. Two mangled aluminum saucepans full of porridge are pushed at us on the courtyard floor, as you push food to naughty dogs. The gate is swiftly slammed shut and violently locked behind us. I ask Alex:

"What's the matter with them – Why do they push and bang the poor doors? Why are they so angry?"

"Forget about them Doc; relax and let's try today's porridge," Alex replies.

It's the word 'try' that unsettles me. And I'm not really hungry; but even if I were, the yellowish shit-like watery porridge, which swills in the saucepan that Alex calls *bakuli*, hardly sharpens my appetite. He continues cheerfully: "Now Doc, there are rules for taking porridge in his excellency's VIP section of Mikuyu prison. One – do not look at what you're eating. Two – do not chew it. Three – do not smell it. Four – just hold the *bakuli* high, close your eyes, nose and whatever, then sip and swallow as much of the contents at a time as you can. I'll lend you a bit of my sugar to flavour your porridge. You can give me it back when you get on the prison's special diet later." I have already had a glance at the porridge, I tell him, and what I saw is not nice at all. Nonetheless, holding the *bakuli* with both hands, I raise it to my mouth as delicately as a priest takes to his lips the consecrated chalice at the altar. And without looking again, smelling or chewing, I sip and swallow a little of the porridge. Suddenly my whole body goes into spasm, my mouth fills with unexpected bile, I run straight to the pit latrine to throw up. When my body stops shaking, I take a long hard look at what I tried to eat. Yuck! Yuck! Yuck! Maggots, maggots, maggots floating everywhere! What I thought were mere lumps of badly cooked porridge are in fact maggots! The maize flour they used was obviously rotten, the porridge uncooked and stinking of putrefaction, but Alex reassures me:

> "Doc, I think today's porridge is very bad, but you should try to eat. You have to survive here; it's the only way to beat the dictator. It can be done".

And as if to prove his point, Alex holds his breath, closes his eyes and pinches his nose with the one free hand, sips a mouthful and gulps down the lot. I want to run into my cell to weep. Instead I decide that I must either go on hunger strike or simply stay without taking breakfast. Alex warns: "Don't let them beat you twice, Doc; eat their poison; God will provide the antidote; He always does; that's why you found us alive". I wish, oh how I wish I had Alex's resilience and hope! Where does he get the constant smile that would crush any tyrant? Our morning chatter moves to birds. The wire mesh we see above the courtyard becomes a home for thousands of wagtails at night. As soon as the beams of light surrounding the prison are switched on – after lock-up – the wagtails flock onto the wire mesh. While there, they deposit their droppings in the courtyard below, making it impossible for us to sit without discomfort the following day. So, our first duty after breakfast each morning is to scrub all bird shit off the floor, to make the courtyard habitable. He continues: "Take this mop with water from my *bakuli*, therefore, and wipe clean wherever you see wagtail shit. I'll start from this end if you start from the other end. We'll meet in the middle. When we've finished, we'll move to your cell to scrub the floor and walls clean."

Alex's mop is made from blanket shreds tied with strips of *foya*. The idea is to hold the mop in one hand, dip it into the *bakuli* of water and clear all wagtail droppings that foul the yard. The point of the exercise is evident. If we do not scrub clean the courtyard, wagtail shit will pile and pile, and the stench will intensify until we are forced to retreat back into the dreaded cells. With wagtail-shit scrubbing, mopping and cleaning every day, we do not need other forms of punishment in his excellency's prison. As for torture, Alex continues, you might be glad to hear that the prison authorities have temporarily suspended the use of physical torture because of pressure from human rights activists outside the country. These days, torture by electrical tongs and other dangerous objects is reserved only for those who break prison rules, such as those who go on hunger strikes, or try to commit suicide, or to jump over the fence for dear life. According to Alex, those who have imprisoned us will be happy if we die here; if we survive, then we must come out of here paralysed both mentally and physically – that's what the leader and his heartless cabal want. So, since Banda, his coterie, their security officers and the prison regime do not care whether political prisoners like us live, die or are paralysed, it's foolish to give away your life to them so easily. At any rate, in general, political prisoners in Mikuyu are determined that they will survive Banda's tyrannical conditions. Everyone believes that survival is the most effective way of fighting dictators – if you die in prison, the dictator and his minions have achieved what they set out to do, they have won; if you survive, you will live to tell your story; and even if nobody reads it or never believes you, you would have said your bit and won.

The Following Dawn The Boots[*]

The following dawn I woke up to the reality of prison
Boots, jangling keys and streaks of the golden sun
My bones, muscles and joints –
My whole new plight stiff:

---

[*] First appeared in *Skipping Without Ropes*, Bloodaxe Books, 1998.

The most dangerous rebels start out here
They may then be moved to other minor prisons
Or perhaps promoted to the general cells inside;
Even that legendary 'gang of four' came here first
At dusk, after lock-up; I commanded my guards
To chain them to the stocks in the cell you slept last night
(You have never heard notables
Crying like naughty children!)
The next day the rebels were released
Although the Special Branch who liberated them
Refused to inscribe their names and signatures
In Mikuyu prison gate books
As they had done when they brought in the prisoners,
That's when we saw something suspicious
About their kind of liberation.
So when we heard radio announcements
About their intention to cross the border at Mwanza
And their supposed accident there,
The guards on duty hastened to bear witness
To the Mikuyu Gate Book inscriptions
Of the Special Branch who had freed their eminence –
But, truly, men have been reprieved within days here –
Welcome home!
The guard commander had intended
The tale to chill me into submission
From the first day of my arrival
He wanted no hunger strikes
No jumping over prison fences
No protests, no nonsense in his prison,
He invoked my university mentors
The country's most 'notorious' rebels
Demagogues and others who had felt
The sharp grip and blister of his Sheffield
Handcuffs, leg-irons, chains, without blinking –
I embraced only his tale of the Gate Book engravings
Imagining someone found it mattered someday.

8

Of CCAM, Lunch and the Dancing Chief

I am not getting any wiser as I think about my prison. Although I refuse to be superstitious, there are three events that occurred in September 1987 before I was arrested that surprise me. I am beginning to regret that I did not consider them serious warnings for what was to befall me. Perhaps I would have taken firmer action to protect myself. The first event happened immediately after my arrival from the University of Zimbabwe linguistics conference. I am sitting at my desk, writing a report on the conference for my vice-chancellor, with a copy to my principal, when the telephone beside me rings. I pick up the receiver and instantly recognise the voice at the other end of the line: "Do you know that there's a conference of 'Chitukuko Cha Amai m'Malawi' (CCAM – Women in Development in Malawi) in our Chancellor College Great Hall?" Zimani Kadzamira asks.

"No, sir," I answer with some trepidation. The truth is I have heard in general terms that CCAM are holding a conference in college, but I have not got all the necessary facts to make sensible statements to my principal. I want to hear the story officially from the principal himself in case I am out of step with events. Besides, his sister, who is believed to be the real power behind the president, heads CCAM; one must, therefore, be careful what one says about her organisation:

"Well," Kadzamira tells me, "CCAM participants are winding up their conference with resolutions for the press. They've asked

51

for help from the college. Could you suggest two names of responsible academic staff who can help them in this?"

"Do you want me to go and help them, sir? I'd be delighted to go," I answer, hoping he will let me go so that I can confirm the stories I have heard from the public houses whether or not CCAM is another camouflage for a political party led by the president's permanent companion.

"Just suggest two names of responsible academics, I'll choose one myself," he says.

"Both to come from this department, or does that not matter?"

"One from English, another from any other department, would be fine."

"I suggest you consider Anthony Nazombe from this department and Francis Chilipaine from the department of French – both have been excellent rapporteurs at various UNESCO seminars at home and abroad."

"Thank you," he says.

"May I suggest further that whoever you choose between the two should get *Roget's Thesaurus* from my office? A dictionary of synonyms and antonyms is always useful in resolution writing, to avoid unnecessary repetition of phrases."

"Many thanks," he says and rings off.

I am agog with suspicion. Why does my principal ask me to suggest the names when he could do this himself? He often merely asks us to carry out whatever duties he wants us to perform and we perform them without question. And the word 'responsible' is critical in this instance. Kadzamira is suggesting that there are academic members of staff he considers irresponsible. Who might these be? Besides, when did CCAM begin to involve academic staff in its activities? Might this be the organisation's subtle way of getting university backing and acknowledgement? Might the rumour be true that CCAM is a craftily disguised political party led by Banda's mistress? Does Banda know about the true origin of this organisation? Has he perhaps sanctioned it? The public houses are rife with character assassination of the poor woman: every cockroach is competing to rule Malawi after Banda, they claim; the latest entry is the so-called official hostess, the Mama; and having been close to Banda since his return to Malawi after 40 years abroad, and being a woman, many people fear that she might succeed where the men vying for the country's political leadership after Banda – including her uncle, John Tembo – have failed, some having died mysteriously. Speculations for the true reasons for the emergence of CCAM are countless. At the Zomba Gymkhana Club the other day a fellow who works at Sanjika Palace even boldly claimed that the Mama was taking private tuition on the art of public speaking in readiness for the country's political leadership. The CCAM seminars and conferences she had embarked upon in Blantyre, Zomba, Lilongwe and Mzuzu are supposed to give her the necessary practice to improve these skills, he claimed. Of course, all this might be one pack of malicious lies, calculated to destroy the woman as a future presidential candidate; but since rumours are the only truths we live by in the Malawi they have created, and in the absence of any proof to the contrary, it is foolish to dismiss them so easily. Those of us who frequent the public houses hear these stories all the time; even the famous Malawian journalist Mkwapatira Mhango exiled in Zambia is apparently reproducing these stories freely in Lusaka papers. But knock, knock, knock! Enter Francis Chilipaine who, without the usual greetings and other preliminary friendly gestures, declares:

"The principal has asked me to get a dictionary of synonyms and antonyms from you. Have you got it?"

"Oh yes," I reply, "he phoned a few minutes ago and asked that I suggest two names of responsible staff to help CCAM with resolution writing for the press; as he seemed reluctant to accept my offer, I could only think of you and Anthony as the best. I hope you don't mind – here's the *Roget's Thesaurus* that I suggested."

Francis simply seizes the book from me and bangs my door behind him without another word. I feel like a scab. I should not have suggested his or Anthony's name – they too are exhausted from the two Harare conferences they attended. I should have insisted that I help CCAM myself, but why was Kadzamira reluctant to take my offer? Why did Chilipaine seem angry? Is he still smarting from the inexplicable quarrel we had in Harare? And why did he take such a short time to walk to my office after I had put down the receiver? Where was he when the principal and I talked on the phone? And he looked impeccably spruced up in his favourite striped black suit – almost ready for the job at hand – am I wrong in feeling rather cheated? Or in asking what's going on? Hasn't he told Kadzamira about the Harare book launch of Chinua Achebe's latest novel *Anthills of the Savannah* and the gathering of African writers to which I got him invited? I remember college drivers and cleaners warning me once that I should be careful what I say to Francis Chilipaine, Francis Moto, Chris Kamlongera, Benson Kandowole and other colleagues; they are tracking down the subversive activities of radical lecturers and will report me and others to Kadzamira or his uncle. Were these rumours true? Were they germane to my arrest? However true or not true, relevant or irrelevant they might be, the truth is I am getting desperately confused about why I have not been tried or charged. The trouble with living under Banda's patronage and his Kadzamira-Tembo clan is that we rely too heavily on conspiracy theories; we spend too much of our precious time spying on one another, often suspecting even our best friends of betrayal – which suits Banda and his cabal perfectly. At the moment, my gut feeling is that my principal is setting up a trap for Francis or me or both. Having heard that the Harare linguistics conference was successful and our lecturers' performance was exceptional, the Kadzamiras now want to test whether our loyalty lies with the regional academic organisation or with the local CCAM. If Chilipaine does not help CCAM, he will be branded another ungrateful brat who bites the hand that feeds him. If he offers his help genuinely, as doubtless he is going to do, he has to be careful not to make any derogatory remarks about the goings-on at CCAM meetings afterwards – and if he is not one of their agents, he is trapped. Or could that be the trap into which I have fallen? Could I truly have avoided this imprisonment? The honest answer is I don't know.

The second event happened after my encounter with Chilipaine and Kadzamira over the CCAM conference report-writing. Blaise Machila and I are leaving the Senior Common Room (SCR), heading home for lunch. University Registrar (UR) Robert Mbaya blocks our way out of the SCR and inquires:

"Is the head of English back from the Zimbabwe linguistics conference then? How did it go?"

And before I reply, Mbaya whispers:

"You two are not going anywhere; University senate has finished its meeting, the senators are having lunch in the SCR. As some of them have already gone back home to Blantyre and Lilongwe, there will be lots of food. Please join us for lunch."

"But, Mr UR," I protest, "we are neither senators nor are we spruced up for the senators' lunch. Besides, having been a senator once myself, I know that invitations to senators' lunches come from the principals of colleges that host the meetings, not from university registers or vice-chancellors. So, thank you for your generous invitation, but we are sorry we cannot come; our lunch is waiting for us at home, anyway. Please let us pass."

Mbaya will have none of it; he shoos us back into the SCR dining room, where my colleague and I are eventually made to sit at the edge of their large table like naughty children. When Kadzamira walks in, he immediately casts his red eye on Blaise and me; I decide to apologise before his rage pours out.

"I am sorry, Mr Principal, but it's the UR who dragged us here . . . " Mbaya cuts in with abundant apologies to the principal on our behalf, but his intervention seems to fuel the tension rather than abate it. The senators seem to notice what the two of us have already noticed – that the principal is choking with indignation about something. After a short while, he adopts a softer tone and asks me about the Zimbabwe linguistics conference, which I had already told him about by phone when I returned; I had even told him informally about the Zimbabwe writer's residency which I had applied for and had been offered after a rigorous interview at the University of Zimbabwe; I told him I would write to him formally about it. But now, for pragmatic reasons, I am obliged to declare that the conference went very well, our delegates did the university and the country proud, they presented papers that generated hot discussion. But as if he was not listening to my story, he asks me an impossible question about some person whom I do not know – how is he doing? I hesitate and mutter something incomprehensible as I try to recall the scholar he might have in mind. He must have taken my hesitation as deliberate unwillingness to co-operate, for, with discernible impatience, the principal suddenly raises his voice above everyone's around the table:

"You mean you do not know the guy who's been terrorising the pubs of Bulawayo and Harare?"

Taken aback, and rather irritated by the implications of his question, I decide not to answer. I recall that my principal follows the politics of Zimbabwe more closely than I do. He grew up there and speaks the national languages of Zimbabwe, Shona and Ndebele, better than he speaks those of Malawi. I do not understand why he is shouting such a dangerously loaded question at me; and at lunch too, when we've never crossed words about anything in public before. The implication of his question, that I associate myself with Zimbabwe terrorists, is patently far-fetched, bizarre and dangerous. I do not know how to defend myself or how to react to this kind of public affront. Blaise is ill at ease. The senators enjoying their lunch are obviously listening in with interest. The principal of Bunda College of Agriculture, Professor Brown Chimphamba, tries to come to our rescue – he was our principal and was expected to become the next vice-chancellor, but he was unceremoniously transferred to Bunda College of Agriculture to give room to Zimani Kadzamira who was being groomed for the post. Unfortunately, Chimphamba speaks in riddles, whose double meanings and relevance to the matter at hand we fail to decipher. He looks at both of us and grunts: "It pays to hang around." Blaise does not like the insinuation of his remark and wants to walk out in disgust. I press his toe down; it would be disastrous if we walked out now. Everyone at the table seems convinced that the principal knows something we do not. After their tasteless lunch, Blaise and I leave the table, bothered by the principal's question.

The third event happened on Thursday, 24 September 1987. My colleague Anthony Nazombe, assistant university registrar Sebastian Musa and I are playing a game of darts at the army's Turf Club, some four miles from the university. Chief commissioner of prisons Chikanamoyo arrives and generously greets everybody in the lounge, at the bar counter and us playing darts. Soon he begins to sing his favourite mask dance song to which he always shamelessly dances. Some spectators roar with laughter, others clap their hands to the commissioner's performance. We refuse to be drawn in, we know the commissioner's antics well. Instead, Anthony responds by publicly declaring: "Barman, tomorrow's payday in the university – treat the entire counter and lounge to one round of drinks on me." There is a loud cheer of gratitude from everyone. But the commissioner won't be beaten. He reciprocates Anthony's round of drinks by offering his own to everyone.

As more people shout and clap their hands in gratitude, the commissioner approaches me from behind and suddenly grabs my neck with both hands as if to throttle me to death. I yell for help and struggle for breath. Everyone cries out for mercy. The commissioner lets go of my throat as instantaneously as he squeezed it. He laughs sharply like a mad man and, clutching firmly at his bottle of Carlsberg, he gulps the beer down in a couple of large swigs, characteristically burps several times and shouting the popular saying, "To kill a baboon, do not look into his eyes," he marches out of the club feeling triumphant and satisfied with himself, dancing and whistling another mask dance song. Everyone roars with shock and mocking laughter, castigating the commissioner's disgusting behaviour. Someone in the crowd asks what wrong I have done the commissioner. Another wonders what I did to his girlfriend. I protest that I am innocent of both the charges and ignorant of the motives for his action; and we stop our darts, we drink up and, perplexed, decide to visit Chipande's Joint & Bottle Store about five miles away. The following day I am arrested and brought into this dreadful prison.

From the stench of this prison today, as I search for the reasons for my arrest and imprisonment – indeed, as I condemn myself for the crimes I have not committed against my country, my president or his intimates – I am sure the chief commissioner of prisons was told beforehand that I'd be dumped in his prison before he tried to throttle me at the Turf Club. Perhaps that's why he refuses to come to hear the problems I have in his prison. But I will soldier on; I will continue to speculate on the many events that could have caused conflict between the authorities and me. I cannot see why what I describe should lead to my detention, despite the times that are politically out of joint. I feel demoralised and helpless; but I will not despair. As I enter my bed I remember to pray the three Hail Marys that police commissioner Lunguzi suggested, for Banda not to forget me in prison.

9

Transfer

17 October 1987, Saturday. The noisy bunch of keys I am trying to get used to threatens again at my door; the night shift commander must be wanting to open my cell, though what message he brings well past lock-up hour, I have no idea. Alex believes that political prisoners are sometimes abducted at night without notice from here; some are never heard of again. This could be it; they could be coming to take me to be 'disappeared'. And why am I already shivering? What's the matter with me? I wait, nervously, gripped by fear. The door suddenly flies wide open. I hear a barrage of orders from several guards at once: "Transfer. You are moving house. Immediately. Pick up your stuff and leave. Quick. It's a directive from officer-in-charge Sitima. We are transferring you to D4 near the kitchen. Now! Where you'll be happier. Man, hurry! Do you hear? You can now stay with other yes-yes friends." I am confused. The orders come with obvious disdain. Alex Mataka has told me that the prison regime calls political prisoners who speak English 'yes-yes men'. But so what? I can handle mockery and innuendo; I love moving house too, particularly on my own terms. With the *foya* that I now use as pyjamas already on, I just need the rags of blanket, the *bakuli*, with the mug that accompanies it, and I am ready to move. Prison transfers are abrupt – to give us no time to plan escapes or grab anything precious with us, they say. That's a fact. The commander pushes me out of my cell into the courtyard, slams shut what was my door and locks it behind me. "Doc, remember me when you are in your new kingdom!" Alex whispers through the spy-hole. The commander threatens him with his

truncheon, but I raise my thumb in response as the guards push me out of the New Building Wing, where the first chapter of my prison life began. The wagtails that had been disturbed by the commander's violent gate opening and door banging, fly back one by one to settle on the wire gauze above the courtyard. Goodbye, wagtails, we were becoming great chattering mates; we'll probably meet in another world. Shame about Alex, he gave me company and cheer; now he'll have to stay alone as I found him.

The moon is shining bright outside. The huge beams of light placed strategically in the corners of the prison are glaring at every nook to expose the rats, bats, lizards, geckos and cockroaches that were my acquaintances. Anyone who dares to jump over the prison's fence will be shot on sight, they say, but I won't run, it's not worth the trouble afterwards. Armed guards surround the entire prison anyway. A gentle breeze is blowing from the prison compound on my right; it's cool and fresh, probably emanating from Lake Chilwa and Mozambique yonder; it contrasts sharply with the stench of the New Building Wing that I am leaving behind. A dog is barking in the prison compound and whining at his night witches, making the night feel spooky, or is it protesting at our interference? But my mind is set on D4 where life is different, they say; and we must go through numerous gates to get there. In the two weeks I've been in the New Building Wing, I've learned that D4 is the most coveted cell in prison; cellmates there have more freedom of movement than in any other cell; and, best of all, they are taken to Zomba General Hospital for treatment when they fall seriously ill. I intend to fall seriously ill – and very soon – maybe I could tell our friends at the hospital that I am at Mikuyu, so they can then pass on the message to my family, who still do not know where I am. Alternatively, through them, I could smuggle out a note for Mercy and the children to come and see me from a distance. Fr Pat at the university could even summon those elusive Irish Republican Army tactics and arrange for me to be abducted from the hospital to Zambia or Tanzania or some other neighbouring country, which would really shock Banda and his underlings. Alex also intimated that some 'politicals' in D4 are able to communicate secretly with human rights activists and organisations outside the country – I want to join the rebels at the earliest opportunity.

The commander opens D4, bellows my name at the door, pushes me in and orders the cell's leader, the *Nyapala*, to deal with me. He slams the door behind me and locks it from outside, his boots crunching into the night. He'll come back later to put out the light. I am stranded and helpless at the door, the focus of about a dozen curious stares. An old man staggers across the floor, extends his hand to me, whispers a greeting in my father's native tongue, chiYao, and says his name is Alidi Disi. He helps me with my property, takes me to a heap of blanket rags he calls his bed and apologises for it being unkempt – he was making the bed when the door opened. But there are no beds here, no mattresses, no mats, no pillows, no lockers either. Only two parallel lines painted white on the cement floor, five and a half feet long, separated by a foot – that's the bed in D4. There are forty-five such beds altogether, three rows of fifteen beds each, and only about a third of them are currently occupied. Disi draws everyone's attention to my presence and starts: *"Ambuje"* which is my favourite chiYao honorific form of address for a person who deserves respect, "welcome to D4, you are the youngest detainee in this cell!" An outburst of laughter ensues from the other cellmates, triggered by his deliberate use of the word 'youngest' – he means I am the newest arrival – Disi's sense of humour strikes a chord immediately, I secretly adopt him as my uncle. Then, beginning with those who have stayed longest, he makes brief introductions: James Mkwanda from Machinga district, southern Malawi – I think he is in his mid-seventies; Aliki Kadango in his late sixties, I remember him: he owned a bottle store on Devil Street, old Lilongwe city market, where I used to visit; I haven't seen him for years. Is this where the man is rotting? What crime could he have committed? Then Disi himself in his early seventies, the *Nyapala*, the trusty, the cell's prefect, originally from my home district of Mangochi, but he was a butcher at the old Lilongwe city market when they arrested him:

"We three have been here for over fifteen years, without trial, without charge," he announces. "Lord have mercy!" I exclaim to myself, "I've been here only two weeks and it already feels like a lifetime; what of them?" I am appalled. Another glance at them reveals Mkwanda and Disi to be six foot plus tall, skinny, with wobbly knees, brittle spindly legs and bony feet – altogether looking tired and malnourished in their oversized *foya*. By contrast, Kadango is skeletal, with sturdy bones and muscles, like someone who spends most of his time jogging. It's his *foya* shorts and shirt that attract my attention, they are so short and tight you would think they were specially made for him – I discover later his tricks when he shows me how to make sewing needles from fish bones and how to pull thread from the *foya* as he shortens and tightens his *foyas*. I gather that Kadango, who can neither read nor write, wants to look like British colonial district commissioners in their white and tight shorts and shirts. This is his way of protesting against Banda's constricting dress code. He thinks the British district commissioners' tight colonial dress was better than the suits, ties, overcoats and bowler hats that Banda would have us wear in the African heat – I begin to respect the guy. Everyone refers to Disi's deputy *Nyapala* by his initials only: TS. He's middle-aged, hefty, comes from Ntchinji district, central Malawi and has been here eleven years. He was stores manager of the Canadian funded Malawi-Zambia Railway Link when they arrested him. There are four other middle-aged rather strong-bodied cellmates: Martin Ndovi, who's bald-headed, has a small mouth, sharp lips and is rather stout – must be the fellow who wrote the graffiti tribute to Orton Chirwa at the New Building Wing – and chunky Daniel Chunga. Both come from the north and have lived in Zimbabwe and Zambia – countries that are considered dangerous because they harbour Banda's political opponents – Banda's security officers assume that Malawians who live in these countries are agents or members of exiled political parties like The Socialist League of Malawi (LESOMA) or Malawi Freedom Movement (MAFREMO) and others that operate from outside Malawi.

Stephen Pingeni looks dark, rather frail, with large eyelashes; he was once a Malawi young pioneer (MYP) driver and comes from Dowa district of central Malawi. Brown Mpinganjira is a well-known journalist and broadcaster from Mulanje district in the south. I now understand why we no longer heard his popular discussion programme on the Malawi Broadcasting Corporation. What crime could he have committed? His chocolate brown complexion and Afro-wig hairstyle marks him out. These prisoners have stayed here between two and seven years respectively; in general they look better fed; as if they ate from a different pot from the others. The youngest prisoner, Ian Mbale, is twenty-five, well built and tall, his dark complexion contrasts brilliantly with his white teeth. He was working in a clothing factory in Lilongwe. On his return from Lusaka, Zambia, where he was visiting relatives, Malawi security officers at the Zambia/Malawi border found books and magazines on communism and socialism in his suitcase; that was enough rebellion for them to punish him indefinitely here – and he was only twenty at the time of his arrest – shocking. The list continues until all the fifteen or so cellmates are briefly introduced. Then Disi suggests that I should not bother to probe the details of the crimes that people have committed, beyond the sketches he will provide; cellmates do not like to talk about the 'crimes' that cost them their freedom; no-one has been tried or charged with any specific offence anyway; that's why they resent discussing these matters. But every prisoner has a story. Maybe I should talk to each individual privately and find out why they think they were imprisoned. I might understand better why I think I was imprisoned myself. The truth is that nobody knows why they are here. He concludes with: "TS will give you the rest of the rules by which we survive. Just one warning: nobody spends his time crying here. No authority listens to anyone's cries. Nobody has been released for crying. Otherwise, welcome to D4."

It's my turn. I thank them for their warm welcome, mention the college where I worked, when and how I was arrested and the New Building Wing where I've come from. Everybody returns to their bed, tittle-tattle or their brooding. TS takes me to the corner of the cell to show me the toilet. Imagine a structure that's two paces by one, about fifteen layers of brick high, stuck to the cell's wall in the corner opposite the door. That's the toilet. It's placed in such a way that anyone using it is visible only to whoever stands directly at the door. No-one remembers when the cistern's chain was broken, but you can fiddle with what's left and pull to flush the toilet. And to pee, you sit with your back to the door so that no urine is scattered below; for the big job, which must be avoided at night for the convenience of all, you sit naturally facing the door. The tour over, TS and Brown offer me extra rags of blanket each, show me how to make my bed and outline a typical day in D4. The night shift commander and his guards open the cell at about four in the morning; three cellmates, who are democratically chosen each week, get out to cook the porridge for the entire prison; the cell is locked up again until 6 o'clock in the morning when the morning shift gang takes over. Under strict escort we dash to A-Wing for ablution, wash our faces and brush our teeth in the communal pit latrines and communal showers there – apparently they had to fight protracted battles to get the privilege. We come back to help in the distribution of porridge to the cells before taking our own. Another three cellmates, again democratically chosen, enter the kitchen to cook the lunch, while the rest of us collect the *bakulis* used for the porridge from the cells and wash them, ready for lunch – we have no evening meal and lock-up time is about 5 p.m. "That's it," TS concludes, "and for the rest just drift with the wind!"

Brown takes over and begins by announcing publicly that TS and he are adopting me as one of their team; there are no ambiguities as to where my loyalties belong. The rest of the communication is largely in whispers. We'll share news about home and the world, medicines and food together. I thank them. And discover it is these two who instigated my transfer. They persuaded the officer-in-charge to have me moved from the New Building Wing for fear that my health would deteriorate. Anyone who stays at the New Building Wing for more than a month is in danger of going mad. Because he was never taken to court, tried or charged, he begins by talking aloud to Banda, his lieutenants and whoever is presumed to have brought him into prison. He wants to defend himself against his having been dumped here unfairly. Then he begins shouting at or singing to himself or to his presumed enemies, challenging them to duels. Often this is the beginning of some kind of madness, which these two did not want me to go through. I thank them again. I discover the true motives for their wanting me to transfer here later. They have been sending surreptitious messages about our sub-human living conditions in prison and exposing Banda's politics of elimination to human rights organisations abroad. They now want my connections as a writer and academic to take the struggle for our freedom beyond the bounds of Banda's expectations – I can't wait to be of some use to my country.

As TS and Brown move to their respective beds, I cast my eyes across the cell and see despair everywhere. There's what they call the prison's survival kit at the head of each bed: the famous *bakuli* and its companion silver mug, an extra pair of *foya* and extra rags of blanket – used as the pillow – the odd toothbrush placed across the mug beside crumbs of cheap red soap on selected beds; as well as the *foya* they are wearing; that's the entire property for each political prisoner. As I soon find out, there's a pinch of salt in most *bakulis* and a little sugar in some mugs for the better-off prisoners. What is maddening and disheartening is to see how everyone lies on his back, knees up, brooding or watching the cobwebs or counting the cockroaches and geckos on the rafters of the ceiling. When I imagine this cell packed with political prisoners as it apparently was in the late 1960s and early 1970s, the picture of African slaves packed like sardines on the decks of European slave ships, which I saw in Secondary School history books long ago, naturally comes to mind. I am disturbed and scared. Will I fit in here? Will I survive? How am I going to cope? The thought that I would be forced to mingle with strangers never occurred to me. I suppose I just have to behave like everyone who has been abducted from his otherwise cosy home without rhyme or reason. Life will not be easy, but we will soldier on.

10
Prison

I did not expect whatever I was doing in the university to lead to this rectangular configuration of the dungeon, which is effectively the New Building Wing writ large. My jail is made up of two parallel blocks with four cells in each block. The block on the left has cell A-Wing with a courtyard of its own; this is separated from cells C-Wing 1 and C-Wing 2 that share one courtyard; and these are separated from cell B-Wing, which has a courtyard of its own. The block on the right has cells D1, D2, D3 that share one courtyard and cell D4, which is separated from the three and shares a courtyard with the kitchen – these two blocks constitute the lengths of the rectangular structure. While D4, the kitchen, the ration store and A-Wing form the northern width of the rectangular pattern, D1, the office block and several punishment cells that share a wall with B-Wing, form the southern width – a quadrangle in the middle crowns the rectangular profile. That's Mikuyu prison. And here life revolves around the kitchen, which is immediately to the left as you step out of D4. It is a simple and ugly contraption of a wall, sixty-seven layers of red brick high, at my last count, an open entrance in the middle with two large open windows on either side, and corrugated iron roofing that slants backwards to the world outside. The builder must have got stuck on this northern wall of the prison and left it yawning purposelessly, incomplete, as if in disgust. There are two types of prisoners here: the condemned prisoners whom I call our 'terminal friends' and us, the political prisoners. Both depend on the kitchen for survival. When TS takes me there he starts by showing me a shallow drainage, which runs alongside the floor, through the back wall in the corner, leading outside where a swamp has apparently developed. Frogs used to stray from the swamp into the kitchen through the drainage once, and for several months TS tamed them in the kitchen; but that's a story for another time, he says.

Three huge electric pots are bang in the middle. When TS takes the lid off the first, I see lumps of boiling porridge springing as high as the kitchen's sooty ceiling. These will be restrained only when the lid is put back on or when one fellow on duty pours maize flour into the boiling porridge and another stirs it with the kitchen's long and heavy wooden ladle to cook the porridge into thicker *nsima* for lunch. The up-and-down rhythm that the wooden ladle makes as one stirs the pot can be heard many miles outside prison, TS claims. When he lifts the lid off the second pot to check if the red kidney beans are cooking, weevils floating on the red froth greet us. The monsters simply refuse to dislodge, TS says, however much one tries to remove them before the beans are cooked. The third pot has a crowd of saucepans dancing above the boiling water. Food for the prisoners on 'special diet' is steam cooking in the saucepans. Steam cooked in this manner the food is believed to improve its texture and flavour somewhat. So, the chief privilege that occupants of D4 enjoy is that of steam-cooking their food in small saucepans, while food for the rest of the prisoners is cooked directly in any one of the massive electric pots. And the fellows squatting in the corner of the courtyard are extracting weevils and other pests lodged in the red kidney beans that they soaked overnight. Having had their red skins and weevils removed, the lobules will be boiled and mashed, making Mikuyu version of the delicious dish popularly called *chipere*. "So, if some D4 prisoners look healthier than others, it may be because they eat steam-cooked food and *chipere*!" TS says, rather triumphantly. This is why even officers and their guards bring their own food into the kitchen to be steam-cooked – though this is not officially sanctioned. I tell TS I love the kitchen for the electric pots. When I was told to transfer to the kitchen I feared the eyesores that come from wood smoke. We are spared that with electric pots.

The second, arguably most important, feature of Mikuyu is the ration store, which is located between the kitchen and A-Wing. When the ration store officer comes, TS takes me there to see how the *Nyapalas* and those allowed into the store share out the prison's food. A pungent and agonisingly foul smell instantly hits me. I see six bags of maize flour leaning against one wall; there are four bags of red kidney beans, two of pigeon peas, two-and-a-half of rice, five of salt, three-and-a-half of brown sugar, a carton of cheap red soap and a box of toilet rolls. Three green bunches of bananas for those on special diet are heaped in one corner. My attention is immediately drawn to the weevils, pests and maggots crawling on the bags of beans and maize flour. I do not understand how we survive eating this poisonous food. One bag of salt and another of brown sugar are rock solid and stink. Apparently the rain seeped through the rusty corrugated iron roofing above and fell on them, hardening its contents, making it toxic in the process; why the bags are not disposed of is hard to comprehend. Anyone can see that the food, the toilet rolls and the tablets of cheap red soap are not adequate for the one hundred or so condemned and political prisoners who live here. And whatever method you choose to cook the flour or the red kidney beans, the result looks, feels and smells lethal. I see why I threw up after sipping a little of my breakfast on my first morning at the New Building Wing. It must be a miracle that we survive after eating this stuff. Banda and his cabal should be ashamed of themselves for choosing to feed us this rot in a country where the prison services could be self-sufficient and growing their own food. And Brown is right. If the British had given Banda and other Malawian nationalists this kind of food at HM Prisons Gweru, Khama and other prisons in the then Southern Rhodesia, and at Kanjedza Detention Camp in Limbe during the struggle for our independence, none of them would have returned home alive.

I soon notice that I am not alone in thinking that we should find ways of changing our condition. The cellmates do not accept this food without doing something about it. Throughout the years the *Nyapalas* have persuaded the ration store officer to let D4 keep the following day's ration in their cells at night. This allows the friends on dawn duty to push some of the rotten food through the kitchen drainage to the world outside, so that fresher provisions can be brought in faster. And when the prison staff, some of whom are on wages too small to feed their large families, crave for this rotten food, the mates in the kitchen encourage them to take some. A good deal of trafficking goes on between those who work in the ration store and those on dawn duties on the one hand, and the prison staff on the other – often cellmates readily offer this rotten food to prison staff in return for minor freedoms and privileges too. When I challenge TS about the morality of the trafficking that goes on, he dismisses my point with a smile and concludes on a rather sombre note: "Doc, don't you think this form of justice is better than their imprisoning us here without trial and without charge? Mustn't we sometimes take drastic measures to beat the dictator who expects us to return home dead? Or at best paralysed? And anyway, we have complained to the prison authorities about this rotten food; no-one at the prison headquarters or here seems to care. Let me make a suggestion, Doc; don't be quick to dismiss or judge; look and listen, then respond accordingly. Do you want to die here? Don't you want to see your wife and children again like all of us?" I shake my head in agreement. "There I rest my case," TS concludes.

Then he changes the subject: "And Doc, because we have no library, you should be prepared to share some of the most boring stories we tell one another here. People tell the weirdest stories on earth. Often the same stories are told over and over again, sometimes without changing anything, sometimes taking away this and adding that. But nobody interrupts the storytellers when they are in business. Have you ever thought that listening to stories that you know to be downright lies can be fun? And Doc, everyone is looking forward to hearing your stories. Even telling us a couple of lies will do; your lies will be fresher to most of us who have never been to university, anyway; they are bound to be interesting. And as I say, don't worry if the stories you tell us are true or not: given Banda's kind of politics, perhaps there's no difference between lies and truths, don't you think?" I don't know what to think; I wish I could think, laugh or cry.

11
A-Wing

There is a cell in Mikuyu where no political prisoner wants to go. It's called A-Wing. Its courtyard is flanked by two famous rooms: the first has a dozen communal showers with reeking, slimy floors and walls with green moss and brown lichen – only six of the showers work; the second has a dozen open communal pit latrines, six of which work and the rest are permanently blocked by excrement. The stench that pours out of these amenities into A-Wing courtyard and the entire prison is excruciating. These rooms are scrubbed clean only when the chief commissioner of prisons visits, which is not often; but some of the guards tell us that the stench is the central part of the punishment we have to suffer. And A-Wing's origin is curiously intertwined with the oral history of the wars that people have been unsuccessfully waging against Banda's despotic regime since independence. There have been two major armed rebellions against Banda. The first came from my home district of Mangochi in the south. After Banda had sacked six cabinet ministers, he instructed the police not to give the ministers he had sacked platforms to put their case to the people against him. Henry Masauko Chipembere with his stubborn lieutenants Evance Medson Silombera and Kumpwelula Kanada waged protracted guerrilla warfare, engaging Banda's army in the mountain ranges of Mangochi district. The rebellion was eventually quelled and some foreign diplomats at the time allowed Chipembere to leave the country secretly for the US. His lieutenants boldly continued their guerrilla war until they were captured and publicly hanged – that's why Banda and his henchpeople consider Mangochi a rebel district and anyone who comes from there a rebel until proven otherwise. Yatuta Chisiza from Karonga district, northern Malawi, led the second armed rebellion with a batch of eight or so tough rebels, who entered Malawi through the Zambia/Mozambique border into Mwanza district. These wiped out Banda's battalion until British officers rescued them, killing Yatuta for them.

The third rebellion came from the central region. It was in effect an alleged bloodless plot to overthrow Banda rather than a full-blown rebellion. The MCP secretary general and administrative secretary, Albert Muwalo, aided by the head of Special Branch Focus Gwede, led the plot. Supporters of the cabinet ministers that Banda had sacked were indiscriminately detained and imprisoned, mostly at Dzeleka prison. When Banda got himself elected as president for life at the MCP convention held at Mzuzu in 1971, opposition throughout the country grew. Muwalo and Gwede imprisoned *en masse* those who did not support the life presidency. Anyone who was considered radical or too independent minded, including at one point journalists, statisticians, economists, church leaders and others, were rounded up and dumped in Dzeleka, Maula, Zomba Central, Chichiri, Msanje and other prisons throughout Malawi.

In the university, Focus Gwede is alleged to have liaised with the Chancellor College registrar, Alex Meke Kalindawalo, a Boston University political scientist and strategist, who, supported by assistant university librarian Ralph Masanjika, is believed to have masterminded the imprisonment of more than a dozen Malawian academics and university administrators, mostly from the north. The first Malawian principal of the University at Chichiri campus Peter Mwanza, Alifeyo Chilibvumbo from the Department of Sociology and Anthropology, James Chipasula from the Department of Public Administration, Chifipa Gondwe from the Department of History, Bernard Harawa and Peter Chiwona, both from the Department of Education, Felix Mnthali and Mupa Shumba from the Department of English, the agro-economist Alan Mtegha from Bunda College of Agriculture and

John Banda, the first Malawian university registrar – these and others were imprisoned for security reasons which were never explained. It was believed that after the expected change of government Kadzamira would become vice-chancellor, Kalindawalo university registrar and Masanjika university librarian; and the country's education would no longer be in the hands of northerners but academics from the central region.

And the Muwalo-Gwede-Kalindawalo strategy was rather obvious. Banda was to be ousted from power at a political rally during one of his crop inspection tours. Muwalo and Gwede would then release the tens of thousands of political prisoners they had thrown into prisons, some of them since the cabinet crisis, thereby making themselves instant liberators of the innocent and gaining the political support they badly needed, especially from the north and the south. And because the plotters had come from the central region, Kalindawalo, allegedly from Banda's own home district of Kasungu, Muwalo and Gwede from Ntcheu district, and Masanjika from Ntchinji district, Banda's suspicion was never aroused. But the plot collapsed. Apparently the other central region contenders to Banda's dominion exposed it before Banda's political rally began. And the plot was credited to Muwalo-Gwede-Kalindawalo only after it had failed. Otherwise it was generally thought that other central region powers-in-waiting were going to share out cabinet and other posts in government and in the university. The then Governor of the Reserve Bank of Malawi, John Tembo, obviously with the support of his niece at the state house, would have liked to return to politics after his record as minister of finance had not impressed Banda. Inspector General Mac Kamwana and secretary to the president and cabinet, and head of civil service John Ngwiri were supposed to have known of the plot. The exact details of the central region opposition to Banda's totalitarian rule, and whether or not these authorities independently or jointly sanctioned the plot to overthrow Banda, will probably not be fully known. What was clear is that the triumvirate of Tembo, Ngwiri and Kamwana, individually or collectively, would have reaped the rewards of the *coup d'état* if it had succeeded. The New

Building Wing in Mikuyu was apparently built to hold Banda's closest cabinet ministers after the *coup d'état* – hence it was referred to as the VIP section of the prison. A-Wing was supposed to hold Banda's junior cabinet ministers if the attempted government overthrow had succeeded.

To crown the never-ending ironies of our times, however, it was Muwalo and Gwede who officially opened the New Building Wing of Mikuyu as prisoners. Kalindawalo was imprisoned at Zomba Central, where some of the university academics he had recommended for detention welcomed him with a good beating on arrival. For the rest of his time in prison he was protected by the guards until he was released and exiled himself in Zimbabwe, where an old university friend of his recommended him for the position of assistant registrar in one of the faculties of the university. Today only the most dangerous political prisoners are admitted to A-Wing or the New Building Wing. At present only Banda's longest living prisoner, Martin Machipisa Munthali, occupies A-Wing.

12
Hold Them Tight

31 October 1987, Saturday. It's more than four weeks now, I've had no news of my family and I know they've had none of me. I am getting worried, very worried. Obviously rumours of my whereabouts have been flying about, judging from the numerous stories that are reverberating within the walls of my prison. I was murdered like 'the famous gang of four', but unlike them, Banda's hungry crocodiles in the Lower Shire Valley chewed me up alive. I was dumped at the Zomba Central prison, Chichiri prison in Blantyre, Maula prison in Lilongwe, the Dzeleka prison in Dowa district, the isolated notorious prison in Nsanje district – the speculations have been worryingly endless, one of the most dislodging of which is that I was murdered and my bones are buried at St Mary's cemetery in Zomba town. The truth is nobody knows where I am. That's a fact. As nothing new seems to be happening after my transfer to D4, I find myself fretting more and more. And the questions that haunt my sleepless nights are many. Has my wife lost her job? Have the children been expelled from school? Has my family been thrown out of the university house? Where exactly is my family? How is my fragile Mother? Are my colleagues in the department being harassed? I know I am not indispensable, but how has the redistribution of the courses I teach gone? How is the colleague who joined the department from Australia coping? Is my course in pragmatics being offered? I pluck up courage and consult TS. He suggests I have a private word with Brown who, lying on his bed, listens empathetically to my fears. And with that extraordinary generosity which fills the

'Republic of D4', he fishes out two Lifebuoy Soap wrappers from his pillow of blanket-rags and a short pencil lead from his kinked hair – so kinked hair does have its use after all, I think to myself. "Hold them tight," he says, shoving them into my right hand; into my left hand, shoving his roll of toilet paper. I know his kind of game. I am about to join the famous African writers who have used soaps, soap wrappers, toilet paper and other unlikely objects to communicate with the outside world – Dennis Brutus, Wole Soyinka, Ngũgĩ wa Thiong'o and Breyten Breytenbach among them. Why didn't I ask earlier about this? Why didn't anyone tell me about this? Perhaps Brown was just waiting for me to ask. But any feelings of getting above myself quickly evaporate as he announces loudly to the rest of the cellmates: "Sorry, fellows, but our professor here wants to use the toilet".

I am embarrassed, but when Ndovi and those whose beds are nearest the toilet in the corner leave the cell and join those playing Ludo or Draughts in the courtyard – to give me privacy – I understand why Brown made the announcement. Pingeni, reading the Bible on his bed at the other end of the cell, declares that it's too hot for him to sit in the courtyard outside: "I don't mind hearing the 'bombs' to be blasted from the professor's bottom," he says. We laugh as Brown shows me how to jam a long broom handle from the kitchen against the door to keep it half-closed, a sign to those in the courtyard that someone is using the toilet; that way nobody should barge in. I begin by flushing the toilet so that Pingeni won't hear the rustle of paper as I straighten the Lifebuoy soap wrappers, though I'm more afraid that prison guards will burst in and find me committing the unforgivable rebellion of writing to my wife. Comforted by the thought that Brown and TS will be watching out for me in the courtyard, I sit down on the toilet, rest my Lifebuoy Soap wrappers on the toilet roll and begin the first of many notes to my wife, using our own intimate names for each other:

Dee, I am alive. Thank God. They took me to Mikuyu prison from where I am writing this. I am well. How are

you, the children, Mother? Still staying in the university house? The children still at school? Not lost your job yet? I pray every day; hope and cry. No idea why I was arrested. Have not been charged with any crime. The authorities hinted that someone at the university reported me directly to the life president, without telling the police authorities. If you can, find out from CC principal K or university council chairman JT – they'll know if anybody does. Probably easiest to find out the official position from V.C. John Dubbey. Send your reply through Fr Pat but do be careful. Tell Lan & Alice in York, that I am here and have been in touch. Pepani (sorry) for the pain you and the children will suffer because of this. I repeat I am well. But miss you all very, very much.
Lots of love.
Daa.

The second note is to Fr Pat O'Malley, a veteran of troubled times. Having been in Nigeria during the Biafran civil war and survived the experience there, he came to Malawi where he's known as a doughty fighter for civil rights. When my university teacher Felix Mnthali, my colleague Mupa Shumba and other local academic staff mostly from northern Malawi, were imprisoned in the 1970s, it was Fr Pat who looked after some of their families. That he arrived at my house just before the police dragged me away for interrogation the day I was arrested and brought here, is typical of his honour, selflessness and generosity:

Dear Fr Pat, Greetings from Mikuyu prison. Thank God I survived the ordeal the day I showed you my cuffed hands. Gave me hope to see you at the house before I was 'taken'. Maybe you've already told Landeg White at the University of York, David Munthali on sabbatical at Newcastle University, Neil Smith at University College London, Felix Mnthali at the University of Botswana, Hangson Msiska at the University of Stirling, Lupenga Mphande at Ohio State

University, Frank Chipasula at Brown University and other colleagues, compatriots and friends all over the world about my imprisonment. Looks like someone reported me directly to the H.E. without telling the police – and you know who – otherwise, I was not tried or charged with any offence. N.B. This courier has taken incredible risks; might need some help for transport; more of him in future, God willing, but can be trusted completely. For all our sakes, please keep his identity and our correspondence under wraps. I hate to think what would happen to us all if either were discovered. Kindly pass on the note to Mercy. Tell David Kerr about the courier, stressing the secrecy needed; hope nobody is harassing him in the Department of Fine and Performing Arts, or you and other colleagues, or the students in the English department. Send us your news, any news, please.
Love & Peace.
J.

Not exactly in the class of Brutus, Soyinka, Ngũgĩ or Breyten Breytenbach, but as I pull up my *foya* shorts and flush the toilet with much force and noise carefully folding my notes of Lifebuoy soap wrappers, I feel the first shiver of pleasure and self-satisfaction since I landed in this hell-hole. I return to my bed in a self-congratulatory mood. I believe I have taken the first step to connect with the world outside, though yet again Pingeni punctures my complacency:

"Doc, what university bombs I heard there! But next time you use the toilet, flush only after the big job; the water is erratic here; you were lucky the toilet worked again after the first flush; you'd have been embarrassed."

All this said in a quiet voice without looking up from the page of the Bible he's reading. I accept my oversight with a grin as I return the broomstick that was holding the door half-closed to its original place. Brown comes in and takes back his roll of toilet paper and his pencil lead. He takes my neatly folded notes and rolls them in the hem of his *foya* shirt and whispers that he has a partner at the Centre for Social Research in the university who knows Fr Pat and will ensure he gets the notes. Brown simply fills me with confidence and hope; even in these conditions the respected journalist and broadcaster is informed and organised – more than enough reason to be jailed in this culture of secrecy and corruption.

That night I have the first series of disjointed dreams. All I can recall is what's centred on my eldest uncle, without whom my brother and I would not have gone to school. He had shot himself and died without proper explanation while I was a student at University College London. It later transpired that he had been frustrated by the famine of 1980, which life president Banda's government had claimed, typically, did not exist – no-one in Banda's villages up and down the country was starving, no-one had died. But in a letter to me my uncle begged to differ and wrote about how our extended family in the Lower Shire would starve to death if I did not intervene. Despite the pledge he had made when I was young, that he would never seek help from me when I grew up, on this occasion he shamelessly sought my help and declared that the situation was dire. My student grant was too small for my family of four, but I sent him two lots of £60.00, the first through his son and the second through the nephew he had adopted as his son. I was to discover after I wrote him a letter to explain the two lots of monies, and long after his death, that he had not received the money. Both sons had taken the money in order to buy food for their own families instead of sending it to him to feed the larger extended family. I suspected that he had taken his life in order to show the two sons what a horrible act they had done. However, the guilt I felt for his death followed me wherever I went. I kept telling myself I should not have trusted my cousins with the money. But in the dream my uncle reproaches me: "Forget about me; you are not responsible for my death; I want you to introduce your two friends Brown and TS to Mpokonyola Village to see the people there," he says and suddenly disappears. I wake up to the guard's truncheon poking

80

at my side. And as I watch the guards beat up those who want to continue sleeping, I begin to puzzle about the meaning of my dream. I am only certain about one possible interpretation: my uncle has endorsed my relationship with Brown and TS. I can therefore trust them.

Book Three
Lion of Mikuyu

13
More Political Prisoners

My transfer to D4 opens the gates for more political prisoners whose crimes against the state are more bizarre than mine. Take Rodney Masauko Banda, who is brought in one Saturday afternoon looking absolutely drained of all energy. He comes from Mpemba area of Blantyre district, southern Malawi, is twenty-two, about five-foot-six, small build, stiff neck and walks with a slight bend in his back; but everyone considers him to be so handsome that it is understandable if girls ran after him outside. Rodney was a clerk in one of the local banks in Blantyre city and was rather tactless in his relationships with the girls he loved. He should not have prematurely abandoned his Malawi young pioneer sweetheart for another he seriously loved. For in frustration the wounded sweetheart invoked the tricks which the Special Branch exploit to catch the dissidents they invent for their life president. She persuaded one of her young pioneer friends to write Rodney a letter that appeared to have been written by Banda's political opponents exiled in Tanzania. The letter invited supporters of one exiled political movement to come in their thousands to witness Banda's assassination during his forthcoming crop inspection tour of Kasungu, his home district. It was posted in Tanzania, where Banda's young pioneer High Commissioner works tirelessly to report home the political activities of Malawian exiles. Then Rodney's sweetheart alerted the post office sorting centre in Blantyre about the letters 'from a neighbouring rebel country', which her boyfriend often received. When the letter 'with a foreign stamp' arrived at Rodney's letter box, the young pioneer's security officers swooped down on his house, ransacked it, 'discovered' their booty, and waited for their culprit to arrive from work. Rodney could not defend himself. They brought him straight to Mikuyu without trial and without charge. And the security officers have told him he would be released only at the president's discretion. Brown, TS and I are so disgusted by the triviality of Rodney's crime and his becoming Banda's political enemy at such a tender age that we adopt him as one of our team. And by way of cheering him up I suggest that his story sounds familiar, for in the 1970s, Mupa Shumba, a colleague in the English department, was arrested and imprisoned for an almost exactly similar 'crime', except that in his case it was a young pioneer employee who 'discovered' the rebel letter under Mupa's pillow – informers, agents, spies and security officers planting subversive materials to catch the political dissidents they want to catch is common practice and threatens to continue long after Banda's political career. After a few days, Rodney confides in me and suggests that his parents had named him after Banda's arch-political enemy Henry Masauko Chipembere; it might have been his middle name 'Masauko' that caused his arrest.

Charles Mnyenga, about six-foot-five, in his mid-sixties, was born on Likoma Island, northern Malawi. He's brown in complexion, well built, and the cellmates say he would win Mikuyu prison beauty contest for men even in his torn *foya*. When the commander pushes Charles into D4 one afternoon, it's obvious to all that the panic-stricken man could not possibly have been a threat to Banda's leadership or to the political desires of his cabal. Charles has worked in the accounts office of the Tanzania National Railways all his life. Upon retirement, he returns home on the island, to live quietly on his pension and die in peace, he says. But anyone who has worked in countries which the security officers believe to harbour Banda's political opponents, real or imagined, is under immediate suspicion on arrival in Malawi. Likoma Island security officers must have been jealous of the 'wealth' that Charles had brought home, and decided to implicate him in the local politics in order to force him out of the island –

not an uncommon occurrence since Banda's cabinet crisis in the 1960s. Charles himself confirms that at his bogus interrogation he failed to explain the close relationship he was presumed to have had with Malawian exiles in Tanzania – because he had none. No security officer believes whatever he says in order to exonerate himself; so they bring him to Mikuyu to punish him for nothing.

AMdala aLongwe (Old Man Longwe) is brought into D4 one afternoon looking bruised and pathetic. He is bony, his hair dishevelled, and walks as if he still needed the walking stick he might have left behind the day they arrested him. Apparently, the security officers beat him up and blindfolded him as they brought him to Mikuyu. And having lost one of his front teeth, his lined cheeks and toughened face make him look older than his age, which must be about fifty, but he looks almost as old as Mkwanda. Whatever district prison he has been transferred from, Longwe bears all the marks of a prisoner who was being slowly starved to death. And all he remembers is this quarrel over land in his village in northern Malawi, but has no clue how the matter infuriated his Malawi Congress Party area branch authorities, who pronounced him another of Banda's political enemies. We think that Longwe was one of the most hardworking small-scale farmers in his village; he might have been imprisoned because he was a stubborn fighter for village justice. Longwe himself claims that although he was not sufficiently educated and not rich, his family was not starving, he sent his children to school; some of his fellow villagers did not take kindly to this sort of success. He too was brought here without proper trial or charge and will be released at the discretion of the president. D4 is demoralised by the arrival of these new prisoners, whose cases are too trivial to deserve incarceration at Mikuyu – if people enter prisons for such crimes, those of us who are presumed to have committed more serious crimes have no chance of being released from here. But while some of us weep at the hilarity and triviality of the crimes that have brought us into prison, there is despair for those who think they have over-stayed their time here; our arrival has destroyed their hope for possible liberation, despite the fact that they do not know when they are supposed to be freed. Other speculations begin. Kadango declares: "This is how the Kadzamira-Tembo clan justify the people they imprison; when the main prisoner they want is detained" – and he is thinking of me – "they imprison others with minor crimes to give Banda and the country the impression that the rebellion, for which their enemy has been apprehended, is widespread". Although Kadango has not entered school, college or university, his interpretation of political events is incisive. I feel uncomfortable that I could have got people arrested, perhaps even killed.

14

Why did I Return Home?

My folly is crystal clear from this prison. I should not have returned home after the publication of my book of poems *Of Chameleons and Gods*. When the book appeared in 1981, as I read for my doctorate degree in linguistics at University College London, it had a couple of favourable reviews, including one by Peter Bland in *London Magazine* and apparently caused a stir that I had not anticipated at home. In other African countries the publication of the book would have been good reason for celebration. But no-one cared that *Of Chameleons and Gods* was the first book of poems from a Malawian to appear in the then famous Heinemann African Writers' Series. Or that the book put my country, my university and me on the literary map of the continent. This was thought to be the kind of 'showing off' that did not impress those in power. I was not surprised, therefore, when I received stern admonition from relatives, colleagues and friends that the poems had displeased 'people in authority' back home, and that I had to be careful what I said or wrote, which countries I visited and what I did while I read for my doctorate degree. Meanwhile, nobody in Malawi's *Daily Times* or the weekly *Malawi News* reviewed the book – though, to be fair, book reviews were alien to these papers at the time. The commentators, who often made their point orally, having only heard about what the reviewers from abroad had said about the poems, claimed that the verse was critical particularly of the self-appointed heirs to the country's leadership – Banda's permanent mistress and her uncle. And predictably, the oral reviewers claimed that even the politically neutral verse in the book made a mockery of the president and his coven. Of course, nothing under Banda – indeed under any dictatorship – was ever neutral. However remotely radical the writings under despotic regimes might be, they gratified potential political opponents, who exploit them to justify whatever they cannot express under normal circumstances – that's the nature of life under despotic regimes.

But I will concede, one of the poems, 'Making Our Martyrs Clowns', does mention the traditional rock paintings of Mphunzi Hills and the leopards of Dedza Hills – places that are close to the homes of the Kadzamira-Tembo family. Almost every Malawian reader of the poem took these landscape references as veiled criticism of the brutality of Banda's cabal because they have homes there. But I had taught at Mtendere Secondary School, near the place, long before the poem was written and with American Peace Corps and British VSO teachers, I used to visit the rock paintings of Mphunzi Hills. I exploited the landscape of home in my verse as any writer would. What I had claimed in the short introduction to *Of Chameleons and Gods* might also have brought the kind of controversy I had not imagined. I had said: 'The verse in this volume spans some ten turbulent years in which I have been attempting to find a voice or voices as a way of preserving some sanity. Obviously, where personal voices are too easily muffled, this is a difficult task . . . But the exercise has been, if nothing else, therapeutic; and that's no mean word in our circumstances'. The various implications that these words carry in a totalitarian regime like ours might be the reason my relatives, colleagues and friends suggested that I think again about my intention to return home after my studies, though nobody seemed able to spell out precisely whether it was these words that seemed to be giving offence, or the poems or both, or something else I had done or said. And, rather foolishly perhaps, I did not take any of these warnings seriously. It seemed nonsense to say that I shouldn't use part of the landscape of my country in my poems because some politically ambitious people lived there. I was confident, perhaps in my naïveté that, if the security officers took me to court, I would easily defend my writing. There were several levels at which the poems – almost any poems – could be read. But from this prison the question still glares at me: Would I not have been arrested and dumped in this stench if I had taken the matter more seriously? Frankly, I do not know.

Today, we live in dangerous times, when writers' clubs, debating societies, cultural groups and associations are proscribed for fear that its members would be considered supporters of Banda's exiled political opponents. Today, whatever we think, say or do is closely monitored and scrutinised. Whoever is presumed to be a potential dissident is hunted down like an animal until he is brought down to his knees. This is a fact. I remember one of the original members of the writers' group at the university's Chichiri campus, Frank Chipasula, who literally ran across the border into Zambia being pursued by the Special Branch, for whatever he was presumed to have said about Banda's autocratic regime. Frank was lucky eventually to finish his first degree at the University of Zambia and his masters and doctorate degrees at Brown University in the US – he is the finest and most prolific poet of our generation, writing from exile in Zambia and the US. The university publications that I was involved in might also be the reason for my being brought into prison. Student magazines such as *Expression, The Jacaranda Tree* and *Odi,* the newsletter *Vanguard* or the first slim anthology of poetry from the writers' group, *Mau 39 Poems from Malawi,* where my creative efforts first appear – these and others are among the publications I helped to edit, I edited or I contributed to, and may have caused some disquiet in higher places; although I must admit we often sent the manuscripts of these to the censorship board for vetting before publication. Of course, there were occasions when we were rather bold and circumvented the censors. For example, one issue of *Odi* included the fine poetry of the eminent South African anti-apartheid activist Dennis Brutus. If the censors had known this fact the guest editor, Blaise Machila and his committee would have been expelled or imprisoned. Banda and his university cabal frowned upon Malawians who even edited or co-edited anthologies from abroad.

A good example is *Summer Fires: New Poetry of Africa*, which was co-edited by the Scottish historian, critic and fine poet Angus Calder, the South African writer Cosmo Pieterse and myself, and was published for the BBC in the Heinemann African Writers' Series. The anthology was based on the 1981 BBC World Service Poetry Competition for Africa, to which the BBC's own poet, David Sweetman, had invited the three of us as judges. Our brief was to explain to listeners of the BBC World Service for Africa how they could enter for the competition, what type of poems we liked and why, although the competitors could submit work on any subject of their choice and present it in any style or form they liked. Those who listened to the BBC programme in Malawi included government officials, security officers, the president's cabal, as well as ordinary people. Naturally the spies, informers and agents were quick to fabricate the view that I had given up my doctorate studies at University College London, was employed by the BBC and had joined the ever-growing numbers of Malawi exiles abroad – none of which was true. And, as if to underline the point, on arrival at Chileka Airport after my studies, one immigration officer greeted me with: "Have we decided to come back, then? Whatever happened to the BBC jobs we used to hear about?" Cynicism was written all over his face as he checked my passport and grinned his welcome back home. After my doctorate degree I should have taken the job I was offered in one of the Nigerian universities. I would not have been spending my precious time accusing myself for nothing, and wildly speculating on the reasons I have been chucked into this jail.

15
Republic of D4

More than two months in prison and still there is no indication why I am here, how long I will be, whether I will be taken to court, when my family will be allowed to visit me and why chief commissioner of prisons Chikanamoyo refuses to come and hear my problems. I do not know what to do. I am desperate, very desperate, which probably suits Banda and his coven well, as they always want us to despair until we crack up. Some cellmates have already begun to lose hope on my behalf. I might stay in prison longer than they anticipated, they say; I must prepare for the possibility of a long drawn-out incarceration. Others have begun telling me stories and creating situations that are meant to help me get accustomed to the idea of a long prison term. For example, after lock-up today Brown, who has been more animated by my transfer to D4 than most, introduces a subject he knows will generate discussion that will stimulate my mind – I am clearly dealing with a shrewd set of political prisoners:

"So, professor," he begins, "welcome again to Bandaland. And what, may we ask, did you do to annoy the self-styled royal family for them to bring you here? After about two months in D4, our intelligence services have uncovered one or two facts about your abduction and imprisonment. You may have annoyed Banda's private secretaries at Sanjika Palace – the Kadzamira sisters, Cecilia and Mary – or their uncle and your chairman of university council, or your college principal. What did you do in the university to annoy them?" he says. I recall the brief interrogation I had the day I was arrested and inspector general

93

Mbedza's question about what we had done to each other in the university, and tell him I haven't got the faintest idea what I could have done to infuriate the president's coterie. Then he turns and appeals to the rest of the cellmates: "People, look at our professor. Do professors like these deserve to wear torn *foyas*, eating rotten food, from crumpled *bakulis* and holed mugs, and sleeping on cold cement floors, without proper blankets, without pillows? What's happening to our country?" He suddenly laughs loudly; and everyone joins in the raucous laughter and merriment; even I begin to laugh at myself, especially when I see how, in such a short time, prison has reduced me to bones.

Mbale picks up the story: "But this is no ordinary joke, people," he says, "this is a serious matter. Indeed, why is Banda still imprisoning people who should be helping our young men and women to become better citizens of this beautiful country? When is this waste of human resources going to stop? Why do we allow this to happen?"

Old Man Mkwanda in the corner responds. "It's madness; lack of brains and jealousies Mbale," he says. "Banda is mad, he has no brains; his concubine is mad, she has no brains; her uncle is mad, he has no brains; their entire extended family ruling us illegally are mad and they have no brains; so they arrest and imprison people who are not mad and have the brains; it is their madness and jealousies that bring us here, pure and simple!"

Brown agrees: "And that's the tragedy of our African educational system, Big Man: our leaders send their young men and women to national universities or to universities abroad to get advanced qualifications, skills and experience necessary for the development of their countries. But when these young people return home, they are never trusted to put into practice the skills they've acquired; they are arrested and imprisoned instead; how can Africa progress like that?"

Ndovi near the toilet shouts with impatience: "Why don't you people believe what we've been saying all along? Banda's dislike of clever Malawians started early. Didn't Dunduzu Chisiza die in a car accident that Banda invented at Thondwe Bridge, after we

94

got self-rule from the British in the early 1960s? And you may disagree with me if you like, but wasn't Du the best-known economist in southern Africa and all the independent countries of the African Great Rift Valley, from the Somalia peninsula to the South African tip?"

Daniel Chunga concurs: "And after Du's death, Banda sacked six ministers he himself chose at independence, including the very people who invited him home from abroad to help in the political struggle against the British. To fight Banda the ex-ministers crossed the borders and formed political parties like the Socialist League of Malawi [LESOMA], Malawi Freedom Movement [MAFREMO] and others. Aren't some of us rotting here because we were thought to be members of these political parties?"

Disi tries to change the subject slightly: "Professor," he chips in, "did you know that several years ago, your university colleagues, most of them from the north, languished with us in this very prison?" I nod my head in agreement. He continues: "And I remember four students from your college: Fidelis Edge Kanyongolo, Zangaphee Chizeze and two others ... does anyone remember the other two boys from Chancellor College who suffered with us in this very prison?"

Kadango answers. "*Amwene* cheDisi, how can you forget Michael Mbwana whom we called aThube and his friend McWillie Kilion?"

That's it. Kilion and aThube," Disi recalls. "How could I have forgotten those delightful boys who were so good and so funny? They cheered us up with their stories about how their teachers or fellow students at Chirunga campus wrote and talked about the future of this country. Of course, some of us did not understand their degree talk, especially when they fell into long trances thinking about what they called important matters about the future laws of Malawi. Often we wondered whether they had smoked *chamba* or they were going mad just like everybody; but those boys really cheered us up and gave us hope that we too, would be liberated from Banda's claws one day."

"And now, we have this professor," Chunga cuts in. "Look at him. What could that man have done to be dumped here?" And raising his voice and pointing at me he asks: "Does this man even know what an AK47 looks like, let alone know where to pull the trigger?" Rasping laughter ripples within the walls of D4. TS enquires: "When will our political leaders stop amassing wealth for themselves, their relatives, their district and their communities and begin improving the lives of all the people who vote them into power? When we voted these people into power to become our MPs, we hoped that they would help us improve our lives. Ask me what they want now. They want us to serve them, not them to serve us! What kind of people are we dealing with?"

Kadango observes: "I remember when Banda first arrived in Lilongwe. He came with very few clothes. Often he sought the help of politician and businessman Chester Katsonga to help him out with transport to travel to the various places he wanted to visit. Ask me how many overcoats, bowler hats, striped suits and sunglasses Banda has now."

"Don't forget the Rolls-Royce," chimes in Mbale.

"I was forgetting that indeed!" Kadango continues: "And does a man who sleeps with a woman he refuses to marry need thirteen palaces to sleep with her in?"

Cheeky outbursts of laughter and mockery ensue. But Kadango will not be deterred: "As for you, professor, I agree with *Amwene* cheMkwanda, it's jealousies that have brought you here. It's John Tembo, his nephew at Chancellor College and his two nieces at Sanjika Palace that have got you into this trouble. These people could not do the things you can; you were too clever for their liking: that's why you are here. I was a businessman once; I know how these people destroy whoever performs better than they do – this country is going to the dogs with jealousies!"

"That's why the very word 'jealousy' is enshrined in our national anthem," Pingeni observes from the furthest corner of the cell: "Everybody must eliminate ignorance, hunger, disease and especially jealousy, says our national anthem, if I recall correctly!"

Ndovi immediately cuts in: "Pingeni, do you have to bring into this discussion your so-called national anthem and whatever your Malawi young pioneer bases taught you? Why can't you, for once, think of this innocent man without reminding us of your stupid national anthem? If you have nothing to say, just shut up, but please don't remind us of your MYP and what your stupid national anthem says."

Pingeni won't take Ndovi's irritation lying down; clearly incensed too, he stands up and shouts back:

"Ndovi, listen to me – nobody is talking about Malawi young pioneer bases here. As I've told people many times before, I admit I was a young pioneer driver for many years, but in prison I want to be treated as a human being, not as a MYP driver; I don't want the MYP experience to be used against me; I want to be treated as I am. And I come from Banda's central region, not from the north or the south, yet where am I? Am I not suffering like everyone else in this prison, and for nothing? Was I planted by the MYP more than six years in this pit? No, I would have been released a long time ago if I had been their spy. And I don't talk about your past, Ndovi. How would you feel if I talked about your involvement in Dr Attati Mpakati's assassination at Stanley Hotel in Harare all those years ago? Were you or were you not involved in the assassination of the LESOMA leader? Didn't you northerners who did not want the southerner to lead the opposition party plan his death? And let me remind you of this, Ndovi: you cannot shut me up; I have as much right to speak in this cell as anyone. If people want to fight, they should just say so – we can fight!"

Pingeni boldly announces this as he walks towards Ndovi with fists ready for battle. Kadango intervenes as people leave their beds to stop the imminent fight. Everyone shouts Pingeni and Ndovi down. "Quarrelling amongst yourselves will not beat Banda, his cronies or our despair," Old Man Mkwanda declares. The prison guard who is patrolling outside D4, and must have heard the commotion, hits the wall of our cell three times with the butt of his gun. We shut up at once, everybody returning to his bed. Lying on my back, with knees up, on the cold cement bed and watching the geckos and cockroaches on the ceiling and the rafters of my cell, I begin to reflect on the discussion we've just had, and how lively and revealing it was, although I was not given any opportunity to contribute anything to it. I marvel at the various points of view that each participant provided. It was as if they were all dying to give their opinions without my intervention in the subject that was close to their hearts. But I have no illusions. I have been transferred to a cell where people's tempers are short. Pingeni and Ndovi almost hate each other; we could have witnessed a nasty fight. And yet I consider my transfer a blessing. This must be the kind of freedom Alex was referring to at the New Building Wing. I particularly liked how everybody contributed to the discussion without fear, naming names and events we'd not dare to name outside prison. No-one is afraid of anyone; everyone wants to fight for his own patch of land, as it were; everyone wants his dignity restored, his story told and heard. The observations that cellmates made, the young or old, literate or illiterate, were so astute and their memory of historical events so sharp that I cannot help feeling the breath of fresh air that D4 provides. I admit some of the discussion might have been exaggerated, but I wonder if we'll ever have a political leader who allows this kind of freedom of speech without fear of arrest, prison or death. I am beginning to understand why this cell is called the 'Republic of D4'.

Scrubbing The Furious Walls of Mikuyu

Is this where they dump those rebels,
these haggard cells stinking of bucket
shit and vomit and the acrid urine of
yesteryears? Who would have thought I
would be gazing at these dusty, cobweb
ceilings of Mikuyu prison, scrubbing
briny walls and riddling out impetuous
scratches of another dung-beetle locked
up before me here? Violent human palms

98

wounded these blood-bloated mosquitoes
and bugs (to survive), leaving these vicious
red marks. Monstrous flying cockroaches
crashed here. Up there cobwebs trapped
dead bumblebees. Where did black wasps
get clay to build nests in this corner?
But here, scratches, insolent scratches!
I have marvelled at the rock paintings
of Mphunzi Hills once but these grooves
and notches on the walls of Mikuyu prison,
how furious, what barbarous squiggles!
How long did this anger languish without
trial, without charge, without visit here and
what justice committed? This is the moment

we dreaded; when we'd all descend into
the pit, alone; without a wife or a child
without Mother; without paper or pencil
without a story (just three Bibles for
ninety men) without charge without trial.
This is the moment I never needed to see.

Shall I scrub these brave squiggles out
of human memory then or should I perhaps
superimpose my own, less caustic; dare I
overwrite this precious scrawl? Who'd
have known I'd find another prey without
charge without trial (without bitterness)
in these otherwise blank walls of Mikuyu
prison? No, I will throw my water and mop
elsewhere. We have liquidated too many
brave names out of the nation's memory;
I will not rub out another nor inscribe
My own, more ignoble, to consummate this
Moment of truth I have always feared!

16
First Contacts

7 November 1987, Saturday. It's boiling hot in the courtyard outside, the sun is burning directly overhead and the order of the day is as little movement as possible. Pingeni is admiring the antics of what he calls 'Mother wagtail', which is chattering on the roof of A-Wing; it's twitting and stretching its fluffy wings, dancing and singing on the roof. To him and the prisoners who have stayed here longer this can only mean that someone would be getting important news or visitors today, particularly the person who first saw the wagtail. I think Pingeni is mad; he has probably run out of speculative narratives to tell us. I cannot see what chattering wagtails have to do with the arrival of news or anyone's visitors. So lying on my bed, knees up as usual, I continue reading the Bible. Then Brown walks in from the courtyard, throws himself on his bed, and with limbs sprawling, despairs about the weather:

"I cannot bear today's heat outside, but this hard cement is no better," he complains, and casually but softly whispers: "May I borrow your Bible?" I hand it over. He opens it and slips what he calls 'bulletins' between the pages. He reads on briefly as if he were looking up some verse he'd forgotten, and passes the Bible back to me with instructions, as he looks out for guards from his bed: "Read them quickly. Store the critical events in memory. Chew the notes well. And flush them down the toilet afterwards." He runs to the courtyard to keep sentry.

My hands shake as I open the first 'bulletin'. From Fr Pat. He's delighted to connect. Passed on the note to Mercy, who's writing her community nursing examinations in Lilongwe. Family still in the university house. Vice-chancellor John Dubbey has managed to get my salary paid into my bank account for a little longer. "Praise the Lord," I hear myself whisper. Salaries of detained academics are stopped from the moment of arrest. This is a miracle. What did Dubbey do to convince the university council chairman, the finance officer and the university housing committee? God bless Dubbey! There's more. After he saw me handcuffed at the back of the police vehicle, Fr Pat first cheered up my children and Mother; then he drove to my old school, Zomba Catholic Secondary School. And ignoring the fact that most offices were bugged, he phoned his friend, Fr Leo Morahan, at Galway Parish, The Republic of Ireland. They spoke in Gaelic. I had been arrested, he'd actually seen me at the back of the police vehicle, but did not know where we were headed for. Could he pass on the message to our mutual friend Landeg White at the Centre for Southern African Studies, the University of York, England? He would know what to do. Landeg informed the BBC instantly, *Index On Censorship Magazine* editors and Writers in Prison Committee of International PEN in London. Within twenty-fours hours of my arrest, I had my two minutes of fame as radio commentators in Africa, Europe and the US reported my arrest. Colleague and friend Steve Chimombo even went to my house to tell Mother and my children that the story of my arrest was broadcast on the BBC World Service for Africa and on other radio stations.

A chunk of disbelief sets in my throat. Suddenly the rags of blanket on my bed sticking to my sweating body do not matter. Let the cellmates sweating in rows on their cement beds without their *foya* in the heat, conjuring up another pathetic image of slaves on European ship decks during the African Atlantic Slave Trade years ago – let them sweat. But when I envision Fr Pat speaking in Gaelic to his friend in Galway, I want to laugh and shout victory! The Gaelic must have delighted the ever-present informers listening in at the national post office sorting centre, which is headed by another one of the Kadzamiras. The news is too good to be true. And Fr Pat had already informed the friends

I had listed in my note as well as David Kerr in the Department of Fine and Performing Arts about our 'privatised' post office. David himself has sent a note, which says: 'As soon as I talked to Anthony Nazombe about your being abducted, I informed Amnesty International in London about it. The fight for your liberation began as soon as you were abducted.' I feel utterly humbled and cannot find the words to thank these two. Tears begin welling up in my eyes. And taking the Bible with the bulletins with me, I stand up, shake myself free and give Brown and TS the Bible while I join the rest of the cellmates playing games of Draughts and Ludo in the courtyard.

Commander BK suddenly appears in the courtyard and invites Brown to the office, where visitors have come to see him. Pingeni reminds us about the wagtail that was singing on the rooftop of A-Wing this morning. His madness has been vindicated, he says. And I recall the bulletins brought by Brown today that might justify Pingeni's claim. As Brown prepares to see his visitors, one or two people shout their messages for his visitors to take to their relatives, if BK allows him to do so. We love BK because he is the kind of commander who can do this. He is fearless. Soon BK shouts for me to take a bucket from the kitchen for Brown. "This is good news," says TS, "it means Brown is being allowed to let you see his visitors." I take the biggest bucket to the visitors' room, which I see properly for the first time. I find Brown sitting on the visitors' bench, talking to the man who has come for him. He stops when he sees me and says:

"Jack, this is my dad, Bambo James Mpinganjira. Dad, this is our new arrival Dr Jack Mapanje, head of the English department at Chancellor College."

"Oh, how are you, Dr Mapanje?" he asks.

"I am well, sir, and how are you?"

"I am fine. Only the other day was I listening to the BBC World Service for Africa, where they were mentioning your name. These days, radio stations in Europe and Africa continue to talk about you."

"Thank you for the news, sir," I answer.

"Take courage, it will be all right in the end," he concludes.

"Thank you for coming to see us, sir," I reply.

Brown gathers the pineapples, bananas, loaves of bread, five one-kilo packets of sugar and five of rice; he shoves them in my bucket; I say goodbye to Brown's dad; BK opens the door to the quadrangle for me; I return to D4, delighted with the news Brown's dad has brought. It confirms what I have read in the bulletins. When Brown, TS and I take stock of the day's events that evening, the news in the bulletins becomes our main subject of discussion. "This is beyond our expectation," whispers Brown. "The struggle for our possible liberation has truly begun; this is why we wanted you transferred here; what we need now is to record everyone's story and send it abroad to human rights activists."

From now on Brown, TS, Mbale and others begin to gather as much information as possible about the crimes the political prisoners are presumed to have committed. We will compile these stories and pass them on to David, Fr Pat and Landeg. They in turn will pass these to human rights organisations abroad, some through diplomatic missions in Malawi. The window to the world is open forever. That radio stations in Africa and Europe still report my abduction is a humbling and reassuring achievement. But, intrigued, I ask TS and Brown who the courier of our bulletins might be. "For his daring we've nicknamed him *Noriega*," Brown says. "Safer than any post office courier, the real lion of our lives, the true Ngwazi for political prisoners in Mikuyu, you'll recognise *Noriega* by his squeaking boots, and you'll understand what he does for us in time."

For weeks *Gossip International*, as I call those who share the clandestine correspondence with the outside world, is particularly delighted by the speed and courage with which Fr Pat, David and Landeg passed on the news of my detention to the world. Fr Pat's telephone call has patently saved my life, brought credit to himself, his missionary society and, above all, to the Catholic Church, which is known for showing little enthusiasm in defending the sheep it claims to shepherd. Indeed, the assassination of Malawi's 'gang of four' is the classic example of Banda's method of elimination of political dissidents. Anyone who is deemed by Banda's security, or that of the Kadzamira-Tembo cabal, to be radical, popular with the people, or closer to Banda than they are or, all of these, is abducted and held incommunicado; the world's media is monitored; if no serious protests are forthcoming, the presumed 'political enemy' is murdered and the death pronounced an accident; the fellow is said to have been 'accidentalised' – a term invented at the workshops of the writers' group. The beginning of correspondence with my family and colleagues diminishes the fears I had for their safety, bringing hope where there was despair. These happy contacts are most inspiring:

The Speed is What Matters, My Dear Padre[*]

It's the speed, my dear padre, the speed with
Which you risk to save one's life that counts;

The chameleon hesitates, often three times,
Before putting his foot down, the squirrel

Lashes its bushy tail before it leaps onto its
Safer baobab branch, the spotted cheetah

Stalks the undergrowth, smarting for her
Final pounce, but nothing happens without

The speed with which they do their deed,
My dear padre, the speed is all – for it was

The speed with which you chose to telephone,
Speaking in Gaelic, so our tyrant's surrogates

---

[*] First appeared *Stand Magazine, new series, Vol.1, No 2, 1997:89–90.*

Could not decipher your word – that you had
Seen this bumblebee chained behind their

Security van; it's the speed your Galway Parish
Friend sent the word to our friend in York

To shout to the world for another who'd been
Taken; it's the speed the radio waves recycled

The word across the globe the following day,
Shaming our Life Excellency and his minions,

Shattering their designs to kill; it's the speed
That saved the bumblebee which matters, padre.

17

The New Censorship Board?

One institution that might have brought me into this dungeon directly or indirectly is the newly constituted censorship board, a tragicomedy in itself. When the life president visited the US he was presented with a book on democracy. On his return home he ordered all his members of parliament to read the book so that they could see how he interpreted democracy in the context of Malawi politics. It fell to the incumbent secretary to the president and cabinet to remind his president, however, that his own censorship board had banned the book long before his visit to the US. Banda was furious and is believed to have sacked the entire censorship board. Whereupon his permanent companion asked her uncle and her brother in the university to help the president. The situation must have seemed God-sent to them. It suited their expectations well since it gave influence in an area that counted – the assumption at the time being that whoever controlled the university controlled the country. Zimani Kadzamira, who had just been appointed Chancellor College principal, effectively reconstituted the board with the academics he trusted, including Adrian Roscoe my colleague in the English department, Enoch Timpunza from the chiChewa and Linguistics department, Willie Nampeya from the Fine and Performing Arts department; and academics from other constituent colleges of the university, such as the fine poet and linguist Lupenga Mphande from the English department at Blantyre Polytechnic. Some members of the university's alumni working in the country were appointed to the board too. Naturally, Zimani Kadzamira appointed himself chief representative and university spokesman on the reconstituted censorship board – a position he had hitherto been occupying unofficially.

But when I submitted *Of Chameleons and Gods* to the reconstituted board, the censors must have been disappointed that the reports from their readers were more positive about the book than they had imagined. Roscoe suggested that the poems contributed to the cultural development of the country and did not recommend a ban. Mphande had no problems with any of the poems. Other readers first independently agonised over the notion of 'banning poems in a country that had so few poets' and voted against a ban. Of the reports that had been smuggled to me, only Enoch's was negative: it suggested that some of the verse in the book 'pokes at wounds that are still raw in Malawi history', though it was silent as to which poems or how they did their 'poking'. When other unacceptable reactions to the book reached me at University College London, I was enraged and wrote to the chief censoring officer, Catherine Chimwenje, asking for the official clearance of the book, which I enclosed with my letter.

I boldly suggested to her that there was nothing dangerous about the poems. I could not recall any book of poems that had brought a nation down to its knees. And exploiting their readers' reports, I pointed out that my writing had been influenced by our oral culture, which the verse was trying to preserve. Catherine's reply came sooner than I had anticipated. Her letter read as if it had been dictated by my principal, whose language and logic I was familiar with. Why had I not submitted the manuscript of the poems to the board in Malawi first, before sending it to the Heinemann African Writers' Series in the UK for publication? She asked. The point seemed somewhat bizarre. It was particularly puzzling because the tradition of sending manuscripts from abroad for the censorship board in Malawi to vet before publication had not been established. Was the board perhaps considering introducing it? However, within a few days of her reply, I received the following letter from an old university friend James Ng'ombe, who was the managing director of Dzuka

Publishing Company Ltd at the time. The letter, which came on Dzuka Publishing Company Ltd headed paper, clearly reveals what might have been going on behind the scenes amongst the proprietors of the publishing establishment, and it reads:

April, 1982.
Dear Jack,
Before breaking for Easter, I received on my desk publicity material for The First International Book Fair of Radical Black and Third World Books. That automatically tells you my predicament since this was about five days after the event had already taken place. Steve Mwiyeriwa passed the material on to me after long delay resulting from his waiting for one official to look at it. My apologies are due to you and we would like to thank you for remembering us. Dzuka can do with more such publicity. Keep on doing us that favour, Jack.

On a more business-like tone: I have been contemplating a Malawian version of "Of Chameleons and Gods" which should give our literary series a blasting send-off. This is an area I am trying to develop. I need something powerful to start us off with. Should you give us consent to proceed, it would mean, sadly, deletion of certain titles which, to quote one anonymous analyst, "pokes at wounds that are still raw in Malawi History".

The following are the implications of this request. Malawians will have a chance to read freely at least eighty per cent of your poems from this collection, and I think both you and the Malawi readership do deserve to share the experiences contained therein. For this to happen, of course, we will need to buy a licence from Heinemann after you have given us a written consent to proceed, and publish it with the omissions I am yet to indicate upon your acceptance.

*Pass my regards to Mercy, Judy and Lunda and tell
them we remember them all.*

*I hope you will write soon even if to say 'No thank
you' to the suggestions above.*

Yours sincerely,

Signed

James.

The origin of Ng'ombe's letter is intriguing. John La Rose, who
chaired the committee of Race Relations in London, and his
colleagues organised the first international book fair of radical
black and third world books. I was invited to read from my
poems and consulted on which publishing houses from southern
Africa they could invite to the festival. Among others, I mentioned
the newly formed Dzuka Publishing Company Ltd in Malawi,
little realising that the invitation would need to be officially
cleared by principal Kadzamira and university librarian Steve
Mwiyeriwa before Ng'ombe and his publishing company could
attend the festival. And Dzuka Publishing Company itself had an
atypical origin. One day, the powers that be decided that Malawi
was going to have a publishing house of its own, which would
control the buying and selling of school textbooks throughout
Malawi – this was an extraordinarily lucrative market, which
they needed to capture. The representative and managing director
of the Malawi branch of Longman Publishers UK, Collins
Malinki, who was responsible for the order and sale of such
schoolbooks, was ordered to pack up and leave his office at once.
Malinki did. And whatever constituted the local branch of
Longman Publishers UK became Dzuka Publishing Company
Limited. An executive board was drawn up with John Tembo as
chairman; Zimani Kadzamira and their closest friends were
invited to the board too.

Then Tembo flew to London. And stayed in a flat at the top of
his favourite hotel off Edgware Road – apparently he always
stayed there when he was Governor of the Reserve Bank of
Malawi. He asked the education attaché at the Malawi High

Commission, Marvin Kambuwa, to invite James Ngo'mbe and me for interview. We went. We had no choice. We were told that Tembo had been reliably informed that one of us would make him the best managing director for Dzuka Publishing Company Limited. Whoever got the job would have a massive house with a swimming pool, company car, electricity and water bills paid for, and a gardener to look after the house. We were not to worry about being seconded from the university to the publishing company. He would sort that out, as he was the chairman of both organisations. I was in the second year of my doctorate degree at University College London and did not want to disrupt my studies, however lucrative the job offer might have been. I suggested that the chairman consider my friend Ng'ombe, who had already submitted his PhD thesis at the University of London Institute of Education and was waiting for his viva voce. I dared to suggest further: since this was one of the most important jobs to the nation, the chairman might like to advertise the post internally, to give other qualified lecturers a chance to apply and to forestall future queries about how people were appointed to such important jobs without contest. Tembo gave the job to James Ng'ombe without the internal advertisement I had proposed.

Was the chairman of Dzuka Publishing Company Limited so angry with my suggestion then that he has decided to punish me with imprisonment now – more than six years later? How very odd! However, what is patently obvious about the above letter is that it seemed to have been written under duress – and it isn't hard to guess who might have pressurised my friend. The company's proprietors knew that James and I had been students in the University of Malawi; we were original members of the writers' group; and after our studies he went to teach at Bunda College of Agriculture, while I joined the English department at Chancellor College. And we remained friends throughout. I knew that Ng'ombe would be in trouble if I ignored his request, so I replied quickly, suggesting that we delay his project until I returned home after my studies, which would be soon. This would give us the opportunity to edit together the poems that seemed to be giving offence. When I returned home, however, only my dear friend Joe Masinga, working at Manica Travel Headquarters in Blantyre at the time, mentioned the matter: "Watch out, my friend," he warned, "you refused to be published by Dzuka Publishing Company Ltd – the proprietors of that establishment will punish you for it. Remember Banda's cabal never forget those who snub them. And before they slaughter the chicken, these fellows wait for it to hatch eggs for them," he concluded.

As I recall these events from the walls of my prison today, I realise how stupid I was, how mischievous what I did must have seemed. It was not the idea of my writing the letter to the chief censoring officer that seemed daring. I had no serious problems with her. I knew Catherine Chimwenje well. I was chairperson for the English syllabus committee of the Malawi Certificate of Education, and Catherine was one of the most competent chief examiners in the literature aspects of the syllabus. What I wanted was an official response to the poems in order to prepare myself for any eventualities when I returned home. Our security officers often quizzed students returning from their studies about the countries with communist or socialist connections they had visited as part of their education. Routinely, returning students would be asked about their contacts with Malawian exiles too, hoping they would find out what programmes for returning to Malawi the exiles had. Yet today, I refuse to accept that these ramifications of the newly constituted censorship board can be the true cause of my imprisonment. Somebody, tell me why I am going mad in this stinking prison?

18

Detention Order

21 November 1987, Saturday. I have been gazing at the prison's brick wall in the courtyard, counting the holes that hide people's secret notes, broken razor blades, needles manufactured from fish bones, newspaper cuttings and other items prohibited in prison, when commander BK shouts: "Professor to the office!" My name ripples within the prison walls. From the prison's office block BK repeats: "Officer-in-charge wants to see professor!" I put on cleaner *foya* in case my wife and children, relatives or friends have finally been allowed to visit me, more than three months after my imprisonment. The cellmates wish me well. "Doc, don't come back," shouts Pingeni. "Remember to fight for us when you're gone," concurs Chunga. "Just tell the world how boring and inhuman it is here," declares Mbale. But I know this can't be my release, and before BK closes the gate behind us he whispers that the man who wants to see me has come from the police headquarters. My heart jumps, wondering what the police would want me for; they have not come to see me as they promised when they dumped me here; why are they coming now? But I thank BK and prepare to face the fellow boldly. We head for the visitors' room, where I instantly recognise the man that even BK fears. In his forties like me, it was this fellow who disposed of the African National Congress bumf, which would have implicated me in the real politics of the region when they searched our bedroom. He also came to see me last month on a mission he did not know I had initiated. Mercy and the children did not believe the surreptitious correspondence we had been engaged in for some time. So in a note I challenged her: 'If you want to prove that I am still alive and at

Mikuyu, find my cheque book; take it to the eastern division police headquarters; tell them Mother, the children and you are starving; you need cash urgently; could they take the blank cheques for me to sign? You can then deposit the cheques into your account and buy the food you need for the family. You'd thereby have proved I am alive and at Mikuyu!' I told her. It was the perfect trick. The police fell for it and sent this man to get me to sign my cheques for Mercy, although I do not believe he is a harbinger of good news just now. And how dare he smile at me as he extends his filthy hand for a handshake! I mumble something incomprehensible and immediately attack:

"Why are you people refusing to give my wife and children visiting permits to see me? Every political prisoner here is being visited. Nobody visits me. What wrong has my family done to you?"

"The higher authorities are looking into those matters," he answers and continues, "Dr Mapanje, how are you?"

"How can anyone be within these stinking rotten walls? I want to go home. That's how I am! How can you help me?"

"The higher authorities are looking into that too," he answers.

"For how long will your higher authorities go on looking into whatever it is they are looking into?" I ask.

"I don't know, Dr Mapanje; anyway, I came here because I've been sent by the higher authorities to ask you to sign this."

"Sign what?"

"His Excellency's order for your detention."

"What?"

"The H.E's detention order for you."

"The D.O. for me to sign?"

"That's right, the D.O. for you to sign."

My head reels as if a deluge of truncheons from several prison guards has hit me at once. I feel sick and begin sweating profusely in the oppressive heat. A cockroach from the rafters falls on my visitor's lap; he mechanically pushes it aside and watches my response. It's only last week that TS and I joked about my signing Banda's famous detention order. "If it should come to signing the D.O.," TS suggested, "you should protest once or twice but sign it in the end. In the eleven years or so that I have been here, I have known lots of political prisoners who were abandoned by the Special Branch for refusing to sign Banda's detention order. You should not demand lawyers either, because the Special Branch regards such demands as being confrontational to authority." I did not like the self-censorship which TS's propositions entailed, but we are dealing with people who do not care whether we live or we die. And now this. The bench squeaks. On the dirty wall near the window someone crushed a mosquito that must have sucked his blood and left the bloody spot there glaring; I protest:

"But if I sign this D.O., I am accepting that I've done my country, the president or someone in authority wrong. You know very well I have not done anyone wrong. Why do you want me to accept that I have committed a crime when you know I have not?"

"Dr Mapanje, you must ask the higher authorities these questions, not me."

"But your higher authorities refuse to show up here. You were there when the eastern division commissioner of police promised to come to see me the day you dumped me here. To date, no higher authority has put his foot in this prison. Even chief commissioner of prisons Chikanamoyo refuses to come and hear the problems I have in his prison. When do your higher authorities plan to come? And which higher authorities are you talking about, anyway?"

"Look, Dr Mapanje, I've only been sent to ask you to sign the D.O. Your signing it will solve a lot of problems. Everybody will be happy."

Everybody? Happy? What's this man talking about? "Mister, I thought you were talking about the higher authorities a minute ago. Who's this 'everybody' you are talking about now? And why does your 'everybody' not care about what I think, what I suffer, what my wife and children suffer, what my aging mother suffers?"

"Look, man," he says with irritation, "I am only a messenger!"

He's right. There's no point wasting my energy quarrelling with this character; the so-called higher authorities have sent this junior officer precisely for them to avoid my challenging these cockroaches!

"Where do you want me to sign?" I ask, humbled.

"Just here, next to H.E.'s own signature, here."

I note that Banda's signature is the usual photocopy of the original signature of the 1960 Malawi Congress Party Card that we all carried when the party fought the British for our independence. My detention order is No. 264 and the stupid piece of paper reads:

IN EXERCISE of the powers conferred upon me by regulation 3 of the Public Security Regulations, 1965, I, H, KAMUZU BANDA, President, considering it to be necessary for the preservation of public order so to do, hereby direct that you,
  JOHN ALFRED CLEMENT MAPANJE
of N.A. Makanjira, V.H. Kadango, Mangochi, be detained at any place within Malawi for the time being approved by me as a prison or detention camp for the purposes of the said Regulations.
  signed
  H. KAMUZU BANDA PRESIDENT

I sign my name; feel sick and disgusted; and ask BK to take me immediately back to D4. I don't want to look at the Special Branch fellow again. I return to the cell choking with rage. Everybody knows that the meeting was disastrous; some assume I went to hear about death in the family; others think this will eventually lead to the punishment cell for somebody; before yet others begin speculating about another strip-search that might follow, I shout for all to hear:

"I am sorry, gentlemen, but I went to sign the D.O." I take a deep sigh in despair. "It was the fellow who searched my office and my house more than two months ago who brought it; and I've signed it; so, please leave me alone; I want to think; OK?" My voice begins to break. D4 is suddenly dead. Those playing games of Draughts and Ludo in the courtyard or in the cell stop. Shock and despair are written all over the cell's walls. There's a paradox here. While I had not signed the detention order, there was hope for me to be released.

Some cellmates even believed that my being freed quickly would be good for them. I would be forced to fight for them. I had known the subhuman conditions we live under at Mikuyu; I would, therefore, make the perfect ambassador for them. These expectations are permanently dashed now. But D4 refuses to leave me alone; for the rest of the day the cellmates come one by one to offer their condolences for my signing Banda's detention order – I feel desperate, helpless and shattered, as if I had truly signed a warrant of my death. Soon TS, Brown and I decide to take conference and resuscitate whatever hope might still be about. We must write a note to tell our friends outside prison that I've signed the dreaded D.O., which means I am here for a very long time indeed, unless somebody out there begins to shout on my behalf. I know that Fr Pat, David, Landeg, relatives, colleagues, compatriots and friends will intensify the struggle without their being told to do so. But we must still inform them, which Brown says he will. When I lie down in bed that evening I compose a prayer, which I will say regularly in addition to the three Hail Marys that Lunguzi suggested, until God opens the prison gates for me.

'Almighty God, too many, nobler than I, have perished for the liberation of this country. Please, do not add my name to their number. Lord, do not let my torturers triumph over me, my family, relatives, friends, these innocent prisoners, those suffering in other prisons throughout the country, and those fighting for our liberation. If you will, Lord, I ask for survival not death as the major statement of protest to my torturers. And let my enemies see your light, on your own terms, not on my terms or theirs, through Jesus Christ, I pray. Amen.'

That night I have the second dream, which I recall the following morning in its entirety. I am strolling along a thickly wooded valley between two mountain ranges, thinking how difficult it would be to cross the river that lies in between. In a nearby cluster of reed and grass on the riverbank I notice noses of what can only be crocodiles, poking above the gently flowing water – anyone who crosses the river will obviously be meat for these crocodiles, I think. But suddenly, between two branches of a nearby tree above me, I see a leopard hunched up ready to jump at anyone walking below. Before I begin to run, the beast turns to me, its jaws and paws bare and ready to attack. I instantly begin praying for God to spare my life. The beast leaps at me. I quickly swerve to face it, ready to fight back – though goodness knows how. All in a flash, the creature and I are down, fighting and struggling.

The beast is trying hard to pin me down on the dusty ground with its paws; I have gone for its jaws, the two sets of teeth should not close in on my hands, otherwise I am a dead man, I tell myself. Where I find the strength of a monster larger than the beast, I cannot tell. But I am suddenly struggling and pressing firmly at the beast's lower jaw with my right foot, while both hands pull more resolutely at its upper jaw. I am pressing down hard and pulling up harder until the beast begins to tear apart in two halves. The monster in me continues desperately to fight the beast that is now kicking and writhing to its death. Eventually I notice I have, in effect, ripped the animal in half from the mouth along the ribs to its tail; its insides are out, blood is pouring all over. Breathless, sweating and covered in the beast's reeking blood, I gasp for life feeling triumphant and wondering how I'd managed to kill the fearful creature.

I wake up covered in sweat, trembling with fear, my heart still pounding fast, but delighted that I am alive. One guard who poked at my side with his truncheon shouts that the morning is here. Indeed, the commanders have already opened cell D4 and the rest of the guards on their shifts are going home or taking their places in and around the prison. They have done their handover after confirming that our number is right and we are all alive – the kind of roll call I am trying to get used to. I stand up but find it difficult to walk. The toe on my right foot is swollen. And this is the toe that took most of the weight when my foot pressed firmly at the beast's lower jaw, as my hands tore the beast's mouth apart, in the dream – for two weeks I am unable to walk.

19
Lion of Mikuyu

5 December 1987, Saturday. We are playing Draughts and Ludo in D4 courtyard; our teams are shouting, cheering, jeering and encouraging the teams we support when the gate to the office block squeaks open. We hear boots that seem to be crunching towards the ration store or the kitchen courtyard where we are. We ignore whoever is coming and continue playing our games. "Perhaps it is another guard looking for yesterday's rotten leftovers to smuggle out to his starving children at home," suggests TS. It happens all the time; that's why prison officers sometimes fear prisoners who work in the kitchen: they wield a lot of power as controllers of the ration store. "Perhaps some officer is coming to tell us the latest lies that he might have heard about us on foreign radio stations last night," declares Pingeni. The relationship between the 'politicals' and the prison authority is complex and continues to astonish me. Most prison guards know that we know that they have no radios; most of them know that we know that they don't understand European languages; but we all play the 'news' game designed to make us feel good. But listen! Squeaking boots! Must be *Noriega*! I hope it's not another search, we had one only two days ago. Anyway, we've been warned. Pingeni has already run into the cell to announce the arrival of the squeaking boots in case this is another search. You can never predict the time of prison searches. That's the point of them, I suppose. And it is *Noriega*, the famous joker, who suddenly stands before us. He stamps his boots to attention, salutes us as he always does and begins shouting at us:

118

"What are you stupid political prisoners doing in this prison, shouting, jeering and cheering up your players at games like children? And what messages are you people sending abroad? Do you think you can overthrow anybody's government from here? How do you hope to topple especially the life president's government? Haven't you heard what happened to the man you call your hero, Orton Chirwa, at Zomba central when he tried to smuggle out a letter to his rebel friends in Tanzania? Look at you, rebels, dissidents – What rebels? What dissidents? There were proper rebels and proper dissidents here once, men with a fearful education, rebels with huge bushes of beards. Fearsome dissidents. Not fools like you, wearing worn-out *foyas*. What kind of government can feeble flying cockroaches like you hope to form?"

There are times when it's hard to know whether *Noriega* is joking or not; he doesn't seem to be joking now. He must be fuming about something that's gone amiss. Maybe one of our notes has been discovered at the office. His fragile chest heaving with rage and the teeth grinding aloud, *Noriega* suddenly lands his bloodshot eyes on me:

"You, come with me! Quick! The officer-in-charge wants to see you. Why don't you people behave? What have you been doing in this prison? And they say you are a professor – what, professor? Come on, to the office, double march!"

I stand up dismayed, but *Noriega* rants on.

"Professor, professor, what kind of a professor are you? There were real professors here once, professors with grey beards and sharp moustaches like British colonial district commissioners. They opened their mouths and massive knowledge poured out. They are all gone. What can you hope to do where they failed? Come on, quick march to the O.C.!"

I am horrified and painfully reminded of the day I was arrested as he pushes me towards the office. The other cellmates stand up dismayed and stupefied. Disi and TS try to put in a word for me in defence. This is their duty as *Nyapalas* but *Noriega* pushes them back, dismissing their protection abruptly with: "The O.C. does not need your *Nyapala* defence."

119

They retreat, cowed by *Noriega's* harsh tone and threatening truncheon. But the kindest guard that we have cannot come in this manner without good reason. Some cellmates have already gone to join Pingeni in the cell to hide whatever proscribed materials they might have on their beds. Scenes like these always end up with an army of guards marching in large numbers to pull the cells to pieces, demanding strip-searches that have neither reason nor rhyme. *Noriega* opens the gate to the offices, bangs it to close, locks it behind us, and pushes me into the little telephone exchange room on the left. I've heard that punishment cells are behind this telephone exchange; I see the corridor leading to them now. I've done everything possible to avoid the punishment cells I see; I'm a coward; I desperately want to be alive; these people can kill you anytime, and nobody will raise a finger in protest. Still fuming, *Noriega* grabs the telephone receiver and shouts into it. I'm still trembling, standing next to him:

"Hello, are you still there? Can you wait just a moment, please?"

Then he swings around, faces me and whispers:

"Professor, here, you've two minutes to talk to your wife!"

"What?" I shout, almost collapsing, totally thrown; but I quickly come to and grab the phone and speak softly into it:

"Hello," I recognise my wife's voice. "Dee, it's Daa. How are you and the children, Mother – all OK? I am fine. Don't worry about me. Keep praying."

She's obviously as shocked as I am, but I give her time to recognise my voice. When she's sure she shouts back:

"OK, OK, OK. We are fine too, thank God! Oh, my God, you're alive! Thank God! But don't ring again, please. Do you hear? I understand, we all understand. God will protect you! Do you hear? We are all fine: Mother, the children, everybody. But please don't ring again. We all understand. Do you hear?"

"Dee, I hear you, and oh, how I miss you..."

She's gone. My hand is still trembling, holding the telephone receiver. I look intently at *Noriega*, who was standing at the window all the while, looking out in case someone was coming towards the main gate outside. He catches me watching him. I want to give him a huge hug. He dismisses my approaches, chuckles something incomprehensible and merely grins at me. More than two months have past since I was arrested. The whole heavy-handed apparatus of the state has kept me from contact with my wife, refusing her and all my relatives, friends and colleagues visiting permits. I've sent notes through this man and other prison guards to my wife and children and to Fr Pat and David. Not in my wildest dreams could I have expected a favour like this. One courageous and wily guard has beaten Banda's entire despotic structure in one simple swoop. No political prisoner is allowed to use the telephone! If this and what *Noriega* does for us were discovered, he would be locked up forever, or worse, tortured to pulp. He advises me:

"Professor, your wife now knows you are alive; but your friends inside are expecting a good story from you. Tell them the officer-in-charge wanted to warn you to be careful that the Bible readings and discussions, the prayers and choirs you are organising, the games you have created for yourselves – ensure that none of these turn into political parties. Tell them that the O.C. said some prison officers might report you to the 'higher authorities' that you are organising political parties in prison. And that you have not repented. Or invent something better. Aren't you a professor?"

He opens the gate, pushes me into the quadrangle to the full view of the cellmates sitting between the ration store and A-Wing, and banging the gate shut behind me, lets me return to my mates alone. I decide to look as miserable as I can possibly be, but D4 cellmates will not leave me alone. What happened? Is everything OK? Why were you summoned? Are they finished with you? Is strip-search on its way? Are you about to be released?

I tell them a story whose origin only God knows. "I knew it," I shout, "that idiot has always wanted to embarrass me before the officer-in-charge from the day I walked into these stinking walls. The bugger was expecting the O.C. to send me to the punishment cell for the note I'd sent. He was ashamed of himself when he discovered that I had asked the O.C. to let me have my shoes back because of the blisters under my feet. Gentlemen, the O.C. invited me to his office for me to show him the nature of the blisters for which I want my shoes back. When he saw my blisters he phoned the headquarters to get permission for me to wear my shoes. The authorities at the headquarters have granted my request. So, my dear friends, the good news is I've been promised my shoes back any time from today!" I declare triumphantly. The cellmates sigh with relief, as some retire back to their games of Draughts or Ludo. The others go about their brooding uninterrupted, as yet others enter the kitchen to cook the lunch. And as usual it is Old Man Mkwanda who cannot help commenting:

"*Baba*, good news! And if O.C. has got permission for you to have your shoes back, everybody will have their shoes back. I know the rules by which Banda's prisons run. *Baba*, good news, Banda's prison rules will be disappearing one by one! *Chimthakati*! – bloody murderer!"

When TS and Brown visit my bed for the post-mortem of the day's events after lock-up, I tell them what actually transpired at the telephone exchange. They laugh, laugh and laugh with delight. Brown whispers in a solemn tone:

"You put on a splendid show, professor, we have no choice but to pronounce you now duly circumcised into Mikuyu prison communication systems."

"Man, even I was taken in," TS comments.

"That's *Noriega* for you!" They both chorus.

I begin to see *Noriega* in a new light, but still do not understand why he should take such risks for political prisoners like us. Surely he deserves a nobler nickname than that of a brave dubious South American cowboy. We should have named him after our traditional hero, *Kalikalanje*, the all-knowing, the already-fried one. Or perhaps we should have called him after one of the heroes of classical Greek legends, Hector or Achilles. How does that feeble body carry such a robust rebel mind? *Noriega* is frail, five-foot-six and wears loose huge-legged khaki shorts that are unevenly starched and always look badly creased. He seems permanently absent-minded and far too sloppy to be a dictator's prison guard. Hanging his head low, he wears his battered cap as if he hated it. He seems to shiver all the time, even in the scorching wind that is trapped within these smelly prison walls – every fibre of his being cries out fatigue.

But *Noriega* has the heart of a hero. The holed pockets of his shorts are used to slip notes that link us to hope. He greets us with a salute, a privilege normally reserved for the chief commissioner of prisons. He communicates with his hands and feet as well as with his eyes and mouth. You must watch every body movement *Noriega* makes to get the full message he is carrying for you, or the dangerous proposition he intends to carry out on your behalf. He reckons he will be more important than his prison chief some day. He says if he had his way he would liberate one political prisoner every day until the prisons of Malawi were emptied of all 'politicals'. He would then look for a job amongst the 'politicals' he had released:

"The fellow is sheer poetry," Brown declares. "Every time you hear his holed boots squeaking towards D4, the kitchen or the cells, it's a warning for us to hide our contraband, for the strip-search is on its way; the guy is a genius."

Book Four
Birthday in Prison

20

Our Terminal Friends

8 January 1988, Friday. I wake up to noisy wailing sirens, and suddenly think some important person must be arriving in prison. It's still dark. Thursday night, or dawn on Friday. I have no idea who could be coming into prison with such fanfare in the middle of the night. There couldn't be a *coup d'état*. No, it may be a very imaginative thought, but coups are not likely to happen here. Listen; some officer is shouting to attract attention; the guards are thumping their feet on the ground and marching left-right, left-right, left-right. What kind of a ritual takes place at night with guards and their officers marching up and down, their boots breaking Mikuyu's tired cement floors? Is this a dream? Is it reality? Why was I not told about these devilish night rituals? It can't be another visit of the chief commissioner of prisons surely? He came in the middle of the night about a fortnight ago, totally sloshed, if we accept *Noriega's* version of the story. "He found one of his staff as drunk as he himself was," says *Noriega*, "except that his guard was fast asleep on duty besides." The poor fellow was sacked on the spot. Yet the chief could not be creating all this ruckus if he were carrying out a snap inspection. There comes the shouting, the marching and the feet thumping guards again...

"Oh, bloody shit," shouts Pingeni in the corner.

"God help us," says TS.

"God protect them," Mbale says nervously.

"What's happening?" I ask, after discovering that everyone is up and listening from their beds.

"Doc, that's the condemned prisoners going," Pingeni answers in a muted voice.

TS definitively explains: "That's chief commissioner of prisons Chikanamoyo, coming to take condemned prisoners from block one for hanging at Zomba Central prison tomorrow. The chief comes like this to take usually six prisoners for hanging in January and August every year." TS concludes with a rather cynical prayer: "Please God, forgive the poor bastards, and welcome them into your kingdom. Most of them are only naughty children, Lord, please!"

"Amen!" I add quietly.

Then the condemned prisoners in block one suddenly – and chillingly – begin to sing the famous hymn *The Lord Is My Shepherd*. The cacophony of marching boots and shouting officers falls instantly dead. With the jangling chains that the guards are carrying, the disturbed crickets and wagtails flying about nervously a moment ago, the frogs singing tunes in the swamp outside – everything stops abruptly, as the condemned prisoners' choir reaches its crescendo. The silence is killing. I feel my lot as a political prisoner lighter compared to what the poor condemned criminals must be feeling now. As soon as the haunting requiem stops, the cacophony starts up again; chains clatter, the wagtails fly about, the crickets wail their tunes, as the army of prison staff marches from the office towards the block where the condemned prisoners are waiting to be chosen for hanging. I am scared; my knees are already knocking, one against the other; I am trembling all over with fear. I imagine the prison regime coming to take the condemned prisoners for hanging, but abducting us with them as well; in principle, nothing could save them.

The marching gang grinds to a halt at the first cell, where the condemned prisoners, with throbbing hearts and flabby sweating bodies, must have lost all hope and energy to live. They wait to hear if their names are on the list for hanging this time around. The prison is on edge. Totally. My heart continues to pound with fear. I begin to panic. Anything can happen in this country. It could be me they have come to grab for execution. I hear the keys open the first cell and feel as if the commander was at our door. If I have been shivering with fear so, the poor fellows must be shitting in their *foyas*. I hold my breath and strain my ears for the names being ticked off. My heart continues to thump with fright. Whatever energy I had has evaporated. I cannot hear what I want to hear. The first name is called out. I miss it, too nervous.

Pingeni explains: "Doc, the prisoner called out is bound hand and foot with the heavy chains you can hear; he's lifted up high and passed from officer to guard down the gauntlet that starts at the cell's door, past the courtyard, out into the quadrangle, through the gate to the office block, until the fellow is dropped like a rabid dog in the back of the waiting truck whose engines you can hear, chewing and chugging at the office. The next name is called out, again I fail to catch his name, but this fellow starts howling for his mother. Pingeni and Chunga seem to recognise his voice; they call out his name and pray that his soul rests in peace. My heart sinks further. The morbid business of passing him down the gauntlet is repeated, until we hear the clang of his chains and his muffled voice as he's dropped into the truck grinding its teeth outside the office block. The death march moves to cells C-Wing 2 and C-Wing 1, where the gruesome ritual is repeated again and again and again until the sixth prisoner is thrown into the back of the truck. *Consummatum est*. The grim lottery is over for another six months.

The vehicles disappear as suddenly as they came in. I feel relieved and safe. Mbale wants us to discuss why we are subjected to this kind of torture. Why the authorities brought condemned prisoners into a prison that was meant for political prisoners. But *Nyapalas* Disi and TS refuse to entertain any discussion at this hour. The following morning *Gossip International* debates the whole issue of men playing little gods with other people's lives, whatever their excuses – in a future Malawi there will be no hanging of any kind, we declare. I cannot remember what excuse I invented for not delivering porridge to block one that morning. The truth is, I was afraid to know who was gone and who was still around; I feared being affected forever. Disi and the others come back demoralised after discovering which prisoners have been abducted for hanging. He says it was the senior assistant chief commissioner of prisons who headed the grotesque cavalcade last night, and ticked off the names of those who went for hanging from the list he brought from the headquarters. TS adds: "Our *nsima* was not popular today, the better cooked fish, notwithstanding. Nobody wanted to touch the food when they knew that the person who was sleeping next to their bed has been hanged...And we'll never see them again... Never...I grew fond of feeding the buggers, you know, like my own children...I can put up with the pain and blisters of handcuffs, leg-irons and chains but this mental torture...Why does Banda let us see all this? Why does God allow this brutality to happen? When will it end? Even I have no answer.

Gossip International is concerned about the treatment of the condemned prisoners in general too; for, our 'terminal friends', as I prefer to call them, have no rights, no privileges, and only one advantage over us – they were tried and charged before a court, however corrupt the procedure might have been. In principle, therefore, our terminal friends know when they'll go for hanging, whereas we do not know if and when we'll ever get out of here. And we are not supposed to have any contact with our terminal friends – no exchange of stories, news, ideas, food, even smiles. The guards insist that these rules apply for our own protection because these condemned prisoners are so dangerous that they would wring our necks within minutes, if we were left alone with them. But, of course, I disagree. I find our terminal friends keen to have contact with us. When one younger 'terminal' nicknamed Madala discovered that I was a university teacher, for example, he begged me to write about his innocence if I were freed before he was hanged. If I were allowed to meet him, I would record his story and get it published under a pseudonym. But it's the lottery of the wait to be named for hanging that is obscene. One terminal friend has waited for his death for fifteen years and he is still here – thirty times has he heard the guards march up to his cell; and thirty times has he waited for his name to be called out; but thirty times in vain – can you get more cruel and more evil than that?

21

The Research in Orality?

Could it have been the research project in orality that I directed at the university which brought me into this reeking prison? I do not know, but the idea is becoming increasingly probable. The History department at Chancellor College embarked upon research on the oral history of Malawi. The well-known Canadian historian, Professor James Webster, directed the project, which came under the title of Malawi oral history research project. It was well funded, more elaborate, officially cleared and blessed by Zimani Kadzamira before he was appointed principal of the college. History staff and their students were seriously engaged in the research, whose results were presented as papers at what became popular staff-student history seminars. Some of the papers generated heated debates, particularly when they seemed to accept blindly Banda's views about the nature of Malawian identity. In his many attempts to control the country, Banda shamelessly claimed that every community in Malawi had its origins in his own Chewa ethnic group, which in turn had come from the Congo basin in central Africa. In order to justify his claim Banda produced two very short people, the Batwas, at one public gathering, then claimed that these were the Chewa ancestors who had come from the Congo basin; all ethnic communities in Malawi originated from them. Although most academics knew that Banda's claims were misguided or downright wrong, no-one dared to challenge him for fear of what might happen to them.

The English department was engaged in the Malawi oral literature research project long before the history project. It was initiated by Mupa Shumba and later directed by me, with the assistance of Enoch Timpunza of the chiChewa and Linguistics department. I had applied for a grant from the University's Research and Publications Committee in order to conduct the research. My application was successful. And through the English department I acquired cassette recorders and cassettes and distributed them to students, who interviewed their own parents and relatives during university breaks. They recorded ancient stories, riddles, proverbs, songs, chants and other interesting oral material, and brought these to college to translate into English, analyse their meanings and write out research papers or reports that were submitted for assessment, including appendices of the resource materials they had collected and used.

What might have annoyed the authorities about this was the fact that our oral literature (what the Ugandan scholar Pio Zirimu called 'orature' – to avoid the apparent contradictions imbedded in the term 'oral literature') project did not have government official clearance, although we were vigorously engaged in it. Our argument was logically acceptable but perhaps politically dangerous. We thought that it was absurd to seek government clearance for students and local staff to ask their grandparents, parents, uncles or aunts and others about the folk stories, riddles, proverbs, and the songs they sang at initiation ceremonies, weddings or beer-drinking parties, including the games they played during their childhood. Our project might have displeased the local authorities in the university, as it seemed to be in direct competition with the Malawi oral history research project. Of course, we did not seek to frustrate or challenge the history project: most of us even attended and enjoyed the staff-students history seminars. We had a larger and more ambitious aim. We sought to collect, analyse and publish the oral materials in order to provide a theoretical framework for its collection and interpretation, and speculate whether this would help in the interpretation of African literature in general. We saw two ways of analysing African orature: by borrowing already existing theoretical frameworks, which tended to be European, and extending them for the interpretation of

African texts; or, more importantly, we hoped that structures and themes, which could provide the basis for some form of theoretical framework, might emerge, or be uncovered as we critically examined the texts themselves – to all intents and purposes, the search for multiple Malawian identities was incidental to our principal concerns.

The idea that the two research projects could be considered in conflict is obviously far-fetched, though to be sure we live in such despotic times that it is not odd to consider it feasible. What my local employers might have thought about our project was revealed when the best research papers, reports and appendices were published in an interdisciplinary journal we called *Kalulu: Bulletin of Malawian Oral Literature*, which I founded and edited with the assistance of Enoch Timpunza. The first issue of *Kalulu* included speculative articles (on the relevance of orature to modern society in Malawi and Africa); these came from staff and students of the departments of Law, History, Sociology, Philosophy, French, English, chiChewa and Linguistics. Reverberations around campus indicated that the interdisciplinary structure of the bulletin and the articles therein caused concern among some colleagues who toed Banda's official line; although none of the articles spelt out or sketched the broader non-Chewa-based Malawian multiple identities. Perhaps the implication that Banda's assumptions on the origins of the Chewa were flawed was too obvious.

When Zimani saw *Kalulu* being sold in the Senior Common Room, he mocked it with the declaration: "Another bulletin from the English department: we hope this one lasts this time around! The renowned Edinburgh-trained social anthropologist John Kandawire, who was present when the deputy principal made this remark, warned me sternly afterwards that I should be careful how I reacted to Kadzamira's apparent jokes about our bulletin. Everyone who heard the joke was afraid of what Kadzamira might do. They knew it was he who often killed imaginative projects like *Kalulu* because of the influence he exerted on what the censorship board banned or did not ban; though how he had

133

managed to appoint himself as university representative on the board is mind-boggling even from these prison walls today.

Of course, there was no dispute about the important offshoot of our Malawi Oral Literature Project: Oral Poetry from Africa: an Anthology, which I later compiled and edited with Landeg White, and was published in 1983 by Longman UK. The anthology might have given Landeg and me the exposure that the authorities had not anticipated. For several years it was adopted as the standard text for the introduction of modern African literature in African schools, colleges and universities, including our own. I was not surprised, therefore, when copies of the anthology suddenly disappeared from our university bookshop one weekend. Apparently the police had bought all the copies that were left in the university bookshop, only to drop them down pit latrines at the police headquarters afterwards. As I later gathered, they had been instructed to buy the last copies of the anthology, because the authorities did not like the publicity the book was giving the editors. Besides, it was believed that the anthology was drawing attention away from the president and his cabal to the African countries from which the materials we included had come. However, that I could have been sent to prison for compiling and editing an anthology of African orature, which was not politically contentious, is utterly incomprehensible – though, again, perhaps likely, given the nature of the despotic world in which we live.

Pen Writers in Prison Committee protest at the Malawi High Commission London. Harold Pinter reading from Jack Mapanje's book: *Of Chameleons and Gods*; the president of International PEN Ronald Harwood and others carrying the poster in the background, December 1987.

22

Word Mightier

We've been subjected to another ruthless strip-search for the wrongs that the condemned prisoners in block one have committed. A plan for their escape from prison has been unveiled. Our terminal friends are forever planning to escape from Mikuyu. And who wouldn't, when the courts that tried them and brought them here were corrupt and the walls, doors and gates of the prison are wobbly and squeaky? Anyway, I am feeling totally demoralised for most of the morning after the strip-search, when later in the day *Noriega* brings "the bundle of bulletins I have been keeping for a long time," he says, "waiting for the right moment to bring them all in." I thank him, quickly roll the bundle under my arm, borrow the Holy Bible from Pingeni and lie down on my bed to enjoy the newspaper cuttings, one by one. TS and Brown are watching out for me in case the guards barge in unannounced. The news is not fresh but very exciting and welcome. Soon I feel rejuvenated and begin to tremble with disbelief as I am transported to a world I least expected to visit.

'... Men and women of letters gathered in front of the Malawi High Commission in Grosvenor Square on 17 December to appeal for the release from detention of the Malawian poet Jack Mapanje. Among those who took part in the protest... were Antonia Fraser, who chairs Pen's Writers in Prison Committee; Ronald Harwood, Dannie Abse and Alan Brownjohn, the Chairman of the Poetry Society. Harold Pinter read from Jack Mapanje's book *Of Chameleons and Gods*.' Thus starts the piece from the *Times Literary Supplement* of 8-14 January 1988, in an article from the pen of the Nigerian radical scholar Chinweizu, who continues by quoting, as part of the campaign, Somali's foremost writer Nuruddin Farah:

'African rulers want national flags, national airlines and national poets as items for display in their parade of power. Anything remotely individual is, by definition, potentially subversive... those of us who are not Malawians, and who are not in detention, must remember that it is our consciences that are imprisoned, not just a poet. In making our appeals we are not just helping Mapanje, we are clearing our consciences.'

A strange sense of relief overcomes me. My heart begins to throb faster and faster. How could such renowned writers and scholars stake their honour and time for a person like me? How selfless, how generous! But Chinweizu goes on to quote the eminent Kenyan writer Ngũgĩ wa Thiong'o who says:

'As a person who has been in detention myself, and whose final release was as a result of international pressure, I know how important even the smallest one-line letter of appeal can be.'

This is awesome support, I think. I don't believe it. The second cutting is from *The Guardian* of London, of 18 December 1987, and again tells how on 17 December English members of International PEN, including their Writers in Prison Committee, protested about my continued imprisonment. The article is illustrated by a photograph of Harold Pinter reading from my book of poems *Of Chameleons and Gods*; Harold Pinter is surrounded by a host of British writers, scholars, broadcasters and journalists. The English president of International PEN, Ronald Harwood, is in the background, carrying a huge poster with the words:

P.E.N. PROTESTS.
RELEASE JACK MAPANJE – NOW!

I am confused with joy. I pinch myself and ask: "Could all these fine writers have been protesting on my behalf? Is this true?" I have heard through previous bulletins that the publisher of New Beacon Books, John La Rose, is also getting the London

African and Caribbean community of writers, journalists and artists involved in a vigorous campaign for my release. The other day, I saw a photocopy of a letter sent to president Banda from London's first black woman MP Diane Abbott. How did David, Fr Pat and Landeg manage this? Has the campaign grown so big? And from other cuttings of some US journals and magazines, I can tell that there has been a series of exchanges between brother and compatriot Frank Chipasula and the editors of an American literary magazine called *A View from the Loft*, which carries a short article about my case with my verse published next to it. This is awesome.

And here's a photocopy of a letter from the President of International PEN American Center, New York, Susan Sontag, telling me they have made me an honorary member; the membership card is enclosed. And here are snippets from the January issue of the *Literary Review* in London, where a Siobhan Dowd has highlighted my case, among others, in an article she calls 'Writers Detained'. Next to it is another batch of poems from *Of Chameleons and Gods*. I recall months back getting from Fr Pat and David, *Index On Censorship* magazine cuttings, with messages that I had also been made an honorary member of International PEN, English Centre, London; the membership card was included. And now this. Do I deserve this? Could I have dreamt of a better honour?

And this other note says the Canadian Centre of International PEN has adopted me as their prisoner of conscience. Human rights activists there have either already produced or are about to produce a postcard for their members to send to the Malawi authorities as recommended by London's *Index On Censorship*. Whether this is because of the influence of my Canadian teachers at Zomba Catholic Secondary School or the Canadian writers Graeme Gibson and Margaret Atwood, whom I met at the 1986 Edinburgh Commonwealth writers' conference, when I was with the Zimbabwean poet Musa Zimunya, I do not know. And Fr Pat adds that Pen Scottish Centre, Amnesty International centres in Dublin, Bristol, Derby, Edinburgh and Glasgow, Africa Watch in

London and Human Rights Watch in New York have adopted me as their prisoner of conscience too. Other human rights centres throughout Europe and Africa are likewise planning to adopt me as their prisoner of conscience. Some may have already done so by now. Sweet heaven! How expansive is this campaign? This is too good to be true, and, quite frankly, I can't take it all in; and I know the news will give real hope to other cellmates in D4.

But watch this belated news about students of the University of Zimbabwe who, apparently led by poet Musa Zimunya and other writers and academics at Harare campus, marched to the Malawi High Commission offices in Harare, demanding that I be taken to court or be released. And did University of Zimbabwe professors Micere Mugo and Emmanuel Ngara really refuse to come as external examiners in our department in protest over my detention, as this note declares? Comrades, how can I thank you for this, when a mere 'thank you' is not sufficient to explain my gratitude and the privilege I feel? But there is more: compatriots, colleagues and friends, Lupenga Mphande and Sam Mchombo among them, are appealing to the African Studies Association, and other writers' associations in the US, to write letters of appeal to the various Malawi authorities on my behalf. My God, who has been left out of this protest? Why me? *This* is most humbling. I do not know how to thank God or any of these people. I know I have a long way to go before I get out of here, but with such campaigns for my liberation in progress, the time I am expected to stay here can only be shortened. And where was *Noriega* keeping all these bulletins? I love the fellow for bringing them in now.

Shivering with joy tinged with genuine worry, I pass the Bible with the bulletins to Brown and TS in the courtyard for them to enjoy. The worry concerns my debt of gratitude. How could I possibly thank all these people, who are working so selflessly to get me out of here? What have I done to deserve this kind of solidarity? I have only published one book of poems and co-edited two poetry anthologies. I do not know if I will adequately thank all these people: family, relatives, compatriots, colleagues and friends in Malawi and abroad. I consider Landeg, Fr Pat and David special; then there are Nuruddin Farah, Ngũgĩ wa Thiong'o, Micere Mugo, Emmanuel Ngara and Chinweizu and others who I have had the privilege of knowing. Many of these fighters for my freedom I know through their work or reputation as writers and critics. Some in the long litany are stars I have admired from a distance. I know Harold Pinter, of course, through his plays, which I studied as part of drama and theatre studies for my first degree. I remember enjoying Alan Brownjohn's poetry every time it appeared in *London Magazine*, when I was a student in London. I know Susan Sontag through her reputation as a novelist and critic. Please God, protect these fighters from natural catastrophes.

After lock-up, TS and Brown are so overcome with joy that they want to share the news with others beyond our team. This is dangerous because some of the cellmates could report us to the prison regime. Still, they tell the cellmates who cannot read English the news brought by *Noriega* today. And when people see the newspaper cutting from *The Guardian*, with Harold Pinter reading from my book of poems; when they see the serious-looking Ronald Harwood carrying the poster demanding my release in the background, their faces beam with delight and disbelief. The idea that celebrated writers, critics, artists and scholars both African and non-African are protesting to Banda's regime on my behalf brings the kind of joy that is impossible to describe. Even Mkwanda and Kadango, who felt excluded from the campaign because they cannot read or write English, now think differently about the effect of what we are doing. D4 begins to speak in one language, as it were; we all agree that this kind of protest will eventually puncture Banda's complacency and that of his coven. D4 begins to talk about 'when' not 'if' we are released. Clearly, this is a different kind of campaign from that which the cellmates who have stayed here longer have known. The fact that branches of PEN International and Amnesty International in Glasgow and Edinburgh have joined the protest particularly thrills those who are proud of being members of the Scottish

Presbyterian Church. Pingeni openly declares to the entire cell: "If the campaign has reached Scotland, as your news claims Doc, Banda has no chance; Tembo and the Kadzamiras have no chance: they will have to give in and get you released. And Doc, you'll carry some of us along with you, won't you?"

Boisterous laughter ensues. And suddenly feeling animated at the prospect of his imminent freedom, Pingeni declares: "You can mock me all you like for being imprisoned here as a mere young pioneer driver, but let me tell some of you a thing or two: I definitely understand the relationship between Banda and the Scottish people better than some of you – we'll be released, definitely, very soon, definitely!"

D4 roars with more laughter at Pingeni's excitement, though secretly everyone shares his delight. Tonight there will be no fight among the lads. D4 will buzz with unprecedented hope for liberation, which has not happened for a long time – for the rest of his stay in prison we nickname Pingeni 'Mr Definitely'. When the excitement has subsided and I am at my bed brooding again, I begin to wonder what Banda, Tembo and the Kadzamiras make of these global protests and appeals. How are they coping? Are they still telling the world lies that they do not care? Like the rest of *Gossip International*, I am convinced that the dictator and his minions are listening and that one of these days they will release not just me but the majority of the political prisoners in this and other prisons. Dictators and their henchpeople are often too proud to admit defeat. So, let the struggle continue, dear compatriots, friends and activists; truth, justice and victory will eventually be within our grasp! Suddenly the blisters from the hard cement floor, the stinging mosquitoes or the creeping crawlies that suck our blood at night do not matter. I am a humbled, transformed man, determined to survive my incarceration, if only for the sake of those fighting for my life and freedom.

23

A Scare and a Half

Noriega, who is manning the switchboard again this Saturday, comes to the kitchen to ask Brown if he might borrow his mug for a drink of water. Brown runs to his cell to get it. *Noriega* follows him. I know this is a cover for an important message being delivered. When *Noriega* leaves after his drink of water, Brown looks agitated and concerned about something. I've never seen him in such a state before; I hope it's not news of death in the family. But when I ask what *Noriega* had to say, it turns out to be about my colleague and friend from the English department, Blaise Machila, who has been showing signs of his mental illness again. Since my abduction, Blaise has been calling at the police headquarters in Zomba and Blantyre to seek the truth about my whereabouts. And for his kindness, even in madness, the police have been beating him up and dumping him at their police cells like a criminal. Last night Blaise decided to tell Fr Pat about his exploits and to show him the injuries the police have been inflicting on him. Fr Pat was so shocked that he offered him a bed for the night – although Blaise's house is only about a mile away. But when Fr Pat went out to the shops this morning, Blaise got up and had begun to poke around the cupboards and drawers, where he chanced upon a bundle of correspondence that we've been having. Blaise has spirited away the bundle, claiming he's going to Zomba Mental Hospital for treatment. When Fr Pat returned from the shops, he found the correspondence gone; he does not know whether Blaise has dropped it at the Special Branch or at the principal's office before going to the hospital. Fr Pat has therefore contacted *Noriega* to warn us about the matter and to expect the worst. I am boiling with anger; Brown is beside himself; TS distraught; we feel betrayed. We had instructed Fr Pat and others in the strongest possible language to destroy the notes instantly after reading them. Although most of the correspondence is harmless, asking for food and medicine, the discovery of correspondence between prisoners and those outside is an explosive affair. We will be in deep, deep trouble and must therefore act fast.

We dash to D4 and discreetly remove all the contraband we had secreted away, in case there will be a sudden search or we are transferred to another prison. Trying to act as if nothing had happened, TS and Brown go out into the courtyard to watch Draughts and Ludo. I borrow the Bible and read King David's Psalms, adding a verse of my own: *Dear Lord, save us from the impending wrath of the Special Branch*. There is a problem. If the Special Branch comes across the correspondence, Fr Pat will be deported immediately. The catholic churches in Malawi's southern region, were being vandalised by the Malawi Congress Party youth league and young pioneers before I was arrested; the church in general was being accused of subversion. Our families and friends will be harassed, subjected to outrageous searches; they might even be imprisoned. David Kerr's wife – whose family comes from the north – will be hit badly by the news. For the rest of the day we fret and fidget, expecting the worst to happen. To be honest, we have learned to cope with the worst possible scenarios ourselves – at the moment only death is worse than Mikuyu – but to think that we will be responsible for our loved ones falling into the vicious hands of Banda's security and intelligence services is unbearable.

Before lock-up *Noriega* comes back, demanding tea with lots of sugar from Brown. He is looking distinctly chirpy. Brown obliges and finds out that Fr Pat has been to Zomba Mental Hospital and found Blaise in deep slumber on a bed there. The prison correspondence was intact and carefully hidden under his pillow. Fr Pat has extracted the bundle from the pillow and brought it home. He sends his apologies and promises never to be so careless again. Brown uses Disi's expression, *Allah Jwamkulungwa* (God is great!), to describe his relief; TS and I shout our joy to the brick walls. But what a scare! What a story! I return to my cell to read King David's thanksgiving psalms. After lock-up, Brown distributes sugar to the cellmates who don't have any. Only Mkwanda wonders: "*Baba*, I notice we are overcome by generosity again today; many thanks; but what's the news?" D4 roars with laughter. It is almost impossible to hide anything from the old man!

The following day *Noriega* catches me unawares. "Could I have a word with you?" he asks quietly. I feel disarmed, thinking he wants to share a tragic story about my family, but let him continue. "Do you have a friend who comes from your home district and teaches economics in the university?" he asks. "Yes," I answer, recalling one colleague who comes from what we call the 'west bank' of Lake Malawi. "What's happened to him?" I ask, anxiously. "Nothing," he says. "So why do you ask?" I answer back. "How well do you know him?" he inquires. "Not very well; my wife is supposed to be distantly related to his wife if it is the same man we are talking about," I reply. "There is a story concerning him, his wife, your writing and your principal," he says. "Everyone in college is talking about it." "Fumwe*," I boldly reply, "I am sure that will be another of the stupid stories people are inventing as reason for my continued imprisonment. What have these good people done?" I ask. *Noriega* begins: "Apparently your friend's wife was in the UK recently, taking a course in administration for nurses. And a friend of hers gave her some writing which claims that your poems are supposed to be critical of Banda's regime. And when she returned home after the course she showed the writing to her husband, who for reasons best known to himself took it to your principal; but nobody seems sure whether your principal sent it to the Special Branch or not. Does the story sound genuine?" he asks. "If you tell me where you got it from, I will tell you whether it is true or not," I challenge him. "I got it from Chirunga campus drivers, cleaners, messengers, gardeners

---

* An address such as *Chief, Mister, Comrade*, etc.

144

and others – but the question is; Do you think that's what might have brought you into Mikuyu?"

"I cannot see why anyone would want to expose an article like that to the authorities," I answer, "but anything is possible in this country, and thank you for telling me the story." "When will these jealousies end?" *Noriega* wonders, then shuffles back to his post at the office. I feel disturbed. How did he get such a story? I begin to suspect that *Noriega* often reads the bulletins that Fr Pat and David send us through him, which I expected anyway; but after keeping them for a long time unable to deliver them to us, he probably tells us the stories verbally and pretends he got them from people. For all I know, he may even have invented the story of Fr Pat's missing correspondence; he is capable of creating his own stories to cheer us up too! I suppose that's why we love the guy.

24
Birthday in Prison

25 March 1988, Friday. Today I celebrate my first birthday in prison. I am forty-four and exactly six months in Mikuyu. Today my wife and children would have sung me the Happy Birthday song. Perhaps I would have blown out the candles and shared a cake with family and friends. But it pleased his excellency the life president, the Ngwazi the Dr H. Kamuzu Banda, the Messiah, the father and founder of the Malawi nation; it pleased his Kadzamira-Tembo coven too, to have me dumped in this stench of a prison to punish me for the crimes I know I have not committed against them. Today I am forty-four. And I thank God I am alive. After the ruthless search at my office and my house on the day I was abducted and after their farcical interrogation, I expected only death. But today I specifically thank God for valiant *Noriega*, who again has surreptitiously brought bulletins from Mercy, the children, Fr Pat, David and Landeg to celebrate my birthday. I am pleased to hear that the family is fine and they all wish me good health. My children Judith, Lunda and Lika promise to celebrate my birthday by listening to my favourite track 'Island' from Jerry Raffety's *City to City* album – the track the family has dubbed 'Shalala'. Besides, Mercy and the children have sent me the two toothbrushes I had asked for – it's the 'Reach' brand I used to think was unnecessarily expensive, but many thanks. They have also sent three deep-fried fish, two one-kilo packets of rice, two of sugar and two tablets of Lifebuoy soap to grace my birthday – how very generous. Why should I complain? Why should I lose hope? May the good Lord bless them!

But watch what other goodies have been sneaked into Mikuyu on my birthday – a bowl of minced meat and a whole fried chicken! I will have a feast of minced meat and a freshly fried chicken with rice in prison – the best meal I will have had since I was dumped here. May the God of our ancestors be praised. Of course, I will share these with others: it's my birthday, isn't it? And if you are wondering, Mr life president and your vicious cohort, how a bowl of minced meat and a whole fried chicken were brought here, where you feed us poisonous food everyday; if you ask me how one smuggles these into prison; I won't tell you. What I can tell you is a female colleague in the English department and my student once, prepared the chicken and Fr Pat sent the minced meat, to grace my birthday. Did you expect such solidarity in the world you have created for us? Of course not! May the spirit of our ancestors bless and protect these fighters for my freedom today and always.

Today I am forty-four. And I refuse to welter in the despair Mr president and his ruthless coterie have created for us. No, I will not despair, not today when Mercy says Oxford Professor Megan Vaughan, a certain Dr Malcolm Douglas from York, Mr Patrick Foorte – father-in-law of my colleague and previous head of department – and others have brought news about the progress of the global campaign for my freedom. I hear they have brought a small financial donation from well-wishers in the UK, the US, the Republic of Ireland, Europe and one or two places in Africa. Landeg White says he might even open a modest bank account soon to help with the education of the children in case I am here indefinitely. How remarkable! Could I have asked for better news on my birthday? *Dear Lord of the universe, please shield from the enemy these people who are fighting for my freedom. On my part, I pledge to continue fighting for my survival so that I can thank them in person when I am freed from here; amen.*

But Mercy's bulletin brings unsettling news. The police have again refused to offer her visiting permits for the family to see me, the tenth rejection at my count. It must be tough for the poor girl. But why, Mr president for life? Why, Mr chairman of university council? Why, Mr principal of Chancellor College? Why, Miss Sanjika Palace Mama and your clan? What crime could the poor girl have committed? Why are you punishing my family, relatives and friends for the crime I am supposed to have committed? What wrong could they have done to deserve this? Why don't you take me to court for it? My dear Mercy and children, I suggest you stop applying for visiting permits. They might just bring you more trouble. Let's just keep exchanging these covert bulletins until God opens the prison gates some day. And He will. He never disappoints anyone who asks Him. We are all praying that we should be released. I am sure you are praying for that too. Let's not be despondent; let's allow God to answer our prayers in His time.

After lock-up, the post-mortem of the day's events is intriguing. Brown, TS, Rodney, Mbale and other cellmates gather around my bed. They suddenly break into the Happy Birthday song. I protest. They ignore my protestations. The cellmates who do not know the Happy Birthday tradition are baffled. Old Man Mkwanda is uneasy, inquisitive and bemused: "What does this stupid ritual mean, you uncircumcised people? Why are you gathering there and singing your rubbish? Do you want prison guards to punish us all for your senseless noise?" he asks. No-one takes any notice of him. Brown fishes out a huge Happy Birthday card. "It's yours, with love from your colleagues in the department at the university," he tells me. The card has come from the English department, signed by all the colleagues including the department's secretary. Every member of staff has inscribed brief messages against their initials, wishing me good health and speedy liberation. I am stunned and feel overwhelmed. Could people be so daring? So noble? So altruistic? Again I believe I do not deserve this kind of solidarity; and this is subversion by Banda's reckoning; punishable by imprisonment; I hope the authorities do not discover it.

"People," I find myself shouting, "I am deeply moved; thank you very much indeed for your camaraderie; may God bless you all."

Mbale interrupts my celebration by offering me... "What? What's this? Tiny bottles of Malawi brandy? Go away! Where did you bloody political prisoners get this? The rest I can understand; but this; where...?"

"Never mind where! Just enjoy!" Brown declares.

"I don't believe this!" I shout.

"If you don't believe this, Doc," TS intervenes, "perhaps you should ask Fr Pat to give you back your faith." Further outbursts of laughter, followed by another noisy chant of Happy Birthday; then Brown shouts: "We know you are blushing behind that black skin, although we cannot see it." More riotous laughter ensues, as Brown's stale joke feels strangely fresh and original. Mbale opens the little bottles of brandy and offers one to each of them, as a priest offers host or wine to celebrants at mass. Then offering me the final bottle he says: "Doc, here, have a good birthday swig." I shake my head in protest. I simply cannot see myself doing it, especially when my wife and children are denied visiting permits to see me. I will not have a swig of brandy on my forty-fourth birthday. When Old Man Mkwanda sees the postcard and recognises the mini bottles of brandy, he screams in horror and amazement:

"What are you boys doing to beat Banda and his sycophants in this prison? What on earth is this prison turning into? Can you fools really bring...?"

"Shut up old man!" Mbale threatens him and he shuts up.

TS, Brown, Rodney, Mbale and the others chant the Happy Birthday song again; they are only too glad to gulp down the contents of the little bottles. "This is the first 'drink' I have had since I walked into prison," Mbale says, smacking his lips. I pray that there should be no strip-search when the cell opens tomorrow. How are we going to dispose of these empty little bottles? I must tell *Noriega* to ask Fr Pat to keep the birthday card for me. The signatures and messages of solidarity are too precious to be erased by the stench of prison.

When everybody has left my bed, I begin to talk to my torturers as I have been doing since I entered prison. "Mr life president and your ruthless coven, you have patently done somebody wrong; you have abducted a young burgeoning poet, academic, a dad, a husband and a son and inflicted permanent scars on his young blossoming family. Let me assure you of one thing, therefore: I'll not forget you for this. I repeat, I might perhaps forgive you, but you'll pay dearly for abducting me from my family without committing any crime against you. I will not shoot you. I do not know what a gun looks like. It'll not be me who will punish you. I intend to give God the opportunity to punish you on my behalf. And as He knows you better than I do, I am afraid He will touch you where it might hurt most. Watch."

After a fortnight *Noriega* brings two bulletins, which he says are several months late. He apologises liberally: "I should have brought them on your birthday really, for a fuller celebration; but I misplaced them and could only find them today!" "Never mind," I say, and thank him for bringing them. The first bulletin reads:

Dr Z.D. Kadzamira   *January 17, 1988*
Principal
Chancellor College
Box 280
Zomba
Malawi
Dear Dr Kadzamira,
    Please accept my condolences on the tragedy that has befallen the University of Malawi. I refer to the detention of the head of Chancellor College Language and Literature Department, Dr Mapanje. I have read in the English press that he has been held incommunicado since September 25 of last year. I have read through his book Of Chameleons and Gods *and cannot understand how any of the poems contained in it could have been considered subversive by a government as progressive as that of the Republic of Malawi. I trust that you are exercising your best offices to obtain his speedy release and would be grateful for any*

150

information you could provide on his situation.
Yours sincerely,
(Signature)
Patrick Culbertson
Instructor, American English Language Program,
Woodbury University,
USA

The second is from a Professor Jerry L. Williams, Director of Southwest Institute, The University of New Mexico, USA. I vaguely remember that the fellow was teaching at Zomba Catholic Secondary School. Jerry also appeals to my principal to 'use your office and your conscience to see that these errors in judgment are corrected and that Dr Mapanje is again a free man'. I wonder how many letters of this nature Zimani has been enduring since I was dumped into this dungeon. And does he or his masters have the conscience that these appeals demand? I find these letters particularly fascinating as I had totally forgotten about these two American Peace Corps. Our relationship began in a curious way. In the 1960s Patrick and I taught English at Mtendere Secondary School, Dedza district. At weekends, Patrick with other American Peace Corps, British VSOs and Malawian teachers visited the traditional rock paintings of nearby Mphunzi Hills. We ended up buying demijohns of Portuguese wine from the Malawi/Mozambique border and taking them to our houses for parties at weekends. This was more than twenty years ago; and when we all went our separate ways, it was forever; we did not get in touch again. Has the campaign for my liberation reached even these fellows then? God bless them. But Patrick, I thought you had improved on your impertinence. How can you be so cheeky? Malawi a progressive republic? I don't think so!

25

To Ban or Not to Ban

That's the question. I recall when I first suspected that trouble with the higher authorities was on its way for me. It was an unusually cold Tuesday on 15 June 1985. I was barely a year as head of the English department, but sitting in my chair, I had a strange premonition that my employers in the university had something sinister up their sleeves. I had no proof; I just feared that there was a problem as I picked up a note which Lyscar Chisale had left in my in-tray. It was from my former Canadian teacher at Zomba Catholic Secondary School, Brother Fernand Dostie, who was also my headmaster when I first taught at Mtendere Secondary School. Have I seen the censorship board circular letter, which he encloses in his envelope? He asks. I instantly seize the circular letter, begin to read it, but stop after paragraph one. No, I peremptorily hear myself reply, I have not seen this. I find no energy to read on. The paragraph demands that my book of poems, *Of Chameleons and Gods*, be withdrawn from bookshops and school, college and national libraries throughout the country with immediate effect. My whole body feels as if I have been electrocuted by the touch of the river fish we once hated near our village when I was young. Why has the censorship board not sent me a copy of this letter? Why has my principal, who is the university's self-appointed representative on the board, his registrar, their executive administrators, or the university's central office, not told me about this? Why does it take my schoolteacher outside the university to tell me about it? My heart pounds with fear.

I stand up, stretch myself, walk up, down, across, about my room; the office feels small; I sit down. Across the window towards the university library I see two sparrows fighting on an acacia tree branch. At first I think they are mating, but upon scrutiny I realise they are tussling over a worm that one of them has picked up. I get up again, then sit down again, and for a moment puzzle about the skirmish of the birds in the tree from the vantage of my office. I pick up Dostie's letter again and read it more calmly. Again I stop after paragraph one, and grab paper and a pen; I want to thank Dostie for informing me about the matter. But I decide it's not safe to send the reply through the post office. I'd have to drive to the school and thank Dostie in person later, perhaps then I can find out what verbal reasons the schools have been given for withdrawing the book from circulation. I rip out my note, stand up again, and sit down again; I don't know how to proceed; confused, I sit down again.

One of the sparrows that was fighting the other flies towards my office window, then off and away it goes. Rather flummoxed, I dismiss the bird and shout to myself: "So, the censorship board has finally decided to find something subversive about my poems, although the paragraph I have just read does not indicate what. This is strange; very strange indeed. It's a bold step for them to take. I wonder what I should do now, and what message this sends out?" I shiver at the consequences of the ban and begin to speculate. Since the publication of the book and my return from studies abroad, I've lived in fear of this moment and wondered how I'd confront it. The book was published four years ago, had one reprint and several good reviews abroad – all unacceptable here – and from this paragraph it's patently obvious that the censors do not like the poems at all. My palms, forehead and armpits, the whole of me begin to sweat. I am shaking beyond control, fearing the trouble that looms ahead. I wonder what the sparrows in the acacia tree were doing. What do they symbolise? I feel totally paralysed, sitting in my chair. Then a voice says: "Man, pick yourself up; it's not the end of the world!" No use. I've never been so scared in all my life.

The politics of publishing in my university are complicated. The philosophy of 'publish or perish' prevalent in other universities outside this country is irrelevant to Banda's clique in our university. Their reaction to my book of poems shows that their undeclared philosophy is 'publish *and* perish'. The rumours that *Of Chameleon and Gods* was critical particularly of the self-appointed heirs to Banda's throne, the Kadzamira-Tembo coven, are still rife four years after the publication of the book. But why the board does not indicate what's subversive about the poems, why they merely withdraw the book from circulation, what implications I am supposed to draw from their action; above all, why my principal did not warn me when his office always informs heads of departments and deans of faculties about the books, films, magazines and newspapers that are banned – all this is very baffling indeed.

I cannot help concluding that my principal has been involved in the decision to ban the book, and for all I know, he might even have instigated it. What people say about these people must be true then, that they often get their real or imagined enemies excluded, jailed, tortured and even 'disappeared', while they quietly watch from a distance, as if they had not prompted their enemies' destruction. Another voice tells me to forget the circular letter, and knock on God's door for proper guidance instead; for God's door is always open for the burdened like me in times like these. One of the sparrows that was fighting its mate a short while ago flies past my window again, and lands on the acacia tree branch opposite my office as if to mock my impotent reaction to the censors. Again I wonder what significance I should attach to this. I conclude that birds will always be birds, and anyway, this might be a different sparrow from the one I saw. As for what I should do about the circular letter, I suppose I must ask somebody, anybody; the principal perhaps, or, even better, the chief censoring officer herself. Yes. I might as well hear the tale from the horse's mouth! Check her number; lift the receiver; dial; do not let her detect your angry tone.

"Hello", I begin, "could I speak to the chief censoring officer, please? Is that Catherine? Good! It's Jack here. English department, Chancellor College. Got a minute? Thank you. I'm OK, the family's well, everything's fine, I'm ringing to ask: I gather you've sent a circular letter to all educational institutions, libraries and bookshops throughout the country about the banning of my book of poems, *Of Chameleons and Gods*. Why did you not send me a copy, if only to warn me about the drastic step you've taken?"

"Why should we warn you, Mr head of English?"

Her tone is both jocular and sarcastic. I hit back with the answer I've been rehearsing since I heard the rumours, when I was a student in London, that the book had annoyed Banda's cabal.

"Three reasons, madam censoring officer," I cheekily answer. "First, the book is mine: I expect to be told what the censorship board thinks about it or what they say people should do to it. Do you remember I wrote you a letter when I was in London and sent you a copy of the book for official clearance by the board?"

"And do you remember I suggested that you should've sent the manuscript to us first before sending it to your UK publishers?" she replies.

"Which I could not have foreseen at the time," I cut in, "as I was busy with my PhD, did not know the rule existed, and anyway I imagined a rule like that would not apply when the writer was outside the country." I continue: "Anyway, according to your brief, I am supposed to tell members of staff and students not to use banned books, magazines, films and other unacceptable materials in their lectures, seminars and other academic activities. And, if you recall, you've always updated us with lists of recently banned materials: we expect your office, through the principal and his registry here, to send us such information, my banned book of poems included. So I ask again, why didn't you send me a copy of the board's circular letter, if only to let me update the department's records of banned materials?"

"But Jack, my friend," she answers, "why do you keep referring to your book as being banned? Don't you know we've not actually banned your book; we've merely withdrawn it from public circulation. Shouldn't you be grateful that the board has not taken more drastic measures?"

"Ah, Catherine, my friend, what more drastic measures were you going to take for such a simple case? And what's this difference you seem to assume exists between withdrawing a book from circulation and banning it?"

"There's a difference."

"What is it?"

"Well, technically, anybody can read, sell, buy, borrow or keep your book, at home or anywhere, despite it having been withdrawn from circulation."

"And how could they do that if the book were not available in libraries, bookshops and presumably the home itself in the first place?"

"I still insist, my friend, banning means the book has been listed in the government gazette under the section for banned materials; that means it's illegal to read it, buy it, sell it, possess it, loan it, borrow it and so on; whereas if the book is merely withdrawn from circulation, as we have done with yours, it's not illegal to do all these."

"But Catherine, you forget that detecting implications from utterances is my profession; can't you see that to ban or to withdraw from public circulation is only a semantic gimmick, another trick in the game of interpretation of utterances? I am surprised that you did not suspect that I'd see through that. Anyway, let's forget the academic arguments about what constitutes banning and what doesn't; what do you want me to do now? What does the board want me to do – sprint into exile, perhaps, because you've withdrawn my book of poems from circulation?"

"No, my friend, do nothing of the sort; there's no reason for your being worked up about the matter; don't panic; my advice is do absolutely nothing!"

"Is that so? All right then, I won't get worked up about it; I won't panic, I'll stay put and do absolutely nothing. I am sorry for bothering to ring you; thanks for your time; talk to you later; goodbye!"

I put the receiver down before she discovers that I am fuming and trembling with anger. When I read the rest of the letter, I discover that all persons, libraries, bookshops and institutions of learning that keep Felix Mnthali's book of poems, *When Sunset Comes to Sapitwa,* are being directed to send it to the censorship board for immediate clearance too. I am surprised. Felix's book was first published by NECZAM, in Lusaka, Zambia, before mine and later by Longman UK. After Frank Chipasula's volume of poetry, called *Reflections,* again published in Lusaka, Felix's was the most substantial volume of poems to come out of Malawi. How do the censors hope to get anybody voluntarily to give up their copy and actually send it to them? The irony is that Felix was not only my teacher in the university, but he was Catherine's husband once. He was imprisoned without trial or charge for about a year in the 1970s by president Banda and his coterie. Rumour had it that the Kadzamira-Tembo faction of Banda's inner circle hated northerners and they had been persuading Banda to do the same. They did not want northerners to hold positions of influence in the university. And Felix, who comes from the north, was to become the first Malawian professor of English, as well as head of department. And having been provost once, Felix would have been a more serious contender for the vice-chancellorship of the university. He was arrested before he could read his letter of promotion and appointment, joining the group of local academics and administrators, mostly from the north, who had been arrested and imprisoned to clear the way for Zimani Kadzamira's vice-chancellorship. The university offered Felix's position to Adrian Roscoe instead. After his release from prison, John Tembo and his university council made it impossible for him to return to the university. When the censors were calling for his book to be officially cleared, the poet had already left Malawi and gone to the University of Botswana, where he'd accepted the post of professor and head of the English department as well as dean of the faculty of humanities. They never told him what crime he had committed to be imprisoned; they never told him why he was released; they never told him why they could not re-employ him. Why the censors would want his book of poems for clearance when he is already working outside the country remains a mystery even for me, as I speculate on these matters from prison. Perhaps the censors needed to ban another book to cover up for the one they really wanted!

Jack Mapanje as a student at University College London
where he read linguistics 1979–1983.

26

A Linguistic Sense of Belonging

Our Sunday morning prayers over, *Nyapala* Disi pulls me to one corner of the courtyard and whispers: *"Noriega* gave me this when you were in church, apparently from your teachers." I grab the rolled-up bundle, hold it tight under my arm, whisper back my thanks and look for the Holy Bible and a safe corner to read the bulletins from. Ndovi is reading the Bible right now, therefore I must wait until he is ready to pass the holy book on to me. Meanwhile, I recall how lucky I have been with the key teachers I've had in my life. Dalson Chilimampunga from Mwanza district was the best Maths and English teacher Chikwawa Catholic Mission Primary School ever had. Without him I would not have been one of the top ten candidates in the 1959 Primary School Leaving Examinations for the entire country, earning me the Timcke bursary that enabled me to enter Zomba Catholic Secondary School for four academic years. There I met Brothers Dostie, Raymond, Cajetan, Charles and others, mostly from Canada; these teachers have followed my academic progress even after graduating from the school and entering Soche Hill College, Chichiri campus of the University of Malawi, and – twice – the University of London. I have been lucky with my teachers. When I needed an ankle operation at Queen Elizabeth Hospital, Blantyre, it was the principal of Soche Hill College, Sir Martin Roseveare, my teachers Bryson MacAdam, Brian Hudson, Michael Cuslake, James Kunz, Diana Hantak and others who dipped into their pockets to pay for it. It is with their encouragement and of Molly Michael, another of my teachers and the vice-chancellor's wife that I graduated with a distinction for my Diploma in Education from Soche Hill College. And when I joined the staff of the English department at Chichiri campus of the university of Malawi in 1972 and later published *Of Chameleons and Gods* in 1981, it was Brother Dostie who first warned me that the censorship board had withdrawn the book from circulation. And only last week when I fell ill Fr Pat sent me a note that Dostie and his colleagues at Zomba Catholic Secondary School bought the medicines I had asked for. I've been lucky with my teachers.

At Chichiri campus, I was lucky particularly with two teachers who have remained in touch and are even more precious now: Landeg White and David Kerr. And after the deportation of the acting head of the English department, if it had not been for the support of Chichiri campus principal Peter Mwanza, I would not have gone to the University of London Institute of Education for my M.Phil degree. I have been lucky with my teachers. But when Ndovi passes the Bible on to me and I open the bulletins I realise that *Noriega* does not mean these teachers. He means my other teacher and friend from University College London, Professor Neil Smith. For Fr Pat has sent me a photocopy of pages 1 and 4 of *The Bulletin*, of October 1987, from University College London, where, in a short piece entitled 'A Seditious Chameleon? – Detention in Malawi' Neil Smith makes the following observation, among others. 'In a contribution to the *UCL Bulletin* – "Linguistics and Lizards in Malawi" (Vol. 6, No 6, January 1985) I reported optimistically on the state of linguistics in Southern Africa in general and in Malawi in particular. The occasion for that report was a successful conference set up to inaugurate the Linguistics Association of SADCC Universities and organised by the distinguished Malawian poet Jack Mapanje... He has now been detained without any charge being brought against him, and his book *Of Chameleons and Gods*, published when he was a student here, has been banned... That one can be incarcerated for writing poetry puts our own preoccupation with Academic Freedom in this country in a wider, and chilling, perspective. It also emphasises the tragic and transitory nature of the events which occasioned my previous optimism...Early this year, Jack Mapanje sent me a poem he had just written, with the scribbled suggestion that I send it to the *UCL Bulletin*, as it has not been published elsewhere. I send it in now, in the hope that the more people who know about Jack's detention, the more likely he is to be released from it.' I am surprised, delighted and humbled all at once by these words. I did not expect the poem to be used to publicise my plight in this subtle manner.

April Wishes For Gordon Square (a letter)*

Dear Neil, as the toxic lizards of home crowd
In on us today, I recall those barriers in
Linguistics Gordon Square are so good at knocking
Down. You know how little I cared about those
Concrete gates that suspected me mugger on High
Street Barnet or framed in those hypocritical
Digs of Balham whether I sang about Wimbledon
Strawberries & cream or not. And knowing what
We know about dawns and bonfires, I believe I
Was not meant to map out Africa's dawn from
The dark alleys of London & I make no apology
For being a late visionary. It was kind I was
Spared the Victorian euphoria of bowler hats,
Flywhisks and image-structuring London blitzes
That my fusty ancestors forever drill down our
Throats & flaked by those smoking tongues of
Brixton & Wood Green, it would have been dis-
honest to have pretended otherwise. So, here's
The season's peace for the crowd at the Square.

And dear Harun Al Rashid, as the scorpions
Of Zomba gather at our keyholes to hear what

---

* First appeared in *University College London, Bulletin*, 1987.

They have sewn, the kola nuts you offered me
Now sharpen. Jolting in that rusty, chattering
Citroen from the steel benches of Gordon Square
To the mouldy walls of York, I forgot to ask
Where you got kola nuts to break in the heart
Of London & the gates of York? And today, I
Discovered those photographs you forced on me
Boasting the York linguistics conference (with
Me sampling *Stones* and floating to inscrutable
Punk & you salaaming Mecca by the hour & steering
My 'rough' ways, you said). I hope you understand
Though: on my edge of Africa, without OPEC oil
Or golden stools to show off about, kola nuts
Were merely symbolic fetters, bitter, crumbly
Not like spearmint gum & photographs cold
But as the Shepherds Bush offal we shared &
The *Daily Mirror* cones we ate our chips from
Come back today, I thought you might like to
Look at these bristly negatives, with love?

I recognise the poem instantly; and though it feels different
read from prison, I know this is my poem; I remember clearly
what inspired it. In April 1987 I had an intuition that I would be
in the kind of trouble I had been avoiding for a long time. I did
not know why. I had not committed any crime. I did not feel
guilty about anything. The controversy surrounding the
publication of my book of poems had died down and was
effectively buried. But you know how anxious and desperate you
sometimes become when you have a hunch that something is
about to go wrong; and in order to alleviate your anxiety how
you often hang onto beautiful memories of family, friends and
events you enjoyed once. I just felt rotten and wanted to touch
base with friends whose connection I treasured by sharing with
them the fears I had for my life. So I wrote this letter in verse and
sent it to Neil, with a copy to my Nigerian student-friend Harun
Al Rashid who had been reading linguistics at the School of

Oriental and African Studies (SOAS) while I was at University College London. But the poem was a private matter; I did not expect Neil or Harun to do anything about it. I am surprised but ecstatic to realise that it is now being used in the campaign for my liberation. I know it's not enough to say 'thank you' from this prison, but what can I say? Neil, Landeg, Fr Pat, David and all of you fighting for my release out there, please accept my heartfelt 'thank you'. Even if I do not return home from this ordeal I appreciate your solidarity.

As I read and reread the poem, I begin to shake with joy and disbelief, tears welling up in my eyes; the stench of my prison begins to clear, as it were. In truth, Neil's words and the poem have an unusually cheering, relaxing and overpowering effect on my nerves. I want to devour all these words. I am immediately transported to UCL, and the good times I had reading linguistics with Neil as my supervisor. I remember how Harun's family and mine in Nansen Village, North Finchley, shared the African food we bought at Shepherds Bush Market in West London. I remember how Harun, the Polish classmate Barbara Prangell and I spent hours, days and nights discussing our research and exchanging ideas and references. I recall how we found partic-ularly challenging the more recent work in syntax by Gerald Gazdar, Geoffrey Pullum and others presented at UCL and SOAS; and how we speculated on the exciting direction the discipline was taking, after the influence of Noam Chomsky, his colleagues and his students. I remember my linguistics being influenced by Neil's colleagues – Deirdre Wilson, Dick Hudson, Ruth Kempson and others. This issue of *UCL Bulletin* deserves a special crack in the wall, so I can come back to it whenever I am low. I feel so thrilled that other memories come flooding in. Like the time I spent doing research for my M.Phil degree, supervised by Professor Bruce Pattison at the University of London Institute of Education, and Professor Randolph Quirk at University College London. I recall how classmate and friend John Hartley Williams and I discussed our poems; and my ecstasy when Alan Ross chose three of my poems for publication in *London*

Magazine; and later how my poems appeared in *Stand Magazine* and *Poetry Wales*. But this poem disturbs me for another reason today. What I predicted has indeed come to pass – this is awesome. And where on earth was *Noriega* hiding this belated but delightful bundle of news? How did he let it gather such fish oil and such dust? Was he waiting for my spirits to be so low, after reeling from the shock of my signing Banda's detention order, for him to cheer me up with this optimistic news? I am beginning to love the bugger!

And the rest of Fr Pat's bulletins are just as overpowering. The 'Linguistics Circle' in London and beyond, patently at the instigation of Neil, his colleagues and his students, has begun a campaign that might lead to my liberation, he says. The Linguistics Association for Great Britain (LAGB), of which I was a member once, the British Association for Applied Linguistics (BAAL) as well as the Association of University Teachers (AUT) in the UK have adopted me as their scholar of conscience. I can only thank Landeg and Neil, who are at the heart of the publicity. And David's bulletin says Neil has also brought into the fold Diane Blakemore, whom I remember as having been a fellow student once and now teaching linguistics in one of the universities in the UK. Mark Sebba, a friend from South Africa that I first met at the LAGB conference at the University of York and is now teaching linguistics at Lancaster University has also been invited to help organise petitions for my freedom. So Neil, his colleagues, their students as well as our mutual friends are getting linguists at conferences, seminars and meetings to sign petitions and appeals for my freedom and sending them direct to Banda, the Special Branch headquarters, the Malawi Congress Party headquarters, government officials, as well as the principal of Chancellor College. How noble, how sobering! And did Neil really persuade the eminent American linguist Noam Chomsky and members of the Modern Language Society of America to write letters of appeal to Banda and his Malawi University officials for my release? Was it the influence of my colleague and compatriot Sam Mchombo – with whom I mapped out the idea of the linguistics association for the southern African region? Or was it both? Wherever the truth might lie, I cannot guess what's happening out there or where this campaign is heading. I did not realise that teachers, colleagues, compatriots, students, friends and strangers could be so selfless as to stake their time and honour for my sake.

I heard recently that members of the Linguistics Association for SADCC Universities (LASU) for which I am still chairperson have been protesting on my behalf too. I gather the South African novelist and literary critic Njabulo Ndebele is being sent as an emissary of the Association for the Teaching of Language and Literature in SADCC Universities (ATOLL) to see John Tembo about my continued imprisonment. His visit is to coincide with the celebration of twenty-five years of the establishment of the University of Malawi. It will be a miracle if John Tembo gives Njabulo Ndebele an audience, but I suppose there is no harm in trying, though the question that bothers me now is what song I shall sing from this stench to show that I sincerely appreciate what people fighting for my liberation are doing; and the trouble, pain and shame some of them are going through for my sake. I consider myself lucky to have people who love freedom and care about human dignity fighting for me. I dare to declare: stench of Mikuyu, where is your sting? The support I have from the staff and students of the University of London is not surprising. Nelson Mandela was adopted as the university's prisoner of conscience once. The university hoped that the apartheid regime in South Africa would release him from Robben Island. African and other freedom-loving students from the University of London were proud that they belonged to an educational institution that cared about freedom, truth, justice and human suffering, without prejudice. Have I joined that class of special political prisoners today? Do I deserve it? Do I dare to celebrate? And how am I going to thank Neil, Fr Pat, David and Landeg for passing on information about our fragile prison existence to compatriots, colleagues, academics, friends and human rights organisations the world over?

But watch the contradictory whispers typical of our despotic times. This note says my ex-student Francis Moto, reading for his doctorate degree in linguistics at University College London, is refusing to join the campaigners fighting for my freedom in London. What's the matter with the guy? Is he so desperate to please or so scared of the inner circle that for once he cannot fight for his teacher? Was I such a horrible teacher to him? I sincerely apologise if I did him any wrong. I now understand how foolish I was to ignore what Chancellor College drivers, cleaners and others warned me about Francis Moto and other colleagues who were thought to be informers of the Kadzamira-Tembo faction of Banda's cabal. It was an open secret that some of these colleagues tracked us down wherever we went and wherever our darts club, 'The Scorpions', played and reported our views and activities to the principal and his uncle. On the other hand, I wonder why I should worry about these fellows when more eminent scholars are fighting for my freedom? If indeed these fellows were informers, I have the following message for them: you've got what you wanted by getting me dumped in this dungeon; but we knew the game you played at every stage; we had friends amongst the drivers, the cleaners, messengers and others who often warned us about your machinations; that's why it took you so long to catch us. But the world will change one day, when we will tell our story. And you will not stop us.

But *Noriega* has brought other important messages. Another ex-student and colleague in the English department, Hangson Msiska, is vigorously campaigning for my liberation with colleagues and literary critics Graeme and Angela Smith, historian John McCracken and other academics and friends in the University of Stirling, Scotland. I hear Angela Smith in particular has been fiercely campaigning for my freedom. I feel a strange sense of belonging. I begin to imagine that I belong to a community of relatives, compatriots, scholars, colleagues, friends and strangers who care about human life, although as I said, there is a part of me that feels uncomfortable about these worldwide campaigns – how am I going to pay back all this generosity when I am released from here?

After lock-up, Brown is so pleased with the bundle of bulletins *Noriega* has brought today that he finds himself offering one-kilo packets of sugar that visitors brought him to those who need it. That night I feel hopeful that something good, however ineffable, might result from this correspondence. In thanksgiving I shamelessly say my three Hail Marys as head of security and intelligence services Lunguzi suggested at my interrogation.

Book Five

The Edinburgh Connection

27

Holes in Walls

Despite news of the global campaigns that are being mounted for our liberation, the reality of our condition remains bleak. The food is still dreadful. Even the prisoners on special diet, who have bananas or rice boiled for them, take their food with weevil-infested red kidney beans day in, day out. The pigeon peas we are offered for a change or their sun-dried minnows of fish give us purging stomach-aches, however we cook them. And these days I suffer from malaria almost every fortnight. Will I survive here? Will I see my wife and children again? Am I stuck permanently in this stinking borstal? About two months ago I won the first battle I was forced to fight. I persuaded the prison officers that I do not eat pigeon peas because they give me ulcers. The authorities fell for my lie and granted my request. But does that solve my problem? No. Of course, the prisoners who are allowed visitors bring lots of food; this helps because everybody shares whatever they get with everybody else; everybody wants everybody to survive. But as visitors come only once a month, their contribution is not enough to improve the health of all. Even after forming ourselves into teams, with each team sharing whatever we get to other teams; however charitable we might be, only a third of the political prisoners get visitors who bring food. Our team is probably better than most: TS, who has been here for twelve years now, hardly ever gets visitors; he comes from so far away that his family gave up visiting him ages ago, they can't afford the bus fares from Ntchinji district to Zomba district. Both Brown and Rodney have visitors who bring in food once a month.

And that helps. In our team Brown has more visitors than most of us; he is the envy of everyone; our chances of survival would be considerably reduced if we did not get help from his family and friends.

My contribution to the team is rather erratic. My family, relatives and friends are still not being given permits to visit me. I gather Tembo and Kadzamira in the university are using their influence to stop the police giving visiting permits to those who want to visit me. What I have done to them to deserve this, I have no clue. My contribution to the team, therefore, comes in the form of medicines, tinned food, dried fish and news brought in surreptitiously by *Noriega* from Fr Pat, David, Mercy and the children and Landeg. We have now developed an elaborate system of communication in order to get these provisions; we are extremely grateful to everyone and hope that the prison regime does not discover our tricks. So when I hear that Brown's visitors have been given visiting permits, I tell my relatives to take the food and medicines meant for me to them. But why should family and friends bring us food and medicines as well as feed themselves, when it is the duty of Banda's and his cabal to feed the prisoners they indiscriminately dump into these prisons? Tell us, Mr president and your ruthless thugs, why should our people suffer twice, when it is your responsibility to feed us? Nor have we given up fighting for better food and better medical facilities. Two months ago, we sent a delegation to the officer-in-charge to persuade the prison regime to allow us to start a vegetable garden outside the prison. We don't mind the hard labour that would come with this, even if we worked under armed guard; as long as the vegetables we cultivated kept us alive and healthy, it would be fine. Naturally Sitima rejected our request. This week I have rustled myself on to another delegation seeking a qualified medical officer to attend to our ailments. We will neither give up nor despair. There is one philosophy that keeps us going: if there is no hope, invent it; if the enemy wants you to 'rot, rot, rot forever', as Banda often declares at political rallies when he talks about his political enemies, develop strategies to survive and subvert his wish. I remember Alex Mataka at the New Building Wing saying that the dictator and his cronies are declaring that our family, relatives and friends should not expect us to return home alive; I gather they are creating stories that we have died in prison.

Clearly the authorities will hate it if we survive the ordeal they are putting us through. So we intend to embarrass them with our lives; we intend to survive this prison horror. Come out of hiding, then, our pencil lead; come out of our kinked hair; come out, you Lifebuoy and Sunlight soap wrappers; let's make revolutionary bulletins out of you; let's sit on this toilet seat and show the enemy that his hope for us to 'rot, rot and rot forever' can be sabotaged. We have acquired the craft of writing as many bulletins as possible, hiding them in the spaces between bricks or in the holes in walls, so that whenever the courier is available, we just pull out one and dispatch it to family and friends accordingly. Let's begin with bulletins for David:

Dear Bro, Just a note to say hi! Thanks for your recent news, food and medicines. We are grateful for the provisions you send. Banda and his brutes should be ashamed of imprisoning people they can't feed. But here's another story. Do you remember the white guy from Zimbabwe or South Africa who came to Government Hostel twice a year? He had a bald head and came to hang Banda's condemned prisoners at Zomba Central prison – used to call him Mr Catchpole, I think? Well, there are more than forty-five condemned prisoners in block one of Mikuyu waiting for Mr Catchpole's hammer. In January we witnessed the most frightful abduction of six of them for Mr Catchpole's ropes, scaffoldings and hammer. The event was more ghastly than the death Catchpole inflicts on the poor bastards! It was the most sickening mental torture I have suffered so far. Otherwise, how are they treating you after my abduction? I am sorry for what you will go through because of me; but please send us your tales, any tales.
Love & Peace, Bro.

Dear Bro, your poem on the 'Return of the Chameleon' has arrived with the rest of the provisions, 'many thanks', which does not express sufficiently our gratitude to you for what you are doing to ensure we survive. The poem is fine. Noriega brought it after we'd just had a notorious strip-search. You cannot imagine what cheer it brought us! I have had to explain its meaning to my mates, and TS, who concedes that he does not understand poems, likes the idea in it, he says. So, you reckon the chameleon will return home one day? That will be the day! But please do not publish it. You know how agitated Banda's cohorts get when they see letters or verse dedicated to 'rebels' like me. Did Blaise really photocopy Landeg's long review of my poems from the Southern African Review of Books *and send copies to those who matter in the university and the country? That's dangerous, isn't it? His mind must still be unbalanced, poor soul. By the way, has the censorship board seen Landeg's marvellous book on Malawi's history,* Magomero: Portrait of an African Village, *which came out just before my arrest? I did not finish reading it but the fifty or so pages that I read were brilliant. I hope it doesn't go under the censorship board hammer. Please send us your news, any news.*

Love & Peace. Bro.

Dear Bro, Written in a hurry. Out of my own confusion. Should we perhaps cool down the campaigns for a while? To see if the Martyrs' Day 3 March and Banda's official birthday on 14 May bring us releases? Just thinking aloud. Great to hear about Tony and Angela Nazombe getting married. Your better half must have played a very important role at the wedding! God bless them. Nice to celebrate something different for a change. Isn't it strange how our time is so preoccupied with trivialities and the preservation of the self that we forget there are other people's marriages

that must happen in the real world? Have a belated drink on
me! More news from your end, please, any news.
*   Love & Peace, Bro.*

And then a few bulletins for Landeg, again initially to be stored
in holes in walls until a courier despatches them.

Dear Lan, Today, I celebrate seven months in Mikuyu
Maximum Detention Prison. It feels like seven years. As
David may have told you, I've been transferred to the
kitchen where my job is dishwashing and helping with
cooking nsima in huge vulcan electric pots! There were
twelve detainees when I transferred to what is called D4,
but their number keeps swelling each month. We are glad
that you are trying to get us a place as visiting scholar at the
University of York and contacting foundations and organi-
sations for air tickets and sponsorship. Many, many thanks.
Emmanuel Ngara and his staff at the University of
Zimbabwe promised me the writer-in-residence job; if that's
gone now that I am at Mikuyu, there may be other options.
For unless huge political changes occur in this country, I'd
like to get away with my family, if only briefly at first. These
fellows deserve a huge rest from the ordeal I have put them
in! Please send your news. Any news.
Love, J.

Dear Lan, Delighted about the praise poetry book you are
doing with Leroy Vail. I know it will be, as always, brilliant
and controversial! The long 'Paiva' poem you sent arrived;
it's marvellous; I love every line in it; I've hidden it in a
crack in the wall so I can come back to it any time I feel like
stimulating the mind. Thanks for the financial and moral
support you're giving Mercy and the children. I know
'thank you' is not enough, but then what is?
Love, J.

Dear Lan, Brown's proposal for his M.Phil/D.Phil is enclosed with the application forms for the University of York registry duly filled out. I also enclose my letter of reference for Brown. How the forms were filled out and the reference written, with so much security around, is another story. Because of the sensitive nature of the game of elimination in Banda's politics – Brown's research proposal – please use Fr Pat, David or yourself as contact addresses for Brown's application. University registries everywhere tend to send such material direct to the students concerned. If you give Brown a lot of Jung, Webber, Freud and more recent stuff to read, he'll write you the best psychologically based historical interpretation of Banda's politics of elimination! Brown is a perceptive and disciplined researcher and can actually speak Lomwe, which most of us cannot. But as you say, we hope Banda and his henchpeople understand that these endeavours are meant to get us released. If he does not release us, at least we would have tried – sounds familiar? Antigone *perhaps?*
Peace & Love, J.

Dear Lan, Should we get out of here, and your visiting fellowship for us works out, and your basement is still too damp for our heaving asthmatic chests, as was our flat in Mansel Road in South Wimbledon, London, once upon a time, please get us modest accommodation around college – as long as it's not twenty miles or more from the ancient walls of York city or your home at 7 Newton Terrace. We are fine and still alive. Many thanks for the time you are creating to fight for our liberation. Thanks again for the support you are giving Mercy and the children. Love to Alice, Martin and John & you!
As ever, J.

28
Brown's Punishment Cell

We are sitting between the kitchen and A-Wing, TS and I, with our backs to the ration store door behind us; we are effectively flanked by block one on our left and block two on our right; Mbale comes forwards and announces that Brown is being interrogated at the office. I stop reading the Bible and TS stops dislodging weevils from the soaked red kidney beans that he wanted to mash into *chipere*. We run to Brown's bed to remove whatever *zitakataka* and other contraband that might be around his bed. We are back within minutes. I am nervous. I do not know what to make of it. We are both watching intently the goings-on at the gate to the office block in front of us; the gate suddenly opens and *Noriega* trots towards us. When he comes close to us, he simply whispers: "Brown in deep trouble; you don't know anything; I am very sorry." Then he quickly shuffles back to the office. The commander we've nicknamed 'The Evil One' opens the gate to the office block and calls out my name to see the officer-in-charge immediately. I shiver with fear and reluctantly get up. When I get there I notice that the sergeant who often talks to us about our past is going to chair the meeting, but you can tell that he is wearing a different hat just now:

"You," he says poking his polished cane at my stomach, "we've already heard the story from your friend here; what we want is your version of it. We know that you yes-yes people send letters from here to your wives and your yes-yes friends outside prison. If you give us the name of the prison guard who carries the messages for you, we'll not send you to the punishment cell."

So, when you write your letters secretly, which guards do you trust to take them to their destination?"

My eyes turn towards Brown at the end of the bench. He makes no gesture to help me how to proceed; his head is bowed down. I wish the prison regime knew that detecting presuppositions in people's utterances is my cup of tea – pragmatics was my field of study at the highest research level, PhD. I see myself slowly losing my temper and shouting:

"But you *Bwanas* can be cruel, eh! Where did you acquire this kind of brutality? You know very well that the Special Branch are refusing to give my wife and children, relatives and friends visiting permits, even after signing my detention order. How can you now assume that I am corresponding with the outside world? If my friend here has conceded that he writes letters, that's him, not me!"

"Read this letter and tell us who wrote it!" The sergeant barks in defence, passing me the note 'The Evil One' must have given him. I recognise the writing instantly; it's the letter I had written my wife and sent through *Noriega* several weeks ago; I now understand why she had not acknowledged receipt and why *Noriega* apologised to me in the quadrangle. I read it very slowly as if I'd seen it for the first time. Then I decide to explode:

"*Bwana* Sergeant, this must be a desperate and starving prisoner, political or criminal, struggling to tell his wife to send him much-needed medicines and food; but do you know the person called Dee to whom the note is addressed?" He shakes his head to show he doesn't.

"Do you know the person called Daa, who has obviously written and signed the note?" I ask. Again he shakes his head. I continue:

"Look, *Bwana* sergeant, are we the only people who can speak and write English in this prison? Do you know what my handwriting looks like? Have you considered the possibility that some of the condemned prisoners in this prison write English too? If there's no-one by the name of Daa in this prison, why do you assume that my friend or I wrote this note? *Bwana* sergeant, prisoners here write letters under the supervision of your staff. And if this note was not written under the supervision of your guards, tell me how it's done. I am dying to tell my wife and children, my mother, my relatives and friends abroad that the police abducted me and I am being kept in this stinking prison! Admit it, *Bwana*, you have no proof that this note was written by a political or condemned prisoner, me or my friend here. Admit it if you are man enough, *Bwana*!"

"Take this stupid fool of a professor back to his cell before I get angry!" the sergeant yells to his commander. 'The Evil One' pushes me out of the room before the sergeant's cane cracks my head. I find myself breathing hard in the quadrangle as I return to D4. We hear at lock-up time that Brown has been sent to the punishment cell for three days and three nights – and this for the note I wrote to Mercy, which drunken *Noriega* lost around the offices. I feel the nausea for getting my friend punished for the wrong I had done. The following day we have another unnecessarily spiteful strip-search. The cellmates not in correspondence with the outside world complain formally to Disi and TS that we are bringing unnecessary searches and hurt to the cellmates who do not want to join the struggle for our liberation. We are, therefore, formally asked to stop sending information about our inhuman prison conditions to human rights activists abroad or else they will report us to the authorities. I tell the *Nyapalas* that we sympathise, but insist that the show must go on; we must try every opportunity to liberate ourselves. Banda and his minions want us to 'rot, rot, and rot forever' in this prison; I remind them that those are his exact words. I suggest to both of them to tell those who have complained that we will stop writing forthwith.

When Brown returns from the punishment cell after three days, he congratulates me for not revealing the names of our couriers; our correspondence would have collapsed, he says. "I was hoping that the anger I put on would protect you from the punishment cell my friend," I say. He refuses to tell me how he managed to come back without blisters around his wrists and legs. And as if to cheer us up, the following week *Noriega* brings a special handshake from Fr Pat and David. The despair that set in after Brown's punishment cell vanishes. *Of Chameleons and Gods* has won the Rotterdam International Poetry Award in the Netherlands! On Wednesday 22 June 1988, the distinguished Nigerian writer and 1986 Nobel laureate for literature, Wole Soyinka, accepted the award on my behalf. I recall the Dutch postcard I got several months ago; the Dutch doctor, Dr Van Thiel, whom we befriended at Zomba General Hospital; the Dutch priest, scholar and friend, Professor Revd Fr Matthew Schoffeleers, who married my wife and me at St Mary's Secondary School chapel in Zomba in 1975 and now lives in Leiden. I wonder if these and other friends might be fighting for my freedom in the Netherlands? My spirits are revived; tears of joy trickle down my cheeks in disbelief. When I see the geckos running about the grey wire gauze ceiling I shout to them:

"You silly creatures, stop disturbing people who belong to world communities, you hear?"

The cellmates crack with laughter at my meaningless gesticulation. Pingeni who suspects that something has at last gone right, quietly inquires:

"What's the news, Doc?"

I gaze at him vacantly. He gazes back empathetically and continues: "Doc, feeling so animated for no apparent reason is worrying here, people won't notice the difference between laughter and madness. Please don't go mad, we need you in this struggle."

I laugh hysterically, gazing at the blank wall in disbelief; hysteria is infectious; soon everyone joins in my merriment without control, even the sceptical Pingeni – they do not know why. But the bulletins have also brought a poem that gives me great cheer. For weeks I am thrilled by the news. I bless David who has sent the poem; bless *Noriega* who smuggled it in; and bless the poet himself, Eddison J Zvobgo – a veteran of Zimbabwean politics – for writing it. Who would not feel immensely better reading and committing to memory the following truncated lines of a long poem, given the nature of the prison where we live?

My Companion and Friend:
The Bare Brick in my Prison Cell

We have become friends
Over the long years;
Both of us are deportees
From our homes and friends;
Both of us long to return from death
To the councils of our peers.
Does nobody care to remember
That perhaps these caked grains
Have fed some plant which gave forth
Grain or fruit for man?
Is this banishment to these wedges
Through form and fire deserved? ...
This brick insulates me
From myself, rendering me
As cold as salad.
I bear no grudge against it;
All I seek is a sworn treaty
Between us, so that when its purposes
And mine are done, it may
Cover my bones and, consummate
Our seven-year romance.

29

Sting in the Tail

We are sitting in our favourite spot between the kitchen and A-wing as usual, with our backs to the ration store, watching the main gate to the office block in front of us. The little breeze that occasionally blows here reducing the stench of prison is welcome. But today is special. The armed guard who usually sits on the balcony above the gate to the office block, watching over the prison's entire roof and the four fences of the prison, ready to shoot whoever dares to escape from prison, has temporarily left his post. This allows us to dash to both blocks to run precious errands or to talk to the prisoners we have known briefly and share the news we've heard from outside. But before we begin our errands, the gate to the office block squeaks open and *Noriega* appears, trots towards us and beckons to me to meet him in the middle of the quadrangle. I dash to him, eager for the latest news he might be carrying for me.

"Your principal has done it again," he whispers.

"What?" I whisper back, puzzled.

"He's told the Special Branch to arrest your friend, Blaise Machila, and to bring him here where you are, because since you were abducted Blaise has been harassing Kadzamira over your whereabouts; your friend will be walking into this prison any day from today; I just thought I should warn you."

He dashes back to the offices, leaving me rooted stiff with shock. I am stuck to the ground, my head reeling, the pain on my backside from a scorpion sting the other night and from which I am still recovering, vanishes. I want to cry out 'foul!' but I cannot

182

even do that; the words simply refuse to come out. Brown and TS run to catch me before I fall to ground; they are as alarmed as I am to hear that Blaise is being sent to Mikuyu; they walk me into the cell, where I begin to wonder what has come over Kadzamira, how he could get imprisoned his own academic member of staff that everyone knows to be mentally ill. I throw myself on my bed totally nonplussed. I can neither help my colleague nor have I any idea to whom I should turn to save him. When I come round, as it were, I pick myself up and join Brown and TS again; they are still sitting between the kitchen and A-wing, watching the goings-on at the gate to the offices. I tell them that Blaise had set himself the task of finding out, on behalf of my family, which prison the security officers had dumped me in. He does not know that I have surreptitious correspondence with them. Nor do we want him to know when he arrives. I do not want him to expose our communication system to the prison authorities, Kadzamira or the police. When his mental state is out of balance, Blaise is capable of performing astonishing feats. On one occasion, he walked more than two hundred miles from Zomba to Lilongwe to report to Capitol Hill for duties, he said, and almost got everyone he met to believe that Banda had appointed him minister of foreign affairs. As the head of department, I checked wherever I thought he might be hiding, secretly fearing that he might have been killed; I only rested when I got a telephone call from Capitol Hill that my member of staff was wandering around the buildings telling everyone Banda had appointed him minister of foreign affairs, and could I ask the college to get him? What I fear most when Blaise comes to Mikuyu is the deterioration of his health. He will refuse to take his medication when he comes here. I was one of the privileged few he could trust to ensure that he took his medicines. As we may be separated when he comes here, I cannot guarantee that I will have any control over him. And should he discover how *Gossip International* corresponds with the world outside, he will not shut up about it. He will want to show off his discovery, and will want to expose the vulnerability of Banda's security system. Despite these fears, we decide that he will become an essential part of our team when he arrives. We will also do everything in our power to inform the prison authorities about his health, in the hope that he can be released on medical grounds and be sent to a psychiatric institution in Zambia, Zimbabwe or South Africa. We do not despair.

Late that afternoon the gate to the office block opens again. Commander BK appears, pushing a new prisoner into the open quadrangle. He is still handcuffed and in leg-irons, "which is unusual," whispers TS, "because prisoners are normally unchained before they are brought into cells." The fellow is bearded, wearing the usual oversized *foya*, which makes him look thin, tall and weird. At first we think he is another condemned criminal walking painfully slowly, with the leg-irons clearly hurting him. As he approaches us, however, I realise to my horror that the man we are watching is none other than Blaise, whom *Noriega* was talking about in the morning. I am devastated, and tell my friends I want to run to D4 and cry myself to sleep, but TS and Brown block my way. "Take courage and welcome him," they say. I'm totally drained of energy. Tears of mutual recognition suddenly break out as he drags his leg-irons and handcuffs towards me. I awkwardly embrace him with both free hands. No words are exchanged; just the looks, sighs, tears and the clumsy hug. Commander BK pulls him away from my embrace and takes him straight to A-wing, with a whispered message for us that the officer-in-charge has been instructed by the Special Branch to keep Blaise in leg-irons throughout his indefinite imprisonment. "And the Special Branch are apparently following instructions from your college principal," he says, pointing at me as he leads Blaise to A-Wing. I am horrified. I know Blaise is capable of threatening Banda's cronies like Kadzamira, but he could not have done anything to deserve permanent chains as his punishment. The man suffers from an inexplicable kind of schizophrenia, for goodness sake! How could anyone normal suggest prison to punish mental illness? I feel totally helpless, demoralised and guilty. Brown, TS and I swear that we will find ways of having that decree rescinded. I am upset and wonder how many people will suffer this kind of indignity for merely being my friends; I collapse on my bed, utterly shattered.

After lock-up that evening the post-mortem of the day's events is dominated by the story of Blaise's arrival. When I suggest that students voted Blaise the best lecturer in the English department, everyone wonders why the university allowed such a brilliant academic to vegetate so. The nagging questions which follow reflect everyone's irritation, anger and frustration. Why did the university refuse to send Blaise to a proper psychiatric institution in Zambia, Zimbabwe or South Africa? Why does the government not improve the facilities at Zomba Mental Hospital to accommodate patients like Blaise? Why can't Banda spend people's tax to develop needy institutions, instead of furbishing the thirteen palaces he does not need? Mkwanda makes another of his extravagant threats: "If Banda is bringing mad men into prison, he is playing with fire; his time and that of his concubine's family is up. *Athakati* – witches!" But no-one has the stomach to laugh or comment further. When we enter A-wing for ablution the following morning, Blaise has somewhat recovered from his ordeal and tells his story through the spy-hole. He had been bothering everybody who matters about my whereabouts because he wanted my family to know. I thank him for this, but feel mortified to see him suffering and humiliated for my sake. "Stop your whispering!" Commander BK shouts. "D'you want me to get the sack?" I tell Blaise that he should find out from the Big Man, Machipisa Munthali, how to get in touch with me for further discussion; but I doubt he will, nobody trusts anybody when they first enter Mikuyu. When the news bulletins from Chirunga campus arrive several days later, they confirm what *Noriega* has already told us – Blaise was arrested on the specific orders of Kadzamira, who felt insecure and was unable to answer Blaise's persistent questions about my whereabouts. My heart begins to throb with fear of my principal's power; I am particularly sickened by the thought that he chooses to use it in this manner; all the time I was employed in the university, I had naively trusted that Kadzamira could not go as far as this.

One day, as the heat is unbearably oppressive and everyone is sitting, squatting, standing, or lying half-naked on their backs, knees up, blowing themselves cool with blanket rags or *foyas*, another political prisoner is pushed into D4 courtyard for *Nyapala* Disi to deal with. Disi holds the prisoner's hand and introduces him to us. We stop playing our games and crowd around the new arrival, making him feel at home, and desperately wanting to hear his story. The fellow is charcoal black, tall, in his late twenties, and totally bewildered by the gathering of political prisoners before him. He comes from the Lower Shire Valley, he says, his name is Hector Banda. I do not know what to make of the combination of the Greek hero and the Malawian dictator that constitutes his name. But Hector's story is more mind-gripping than that. For more than thirteen years he has been working at one of the family bakeries in Limbe township. In recent years the bakery has been so successful that the Press Group of Companies, which are controlled by president Banda, Tembo and the Kadzamiras, has decided to take it over. They have appointed another Kadzamira as the new general manager. And he wants to show the world that the Kadzamiras from Dedza district in the central region (though some of them grew up in Zimbabwe to be sure!) have entered the arena to rule the country. He is, therefore, sacking or retiring many employees under the pretext that the company needs streamlining to be more cost effective than it has been hitherto.

Hector Banda welcomes these and other innovations meant for the growth of the company. What he does not accept is that he should return home without being paid a single coin from the thirteen-year pension scheme to which he has been contributing during his time with the bakery. Naturally, he needs an explanation or what the company owes him from his pension; he needs to send his children to school; therefore he makes an appointment to see the new boss. But general manager Kadzamira demands loyalty to the life president, his party and government instead! Hector knows the trick. When authorities invoke people's loyalty to Banda, his party and government in an argument, the case is always lost before it begins. Whatever evidence Hector might provide, the crime of lack of patriotism, which by implication the general manager accuses him of is indefensible. Choking with indignation, desperation and impotence, therefore, Hector is left with no other option but to stand up, give the general manager several solid slaps and punches on the cheeks, the nose and the mouth. When the bakery's security guards come to rescue their new chief, he is already on the floor, spitting blood. The cabal's security officers are on the scene within minutes. Hector is arrested and brought straight to Mikuyu prison, where we are now welcoming him. And no. He was not tried. He was not charged. And yes, he will be liberated from here only at the discretion of the president. We are amazed that such a youthful person could have been prepared to fight for his rights, honour and dignity in this manner. We contribute clean blanket rags to his bed as we envy his daring and his noble temper. D4 and Hector are permanently bonded.

That night after lock-up *Gossip International* engages in the most trivial exercise ever. We start drawing up a chart mapping out which 'higher authority' in Banda's government or party is responsible for whose detention at Mikuyu. Of the recent arrivals, Hector, Blaise and I have been brought into prison in one way or another by the Kadzamira-Tembo faction; Mnyenga and Rodney, by the young pioneers; and aMdala aLongwe by Banda's village cronies. We note that the self-styled royal family top the list. We therefore declare them the most powerful amongst Banda's coven. And from now on we measure the power of Banda's inner circle by the number of imprisonments they can effect. "We have cracked it," Mbale shouts. Everyone takes the exercise to be futile, but it helps to kill time, ease the pain of jail, and somewhat explains where political power lies in Banda's Malawi. But nobody forgets the larger truth: my arrival and that of Blaise, Hector and the others has brought massive despair to the cellmates that we found here. Their hope for liberation has been dashed yet again, although life must go on, no matter what.

187

30

Spider in my Poem

The sign that something was not going right for me started early. Friday, 28 August 1987. I am sitting at my desk trying to write this poem, which I think will become the watershed of my creative career, but my page is blank, the words just won't come, the muse is gone. Everyone goes through such agonising moments in their writing career; but this is stranger. In the corner of my office window, near the ceiling, a spider is trying to come to my rescue; it is offering itself as the subject of my poetry; it has entangled itself in its own web. I watch intently the creature's attempts to free itself, and notice that it is not succeeding; and I do not feel like rescuing it either, with a poem or using a twig. Beyond the cliché about spiders entangled in their own webs, I cannot imagine the kind of poem I could write about spiders. I am on the point of despairing that spiders would make bad poems anyway, when I hear a knock on the door and university librarian Steve Mwiyeriwa invites himself into my office. He seems in a hurry. For, without preambles of greetings and polite smiles to show that we are close friends and colleagues, Steve places a brand new book on my desk, and with all seriousness asks:

"D'you know anything about *this* book?"

I feel threatened by his sudden arrival, the harsh tone of his voice and the emphasis he places on the word 'this'; but when I make out the book in question, I instinctively exclaim:

"What? Has that long-awaited book finally come out then? *A Handbook for African Writers*, edited by James Gibbs! Brilliant!" I scream with delight.

"So, you *do* know something about *this* book."

"Look, my friend," I answer, shifting my position, "I do not want to make large claims about my contribution to the book's existence, nor do I want to guarantee what the editor has decided to include, but I can give you some background information on its origin."

"How did it come about?"

"It was only an idea of a book, as I recall, about three years ago, in 1984, I think. I was invited to read from my poems at a conference on 'New Directions in African Literature' held at the Commonwealth Institute, London. At the close of the conference, an appeal was made for someone to publish a guide for African writers, established and budding, on the art and craft of writing. The book was to take the form of a compendium of the cultural activities that one found in each independent African country. It was to list the number of writers' groups, theatres, cinemas, dance groups, drama groups, literary magazines, publishing houses, newspapers and so on. It was also to provide practical suggestions on how budding writers might get literary agents and publishers, and how their work might be marketed. As far as I can remember, James Gibbs either offered to compile the book or he was commissioned to do so. This must be it. And if Gibbs has kept to the fine objectives of the original idea, this book will be invaluable to creative writers in our departments of English, French, chiChewa and Linguistics, as well as our writers' group – anyone interested in writing, anywhere, should find this little book priceless. When did it come out? It looks beautiful: fine printing, glossy light-green paperback cover, feels practical too – full marks to Hans Zell Publishers!" I enthuse.

"But the question is, did *you* assist Gibbs in compiling *this* section?" Steve interrupts my buoyant reception of the book. I grab it off him again, run through the section he is referring to and instantly see the reason for his mission to my office. I flick through the entire book and note that Gibbs had chosen the writer he considers important for each African country, placed his/her name above the country's, then provided a résumé of the country's political and cultural activities, as recommended by the conference. Nothing wrong with that. Editors have the liberty to present the work they edit any way they like. But Gibbs has placed Malawi under my name and summarised Malawi's politics so as to suggest that it's Banda, his lieutenants and their censorship board that hinder the growth and development of Malawi's cultural activities. Although this is true, fear suddenly grips me cold. This kind of criticism, however oblique, placed under my name has serious political ramifications in this country; everyone who matters will assume that I've written what's below my name, that I am more important than my country – there will be manifold interpretations.

"This section could put you in trouble, my friend, don't you think?" Steve says, gently but sarcastically, his words stinging like a black wasp. I snatch the book again and reread the section in question. And realise that he is right. Given the kind of politics we live under, one can draw numerous political and other insinuations from the two pages. Essentially, Gibbs has presented Banda's politics with the casualness and insensitivity typical of an outsider, which is inexcusable for someone who has worked in Malawi for many years. He should have realised that his glib mention of Banda's politics and the censorship board, highlighting my name above the Malawi section, would bring me into direct confrontation with Banda, his vicious cohort, the censorship board and their ruthless security apparatus. I seethe with rage but offer some form of defence:

"But Steve, you know the endless controversies Gibbs had with the censorship board when he taught drama and directed the Travelling Theatre in this university. At one point he was even told to rip out the entire introduction to the book of Malawian plays he edited because he had mentioned David Rubadiri and other Malawian exiles in his brief history of theatre and playwriting in Malawi, and Banda and his henchmen considered these Malawians their political enemies; they were to be permanently erased in the consciousness of Malawians. Besides, he suggests in this section that Malawi's repressive grip is loosening in general; Banda is now allowing people like you, me and others to travel. Isn't that the central message of this section? Is Gibbs lying?" I ask.

Steve answers: "My friend, you and I know that Gibbs is not lying but I have a problem. If I put this book on the library shelves, the spies, informers and agents will get hold of it, and you and I will be gone, don't you see? Didn't Gibbs know that by placing your name above the country's as he has done here, he would expose you to Banda's wrath and that of his cronies? And will your colleagues be happy to see the hero that Gibbs is turning you into by putting your name above Malawi in this manner? Has Gibbs already forgotten that it's only the life president's name that's supposed to be above anything here? And I swear to God that no informer, spy, agent or whatever would believe you, if you claimed that you had not contributed an iota of information to this section. There simply isn't any proof either way." Then, raising his voice, Steve declares: "This, my friend, is what I do not like about my job. I hate being put in awkward situations of this sort, especially by friends like you. What do you think I should do as the university librarian and your friend?"

Lord have mercy on me, I exclaim to myself, am I being blamed even for this? What's wrong with these people? I think for a moment, and rather irritated, hit back with:

"But Steve, my friend, when you took up this job you knew what you were getting into. Don't ask me what you should do; don't blame me for the wrongs that others do; just do what you've always done in situations of this kind. Do you know that two years ago, in June 1985 to be exact, the Special Branch bought all the copies of my book of poems, *Of Chameleons and Gods*, that were on the shelves at the university bookshop, and then took them to the police mess where they threw them into the pit latrine, after the book was 'withdrawn from circulation' by the censors? And do you know how demoralised I felt? Perhaps you should suggest that the censors throw Gibbs' books in the pit latrine, or, even better, send the copies back to England for others to use – we obviously don't deserve using such lovely books here. How many copies did Gibbs or the publisher send you?"

"Between fifteen and twenty-five."

"Shame if we can't use them."

We are both fuming, each for different reasons; I am particularly indignant when I realise that we are reacting to and making inferences from the two pages in the manner that Banda's informers do for whatever we do or say. We seem to have internalised the deductive principles that the dictator's apparatus uses to oppress us; we are seduced by the politics of our time. When Steve leaves my office, I am incensed that he came at all, and wonder how he is going to resolve the issue. I stand up, tear up the paper I was scribbling my poem on, and notice that the spider on my window has vanished – how did the fool free himself? I wonder.

After about a fortnight, Willie Nampeya, a colleague who teaches art in the Department of Fine and Performing Arts, makes another unscheduled visit to my office.

"I say, Jack," Willie begins, "do you know that I am your representative on the new censorship board?"

"No," I lie, "when were you conferred the honour? Please accept my heartfelt congratulations," I answer playfully.

"Thank you, but I am here on more important business, my friend," he says seriously. "There's a meeting of the censorship board in Blantyre next week, and you are an item on the agenda. It's about the book that Gibbs has written and to which, I hear, you've contributed a chapter. What exactly is the case and how do you want me to represent you?" he asks gravely, looking me in the eye.

I look at him earnestly, infuriated by his apparent wish to represent me as a dedicated MP would to his constituent; but my rage turns into amusement when it is obvious that Willie has neither read the section concerned nor does he seem to know the details of the case where he wants to represent me. After repeating what I had told Steve Mwiyeriwa on the previous occasion, I conclude rather impatiently:

"And for goodness sake, Willie, it's not a chapter we are talking about; it's only two pages – two pages which could not demolish the life president's nation. If the censorship board really want to know the truth about the issue, why don't they invite me to the meeting? Otherwise, this is the heart of the matter: Gibbs compiled the book all by himself. Remember, he taught at this college for many years; he does not need my help, yours or anybody's to write two pages on the barrenness of Malawi's literary landscape in our times. When you come across the two pages, read them; you'll discover that Gibbs has been obliquely critical of the censorship board and by implication the life president. But remember this: like other originators of the university's Travelling Theatre and the lecturers who taught theatre and drama before him, Gibbs had running battles with the censorship board over the plays he put on or taught from. As for how you should present my case, quite frankly, Willie, there's no case here. Perhaps you should suggest that the board rip out the two pages on Malawi from the book, or that they blacken them as they always do to what they call offensive pages. We can then use the rest of the book afterwards."

"You must be joking," he says.

"No, my friend, I am not joking, and don't laugh. I am dead serious; the board has done this before. My predecessor, Professor James Stewart, was forced by the censors to remove David Rubadiri's poems from an anthology of East African writing edited by Cook and Rubadiri. One of Rubadiri's poems in the anthology was dedicated to his friend Yatuta Chisiza, whom the Malawi Army had killed during Chisiza's abortive insurrection against Banda. You must know the story; why am I wasting my breath repeating it? But the point is, after the pages with Rubadiri's poems had been ripped out, the censors allowed us to use the rest of the book, and we did. So, it'll not be the first time that the censors have ripped out or blackened 'offensive' pages from a book."

When Willie leaves my office, I am exasperated and wonder what message he is going to take to the meeting that I know Zimani Kadzamira will chair, and where all this is leading? The role that my principal is playing behind the scenes in forcing Steve and Willie to pressurise me into revealing my contribution to the book, which I honestly did not help to edit, is puzzling and begins to bother me. I suspect that the principal is looking for some excuse to make a major decision about my activities, and he is hoping to blame it on Steve or Willie or me, or all three of us. My ardent representative never comes back to report how the board meeting ended. I dismiss the matter as another of the trivia that one learns to live with in our despotic times. Though from this stinking prison today, I wonder if matters would have turned out differently if I had asked; I see why the rats racing among the rafters of my prison offer no clue.

31

Death of Debate

I am here because of the death of debate. That's a fact. Once upon a time we had debates in this country; hot and sometimes hostile debates; debates that earned us freedom; freedom to break away from the Central African Federation of Southern Rhodesia, Northern Rhodesia and Nyasaland; debates that gained us self-rule and independence from the British; debates by which Malawians around the region were respected and admired. Today there is no such thing. There are no discussions on anything that matters. President Banda cannot tolerate them; his cabal hates them; the powers that be have killed debate and serious discussion. Completely. Before Banda's cabinet crisis, Kanyama Chiume and Henry Masauko Chipembere urged schools through-out the country to form debating clubs and societies, which would compete with one another within each school and between schools. I remember being on the committee of Zomba Catholic Secondary School debating society, and at one point competing with Providence Secondary School debating society in Mulanje district. During school breaks, secondary school students were advised to go back to their villages and form student associations that would go from village to village to help the young, the old and the infirm. They would build or mend their houses, wash their clothes, dig pit latrines for some, work in their gardens and cook for them, even teach them rudiments of reading and writing. I recall, after we had moved from Mangochi district to Chikwawa district, that David Chiwanga, Dan Theka and other senior secondary school students in the Lower Shire Valley encouraged us – Patrick Mandowa and I, then at Zomba Catholic Secondary School, and our friends Boniface Millinyu and Justin Dorben Malungo at St Patrick's Secondary School, Mzedi – to give talks to primary school pupils in our village and the surrounding areas, preaching the virtues of modern school education. Members of the Lower Shire student association scattered around Nsanje and Chikwawa districts teaching arithmetic, English and other subjects in the primary schools that were short of staff. And we enjoyed encouraging the pupils to play football and netball, and to participate in sports and to work hard at their subjects, so that they could pass their primary school examinations and enter secondary schools. We had fun sharing our secondary school experiences with local primary schools and communities.

After the cabinet crisis, however, Banda and his henchpeople discouraged debates, student associations and the community projects we were engaged in. They feared that student associations would become breeding grounds for supporters of the cabinet ministers that Banda had sacked. There were even rumours that the university was on the brink of closure, as Prime Minister Hastings Banda had begun to hate any form of university student association and the radicalism that accompanied it. When the cabinet crisis broke out, Henry Masauko Chipembere was in Canada, seeking funding to support the university. Banda did not want Chiume or Chipembere to get the credit for initiating and developing the idea of the university. It was because of the diplomatic approach of vice-chancellor Ian Michael and his academic colleagues and the huge influence they exerted on Banda that the university remained open. It did not dawn on Banda and his advisers then, and I dare say now, that wherever universities were established, student and staff radicalism could be expected to bloom. Governments of neighbouring Zambia and Tanzania were tolerant of the aspirations of their young nations and proud of the liberal traditions that their universities were establishing. Not us. Today, as *Gossip International* discusses these matters, I do not remember any officially recognised debating society that exists in Malawi schools or institutions of higher learning. Banda's intolerance of debate and freedom of speech and expression in the university worsened, particularly after some students at Soche Hill, Chichiri and Mpemba campuses openly supported the cabinet ministers he had sacked. At Chichiri campus the student newsletter, *Vanguard*, which reported pretty much what it liked from the inception of the university, and tried to set the standards for future liberal thinking within the campus and the country at large, was later banned, and one of its English department staff advisers deported. University magazines such as *Jacaranda Tree* from Soche Hill College and *Expression*, *Odi* and others from Chichiri campus appeared irregularly, as the censorship board impounded some issues.

The death of debate and student/staff disagreement with Banda, his censorship board, his political party and government have a long history. The Chichiri campus debating society was in trouble in the mid-1960s, almost immediately after the inception of the university. The society had been attempting to establish the tradition of university debates in which cabinet ministers, ambassadors and other prominent citizens of Malawi could participate without fear. This was in line with what was being established throughout the new universities of the British Commonwealth in the 1960s. Banda's cabinet ministers, and at one point the American Ambassador to Malawi, were scheduled to debate with Chichiri campus debating society on such topics as 'Africa for the Africans', 'One Party Governments Are Suitable for African States' and 'America Should Leave Vietnam Alone'. The chairman of the university council at the time, John Msonthi, must have known that Banda would consider such topics too radical. And when Brian Roberts, Banda's first secretary to the president and cabinet, was alerted about these topics, the debating society's entire executive, comprising Sam Mpasu, Isaac Valeta, Crispin Ng'oma, Justin Thundu, John Phiri, Han Ng'oma and others, was suspended. Again, it took the diplomatic intervention of vice-chancellor Ian Michael, Chichiri campus principal John Utting and secretary for education Ian Freeman to get Roberts, Msonthi and Banda to change their mind and allow the students to return to college.

When Soche Hill College, Mpemba Institute of Public Administration and Law and Chichiri campus moved from Blantyre to Zomba to form Chancellor College at Chirunga campus, radical students there were harassed too. The case of four students, Michael Mbwana (aThube), McWillie Kilion, Fidelis Edge Kanyongolo and Zangaphee Chizeze, who were arrested and sent first to Maula prison in Lilongwe and later transferred to this very prison, comes to mind. The four students were neither tried nor charged with any offence. After their prison sentence, they were lucky to return to college to complete their education and get their degrees. Nor were dissenting academics exempt from Banda's policy of deportation. Expatriate lecturers who were perceived to have been radical had their contracts terminated and deported without explanation. In the English department alone James Stewart, Landeg White, Robin Graham and others before and after them had their contracts prematurely terminated and were then deported. The only crime they seem to have committed is that of supporting the student/staff writers' group, their magazines and newsletters, as well as holding radical views. Some were thought to have angered either Banda, his censorship board, the Malawi Congress Party secretary general and administrative secretary, Albert Muwalo or later, chairman of the university council, John Tembo – the last two being the staunchest supporters of Banda's autocratic regime.

The first academic that Banda deported, as far as I can recall from this prison, was the well-known American Professor John Pinney of Bunda College of Agriculture, who protested vehemently over the persecution of Jehovah Witnesses in Malawi. In the late 1960s and early 1970s Witnesses refused to buy Banda's badges or his Malawi Congress Party membership cards on religious grounds; so thousands of them were arrested, imprisoned or killed; some ran into Tanzania, Zambia, Mozambique, Zimbabwe and Swaziland. In each case their property and homes were expropriated or burnt down by Malawi Congress Party officials, the young pioneers or the youth leaguers, often on instructions from Party or government authorities. The infamous Fort

Mlangeni Concentration Camp between Ntcheu and Dedza districts on the Mozambique/Malawi border choked with thousands of Witnesses from Malawi – ironically they were rescued by Mozambique, which was still under Portuguese colonial rule. My sister and her entire family suffered in that concentration camp for more than four years for being Witnesses. Gangs of young pioneers and youth leaguers gathered at their lovely house near chiKoko Bay at Monkey Bay and chased them away, stealing their mattresses, beds, the soft furniture, the fridge, the radiogram, records and cutlery. It is these events that inspired the two poems that I wrote when I was a student in London: 'The House That Florrie Intended' and 'A letter from Florrie Abrahim Witness, Fort Mlangeni, Mocambique, December, 1972'. The cabinet crisis itself happened because Banda refused to discuss seriously with his colleagues what was amiss after independence.

Today, as the Malawi Congress Party, Banda and his coven become more autocratic, debates have shrunk further and further. None of us remembers any spellbinding debates that have taken place recently in the Malawi Congress Party, the government, the university, colleges and schools. In parliament Banda has managed to create a society of MPs who are docile, inactive and afraid to offer their honest opinions on any subject of importance. The standard form of discussion for them, even on matters of life and death, appears to be: *whatever his excellency the life president says or decides, we will agree with him.* But in this prison, if we have to be honest, most of us concede that before we came here we did not have enough critical tools for the analysis of our own political environment. Banda's patronage has not encouraged us to provide alternative views on most matters of significance; that is why lawyers are irrelevant here: Banda, his cabal and their despotic apparatus have rendered them impotent. They sack well-qualified people from jobs because they do not belong to the president's or his cronies' district or region or ethnic community; often the victims are not supposed to answer back, argue, protest, or seek clarification; they will join us in prison if they do.

199

I recall two esteemed Malawian academics who could not bear working under Banda's state of siege. During university breaks, Dr Amos Simbeye, the first Malawian geneticist based at Chichiri campus, and Dr Dunstan Malithano, the first agriculture sociologist at Bunda College of Agriculture, simply packed their belongings, jumped into their cars and, taking their families with them, crossed the Malawi borders to work abroad. Today, at international conferences, Malawians even avoid giving their own views on matters that concern them; a colleague who went to an American Creative Writing Center is said to have locked himself up in his room to avoid reading from his work and discussing problems of African writing! Clearly, the development and success of any future democratic government and open society in Malawi will depend on the extent to which its leaders will allow serious debate to bloom in schools, colleges, the university, parliament, newspapers, the radio, television – when it comes – and the communities, without necessarily arresting, imprisoning or killing the opposing participants. As *Gossip International* claims, the situation regarding dissenting Malawians was worse outside the university. Dzeleka prison was apparently purpose-built to punish the supporters of the exiled ministers after the cabinet crisis. Later, thousands of dissenting Malawians, who showed no enthusiasm for Banda's life presidency after the 1971 Malawi Congress Party convention, filled Dzeleka and other Malawi prisons. The lucky ones ran across the borders to self-imposed exile. And many presumed radical politicians, including those who came from Banda's central region, paid the ultimate price. Malawian politicians who seemed reluctant to consult Banda or those who ran their ministries independently of him suffered. John Msonthi from Nchisi district was one central region politician who was first to resign in support of the colleagues that Banda had sacked. Of course, he later withdrew his resignation under pressure from the central region lobby of Banda's supporters, apparently led, in part, by John Tembo.

The dictionary of chiChewa language which Banda commissioned Msonthi to work on marked him out from the majority of the central region politicians and made him more acceptable to Banda as his possible successor to power than other politicians at the time. And if conditions for writing and publishing had been less severe, Msonthi would probably have been the most serious writer using the national language; the title of his only slim book in chiChewa *Kali Kokha Nkanyama* (Only the Animal Lives Alone) is enough to justify this claim. The book struck an unexpected radical chord as the most accurate interpretation of Banda's politics. Its very title was a pointed criticism of Banda's single-mindedness in dealing with the politics of southern Africa. Those who read the book before they came into prison agree that its language is characteristic of Msonthi's surreptitious form of protest against Banda's domestic and foreign policy. It was not surprising, therefore, that John Msonthi was the first cabinet minister to be sacked when he was Minister of Transport; he seemed too independent for Banda's liking; and rumour had it that he was reinstated to his position only after his cabinet colleagues rebuked Banda for behaving like a despot. Banda did not give his cabinet ministers the respect they deserved or the chance to run their ministries the way they knew best. Msonthi also suffered at the hands of the Kadzamira-Tembo cabal. He was a threat to them because he was the best interpreter of Banda's speeches at political rallies. And after Msonthi's death, Gadama became the next best interpreter of Banda's speeches. And both Msonthi and then Gadama became John Tembo's arch-rivals as a result. When the three politicians interpreted Banda's speeches from English into chiChewa, audience reaction showed that Msonthi and Gadama were more articulate and interpreted Banda's speeches in more colourful and refined Nchisi and Kasungu dialects of the national language. Every time Banda threatened his exiled political opponents with death, for example, Msonthi and Gadama often translated Banda's original threats with polished and memorable jokes, watering down the threats embedded in the speeches as Banda had intended them. Even as we discuss these matters from prison today, Tembo's interpretation of Banda's speeches is literal, dull and misguided; and often comes in tangled and bastardised variants of chiNgoni rather than chiChewa.

Furthermore, Msonthi and Gadama cared about Malawi as a nation; Tembo sees only his home district of Dedza, the central region and himself as constituting the politics of Malawi. As for the Kadzamiras, nobody in Mikuyu seems to have heard them translate any of Banda's speeches on political platforms. *Gossip International* believes that they would translate Banda's speeches better in Shona and Ndebele, as most of them were born or grew up in Zimbabwe. Old Man Mkwanda even wonders where these pretenders got the temerity to rule people they despised and refused to understand – nobody in prison remembers seeing them at ordinary people's funerals or wedding ceremonies!

32

Not the Wedding Invitation, Surely?!

Several weeks before my arrest, my friend Joe Masinga invited me to the wedding of Aaron Gadama's daughter; he was the chief organiser of the celebrations. I accepted the invitation and thought I could encourage the couple with a few cheerful words at their wedding or perhaps even read a poem. But Gadama was said to be an arch-enemy of the Kadzamira-Tembo family, essentially because of his many talents, achievements and political influence. Any association with the Gadamas, who were being closely watched, would, therefore, have been dangerous for anyone. The question is whether the authorities intercepted my letter, or overheard my telephone conversation with Joe, and if I am languishing here for that reason. It is difficult to tell. Obviously, if this had been another country, attending anybody's wedding or accepting the invitation to celebrations where pronouncements about politics were not on the agenda, would not have been reason for imprisonment. Not here. And the assassination of Gadama, Matenje, Chiwanga and Sangala was the most brutal event in the history of assassinations of Banda's presumed political opponents. Apparently, at the close of parliament in May 1983 Banda intimated that he wanted to retire from politics and was about to propose that his coterie should rule the country with his blessing but without the elections stipulated in the constitution.

Banda's intention to create a dynasty where his permanent mistress and her extended family would play an important role had remained a rumour from the troubled times of the cabinet crisis up till May 1983, when it was resurrected – it was meant to be Banda's reward to the Kadzamira-Tembo family for their loyalty to him throughout his thorny political career. Three of the 'famous gang of four' are thought to have dared to remind the president that his passing on power to his retainers without the elections would violate Malawi's constitution. Besides, it would be unwise for him to appoint any of the coterie as successors to the country's leadership, as their allegiance was to Zimbabwe, where they apparently still own property; their association with the ordinary people of Malawi was minimal; and the people-in-the-know within the security services associated them, perhaps unfairly, with the imprisonment and elimination of most potential heirs to Banda's throne up till then.

It is believed that Banda was so infuriated by the MPs' protestations that he declared he did not want to see them again when parliament reassembled after recess. This had always been Banda's way of speaking when he was angry, though his cohort customarily interpreted his words to mean 'death to the protesters'. These stories were common knowledge at the time, though no-one dared to talk about them for fear of being considered fit for the hungry crocodiles of the Shire River Valley. Most people knew that it was the president, his Kadzamira-Tembo cabal or both, who instructed the MPs' assassins to carry out their brutal act. And when the government tried to explain away the MPs' death on the national radio, hardly anyone believed the official lies they heard. It could not have been the case that the MPs had been involved in a car accident in Mwanza district; they could not have been running into exile, because they had no reason to do so. Banda and his intimates were unable to explain why the four politicians were running away or what they were running away from. And Banda had not denounced them at his political rallies as he always did. This is why his coterie was believed to have given instruction for the MPs' assassination without Banda's say-so.

Besides, no condolences from Banda, the Kadzamira-Tembo family, the Party or anyone in authority for the death of the 'gang of four' were sent to the bereaved families. When the MPs' mangled bodies were dumped at their homes, the security officers who brought them ordered the families to bury their dead at gunpoint. The expected traditional or church burial rites for them were not allowed. None of this had happened before. And predictably, written documentary evidence on every aspect of their deaths was conveniently destroyed, though one of the assassins from Domasi area of Zomba district lost his head at a village public house when he heard the lies officially broadcast on the national radio. He stood up to explain how he had helped to club the MPs to death and shoved them into a car which they pushed down the slope – he too disappeared within weeks of his declaration. But Banda and his court had miscalculated their political fortunes and underestimated the popularity of the 'gang of four'. When the truth about how the MPs had been assassinated reached up-country, the people in the towns and villages simply refused to endorse the official version of their deaths. Banda and his cohort suddenly discovered they had created enemies amongst the people they least anticipated – this was the turning point of their political manoeuvrings.

Gadama's assassination was particularly shocking and painful to me because I knew him well. He was the hardest working chairman of the National Examinations Council, of which I was a member. I had met him at the Malawi High Commission in London when he and vice-chancellor David Kimble and others were interviewing white teachers for Banda's 'infamous' Kamuzu Academy. At our London meeting Gadama took me aside and confided in me the story of the undeclared wars that were raging in Malawi between the Kadzamira-Tembo clan on the one hand and himself, Tim Mangwazu and Banda's relatives on the other. Gadama had predicted with despair that I would be lucky if I found him alive when I returned home after my PhD. He suspected that he would be murdered by the cabal's hit squads because the rivalry that had developed between Tembo and Gadama had reached its peak. Although I still believed it was unjust to exclude men like Gadama and Matenje from the country's leadership contest, I was shocked but not surprised to hear that the 'gang of four' had been assassinated.

This is why the Kadzamira-Tembo faction in particular would not have forgiven me, or anyone else, for attending the wedding of Gadama's daughter. I must have been drawn into the politics of Banda's succession to power that the Kadzamira-Tembo coven on the one hand played against Gadama, Mangwazu and Banda's relatives on the other. And with Gadama and Matenje disposed of, the only serious contenders to the country's leadership were the Kadzamira-Tembo clan, though two retired civil servants from the central region – ex-police inspector general Mac Kamwana and ex-secretary to the president and cabinet John Ngwiri – were still in contention. When these two gentlemen later died, Banda's cohort lavishly supported their burial ceremonies, causing suspicion among the people who knew the animosities that existed between the two sides.

Despite the assassination of the 'gang of four', the inner circle was still nervous because Banda was reluctant to hand over power to them. For the first time *Gossip International* saw Banda in a different light. When he was in his right frame of mind, which may not have been often during the last ten to fifteen years of his political career, Banda was able to hold his own against his courtiers, whom he knew to be ruthless. But the question that still bothers most people in this prison and throughout Malawi after the callous assassination of the famous 'gang of four' is: If well-liked and liberal senior MPs could be murdered in cold blood so – what of us, whom Banda, Malawi and the world does not know? And could I really have been dumped in this stench because I intended to attend the wedding of Gadama's daughter? If this is true, then we are living under the maddest and most sadistic of witches on earth.

Jack Mapange visits Glasgow & Edinburgh Amnesty International centres to meet those who fought for him. Left to right: Lord Carmichael of Kelvingrove: Revd. Iain Whyte of Christian Aid; Maria Fyfe MP; Donald Dewar MP and Scottish Secretary of State for Scotland; Jack Mapanje, Janey Buchan MEP for Glasgow, Brian Wilson MP; Alex Smith MEP for South of Scotland and Lady Fraser, Chair of Christian Aid in Britain – 1991.

33

The Edinburgh Connection

25 June 1988, Saturday. Another vicious strip-search done. Feathers and dust from blanket rags, *foyas* and contraptions of pillows are flying in the air, entering our noses and lungs without restraint. Everyone is enraged, coughing, sneezing, choking, shouting and crying with impotent bitterness. Even the guards know that the strip-search was unnecessarily ruthless; no-one has broken prison rules; the political prisoners who have recently joined us have brought no cannabis or *chamba* – the famous Malawi gold – into prison. But I have no reason to complain. When *Noriega* left the cell after the search he whispered that I should grab the Holy Bible near my bed before anyone does because he had placed a bundle of bulletins for me there. I have already tucked the Bible under my arm, even as I put on my *foya;* I find myself urging people to clean the cell, make their beds and quickly get out into the courtyard to play Ludo or Draughts. When all is over I choose my favourite spot between the ration store and A-Wing from which I can read the Holy Bible in peace. The bulletins from Fr Pat, David and Mercy report what's going on at home, in the university and the world at large. Brown's relatives will bring the medicines and food I asked for when they get visiting permits or when *Noriega* visits them next, says Fr Pat. But when I open the larger of his bulletins, I instantly whisper to myself: "Hang on, what's this? Banda's letter? A photocopy of Banda's letter? Where did this come from? Has our secret correspondence with the outside world come to this? How did Fr Pat or David or Landeg get this? Did anyone break into Banda's State House or Sanjika Palace to get this?" I can't believe what I read:

Members of Staff
University of Edinburgh
EH8 7HF

State House
Zomba
MALAWI
Central Africa
2nd May 1988.

Ladies and Gentlemen,

Your letters of appeal on behalf of Dr Jack Mapanje were received. It is not necessary for me to burden you with a lengthy reply.

But if you must know the facts, teachers, here, who stick to their professional work of teaching students, are not interfered with by anyone. Jack Mapanje has taught at Chancellor College for a number of years without doing anything wrong, just like all his colleagues, whether Africans or Europeans. But after all these years, he changed his mind, for his own personal reasons and started using the classroom as a forum for subversive politics. This cannot and will never be permitted in this country, particularly, in the University of Malawi. Therefore, he had to be picked up and detained.

This is Malawi in Africa and not any other country. Things have to be done according to conditions and circumstances in Malawi, Africa.

Signed
H. Kamuzu Banda

Pingeni was right the other night. Of all the appeals and petitions for our liberation that individuals and institutions make to Banda, it's the Scottish ones that rattle him and his cabal most. I do not know what's going on out there, but I can speculate what might have happened in this case. Academic and administrative staff of the University of Edinburgh have petitioned Banda that I be charged with the crime I am alleged to have committed or be released. And Banda has responded with this angry letter. But how did the university convince Banda to reply to their petition? He never responds to anybody's protests, even from his closest friends; it's not in his blood, people say. This is a miracle. Banda routinely ignores whatever representations are made on behalf of any political opponent he might imprison. His court, the so-called royal family, simply refuse to tell him about them; often they do not allow even his relatives to see him; they want to protect the president from the truth, people say. But protests, petitions and appeals from Scotland in general and the University of Edinburgh in particular have a privileged status. Banda's coterie daren't stop Banda's Scottish friends from seeing him – hence this letter. Yet the president's defence is flawed on several counts. Why did I have to be 'taken' without going to the courts? And at my interrogation, inspector general Mbedza and his chief commissioners of police did not accuse me of engaging in political subversion in lecture rooms. The IG did not know why the president had instructed him to arrest and imprison me. And he gave me no reason to believe that he was lying, nor did I suspect his integrity at the time. And today, more than eight months on, comes this letter, which suggests that my imprisonment was politically motivated. Who am I supposed to believe? I have no significant contacts or people of influence in Edinburgh. I remember Keith Brown, my doctorate degree external examiner and professor of linguistics at the University of Edinburgh. I suppose Neil Smith would have told him about my plight: otherwise I cannot think who else could have influenced Banda for him to respond in this manner.

The other Edinburgh connection I have is Angus Calder, a friend, literary critic, fine poet and author of the famous *People's War*. He teaches literature at the Open University and lives in Edinburgh. Angus Calder, the exiled South African writer Cosmo Piertese and I once co-edited an anthology of modern African poetry in English for the BBC. Perhaps Angus mobilised distinguished writers and academics in the city to campaign for my freedom. The substantive population of friends of Malawi in Scotland who are mostly connected to the Scottish Presbyterian Church might also have put in a word to Banda for me. The other obvious connection is the general historical one that every

Malawian can claim to have. Dr David Livingstone of the Scottish town of Blantyre, near Glasgow, is supposed to have 'discovered' us in the nineteenth century on his famous journeys across Africa; the country he discovered became Nyasaland Protectorate; and when Banda became leader of the newly independent country called Malawi, Livingstone's Scottish missionary link was permanently established. But the most likely reason for Banda's reaction is his having been a medical student at the University of Edinburgh. This is why on political platforms Banda often calls Scotland his second home and Edinburgh a city close to his heart; he even claims to be an Elder of the Church of Scotland. All these may be reasons for his wanting to explain himself to the University of Edinburgh staff. The truth, though, is that I do not know who caused Banda to write the letter whose photocopy I have before me, though I am delighted that they did – perhaps Banda will be embarrassed enough to consider the possibility of my release, and that this frank letter might be the kicks of a desperate man.

After lock-up that night, *Gossip International* is ecstatic about Banda's letter; we forget the humiliation we suffered at the strip-search. And as we always do with other matters, we begin dissecting the letter and offering weird reasons behind Banda's response. If the letter was indeed written by Banda, which some cellmates claim may not be the case, then he must have been hurt by the discovery that even the university which he reveres has joined the protests and appeals for my liberation. He must be astonished that a mere lecturer's imprisonment can cause so much global remonstration, when this has not happened after imprisoning his cabinet ministers. Brown thinks the text hasn't the feel of the president he once knew; its tone is too desperate. Pingeni declares Banda's signature too steady to come from a senile dictator with arthritis in the knuckles. According to Mbale, the signature was photocopied from the Malawi Congress Party membership card of the 1960s – it is common practice for Banda's henchpeople to transfer that signature onto detention orders for the people they have imprisoned. *Gossip International* seems

211

agreed on one point: however senile Banda might be he would not end his letter on 'This is Malawi in Africa...' For if we asked British universities where Malawi is, wouldn't the University of Edinburgh be the first to know where? Could our life president perhaps have lost his mind completely? Everybody wonders. For me the assumption that anyone could use 'the classroom as a forum for subversive politics' under Banda's autocratic rule is clearly far-fetched. What kind of politics can the English department teach when the History department is not allowed to mention even the nationalists who invited Banda home to help in the struggle for independence against the British? How Malawi got its independence has been distorted since Banda's cabinet crisis. Today, if you mention Kanyama Chiume, Henry Masauko Chipembere, Orton Ching'oli Chirwa, Willie Chokani, Augustine Bwanausi, Yatuta Chisiza, Rose Chibambo and those who fought for our freedom, you will be imprisoned or even 'disappeared'. Children in schools and youths at young pioneer bases throughout the country are told that Banda came to fight the British single-handedly; he was not invited home by anyone.

When Pingeni asks if ever I met the president officially or privately, I tell him I recall only three occasions when I've had anything to do with Banda. First, when he visited Chinkhu and the rural precincts of Dedza district on the Malawi/ Mozambique border. I was teaching English at Mtendere Secondary School and my headmaster, Bro Fernand Dostie, asked me to form a special school choir to entertain the president with praise songs. At twenty-three I did not want to bungle the job and get the sack. So, I solicited the experience of my friend and colleague Joe Masinga, and the music expertise of Fr Kabango from the nearby Mtendere Catholic Junior Seminary. We pinched the church tune of a well-known Catholic hymn, removed the pious key words and replaced them with words about how Banda, the Messiah, the father and founder of the nation, had developed the country beyond recognition.

Everybody played these tricks to survive, though we often wondered why the MCP leader did not see through the lies we told him. But when he arrived at the political rally, after more than five hours of our sweltering in the sun as usual, didn't the lion of Malawi watch just a few of the dances that came from the districts and suddenly decided to return to the headquarters, apparently for more pressing business at Capitol Hill, we were later told. Mtendere Secondary School Choir got only an honourable mention after entertaining the crowds before Banda's arrival: Banda was merely told that our choir was excellent; he did not actually hear us sing. We were obviously disappointed; having gone to the trouble of creating the choir that was meant to entertain him, why couldn't the president at least acknowledge our roasting in the sun as we waited for him?

I met Banda for the second time during my graduation when he presented me with my first degree. At the convocation my name was called out, the huge graduation drum sounded, I stepped up the podium towards the president, I offered him my hand; and for the first time shook the hand of my country's president and chancellor of our university, then received the BA degree with distinction that I had achieved. And as I went down the steps, smiling with satisfaction for what I had accomplished on my own terms, I was bemused by the frailty of the president, who no longer felt like the lion we all feared. Thirdly, I recall dealing with Banda indirectly through the directives and national duties he forced us to perform for him and for the country. Banda vetted the MPs who entered the Malawi Parliament himself. He insisted that candidates who did not have a university degree, diploma or a school certificate should pass proficiency tests in spoken and written English before they became MPs. The tests were prepared by the English department and administered throughout the country by academic staff from other departments with our supervision.

Yet in none of these cases did I tell anyone what I thought about Banda, his cohort or their autocratic regime – nobody would dare. So, who told the president that I had changed my mind? It can only be the president's toadies who dropped their poison into his ears. It can only be Kadzamira, his uncle or his sister who told Banda that

I was teaching subversive politics in lecture rooms. These people have planted spies, agents and informers amongst the academic staff, students, administrative and support staff, who report to them regularly. That's a fact that no-one would dare declare publicly outside this prison. But I will concede one point. If I taught subversive politics in my lectures, it was Banda's fault. He directed his censorship board not to ban any writings by William Shakespeare. The English department took advantage of this and taught the best of Shakespeare, stressing particularly the tragedies – *Julius Caesar, Macbeth, King Lear, Coriolanus* and others whose relevance to local politics was obvious. Yet even then, no lecturer of Shakespeare dared to make direct links with the subject matter of the plays to the local politics. Students made their own connections, most of which were obvious.

I will confess further. I've never liked Banda's politics of ruthless elimination of political opposition. And I will never change my mind on that. If I carried the Malawi Congress Party card and wore Banda's badge when I went to markets or to bus stations or grain-grinding mills or wherever, it was because, like everybody, I did not want to be harassed by MCP youth leaguers or young pioneers for not having them. It's only today and within the confines of these prison walls that I have had the courage to declare my stand on these matters. It is Banda's letter that has incited me into declaring my position. For the days, weeks and months that follow, the Edinburgh connection becomes a major subject of further speculation about how imminent our liberation might be.

It was to take me more than twenty years to discover what the University of Edinburgh had done for Banda to respond to their appeal. It was Alison Girwood who instigated the protest on my behalf. I had met her at the 1986 Commonwealth Writers' Conference held in conjunction with the Commonwealth Games of that year – the games that had been boycotted by some Commonwealth countries. On 20 January 1988, after hearing that I had been imprisoned without reason, Alison wrote a very strong letter to Mr M.D. Cornish at Old College, University of

Some postcards from Holland that strayed into Mikuyu
before Jack was released, October 21, 1988.

215

Edinburgh, bringing my plight to the attention of the staff of the university. She also liaised with Drs Angela and Grahame Smith of Stirling University, who were organising a general petition from the Scottish Universities as a whole. On Friday 22 January Alison met Dr Andrew Ross of Ecclesiastical History and together they drafted the petition on Edinburgh University headed paper, which read:

'To His Excellency, the Life President, Ngwazi Dr H Kamuzu Banda

We, the undersigned members of staff of the University of Edinburgh appeal to you as a former student, on behalf of Dr Jack Mapanje. We respectfully request that he be either charged with a crime and dealt with under due legal process or released from detention. We, the undersigned individuals, wish to express our surprise and concern at the detention without trial of so distinguished a writer and leading academic, and in view of the special relationship and regard existing between Malawi and Scotland, hope that you will understand this concern and re-examine his circumstances...'

Rob D. Leslie of the Department of Scots Law then sent numerous copies of the petition to all the Law teachers of the faculty. In the end, signatures of academic, library and administrative staff were collected from the university under *Name* on the left and *Title* in the middle and *Department* on the right. More than four hundred signatures were collected, scaring Banda into responding as he did.

Book Six
The Escape

34
New Officer-in-charge

We wake up to the news that officer-in-charge Sitima has been transferred. We do not know why, we cannot ask why; that's how prisons work, we are told. When his deputy assumes control of the prison several weeks later there is general unease. He has given us the impression that he is tougher and harsher than his boss. As deputy-in-charge, Mughogho never delegated punishment to his officers and guards: he insisted on punishing whoever broke the prison rules himself, whether the culprit was a condemned or a political prisoner. We are scared, therefore, when he first visits the cells in his new capacity. And although he talks to some of us in a smattering of English, mostly to get our support on delicate prison matters, we do not know what to expect from him. You can imagine my alarm, then, one Saturday afternoon, when I am summoned to his office to see him. But when I get there I am surprised by what he wants me to do. "Could you check the grammar of the letter I have written in English to recommend one of my members of staff for promotion?" Mughogho asks. I am taken aback. I want to laugh at the triviality of the request. Does he have a more serious matter up his sleeve? I wonder. I do not particularly want to help; this is one area I have the right to say no, without being punished for it. But I submit and correct wherever the letter needs correcting, hoping that my co-operating with him can influence the course of events in future – and apparently the fellow eventually gets his promotion.

My second invitation several weeks later is just as curious. I feel nervous as I approach Mughogho's solemn chair, squatting on the cement floor before him as Banda's eyes in the portrait above the chair gaze accusingly at me. When a rude cockroach from the ceiling peeps at the portrait as if to rebuke Banda's gaze on my behalf, Mughogho gravely observes: "You've lots of friends outside this country, Dr Mapanje, haven't you?" Another rhetorical question that I must respond to with care. What is he up to now? I note his cheeky and inquisitive tone. Will he be asking about my contacts abroad next? What has he heard about me? In times like these every prisoner remembers the options that are at his disposal: the right to remain silent or to prostrate himself before authority, toadying and chanting: "I am sorry, sir; I am sorry, sir; I am sorry, *Bwana*" – even if you are not sorry or not responsible for whatever is supposed to have gone amiss. To claim the right to your hostility lands you in punishment cells here. So, concealing my irritation, I remain silent until Mughogho transforms his loaded utterance into a proposition to which I can respond on my terms.

"Look, Dr Mapanje," he observes, "stop looking worried; you've already signed your detention order; what remains now is your release. And I am not sending you to the punishment cell; you've not done anything wrong to deserve that; not yet anyway. I've received two postcards from Europe; they are addressed to you; I thought you might like to see and read them."

He offers me the postcards. The first comes from Holland, a typical tourist postcard, which simply reads *Groeten uit Holland* – someone from The Hague whose signature is impossible to decipher has sent me greetings. "Praise the Lord!" I say, but wonder why of all the postcards that the grapevine has intimated have been sent to me through various authorities in Malawi, why this has chosen to arrive at such an address: 'Jack Mapanje, Mikuyu Prison, Near Zomba, Malawi'. What right has such a postcard got to reach its destination? But never mind the address; never mind the spotless Dutchmen selling Edam cheeses from oval-shaped trays; never mind the men in white selling clogs on stalls; never mind the mother and daughter sharing yellow and red tulips on the green, well-trimmed Dutch lawn; never mind the family of four, strolling along their Dutch avenue – the postcard is truly colourful and I love it. I've never been to the Netherlands and can only recall the English ITV television commercials about Edam cheeses, which in the 1970s we used to laugh about as University of London students; and I cannot quite recollect the jokes about Dutch tulips that were common and became part of our student culture. Months later I feel like saying:

To The Unknown Dutch Postcard-Sender (1988)*

Your *Groeten uit Holland* postcard, with
Five pictures, dear unknown fighter for
My freedom, should not have arrived here
Really; first, your shameless address:
There are too many villages 'NEAR ZOMBA,
MALAWI', for anything to even stray into
Mikuyu prison; then, I hear, with those
Bags upon bags of protest letters, papers,
Books, literary magazines, postcards,
Telexes, faxes and what not, received at
Central Sorting Office, Limbe Post Office
Everyday, later dispatched to my Headmaster
And his henchpersons and the Special
Branch and their informers to burn, file
Or merely sneer at and drop in dustbins;
Your postcard had no business reaching
Mikuyu prison...And how did you guess I
Had recently signed my Detention Order
(No.264), October 21, and I desperately
Desired some other solidarity signature
To stand by (to give me courage and cheer)
However Dutch, however enigmatic, stamped
Roosendaal, posted *Den Haag 23 Oktober*

---

* First appeared in *The Kenyon Review, Vol. XV, No 2, Spring 1993, Ohio, USA.*

1988, to buttress this shattered spirit,
And these mottled bare feet squelching
On this sodden life-sucking rough cement
Of Mikuyu prison ground? But many thanks,
Many thanks on behalf of these D4s too!
...

But however these colours slipped through
The sorters, your *Groeten uit Holland*,
My dear, has sent waves of hope and reason
To hang-on to the fetid walls of these
Cold cells; today the midnight centipedes
Shriller than howling hyenas will dissolve;
We will not feel those rats nibbling at
The rotting corns of our toes; and that
Midnight piss from those blotched lizards
Won't stink; and if that scorpion stings
Again tonight, the stampede in D4 will jump
In jubilation of our *Groeten uit Holland!*

The second postcard has a London stamp and comes from a certain 'Celia (BC)'. I take the bracketed initials to stand for the British Council, though I wonder who Celia is as my British Council programme organiser in London was Sheila. Nonetheless, given the drab red brick walls, the white and red roses on her postcard look gorgeous; they remind me of the 'War of the Roses' that I read about many years ago in order to pass my London A-level History. And the bright green British landscape in the background conjures up the romantic poetry of Wordsworth, Keats, Shelley and others that I read for my first degree. I feel animated at this encounter with the foreign landscape, which contrasts sharply with my dull brown-grey environment.

Mughogho extends his hand to get the postcards back and says: "Well, I thought you might like to see your mail. I'll keep them in your file until your release, when you can take them as souvenirs." It's the last part of his statement that puzzles me as I get back to my cell. Why is he tantalising me with the release when he knows that Banda wants me to 'rot, rot, rot forever' in his prison? I ask myself. Does he know something I don't? Has he perhaps heard about the human rights campaigns being mounted outside the country for our release and he wants to verify whether they emanate from me in his prison? I am truly mystified.

The cellmates are eager to hear what I have to say for myself after this second round at the office. My heart throbs and the mouth feels dry as I tell them I went to read mail from Europe. I can't believe I've seen images of the real world for the first time after a long time. I am sure of one thing: tremendous energy, which I must have bottled up since I entered this hell-hole and signed Banda's detention order, has suddenly been released. Like the surreptitious bulletins from linguists and writers, the postcards have given me formidable cheer, dispelling the fear and despair I've had since I arrived here.

After lock-up the cellmates are euphoric when they hear the story of my postcards; the faces of *Gossip International* light up with hope. "How can strangers as far away as Europe care to continue to send you greetings when Banda and his dogsbodies won't even allow your family to visit you?" Ndovi enquires. Chunga cannot contain his optimism: "Repent, the time for liberation from the beast is at hand!" He shouts. D4 cracks with laughter and applause. Then almost immediately everyone begins to offer his own version of Mughogho's motives for inviting me to his office. "We must infer more relevant information from Mughogho's action," claims Mkwanda, "because mail from out-side the country is never shown to political prisoners." "Mughogho has started well as officer-in-charge," claim Disi and Kadango. "Prisoners from Mikuyu II have already begun digging around Mikuyu I; the vegetable garden we have been crying out for has begun; soon we'll be enjoying sweet potatoes and sweet potato leaves for vegetables from there," says Brown. "Perhaps the clinical officers from Zomba General Hospital that we've been fighting for will begin visiting Mikuyu too," he concludes. The postcards begin to have a mysterious effect on our disconsolate lives. The question: "What exactly did Mughogho say about the postcards as souvenirs?" is asked again and again. Numerous interpretations are offered, but nobody seems convinced with the answers I give. When I declare in exasperation that Mughogho has kept them in my file until my release, almost everyone believes that I had gone to the office to hear about the date of my release, not to be shown postcards. I am uncomfortable, as each dissection of what becomes the 'postcard affair' seems to lead to my 'imminent release'. Soon Pingeni and Mkwanda are locked in an argument about whose interpretation is more plausible.

"My reading of the postcard affair is more reliable than yours, aMdala aMkwanda!" says Pingeni.

"But I've seen more releases than you, Pingeni," Mkwanda replies.

"And why didn't they release you then, Old Man?"

"Don't be rude, young man! More than four hundred detainees were freed from this prison after the hanging of Muwalo; *you* do not know *that*!"

"What has that got to do with the postcards, Old Man?" Pingeni curtly answers.

Mkwanda is furious; he stands up, fists high, walks towards Pingeni's bed, ready for a fight: "Pingeni," he shouts, "You're too young and too dull to understand what I'm talking about." Disi and TS have to intervene to stop the two fighting.

Chunga announces: "People outside are fighting for our liberation. I knew it. I dreamt it. We'll soon be released!" Raucous laughter cracks out again as the speculative interpretations become more and more bizarre. "Doc, when you get out of here, please fight for us too," Chunga concludes. And, as if beaten by Mkwanda's blows, Pingeni relents and declares: "Anyway, quarrels and fights like these are the signs of the times, I am sure we'll be released; I am sorry aMdala aMkwanda, I should have been more polite."

D4's desperate desire to be free is scandalous. Their titillation over the postcard affair continues until two night guards patrolling outside the cell hit the wall three times with the butts of their guns. We shut up. And I begin to think: if this is the first time postcards from abroad have reached their target in prison, Banda's security system must be cracking somewhere. The other Kadzamira supervising how letters are checked for security reasons at the national post office sorting centre is not doing his job properly. And yet I do not flatter myself easily, given the detention-order-signing ordeal from which I am yet to recover. I find D4's fumbling for fresh air as they search for the truth about the postcards rather disconcerting. And I am none the wiser as to Mughogho's precise motives for inviting me to his office, though weeks later I feel hugely inspired:

Season's Greetings for Celia (BC)*

They say when God closes one door
He opens a window to let in the sun

Celia, your season's greetings arrived
In time of despair, after I had signed

My life out by signing the Detention
Order insisted upon by the life president

Who wishes us to rot, rot, rot forever?
In this prison, but your white and red

Roses invoke that War of the Roses I
Battled to comprehend to achieve my

A-levels, the green English landscape
Summons the Romantics I explored

Under the billowing smoke of paraffin
Tin-can lamps once upon the rough terrain

---

* First appeared in *Skipping Without Ropes*, Bloodaxe Books, 1998.

I thought I had left behind; and how did
You hope to be remembered when you

Mark your name merely as Celia (BC)?
If the parentheticals are the British Council,

10 Spring Gardens, London, I recall no-one
By that name there, my British Council

Programme organiser with whom I shared
My *London Magazine* poems was called

Sheila, I think, and why, why of all those
Bags and bags of protest mail which harass

The Post Office Sorting Centre everyday,
As oblique couriers convey, why did only

Your postcard from London and another
From The Hague choose to slip past our

Strict mail sorters at this crucial moment,
What bribe did you provide the officer in

Charge of prison for him to chance me to
His office to peruse your mail from over-

seas, defying the edict from the life-despot
And risking his life and mine? No matter.

Your season's greetings, Celia, have thawed
Our anguish, furnishing these rancid prison

Walls with much sought after night jasmine;
Now the cliché glowers: somewhere some-

one we do not know cares – and that, dear
Celia, is all the prisoner needs to know!

When I read this poem at the Barbican Centre in London, two years after my liberation, the British Council lady who sent the postcard came forward to declare her full name as Celia Leak. She provided the circumstances that caused her to write and send the postcard: Sheila, my programme organiser, had retired at the British Council. She had hoped that I would become someone important when I returned home after my studies. Having been shocked to hear about my imprisonment, she told Celia about it. That was why Celia found it necessary to send the postcard in solidarity. She was delighted to hear that I had got her postcard. Often human rights protesters like her did not expect any form of reward or response from the victims they protested about – they always thought that their letters of solidarity never reached their destination, she said. I thanked her as I autographed my second book of poems she had just bought.

35

What Use Phonetics?!

I have been invited to Mughogho's office again, where he has
asked for a bizarre favour from me. Martin Machipisa Munthali
in A-Wing has asked the officer-in-charge to ask me to show him
how to use Webster's *International English Dictionary*. Since his
imprisonment by the British, Machipisa has been allowed to keep
the Bible and the dictionary. Apparently he has been augmenting
his knowledge of English by using the dictionary throughout his
incarceration, though he has no knowledge of the phonetic
alphabet that the dictionary provides in order to facilitate any
form of learning. Could I therefore visit Machipisa and assist him
with his problem since I am an expert in English? Mughogho
asks. I am puzzled and suspect that the officer-in-charge has a
hidden agenda. Prisoners are not allowed to visit each other
except with the blessing of the officer-in-charge, and that blessing
is rarely given. I wonder whether Mughogho intends to change
that rule so that political prisoners can begin to visit one another
with his permission. Anyway, I accept the job as I am eager to see
the father of Mikuyu, whose stories mesmerise every newcomer
here. I am secretly hoping to see what Malawi's veteran political
prisoner looks like; I want to confirm what I have heard about
him; perhaps I could persuade him to join our campaign of
correspondence with human rights activists abroad, too. Besides,
I am rather pleased that at long last someone acknowledges that
I have skills I could impart to others even in prison – my
knowledge of the phonetics and phonology of English has been
fast rusting.

I find Machipisa planning to have his head shaven – a ritual the guards say he performs once or twice a year to remember his mother and to pray for her soul. The long grey beard and sharp unshaven moustache surrounding his thick lips make him the perfect rebel I have known in pictures. The dignity, power and authority the man wields in prison is striking. He has not only brought me to A-Wing officially, but he dismisses the commander and his guard who brought me to him and tells them to squat at the far end of the courtyard as we deliberate on matters of value. I am stunned by his courage. I notice that he speaks with a bad stammer, but he manages to communicate effectively. First he must take me on a tour of A-Wing, starting with his cell – a pathetic-looking little room, about two paces by one, with blanket rags spread on the cement floor, a pair of *foya* he uses as the pillow, a crumpled saucepan, the so-called *bakuli*, a mug, a broken piece of Lifebuoy soap and a worn-out toothbrush. I note that he is being incarcerated under worse conditions than we are in D4. But Machipisa does not want my pity; he dismisses my shock and proceeds to show me the rest of A-Wing. As TS had said, there are seven small cells including his on the right, seven small cells on the left and a little corridor in between. He repeats the history of the cells as I first heard it on my induction to Mikuyu. When we return to his cell, he picks up the *Webster International Dictionary* from his bed. We have no exercise books, no paper, no pencils. We must sit down to the business of learning the rudiments of English consonants, vowels, stress, accents, intonation and other grammatical signs that *Webster's International Dictionary* provides without them. We will have to rely on memory to learn. The course on lexicology and lexicography that I once enjoyed at University College London with Professor Randolph Quirk comes in handy, clearly somewhat adapted to these weird prison conditions!

Before we settle down to the business of noting the phonetics and phonology of English, however, Machipisa changes tack and excuses himself for beginning with what he calls an embarrassing apology. "If you don't mind me saying so, Doc," he begins, "you are lucky to have been imprisoned when physical torture has been suspended because of international pressure. Prisoners were not just handcuffed or chained or left in leg irons throughout their time here, the stubborn ones were taken to the office block to be 'broken'. There they were forced to mount what the prison authorities called the 'bicycle'. And if you rode one of those, it took you only minutes to break your spine; you were brought back to the cells paralysed." Machipisa stops and begins to wipe out drops of sweat from his forehead. I am enraged by these facts. He recalls primary school teacher Arthur Chipembere from my home district of Mangochi, who came out of here paralysed, only for being a brother to Banda's arch-political enemy, Henry Masauko Chipembere. I tell him I know the teacher and people at home said Banda would have been kinder if he had told his security officers to kill Arthur instead of letting him return home worse than a rotten cabbage.

Machipisa continues. "Mikuyu was choking with political prisoners then – at one point there were more than eight hundred occupants altogether crammed here instead of the expected three hundred. The cells you have come from were so over-crowded that at night when people wanted to turn, the *Nyapalas* woke everybody up and shouted 'All turn!' and they all turned at once. The prison guards picked up at least one dead person each week. The stench, which is tangible from this courtyard, is not just from the excrement in the pit latrines that are before you: the blood of the political prisoners who were beaten to pulp in these cells has left an indelible reek," he concludes. I am utterly shaken by the revelations of the torture that used to happen here. Then he switches the discussion to the subject I should have suspected was the principal reason for his inviting me. Lowering his voice he says he has heard with nervous joy stories about D4's secret correspondence with human rights activists abroad. He says this is good news and wishes us well. He is wondering, though, if we might consider keeping his nephew, Kennedy Msonda, informed or perhaps even making him our representative outside prison. Kennedy visits him regularly and has contacts with journalists outside the country. He has heard independently about the campaigns for our liberation emanating from here. He stops, wipes his beads of sweat from his face again and waits for my response. I tell the Big Man, as D4 prefers to call him, that I know Kennedy from our student days at Soche Hill College in Blantyre, where he was my senior when we read for the Diploma in Education – we used to play table tennis together. However, I suggest that it would be premature to involve him in our surreptitious communication with the outside world at this stage. It would be dangerous to behave as if we had formed a political party in prison; then I relent and update him on the progress of the rest of the campaign for our liberation. And although Machipisa is disappointed that I have rejected his request, he is delighted that I've given him an update of the campaign. Trembling with power and determination he boldly stammers his views:

"You... you young people... are... are onto a good thing; I... I want to congratulate you; I wish you well in your... your... your struggle, which is our... our... our struggle. If there is anything, anything I can do to help, use... use the usual grapevine to get in touch with me. And remember... remember however hard it might be, do not, do not despair, and do not give up. Banda will be forced to free us. He will die and we will live to tell our stories. And mark my words. When I come out of here, I intend to take him to court and win for wrongful imprisonment. And believe me, I will come out of here alive and win; I swear to the God of my ancestors I will win!" He pauses in order to breathe deeply. These are the words that newcomers hear from cellmates in this prison to encourage them not to despair: the Big Man in A-Wing, who has stayed in Malawi prisons longer than Nelson Mandela of the apartheid regime in South Africa, swears that we will all be released by Banda and live to tell our story, therefore, let us take courage and hang on!

When we begin the business of learning English pronunciation, I am amazed how quickly he gets the gist of English consonants, vowels, stress, accents, intonation as outlined by *Webster's*

International. The fear I had that his age, the stammer and the absence of pencil and paper might be impediments to his learning vanishes. And although he has the usual difficulty of differentiating between l̲ and r̲, I assure him this is a problem that all speakers of Bantu languages encounter when they learn English. We decide to meet up again for the second and third session.

36

That They May be One

TS takes me aside and declares that he wants to convert me into a proper Christian; I'm suspicious of his true motives and frankly rather amused. But he's dead serious. Having faith in God is a serious matter in Mikuyu. His plan is simple. As no vicars, priests or ministers – no mullahs either, but TS is speaking only for the Christians – are allowed into prison, we ordain our own. On Sundays, Catholics and Protestants turn D4 into a church, the 'vicar' chosen that week leads the rest in a service of prayers and hymns, and chooses the Bible readings from which he preaches. We don't pray according to the different churches we worshipped in when free men, we pray simply as followers of God's son, Jesus Christ; principally for God to release us from here – that's the bare truth of the matter, though even He must sometimes be surprised by the intensity of our petitions, especially as they seem to be carried up to heaven on our nauseating breath, TS declares, then casually suggests: "Doc, why don't you help us choose the readings for the week; later, maybe you could even preach?"

My initial reaction is to say no, but I recall that I was an altar boy once and loved sung masses and the lovely smell of burning incense, candles and altar wine, which I used to nick when the opportunity availed itself. But when I had family, I must admit, I was a bad Catholic. I often took my wife and children, dropped them off at St Lwangwa's Catholic Church and headed for the public houses, only to come back for them after mass. Not exactly the kind of preparation for pulpit homilies that TS is looking for. And I never really read the Bible. At Catholic schools we were not encouraged to read the Bible; it was a rare book with difficult language, everyone said, and the King James rendition that I was exposed to needed special training to comprehend. I feel uneasy at TS's invitation, but accept the challenge it entails, as there's practically nothing else to do in Mikuyu. And it seems what Banda and his coterie with all their might cannot create outside the prison – a genuine respect for and tolerance of different religions, peoples and ethnic groups – a true ecumenism – these political prisoners can! At any rate, my 'conversion' might give me the opportunity to read with a purpose the Bible I have always wanted to read – God's ways are indeed strange, as they say.

Nyapala Disi, who is a devout Muslim himself, is ecstatic when TS tells him of my 'conversion'. And he certainly knows his Bible as well as the Koran. I listen respectfully when he suggests that I should start by reading the prophet Habakkuk if I have not read the Bible seriously before. "It is Habakkuk," Disi continues, "who has the courage to ask God the questions we all want to ask Him. Why does He allow innocent people to be imprisoned without trial or charge? Why does He let evil flourish on earth? Why do evil people live so long? And many other questions," he concludes. Although I don't understand God's answer to these questions, however many times I read prophet Habakkuk, I soon begin to enjoy working with the 'vicars'. The inevitable jarring note in the perfect harmony appears a few weeks later in the form of Ian Mbale. He has been sent by Brown, Ndovi, Rodney and other members of the Seventh Day Adventists (SDAs) to ask me to leave my church and join them. They are all disgruntled former members of Christian churches, who have embraced the SDA creed in Mikuyu. Their conversion has resulted mainly from reading what else, apart from the Bible, there is in our 'library' – two tattered issues of the 1979 magazine called *Signs of the Times* and two worn-out paperbacks by an Ellen G. White. I decline Mbale's invitation firmly, and tell him if what I've read in White's torn books is typical SDA creed, then I suggest that Seventh Day Adventists are dated and have what amounts to a close-minded attitude towards Catholics and Protestant churches. I've always felt uncomfortable with the whole notion of converting people who are already Christians to join another set that claims to be Christian, anyway.

When I tell Disi and TS about Mbale's visit, they tell me to watch out for the SDAs; they are engaged in an intense campaign to recruit Christians from other Christian churches, as well as those who are not Christians. The *Nyapalas* are dismayed by what they consider to be the dogmatic attitude of the SDAs, who believe that only the chosen few who have got the date of the Lord's Sabbath right can be saved. Indeed, for most of my time in prison after this, I am appalled by the animosities that are generated between the SDAs and the rest of us, making life unbearable for those who refuse to convert. I know too little about SDA doctrine to verify the claims they make about their interpretation of the Bible, but I wholeheartedly agree with Disi and TS that we have enough problems as it is, without squabbling over esoteric religious controversies.

I'm certainly not in a position to solve any religious problems when I'm a living religious contradiction myself. My ancestors believed in one God. When Anglican Church missionaries arrived in Kadango, my mother's village, we became Anglicans. In 1954 Mother took my sister, my brother and me – what was left of my family – from Kadango Village, Mangochi district to Mpokon-yola Village, Chikwawa district, where our uncle had moved to and was living with a large family. There was no Anglican Church in the entire Lower Shire Valley, and naturally no Anglican schools. We were faced with the choice either to convert to Catholicism and apply to a catholic school or convert to Presbyterianism and apply to a Scottish Presbyterian school. In those days, for a child to go to any mission school at all, there was no other option but to convert to their religion; non-mission schools were few and far between.

Our uncle chose the Catholic school for my brother and me because the Catholic creed and practice were closer to the Anglican one that we were accustomed to. He then bought us a brand new bicycle with which we covered the seven miles to

Chikwawa Catholic Primary School and the seven miles back, crossing the massive Shire River from Monday to Friday until uncle was able to pay for our boarding fees at the school. Then my sister and her husband, who were married in an Anglican church with all pomp and ceremony, became Jehovah's Witnesses; our uncle's family had become Scottish Presbyterians, long before we arrived in Mpokonyla Village. So our extended family was made up of Anglicans, Jehovah's Witnesses, Scottish Presbyterians and Catholics. And we were all a happy lot. Did I need to add the Seventh Day Adventist Church to the litany, and in the 'comfort' of Banda's prison? Not me!

Disi explains the prison's pernicious quarrels as he sees them. "What we hate about being thrown together in prison, as we are in D4, are the religious conflicts we have; these come from a few very blinkered SDAs. As *Nyapalas*, we are under pressure to report these quarrels to the officers. We don't want to report our fellow cellmates. They are sent to punishment cells or transferred to other prisons, when and if we do. Sadly, the arguments of those who want to convert others never seem to go deeper than 'my Malawi Congress Party membership card is better than yours' – nobody produces any convincing evidence or guarantees that God only listens to prayers from the SDAs. What we want is that God should forgive the wrongs we have done Him and His creation and return us to the world where we can try again. Fighting amongst ourselves over idiotic religious differences won't help us overthrow those responsible for dumping us here."

For the rest of my stay in prison I am embarrassed by these controversies. I did not expect to find us wasting our energies worrying about outmoded religious arguments, which merely weaken our resolve to fight the injustices that Banda and his inner circle inflict on us. Let me clarify my position once and for all. Like my forefathers, I believe there is one God. I accept His existence without embarrassment and without apologies. I don't need to prove God's existence to know Him or to believe in Him. There are too many things we accept without proving their existence. And proving that there is a mysterious power called

God has nothing to do with believing that one church created to pray to that God is necessarily better than another. Besides, I love the sense of mystery that believing in God brings into one's life: if I knew everything there is to know about God and the world, life in general would be most boring. The Ten Commandments that God gave to Moses, which Jesus conflated into two – Love God with all your might and love your neighbour as yourself – seem practical to me. My ancestors knew and followed them without knowing about European religions. They ordered their lives in a special way, which helped them to survive the catastrophes of the world. At any rate, I love the challenge of modelling my life on some mysterious other. I don't feel inhibited. I feel challenged. Life feels more complete and more fulfilling with God leading every step.

If Banda, who claims to be an Elder of the Scottish Presbyterian Church, and his courtiers, followed these commandments, we would not be languishing in this dungeon. And if you believe that human life is precious and should not be destroyed by dictators and their henchpeople, and yet you don't believe in God, you had better believe in something else in Mikuyu, otherwise your endeavours might lead to the frustration whose end product is suicide. And suicide must not be contemplated in Mikuyu. D4 considers it 'illegal' for political prisoners even to consider the possibility of suicide. We need to win this war against Banda, his vicious thugs and the evil and corrupt world in which they let us wallow. God is not only our true liberator here, but almost everyone invents his own strategies for survival, whose success depends on belief in God.

Months after my conversion, I am selected chairperson of the Sunday praying Christians. I spend most of my time painfully fighting SDA's interpretation of the various sections of the Bible. I find myself constantly defending and protecting my flock from attack and the persistent intrusion of the SDAs. It's time- and energy-consuming to live your life constantly trying to prove the other fellow wrong or right about this or that interpretation, especially when you have spent more than a third of your life reading theories of interpretation of utterances and crafting their practical use in verse. One of the reasons for which some of us were thrown into jail must surely be because God wanted us to be exposed to this kind of intolerance, though I must admit the experience is more painful than physical torture.

37

Echoes of a conference

Today I recall several links in linguistics that I suspect might have brought me into this stench of a prison, in addition to those I have already offered or will offer. Almost two years after its creation, the Linguistics Association for SADCC Universities, LASU, of which I am still chairperson, holds its second conference at the Harare campus of the University of Zimbabwe. Mid-September 1987. Eight of the nine universities of the SADCC region send two or more delegates to the conference, which is so successful that as chairperson of LASU my name is splashed about in Harare and its surrounding cities. A television clip of Zimbabwe's Minister of Higher Education, Dr Dzingai Mutumbuka, University of Zimbabwe's vice-chancellor Professor Walter Kamba and me, appears on the afternoon news. We are interviewed on radio and quoted in the papers about the language projects that we hope the universities in the region will be engaged in, which include research into theoretical linguistics, African languages and the translation of world literary classics for schools in the region.

But this publicity does not augur well for me as the chair of LASU because the life president of Malawi and his diplomatic missions abroad frown upon any publicity that highlights the achievements of ordinary Malawians without mentioning them. The success of the linguistics conference might also not please the local 'higher authorities' in my university – involving myself in regional projects, which draw Malawians' attention away from Banda to places outside the country, is scorned upon by the Kadzamira-Tembo cabal and their cronies.

The local organising committee of the conference might also have blundered without their knowing it. They had not invited Malawi High Commission staff to the conference. Not that the mission would contribute anything substantive to linguistics (they have never had a linguist in the mission), but because LASU's chairperson comes from Malawi, where such courtesy is demanded. My patriotism will, therefore, be questioned at home. Besides, my principal's brother finds himself in Harare witnessing LASU's media success. Will he not pass word to his brother about what all this publicity is doing to make me popular and famous in the region?

There is another issue known only to LASU treasurer general Francis Chilipaine and me. For three years I have been external examiner in the Department of African Languages of the University of Zimbabwe. In the final year as external examiner, I apply for the post of writer-in-residence, which has been advertised. The University of Zimbabwe chooses to interview me for the post during LASU's conference; apparently I had been invited for interview, but the letter had either been intercepted by our ubiquitous security officers or somehow it had failed to reach me. I am successful in the interview and offered the job, which is lucrative by Malawi standards; and I accept it on condition that the university hierarchy back home give me permission to take the sabbatical leave I have not taken since I joined the English department in 1972.

However, the dean of the faculty of arts in the University of Zimbabwe, Professor George Kahari, who was on the interviewing panel, cannot contain his joy when I accept the appointment. He announces the result of my interview in the corridors of the faculty office building, within earshot of Chilipaine and other Malawian linguists attending the conference. I will join their faculty not as a head of department but as a writer-in-residence the following year, he says, citing the amount of stipend I will be getting and the source of external funding for the residency – the Ford Foundation. For anyone who knows what it means to live under Banda's patronage, the dean's announcement, declared before my university

240

authorities have cleared the appointment, is tantamount to my stating that I am running away from Malawi to work in Zimbabwe, which is unacceptable to my Malawi employers.

Another ill omen comes from the popularity of the LASU conference itself: media coverage for the conference attracts six lecturers – five white and one black – from universities in apartheid-era South Africa. They fly into Harare to attend the conference camouflaged as tourists. Upon discovering that the papers being presented are original and fresh, the participants friendly, and the joint regional projects that LASU wishes to be engaged in exciting, they decide to declare themselves and appeal to the local organising committee to allow them to register normally to enable them to attend the rest of the proceedings. The gatecrashers should have chosen better times for their subterfuge. Their apartheid regime has just been destabilising the politics and economy of the Front Line States of the SADCC region – of which Zimbabwe was the hub. We simply cannot imagine the wrath of Zimbabwe's security officers if they discover the trick.

Alarmed by their daring, Norris Dembetembe, Alec Pongweni, Herbert Chimhundu, Francis Chilipaine and I gather the six academics and lecture them on the policy of the Norwegian and Swedish research agencies with regard to apartheid. Unless the Zimbabwe government officially clears them beforehand, we are to exclude delegates from all South African universities from the events that they finance, until apartheid is eliminated – a policy which LASU's entire executive endorses without reservation. To prove my point, I give them names of delegates from Soweto township in South Africa that the Zimbabwe security has cleared and are attending the conference with a free conscience. As chair of LASU I have no choice, therefore, but to ask them to leave the conference before Zimbabwe security catches up with them. Today, from this stinking prison, I am thinking: if those tourists complained to their apartheid regime that the chairman, who comes from a country which is friendly to their apartheid government, has thrown them out of a conference, then my chance of getting out of this prison is non-existent.

Yet another bothersome matter originates from a sister regional academic body, the Association for the Teaching of Language and Literature in SADCC Universities (ATOLL), which holds its conference at the Harare campus at the same time as our LASU. Indeed, it was at the Second Uppsala Conference of African Writers in Sweden, where the ATOLL deputy chair, Emmanuel Ngara and I, sought Norwegian and Swedish funding for the conferences of our respective associations. So having been asked to participate in one panel of ATOLL's conference, in my capacity as a poet, I am invited to attend its jewel: an African writers' party, where Chinua Achebe's novel *Anthills of the Savannah* has its snap launch.

I accept the invitation and perhaps foolishly as I am now discovering, persuade Professor Helge Ronning of the University of Oslo to invite Chilipaine, who gratefully accepts and claims afterwards that he has been honoured to mingle with eminent African writers and critics such as Chinua Achebe, Ngũgĩ wa Thiong'o, Micere Mugo, Flora Nwapa, Kole Omotoso, Emmanuel Ngara and many others, most of whom he has heard about but has not known in person. However, throughout the party, I am nervy and embarrassed. When I talk to Ngũgĩ alone, Chilipaine drops in to listen to our conversation. When I talk to Micere, he sticks around to hear what we are talking about. And so on. I am ill at ease throughout the party and fear that if Chilipaine reports me to Banda's security officers back home, or reports to my employers that we have been brushing shoulders with literary luminaries that they might regard as 'potential' enemies because they are friends of the Malawian poet David Rubadiri and other Malawian exiles, they will scowl at our presence at the party.

The final ill omen concerns Chilipaine himself, who suddenly quarrels with the local organising committee about some matter, which I still cannot put my finger on even from this prison. On the first day of the conference Francis and I have a word with the local conference organising committee that they should allocate more money for secretarial services to ensure that the papers presented are printed quickly and distributed in advance – this is what brought success to the international conferences we had organised in the past. But from Mikuyu today, I am still struck with shame when I remember Francis, enraged beyond comparison, calling me a traitor for failing to see his point of view in the arguments that are advanced on both sides. I have always prided myself on being tough at dispute management and dispute resolution, but on this occasion I fail abysmally to exploit these skills. I do not know if my Zimbabwe colleagues believe me when I say goodbye to them, but I predict that their inexplicable quarrel with Francis does not bode well for my return home. Should anyone report these 'hiccups' to my employers, I expect the Zimbabwe residency to be a non-starter, I tell them.

On the other hand, all these links might be illusory. The truth might lie in another area. Malawians visiting Zimbabwe or giving lectures in the university were always warned about Alex Meke Kalindawalo, who, after being released from Zomba central prison in the abortive attempt to overthrow Banda's government with Muwalo and Gwede, got a job in the University of Zimbabwe and was said to have been reporting Banda's or his court's so-called political enemies to Malawi. But I did not believe the stories I heard about Kalindawalo because I had been with him at Zomba Catholic Secondary School once and we were kind of friends. And although we avoided each other for the three academic years that I was external examiner in the university, I did not believe that he'd do me any harm, though today I am just wondering if I might not have been too naïve; if he might not have met up with Chilipaine and conspired to report whatever I had said or done in Harare to the authorities here. Although I do not believe that these links could provide reasons for anyone to be thrown into jail, I do not think they were sufficient reasons for my imprisonment, even in our abnormal circumstances.

38

Landeg's Despair, What Despair?

25 September 1988, Sunday. Banda's official birthday on 14 May and the anniversary celebrations of our independence on 6 July have been and gone. No release of political prisoners has happened as we expected. There's despair on every face except mine. Mercy and the children have sent another survival kit of antibiotics and tins of beef and sardines, though sadly she confirms what Fr Pat has already told me: that they have had to move to Ntcheu district hospital and they could not take Mother with them because the house in Ntcheu is too small. My precious library has been scattered amongst my relatives in the villages, where the books will be chewed up by insects. Finance Officer Geoff Chipungu has been directed to stop paying my salary, but Mercy suggests that I pray every day, instead of worrying about them – everything at home is under control. Judging from the bulletins I get from Landeg, David, Fr Pat, Mercy and the children after more than ten months, I believe that the campaign for my liberation is in full swing, though I am not so sure about its extent. After working so hard to get me freed, my family, relatives, friends and colleagues are disappointed. There is despair at home and abroad. The following letter brought by *Noriega*, which I must quote in its entirety because it comes from the *de facto* chairperson of the campaign for my liberation in the UK, is typical of these concerns.

York.
20 July 1988
Dear Jack,

It's tough to know what to write. Everything we've tried so far has been a record of failure. I enclose a poem which says what we all want to say – by a newish English poet called David Constantine:

Poem on my birthday for Irina Ratushinskaya

We have the day in common, also verses;
And the cold has lasted beyond what is usual;
By now there should be colts foot. Cold?
It hurts the face a little, the eyes weep perhaps,
But you should see my son brake his toboggan broadside,
You should kiss my bright-eyed daughter cycled home.

Some things are black and white: laws against poems,
A camp on the driven snow. Do the guards enquire
Through the eyes of the line of unspeaking women
Who harbours your verses now? I have read of such cold
That the breath you breathe makes a starry whisper,
It forms on the air, it crackles like interference.

What have you done? They can question you to death,
They can feed your lungs with ice, they can dose
The freely riding waves of the air with dust.
You imprinted the dirty glass with frost gardens,
You muttered of love along the Nissen corridors.
Oh triumph of breath! Oh manifest beauty of breathing!

Just now in the dark, turning a year older,
I heard the rain begin. Soon in our country
The little horns of lilac will butt at the sky.
Our house warms through its pipes. The whisper of rain,

A continuous whispering of verses. Courage,
Sister. Good courage, my white sister.

(4 March 1986)

Other things will come with this letter, perhaps in dribs and
drabs as the situation allows. I'm sending an official letter
from U. of York inviting you as visiting fellow for one year
from whenever you can take it up and naming the sponsors.
It will be kept safely until you are free to use it to bargain
with British HC people etc., but I'm sending an extra copy
for you to see. Also, a copy of a letter to the headmaster of
Eton (no less!) who, I've been told, influences your own
headmaster as much as anyone these days! Apparently HE
goes to see HIM every British visit to chat about schools. It
might work!

Otherwise, the next date we can do something is, I'm
afraid, your birthday. There is a major reading planned at
the poetry society for the 18 Sept, with several people
including myself reading your work - just in time to get the
case re-publicised for the following week. Also, we are
preparing new stories along the line of your last suggestions
about who rules OK? We didn't do anything at the time
because we had messages about the need for silence until the
6th. The important thing here is that we shall be keeping the
two stories entirely separate.

There is also a letter for your comrade offering him a
place here. It's the official letter, but please take note that
the place is available at any time, despite the dates given –
we shall keep it open – and that though it's not possible to
promise a scholarship at the present (because awarding one
means withholding it from another student) the various
bodies do know and are prepared for when it will be
necessary.

I've taken to writing long narratives. My piece on the
Hijack you saw two years ago is appearing in Poetry Wales
and I'm sending with this a thing on Mozambique which

246

might get in to you. At present, I'm writing a book-long
poem about the Bounty Mutiny. Better than articles. A
lecturer and poet here called John Birtwhistle is compiling
the Penguin Book of Prison Poetry, *starting with Walter*
Raleigh and other Elizabethan detainees.

I've told him to keep you a page or two. Gibbs keeps
phoning in great glee about what all this is doing to make
you famous. I suppose that's one point of view. It's certainly
the case that you'll have problems of celebrity to cope with
afterwards, but that should ease the job problem!

We are all well. Alice's business is just taking off. I've
been promoted. We've exchanged several letters with Mercy
who is being wonderful. We've shifted our house around a
good deal so you won't be stuck in the basement when you
come. I'm glad you've at least learned to cook at long last!
It is marvellous to hear from you when the chance comes.
Much love from us all – we'll keep pushing!
Love,
Signed
Lan & Alice

My letter from the registrar is enclosed. So is Brown's. And I've
never seen a man so pleased with himself as Brown for receiving
the offer of a place to do research leading to a doctorate degree at
the University of York. This is no mean achievement, we tell
ourselves; in fact, we think it's a miracle. So, why should I in
particular take the campaign for my liberation to be a record of
failures, when Landeg is contacting even the headmaster of Eton!
Man, which president, which prime minister, which ambassador,
which diplomat, will you be contacting next? And there are those
readings in my honour you are planning – I am humbled,
humbled and humbled most profoundly. The lengths to which
family, friends, colleagues and strangers can sometimes go to
liberate folks like us is remarkable. And this can't be for nothing.
I agree with *Gossip International*: it's premature to despair. After
rereading Landeg's letter I recall the first lines of my favourite

poem 'Carrion Comfort' by Gerald Manley Hopkins, which I often recite in times like these:

NOT, I'll not, carrion comfort, Despair, not feast on thee;
Not untwist – slack they may be – these last strands of man
In me or, most weary, cry I can no more. I can;
Can something, hope, wish day come, not choose not to be.

I must admit I had been feeling despondent after signing Banda's detention order. But Landeg's letter has charged my batteries, as it were, and Constantine's poem is pure gold. It's so touching and meaningful that it contrasts sharply with James Gibbs's wild fears for my global fame. I will keep this bulletin in a special hole in the wall and come back to it whenever I need cheering up. And sure enough, inspiration comes several weeks later:

On David Constantine's Poem[*]
(for Landeg & Alice White)

Your poem for Irina Ratushinskaya
On your birthday has reached these
Putrid African prison walls it
Was probably not meant for;
What cheer distant voices must bring
Another poet crackling in the Russian
Winters of icicle cells, I imagine.
Yet even in this dungeon where
Day after day we fester within
The walls of the tropical summers
Of our life president
And his hangers-on, even here,
What fresh blood flushes

---

[*] *The Last of the Sweet Bananas – New & Selected Poems*, 2004, Bloodaxe Books, UK.

When an unexpected poem arrives,
What fire, what energy
Inflames these fragile bones!
Indeed we have the verses in common,
The detention camps
The laws against poems
The black or white
Traitor or patriot
Binary oppositions
Notwithstanding;
But secure in your
Voices of solidarity,
We'll crush the crocodiles
That crack our brittle bones.
Do not falter then, brother,
Do not waver, dear brethren,
But craft on the verses
Whose ceaseless whisper resonates
Beyond the White Halls of our dreams!

39

What Unquenchable Beauty!

The sun's shining bright in the courtyard outside, the sky's blue, it's not yet mid-day but I am already sweating copiously. I've decided to stay indoors, therefore, where I can continue brooding on why I think I am festering in this dungeon, what crime I could have committed against my country to deserve what I am going through. But standing at my bed is *Nyapala* Disi, who will not let me do what I like. Brooding is a dangerous pastime in prison, he says, people go mad without realising it; I must pull myself together and get out into the courtyard and play Ludo or Draughts, or count the bricks on the walls, or do something; it's too glorious a day to stay indoors, at any rate. He insists that he is holding a special gift for me in his closed palms. Since I love and protect all creatures great and small, why don't I guess what his hands are holding before he allows me to remain indoors? I protest, I'm too hot, and it's too early for guessing games. But as *Noriega* often trusts Disi with the bulletins that are meant for me, I capitulate and enquire in my father's language, chiYao, which we often use for intimate matters between us:

"*Ambuje*, are you carrying *baluwa*?"

"No, it's not notes from your friends."

"What is it?"

"Go on, one more guess."

"But I can't think in this scorching heat!"

"OK, touch it and tell me what it is," he says opening his palms.

"It's a moth." I recognise it instantly. Disi has brought me a moth. "Where did you get this beauty?" I ask. "Plucked it from the courtyard walls outside," he says. It has a charcoal grey body, ashy wings spotted in gold and black, shiny brown eyes surrounded by dots of white. It looks beautiful. When I stretch the wings their delicate structure begins to crumble into ashes in my hands – I hate myself!

"*Ambuje*," Disi continues, "I know you don't feel like joining those playing Draughts and Ludo in the courtyard today, but come and look at the wonder of God's creation outside; it's so colourful, you'll love it."

I take my damaged moth with me to let it fly away. And lo and behold, I see that the courtyard walls are covered in hundreds of and hundreds of insects of every colour, making the drab prison walls look magnificent. There are hundreds of multi-coloured butterflies, dragonflies, bumblebees and moths. Some butterflies have black silk wings spotted with shapely patterns of green, white and yellow. Others have wings with large black dots splashed on their white canvas. There are red-winged bumblebees, green-winged dragonflies, brown- and green-coloured praying mantis, moths of every hue, and a host of other insects I am unable to classify – altogether creating a breathtaking radiance. And the sky, as if in celebration, is not the dull hazy grey we've come to tolerate: it is blue, without any speck of cloud. Why has God decided to tantalise us with the beauty of His creation in this ugly man-made environment? The ever-optimistic Disi says Allah has decided to cheer us up. And he makes another discovery.

"*Male*!" he shouts in chiYao, "look who's flying in the clear blue sky today! I saw them first, so I will be the first to be released."

"No, I saw them first, only that I didn't shout about them," Ian Mbale claims.

"If you two are quarrelling about that flock of geese flying in circles in the clear blue sky, criss-crossing and floating towards the colossal Zomba Plateau," Pingeni declares, "I must tell you, I saw them first; I have already counted their number: it's twenty-two. That means twenty-two political prisoners will be released soon and as I saw them before everybody, I will be among those to be freed." Soon those who have stayed here longer are gazing into the blue sky, counting the geese gently and majestically gliding towards the gigantic Zomba plateau in the distance. Those of us who have recently arrived are puzzled by this sudden child-like elation of our senior cellmates after seeing what seems just like another flock of geese. Disi finds it necessary to justify their reaction: "The spectacle you see on the prison walls and in the sky above is a special and rare occurrence in this prison. On the last occasion this happened in the sixteen or so years of my incarceration, about four hundred political prisoners walked out of these prison gates, free. The seven hundred and eighty-eight or so stinking breaths that crammed these dark chambers were considerably reduced. Now that this sight is here again, our feeling is that soon we are going to have another release of our numbers, perhaps of the order of the geese we've just seen flying above us," he concludes.

I accept their interpretation with scepticism, little realising that it would take two-and-a-half years to have twenty-two 'politicals' liberated from Mikuyu, surprisingly confirming their speculation.

The following Sunday, as if to celebrate the unquenchable beauty we saw in the week, Pingeni presents the most memorable thanksgiving homily ever. It's on the birds of the Bible, a topic I suggested to him in my capacity as chairperson for the Sunday-going Christians. He starts with the mysterious raven that Noah sent from his ark to see whether the floods outside had subsided, which never returned to its master; then the ravens that God sent with bread and meat to save His prophet Elijah during the great famine; he includes stories of doves, sparrows, swallows, vultures and others and ends with a reminder of the relevance of the large variety of insects that covered the prison walls and the geese whose presence we talked about during the week. Now everybody believes that each of us is a raven sent into the world on an errand by our Master; some of us go our own way and never return to base; others are charged with the duty to save God's own starving prophets. The homily stretches over many weeks and I am so

252

flattered by its success that I begin to work on the next set of readings about women in the Bible. I believe that I had been among those who thought that male chauvinism had its roots in the great books of religion – the Bible and the Koran included. But not having read these holy books properly, I could hardly know what stories they told of women. I'm also thinking it could be the start of a series of 'seminars' on 'Feminism and the Bible' for TS, who is enthusiastic about our 'academic' discussions, although he has never set foot in any university building. It's real ravens that first suggested the idea of Pingeni's homily for me. We not only have ravens landing on the rooftops of the cells and crowing, scratching and quaking in the afternoons. But at dawn, just as we are catching up on sleep, the ravens land on the corrugated iron roofs, stomping about, pecking at whatever they have thieved from people's dustbins; they disturb whatever sleep and little peace we have. When I ask Disi why these ravens always came at dawn and where they got whatever they pecked at on our rooftops, he laughs and wonders how I could ask such a stupid question. Didn't I come from university houses with dustbins full of bones? I feel embarrassed by the rich-poor divide that the idea of university dustbins suggests to him.

The Famished Stubborn Ravens of Mikuyu

These could not be Noah's ravens, these crowns
Of Mikuyu prison, groaning on our rooftops each
Day; wherever they wondered after their bungled
Pilgrimages in the aftermath of those timeless
Floods, Noah's ravens could not have landed
Here (they never returned to their master's ark).
These could not be Elijah's ravens either, for,
However stubbornly this nation might challenge
Lord Almighty's frogs, the devouring locusts,
The endless droughts and plagues, today, there's
No prophet God so loves as to want to rescue
With bread and meat from messenger ravens!

These could only be from that heathen stock of
Famished crows and carrion vultures sent here
To peck at our insomnia and agony-blood-eyes
And to club the peace of this desert cell with
Their tough knocking beaks. And why don't they
Choose some other place and some other time?
Why must these crows happen at Mikuyu Prison
Always at dawn, hammering at the marrow of
Our fragile bones and picking at the fish-bones
Thieved from the dustbins we ditched outside?

40

The Escape

"Watch him! Watch the prisoner! Catch him! Catch the prisoner! Prisoner jumps over the fence! Catch prisoner! Prisoner from the kitchen! Catch prisoner! Out there! Catch him! Shoot him! Shoot!"

I wake up to these sharp frantic noises of prison guards shouting outside D4. They have been clicking at their guns all the while, as if they were pulling the trigger at the person they were shouting at but the guns were refusing to shoot. I open my eyes and hear the troubled voices fade into the distance and the noise of trooping boots running in every direction outside the cell. The whole event comes to me as if I am in a trance, but I know I have not been dreaming, nor is it drunken guards returning home late after their booze up that I heard – I've learned how to sleep through such noises these days. Then my heart instantly jumps with recognition of what I might have been hearing. I hear myself involuntarily praying:

Almighty God, if that's the boy then, please God, protect him. He's just another one of us gone astray. Please, Lord, do not let them catch him. These people have no scruples, Lord. They will kill him. He is young, Lord, he deserves better in this brutal and evil world that knows no innocence. I should've been firmer with him when he consulted me about this. Please, God, I am sorry but...

My prayer is interrupted by TS who, knocking on the door softly but firmly, draws D4's attention to the commotion of the prison guards outside: "Gentlemen, this is TS speaking; gentlemen, did you hear the guards shouting just now? *Nyapala* Disi, tell everyone to get up and listen carefully. Gentlemen, I've bad news for you: Ian Mbale has jumped over the prison fence. I repeat, Mbale has jumped over the fence and gone, only Ndovi and I are left on duty in the kitchen. Gentlemen, listen, Mbale has escaped and we are finished! Soon the prison regime will be at our throats, I can already hear sinister boots marching at the office block. So, everybody, throw away your *zitakataka* or you are dead men! God help us! Today, we'll indeed see what shaved the guinea fowl bald! Disi, Mkwanda, Kadango, the young fellow Mbale has declared war on Banda's prison regime for us; their wrath will be on our heads; the freedom we've enjoyed so far is gone. People, take cover, there's war coming from the office block!"

There's pandemonium in D4. Everyone's fumbling for their broken pieces of razor blades, the needles, paper money, newspaper cuttings about campaigns for our release, precious letters from relatives and friends and other odds and ends. These must be hidden in cracks in the walls, in the ceiling rafters above, or torn to bits, chewed and swallowed, or flushed down the toilet. There's the chewing of this, swallowing of that and the grinding of soap that has come here illegally. The toilet flushes every time the water fills up the cistern; soon even the toilet must give way, it's blocked; but Mkwanda, who still boasts about having been 'the best plumber in town once upon a time', uses his bare hands to push down whatever has blocked the toilet. There is mayhem in D4. We are climbing on each other's shoulders, reaching out for the articles that refuse to be kept in wall cracks or flushed down the toilet. We are pushing these through the small windows at the back of the prison wall – having broken the mosquito wire gauze especially for this purpose. And speed is paramount when the gates, doorways and doors begin to swing open ceaselessly in the prison precincts. No siren sounds for the prisoner who has escaped, no prison or police authority wants the world to know that a political prisoner has escaped from Mikuyu, lest Banda and his cohort sack them instantly. The dreaded boots come crunching towards the kitchen, the courtyard and D4, and when Disi peeps through the spy-hole he whispers a warning to us all:

"People, TS and Ndovi are being dragged away, to the punishment cells most likely. Please Allah, protect us from Banda's wrath! My friends, the battalion's here. All go to bed, you've heard nothing; don't open your mouth about anything, even if you knew about this or suspected it coming, please!"

Disi's voice trails with despair as he throws himself on his hard bed. I am shivering, lying on my back, knees up, expecting the worst. The familiar jangling bunch of keys sounds at the door. Everyone is in his bed waiting quietly as if there were no brouhaha minutes ago. At the touch of the padlock to D4, Pingeni and Chunga are already snoring. The door is flung very wide open, the hinges almost separating from the door:

"Search! All out! Quick! Leave everything on your bed! Troop out like Adam! Naked! One by one! Double march! Quick!"

The orders come from every direction as the truncheons beat up those who continue sleeping. At the door we pass through a gauntlet of officers and prison guards who viciously search our hair on the head, the armpits and the pubic hair. With their canes and truncheons they poke at our genitalia. They make us bend, as if to find out if Mbale's designs for escape were hidden in our backside. We are made to stand in the courtyard with legs wide apart and hands on our heads. Soon the pot-bellied and fat-necked chief commissioner of prisons Chikanamoyo, who refuses to come to hear our problems, appears on the scene with an entourage of menacing officers and guards from the headquarters. I have not seen these before. Chikanamoyo pounds his feet from D4, to the kitchen, to the courtyard and back, foaming at the mouth, choking with anger and swearing at us without shame. He watches his prison henchmen perform another protracted ritual of search on our bodies. They merely pull and push us about, instead of beating us up with their truncheons and canes, though I fear blood would flow if the truncheons and canes were used. Apparently they have been instructed not to torture anyone for fear of human rights activists outside the country; they resort to mockery instead; mocking the different sizes of our genitalia – some of our penises are circumcised, others are not, some are thin and others are thick, some like silly sausages, short or long, they say, laughing with rancour. One officer whips with his polished cane what he calls my 'hanging university balls and penis', and asks if it hurts. Vindictive laughter breaks out among the officers and guards. Their canes and truncheons poke again and again at every scar and hole on our bodies as if to show their chief commissioner of prisons how perfectly they can execute their searching duties. Other officers and guards remain in D4 beating up every blanket rag, every *foya* in sight, as if they knew Mbale was hiding there.

Then we hear another sound of vehicles entering the prison; chief commissioner of prisons Chikanamoyo runs to the office block to welcome the visitors. A sentry standing in the direction of the office block whispers for all to hear: the Special Branch! They all stand to attention, stiff, waiting for further instructions. So it is that we are treated to the ugly presence of the life president's top officers of the Special Branch that most of us had not seen – about twenty altogether. Apparently they have been hunting everywhere for Ian Mbale and now they want to confirm where he escaped from. They enter the courtyard, the kitchen and D4 in mobs of four. Some pot-bellied characters have their fat arms resting at each end of the *knobkerries* they are carrying over their shoulders. Others are breathing hard and drooling at the mouth like tired, aged hunters beaten by their nimble prey. Yet others have ridged bellies that seem to defy the sleeveless T-shirts they are wearing. Some come in oversized suits, tromping their way into the prison they'd hoped they would never enter. And others carry ugly tattoos and oily black charms on their arms. 'Thou shalt not enter Mikuyu prison without some outward protection on thine wrists, waists or necks' seems to be their belief – obviously, people will do anything to protect their jobs. If Mbale intended his escape merely to embarrass the so-called higher authorities, may God bless the fellow; his plan has been impeccably executed. With the arrival of the Special Branch the strip-search ritual starts again. Again we are forced to stand on legs set maximally apart, hands on our heads. Again they mock with vengeance our genitalia hanging loose. Again we bend for the pleasure of his excellency's security officers to search our bottoms. It's evident that they want to impress their superiors, to show them how well they can do their job.

After examining D4, the kitchen, the communal shower room and the communal pit latrines in A-Wing from where Mbale must have escaped, the top echelon of the president's security officers and the prison regime from the headquarters return to the office block. Presently *Nyapala* Disi is summoned to the office, patently to explain why and how D4 conspired in Mbale's escape – the prison regime always assumes everyone conspires in such escapes. New rules begin to percolate to D4. With immediate effect criminal prisoners from Mikuyu prison II, another prison situated half a mile away, will cook all the food Mikuyu prison I requires. We lose all the privileges we have hitherto enjoyed by virtue of our being cooks. We are to be transferred to B-Wing next to the condemned prisoners in C-Wing. With two rags of blanket, two *foyas*, one mug and one *bakuli* each, we reluctantly move to B-Wing.

As we transfer, some guards claim that the search for Mbale is being conducted in the manner of ancestral animal hunting. Rows of police and prison officers, their constables and guards, with bloodhounds, guns and clubs, are combing and beating up the bushes surrounding the prison. Roadblocks have already been set up on every road or pathway that leads to Zomba town and Mikuyu. Instructions have been issued that any police or prison officer, police constable or prison guard who sees Mbale, arrests him, clubs him to death or shoots him, is to have instant promotion. Mbale must be brought to the security authorities dead or alive. At first, most of us suspect that this is merely meant to scare us into further submission, but soon we hear that the police have arrested Mbale's parents some four hundred miles up north. His sister's family and any relative who might give Mbale refuge has been taken to the regional police headquarters in Mzuzu and Lilongwe for questioning. Officer-in-charge Mughogho is instantly demoted and transferred to another prison. But Mbale is nowhere to be found. I thank the Lord for answering my prayer so promptly.

That night I have another dream almost identical to the second one I had when I moved to cell D4. I am in a church praying with a large crowd of people. After the service, I am left alone in meditation; suddenly, a huge lion jumps through the church's open window and heads for my neck. I remember how I had killed the female beast in the dream I had when I moved to D4. As the lion comes at me with jaws and paws ready to strike me down, I attack it and push it to the ground, and with the swiftness of lightning, lunge for its mouth; I place my right foot on the lion's lower jaw as I pull hard at its upper jaw with both hands. We struggle, struggle and struggle until the lion's mouth begins to come apart and the lion kicks and writhes on the ground dying, looking as if it had been slashed from the mouth right through its ribs down to the tail. I get up, sweating all over. The commander for the morning shift demands the strip search. We know they want to ensure that we have not brought any proscribed materials into B-Wing. As we troop out, I am puzzled that I dreamt again, with variation of protagonist, the dream I once dreamt. I did not realise that this was possible. I am delighted that my foot is not swollen as it had been after my previous dream. The following morning we hear that Sitima is to return to Mikuyu as officer-in-charge.

Book Seven
After Twenty-Two Months

41

Northerners as an Excuse

After the departure of the Special Branch and our transfer to B-Wing, we gather in the courtyard to take stock of Mbale's escape; we urge Disi to insist that a selected group from our number be deployed to the kitchen to show the new cooks how to steam cook the food we eat. We refuse to be held responsible for Mbale's escape; we do not care whether the prison regime clubs us to death or shoots us dead. If the food we eat is cooked differently because of Mbale's escape, we will incite our terminal friends to join our boycott and make the prison unmanageable – the terminals will be only too glad to join the rebellion that might eventually liberate them too. But to get boiling water, brooms, mops and brushes with which to scald the maggots, fleas, scorpions and other vermin and to scrub and launder dry the mucky floor of B-Wing we have to fight. We now feel what it means to have no rights, no privileges and no hope. B-Wing itself is in a state that no human could be expected to survive. There's an unbearably pungent stench, as if some condemned prisoners had died here and nobody had cleaned up the place. The stench of rottenness is almost palpable. The toilet seat and sides are tainted with excrement that has hardened and is difficult to remove even with boiling water – and that's another source of the overpowering smell we will have to endure. The walls are covered in the shit that the terminals, as if in protest, must have deliberately plastered everywhere. Yawning cracks and gaps – obvious refuge for scorpions, maggots, fleas and other creeping creatures that will suck our blood at night – are everywhere. Rats, geckos, bats and cockroaches roam the cobweb roof, the wire gauze ceiling and the rafters, uninhibited. Mbale's escape brings little respite. Strip-searches are daily instead of fortnightly. The stench refuses to go away.

Of course, the cell stinks for other reasons. The only other drainage that might take liquid out of the entire prison, apart from the little drainage from the prison's kitchen and the communal pit latrines in A-Wing, is under our new cell. When it rains, water flows from the two blocks of the prison to B-Wing courtyard, where the drainage beneath the cell, which is large enough to let in snakes, rats, bats – even cats and dogs – takes the filth to the world outside. And the stench that comes from this drainage is agonising: it is as if some of the dogs, cats, snakes, rats and other creatures that passed here died and were left to rot. As with the New Building Wing, the wire mesh above B-Wing courtyard is refuge to hundreds and hundreds of wagtails, which drop their shit below at night. We'll have to establish a duty roster for mopping courtyard bird-shit, as Alex and I did once at the VIP section of the prison. We continue to scrub the floors and walls with boiling water for many weeks after Mbale's escape until the cell and the courtyard are in a habitable state.

It does not take us long to discover that B-Wing has one advantage over D4: it is closer to the prison's main gate and housing estate; we can, therefore, hear vehicles coming in and out of prison, dogs barking and children crying, and feel closer to the reality of the world we have left behind than we had done in D4. With vehicles constantly driving in and out, we can speculate whether or not they are bringing new prisoners, security officers to get us released, or whatever. B-Wing has two walls that face the main gate and the housing estate; on one of them there are narrow windows covered in broken wire gauze close to the ceiling. The terminals who were caged here widened the gauze so that they could watch vehicles or people coming into prison or going out. We exploit this. One cellmate squats on the floor, the second jumps on his shoulders and both stand up slowly with the help of the others. With other cellmates pushing at his feet, the second person pushes himself towards the window and grips firmly at the windowsill; he propels himself closer to the window and hangs in there to watch, through the broken wire gauze, whatever is going on outside. After satisfying his curiosity he climbs down with the help of the others and tells the others which plants, trees, flowers are in bloom, who is entering or leaving the prison's main gate, which chickens are pecking at which bush and what the weather is like outside prison or whatever. Soon, peeping to see who's coming in and who's going out becomes our major preoccupation. We begin to believe that every vehicle coming into prison is bringing security officers who will release us. This becomes an obsession, which in turn leads to some kind of madness. Where the cellmates are short or the wall very high, three or four cellmates are involved. Peeping at the world outside by climbing on one another's shoulders was a common practice in D4, but in B-Wing the craft has been perfected. We begin inventing new stories based on what we see through the window-sill instead of merely recycling the same old tales as we have been doing hitherto. Some of us begin to feel that we have come closer to the real world and through this we believe that our freedom is not far away. The most sceptical among us think this is the only release we will ever know. But for almost everybody the received moral is patent enough: if the authorities want you to wallow in their stench and die, do not accept it; do not mourn; create some strategy for your survival instead.

One Saturday afternoon TS and Ndovi, who were on the shift when Mbale escaped and were being punished in punishment cells that share a wall with B-Wing, are unexpectedly transferred to Zomba Central prison. *Gossip International* is worried. We had been sharing gossip with them by tapping on the wall, now we can no longer do this. We also fear that the authorities at Zomba Central prison might break them and force them to reveal our communication network with the outside world. We spend nervous days and weeks expecting to be invited to the office to explain our secret correspondence with the world. Fortunately, nobody is asked questions about how Mbale escaped. But tempers in B-Wing fray, fights are frequent, discussions heated and unpleasant. And because Mbale is a northerner, all northerners are being blamed for the suffering we encounter after his escape. Mikuyu prison becomes the microcosmic platform on which regional, district and ethnic politics are played out; what was once one community united in the struggle against Banda and his cabal is in danger of disintegrating; quarrelling about the reasons for and the effect of Mbale's escape on our incarceration is frequent; we are back to the world that Banda and his henchpeople propagate outside. But Kadango reminds us that it was officer-in-charge Mughogho who began improving the living conditions in Mikuyu; we had begun eating sweet potatoes and sweet potato leaves; and he was a northerner, so why should we blame northeners for our troubles? He asks. Pingeni sums up what we feel when he claims: "It's a shame that it had to take a northerner to erase the good that another northerner had begun to bring into prison." Most of us refuse to despair; instead, we intensify our prayers to God and add new hymns to the repertoire of our choir; life must go on.

42

Chirunga Campus Riots

Today's strip-search was different. I detected a change of attitude and tone as the guards went about their business. Clearly, an event obliquely associated with us has happened outside prison. Everybody is wondering what it might be as we clean up the cell and make our beds. Nobody seems sure, but something of interest to political prisoners must have happened. The guards were unusually jovial going about their search, which was not as ruthless as it has been in recent weeks. As they returned to the office, some guards were looking directly at me as if to tell me a story that concerns me. And as one of them pushed me aside he cynically joked with his colleague about what has befallen somebody where I work: after all these years of having it so good, they will now see what everybody has been going through these years. And his friend responds dramatically: "They will see what shaved the guinea fowl bald!" It takes *Gossip International* hours to piece together the various threads of the news. It's an old story. Apparently there were student riots at Chirunga campus several months ago. In November 1988 the *Chirunga Newsletter*, which appears at irregular intervals, published articles that criticised the new quota system for student admissions into the university. When the chairman of the university council was tipsy at receptions he often declared that he did not like the large proportion of students from the north who enter the university, whether they were admitted on merit or not. To rectify the situation he suggested that the university should introduce the quota system, with effect from September 1987. According to this new

267

system students should be admitted on the basis of their district and region of birth. The students' newsletter has exposed the fallacy of these matters. It has also explicitly protested against the introduction of the IMF's fees for university students, IMF's bailing out of the country's economy notwithstanding. The newsletter has also mocked as being essentially myopic the rule that expels female students when they are pregnant.

But the newsletter's most dramatic news concerns CCAM, the organisation that is chaired by the president's permanent companion. Recently CCAM held a convention on Chirunga campus; it pitched tents on the grounds and put up stalls for the display of their doilies and various crops – temporary cooking and toilet facilities were established everywhere. At the close of the convention the participants left filth everywhere and parts of the college grounds have been permanently destroyed. The hockey pitch has been the most affected: it has effectively been rendered 'unplayable'. This is the subject of a narrative poem called 'Lament for the Hockey Field', which is divided into stanzas that are separated by the refrain: 'Come, Come And Mend!', whose initial letters are assumed to stand for CCAM. So, at long last the taboo has been broken: the self-styled royal family, who were believed to be beyond criticism, have been exposed. And because the students chose to publish and sell their newsletter during graduation or when parliament was in session, it has given the issues depicted maximum publicity. When the MPs left parliament, or the parents and relatives left Zomba town after the graduation of the children, they discussed openly the issues that the newsletter had brought to the country's attention. This must be why even the most timid guards have been talking freely about these matters. Predictably, the chairman of the university council was infuriated by the criticism of members of his extended family; he told the British vice-chancellor John Dubbey to expel the writers of the articles and poems. The students' union was so enraged by their friends' expulsion that, for the first time ever, they decided to march to the vice-chancellor's office to get rescinded what they consider John

Tembo's decision. As they marched, they shouted political slogans and sang liberation songs of long ago– the famous *Tiyende pamodzi ndi mtima umodzi* (Let's march together with one objective), among them. The song was popularly sung during the struggle for independence against the British and throughout the fight for the break-up of the Central African Federation of the two Rhodesias and Nyasaland. The first half of the students' procession was allegedly led by the principal's own daughter; her mother had to come and drag her away in frustration, in the hope that the march would stop; but the students marched on past Zomba eastern division police headquarters, disrupting the traffic on Kamuzu Highway for the first time ever. And watch. Some policemen stuck their thumbs up in support.

When the vice-chancellor did not meet their demands, the students returned to campus disappointed, but still singing and chanting their songs of freedom and creating havoc on their way. The police helicopter had to be deployed on campus in order to keep the peace. Policemen, young pioneers and army soldiers, who always keep sentry at the door to the principal's office in times like these, are stationed on campus to restore order and obviously to protect the principal from wayward intruders. The last time young pioneers, army and police sentries took turns to protect Zimani Kadzamira in this manner was when the gang of four were assassinated and the Kadzamira-Tembo clan were said to have given the go-ahead to the assassins. And now, for his incompetence in dealing with the student riots, for the chaos on Chirunga campus and the shame that the events have brought to the president's coterie, Zimani Kadzamira will be demoted and transferred to Bunda College of Agriculture; it is even rumoured that he will be sent on a diplomatic mission as punishment. For Mikuyu political prisoners the news is too good to be true; discussions are animated. The students who have done this deserve supporting; they were brave; their action was obviously dangerous; they could have been imprisoned or even killed. Daniel Chunga is not satisfied that we merely admire the students' courage. He tells the entire cell to watch; he stands up and dramatises the events as he sees them. He tears up tree branches on Chirunga Road, picks up stones, throws them at passing cars, then marches left-right, left-right, left-right, chanting *Tiyende pamodzi ndi mtima umodzi*, which he claims people in Zambia still sing; then he throws himself down on his bed in triumphant exasperation. We applaud, cheer and clap our hands in response.

The usual speculations begin. If the story is true, this is the beginning of the fall of Banda's autocratic regime. The politics of Malawi will have to change sooner rather than later. The inner circle will probably lose their clout. Yet *Gossip International* is not fooled by the open criticism of the Kadzamira-Tembo faction. Banda and his cabal are still intact: one little battle led by Chirunga campus students may have been won; the general war is not over yet. Besides, we suspect that the intelligence services have given Banda exaggerated versions of these events and no political prisoner will be released. For weeks the story of the student riots generates serious discussion on Banda's politics of exclusion, elimination, imprisonment and deportation of presumed political opponents – even the illiterate prisoners among us have original experiences to contribute to the subject; the story is another that brings hope for our possible release.

I have another dream. All the political prisoners in Mikuyu have been released. Banda has invited us to Sanjika Palace for a reception. We are gathered in a large room, sitting around an oval-shaped mahogany table with food and drinks on it. At one edge of the table, Banda's mistress Cecilia Kadzamira, is sitting in a narrow tall chair with a fine, soft red cover. She is watching us watching her. You can tell instantly that she'll be presiding over the proceedings to which we have been invited. Suddenly, Banda and his private secretary, Mary Kadzamira, appear from one end of the room; they are carrying trays of food and drinks. And walking in the space between the table and our chairs, they begin passing around the food and drinks on their trays. Everyone chooses the samosas, chicken wings, sausages, drumsticks and an assortment of finely cut sandwiches that they want and put them on their plates, each taking the drink of their choice. When Banda brings his tray for me to choose the food and drink I want, I refuse. "Don't be like that," he says. "Take one or two, they are quite delicious," he continues. But I say no and tell him I do not feel hungry. "Come on, everyone's taking what they like," he urges. But I insist I will not take any. "Be like that, then," he says, giving up and moving on to the next fellow. The woman sitting next to me whom I do not recognise at first elbows me saying: "What did you do that for?" "Do what?" I ask, looking at her; then I recognise her. It's Alice Nyirenda, a friend with whom I read the diploma in education at Soche Hill College a long time ago. She was a good friend of an American Peace Corps member, who came to Malawi to exploit the experience of the famous Malawi poet, David Rubadiri. Their relationship ended abruptly when the Peace Corps was eventually deported. In the end she was married to Mr Jere.

"And where have you come from?" I ask Alice. "It doesn't matter where," she answers. "If I were you, I'd take what I was offered, put it on my plate and refuse to eat it. I am sure you'd not lose your dignity or integrity that way!" "That's why you cannot be me," I reply. We laugh, as old mates would. Then Cecilia turns and chuckles from her tall chair, staring at us like the queen. Alice whispers: "And what does she want? Who does she think she is? The Queen of England?" We laugh, laugh and laugh until I wake up. The morning shift commander has opened the door and declares that we have no strip-search today; he heads for the office with his gang of guards. I smile to myself, pondering the meaning of my dream.

43

Tobacco Scam Victims

We hear the commander's bunch of keys jangling at the courtyard's gate. Disi quickly scuttles to the cell door, peeps through the spy-hole, returns and throwing himself on the hard bed, whispers in disgust: "The bastards are bringing two prisoners!" My heart descends below the level of hearing, the lights go up, the door swings very wide open, the two prisoners are pushed into B-Wing, Disi is commanded to offer them beds and the prison boots crunch away into the distant night. The commander will come back to put out the lights after an hour. One by one we queue behind Disi to greet and welcome the newcomers, who look dazzled and very thin indeed – mere bones; the taller and obviously older man braves the moment:

"Gentlemen, thank you for your warm welcome. We've come from Zomba Central prison where we've been for over a year. I don't know what crime I committed. I don't know why I am being transferred here. What I know is that about two years ago someone reported me to the Malawi Congress Party headquarters. I owned several shops and ran small businesses around Blantyre city townships. Someone who did not like the success of my businesses simply 'carved a mask against me', as we say. You know, what people do when they want to destroy whatever you try to achieve. But, gentlemen, allow me to appeal to you at the outset. I am not well in the head. I repeat. I often see double. I know it sounds funny but it is true. I am seeing things. I am probably going to that permanent home we all dread. And it is not all due to hunger. Though there's that too. Gentlemen, I fear

I am going mad. I have heard that there are powerful people here, people with influence: please, gentlemen, if you can, help me."

He stops and the younger man takes over:

"Gentlemen, my friend who has been talking to you just now is called Mr P. Chabwera and my name is Laurenti Mtemwende. I come from Salima district in the central region. And gentlemen, like my friend here, I too want to apologise beforehand. I suffer from that big affliction known at home as 'the falling disease'. I want to apologise and thank you in advance for the problems I will be causing you when my epileptic attacks come on. And if you can, please help me too. Thank you."

The truth is, our new cellmates are malnourished and mentally unstable because of it. But they are still largely alert. They have heard, for instance, about TS and Ndovi who were sent to Zomba Central prison after Mbale's escape. And they know what we do not know about Mbale's arrest. Apparently, on the Sunday that he escaped from here, Mbale arrived at Pirimiti Catholic Parish Primary School without a shirt, having thrown away his *foya*. He asked the parish priest for a spare shirt, claiming that he was a poor man. The priest consulted his cook in the kitchen before he went into his bedroom to get the shirt. When he appeared to take his time Mbale thought he was ringing the police to come and get him. So he decided to run. The schoolchildren who arrived early that morning saw Mbale running away and thought he was a thief. They ran after him, shouting: "Catch the thief! Catch the thief! Catch the thief!" Unfortunately, Mbale fell into a ditch that had been dug to make bricks for the school block. When they began throwing broken bricks at him, Mbale decided to give himself up. The priest eventually took him to the police station in his vehicle. No police or prison officer, no constable or guard got a medal or claimed promotion for Mbale's capture. They took him to Zomba Central prison and dumped him in a cell next to the place condemned prisoners are hanged. Both the police and the prison regimes beat him up so severely that he could not speak for weeks. Our new arrivals have also heard about Malawi's famous political prisoners, Orton and Vera Chirwa and know that they are still alive at Zomba Central. That Banda and his minions are still imprisoning innocent people and transferring them from prison to prison, angers *Gossip International*, whose hope for release is dashed yet again. In the weeks that follow, the question 'why Mtemwende and Chabwera should transfer now?' puzzles everybody. One afternoon Kadango offers me his intriguing explanation for the recent arrivals. "*Bambo*," he begins, "do not lose hope at the arrival of Chabwera and Mtemwende. Their liberation starts here. This is how Banda's henchpeople work: they gather the prisoners they want to release in one place and choose a day when they can come to set them free. But more prisoners may have to come before these are released."

After several days I pluck up enough courage and ask Mtemwende what crime he is presumed to have committed. He offers me a sobering tale: "Anyone who wants to be anybody under Banda's patronage goes into the tobacco farming business. If you are a member of parliament you have easy access to loans from the commercial banks. Banda himself has decreed it. You only need to get a reliable general manager and the banks are obliged to offer you a loan, though they prefer that you employ a white ex-Rhodesian or a white South African as your general manager. Although the banks are not explicit about the matter, they offer you enough suggestions to lead to the fact that you must employ white managers from South Africa or Zimbabwe – managers who do not care about the independence struggles of Southern Africa and who do not care about the dignity of their labourers. And this is how the scheme works. Farm owners divide their farms into acres; they employ tenants – that is, men, women, children, sometimes entire families – to grow tobacco on the acres for them. With the advice of the general manager, the farm owner provides the equipment, the seedlings, the fertiliser and the food that the tenants need. The tenants are contracted to look after their patch and at harvest to sell their tobacco to the farm manager, who in turn sells the tobacco at international prices on auction floors in the city with or on behalf of the farm owner."

Mtemwende owned several tobacco farms and chose his wife, who is better educated than he, as the general manager – she is a graduate of Bunda College of Agriculture, University of Malawi. His manager insisted that in order to compete with giant farmers like life president Banda, honourable John Tembo, official hostess the Mama and other important personalities in the tobacco business, she should pay her tenants more for their tobacco; that is, more maize, more salt and better beans to live on than, for example, the white South African or Zimbabwean general managers on the president's or his inner circle's tobacco farms. At the last harvest, however, and unknown to Mtemwende's general manager, his tenants sold her tobacco they had bought from the president's or his cohort's farms without telling her; it was this tobacco, together with the produce from her farms, that she took to the auction floors in the city to sell.

The rules for tobacco farming are simple: tenants of one farm are not allowed to sell their produce to tenants of another farm or to the highest bidder, but the violation of the practice is common throughout the 'tenancy-farming-scheme'. And everything is fine as long as those engaged in the trade are not found out. But when the Special Branch heard that Mtemwende's tenants had bought tobacco from the farms of the 'Big People', they swooped on the head of the family and dumped him in Maula prison before they could hear his case. When they took Mtemwende to court afterwards, they accused him of embezzling the life president's tobacco. He pleaded ignorance. That tenants from the farms of the country's leaders had the nerve to sell their tobacco to ordinary farmers like him was beyond his comprehension. He lost the case and was ordered to pay a K500 fine, which he duly paid and was allowed to return home as a free man. But the security officers came back for him a week later and re-arrested him for embezzling Big People's tobacco; this was political subversion, he was told; they dumped him in Zomba Central from where he has been transferred. "What a virtuous crime," chimes Chunga, who had been gripped by the story. Almost everyone agrees with him, some wishing they had committed as tangible a crime as Mtemwende's.

One day after lock-up Pingeni makes the following announcement: "This is Radio Mikuyu, and here's today's news flash read by Stephen Pingeni. Last night it pleased his excellency the life president, the Ngwazi Dr H. Kamuzu Banda, the father and founder of the Malawi nation to detain the famous Lilongwe businessman Macduff Mthawila Msungama. A notorious scam has been uncovered. Tenants from his excellency's tobacco farms and the farms of his cabal were caught selling their tobacco to the highest bidder. Msungama, who is presumed to have been the racket's chief architect, was apprehended and is now safely lodged in A-Wing of this prison. That's the end of the news flash!" Everyone is stunned. We know that Pingeni has not gone mad. He rarely makes announcements of this kind. Speculations for the true reasons for Msungama's imprisonment begin and go on until the night shift commander and his gang come to put out the light.

The following morning Kadango, who is particularly bothered by the story because he knows Msungama – they both owned bottle stores on Devil Street at the old Lilongwe city market – taps the drainage hole from B-Wing to C-Wing, our type of communication. One 'terminal friend' from C-Wing taps back, Kadango asks the fellow to find out if Msungama has indeed arrived in A-Wing. Moments later, the terminal, who knows Msungama well, comes to the drainage hole; he taps back for Kadango and confirms that Msungama is indeed in A-Wing. The story of his crime and detention seems to be similar to Mtemwende's. Macduff Mthawila Msungama had several tobacco farms in the central region. As on Mtemwende's farms, the working conditions for Msungama's tenants were attractive; he offered his tenants higher prices for the tobacco they grew on his land. Tenants from the president's or his clique's farms sold their tobacco to Msungama's tenants. That's the crime for which he is being held in A-Wing.

Msungama's arrival is another subject of hot debate for weeks to come. The questions that *Gossip International* asks are many:

why was he detained, when he is supposed to be related to Banda's permanent companion? Are they really related? Isn't she responsible for his detention because his tobacco farms and his other businesses are more successful than the Kadzamiras'? Why was he brought into prison, when he was taken to court and paid K1,500.00 for whatever crime he is presumed to have committed? Does Banda know about the scam and those who have been imprisoned for it? The claims and counter-claims for Msungama's detention are numerous; the despair it brings to Mikuyu is incalculable.

44
The Sparrows Return

After about six months at Zomba Central, TS and Ndovi are brought back to Mikuyu. "The sparrows are back," we shout, celebrating with songs of praise to God for their return. They confirm what Chabwera and Mtemwende have told us about Mbale's arrest, adding that he is sorry for having caused us so much trouble; he constantly prays that we should understand the despair that caused his escape, especially after the arrival of Blaise Machila and other political prisoners who kept coming into Mikuyu. But one night another prisoner from Zomba Central is shoved into B-Wing for Disi to deal with. He has a long beard; he is thin and looks rather lost; his name is George Mtafu; he comes from Chizumulu Island near Likoma Island on Lake Malawi in the north. Having trained with the world's best-known neurosurgeons in Germany, and worked for a total of twenty-one years there, Mtafu thought he should return home and help in the development of his country. About two years after his return home the security officers imprisoned him without trial and without charge. And his story is typical of our despotic times. SPC Sam Kakhobwe was directed by Banda's permanent companion to invite senior government officers and the country's top technocrats to Sanjika Palace – George was among them – where Banda dressed them down for their incompetence. What shocked George is the way Banda's permanent companion seemed to take total control of events on the day: how she dragged the frail president to the podium; how she pushed him about without mercy; and how she forced the president to speak on administrative and professional matters he seemed ignorant of. When Kakhobwe gave the participants a reception at Chibisa House afterwards and invited them to comment as honestly as they wished on Banda's warning, the poor doctor frankly wondered why the professionals could not do what was required without dragging the president along with them? What took Mtafu to Zomba Central prison and now brings him to Mikuyu is the criticism implied in whatever comments he was supposed to have made. As he concludes the story, George looks so lost that Brown, TS, Rodney and I decide to adopt him as part of our team. Why Dr Banda, a medical doctor, allowed the imprisonment of the only neurosurgeon in Malawi continues to baffle *Gossip International* for months.

When we later learn that it was George who mended Mrs John Tembo's neck after she was involved in a serious car accident, we wonder why the honourable chairman could not have saved his wife's doctor from the indignity of prison. Soon George becomes an asset to our team. At Zomba Central he was allowed visits from his family, which had direct contact with the German embassy in Malawi. The campaign for our liberation will now be taken directly into Europe, through the German embassy. Indeed Brown, who was a student in Germany once, happily passes all the information we have been sending through Fr Pat and David to the German Embassy through George. B-Wing is particularly delighted that we now have a qualified medical doctor who can offer us advice on the strategies we should adopt for our fight for better medical treatment in prison. Some of us even believe that if we die here George might tell the world how and why it happened.

I have an incredible series of disjointed dreams. First, I find myself landing at Heathrow Airport in London, goodness knows from where. I am still a student at University College London and looking as scruffy as a poor student can be, but Mercy and our three children are so spruced up that I do not recognise them at first. We jump into a black cab bound for central London. Then I find that I am alone in the cab. I don't know where the rest of my family are. Later, I notice that I've been invited to Mrs Margaret Thatcher's house, which, strangely, appears to be in South Wimbledon where we stayed when I was a student in London – she is still the British Prime Minister. What am I doing in her house? I ask myself in disgust. Before long, Mrs Thatcher herself appears; she welcomes me and takes me to the kitchen, where the other invited guests have assembled and are having fun, she says. Then her house is suddenly transformed into one of the three-bedroom bungalows occupied by civil servants in Lilongwe capital city. Mrs Thatcher shows up again and invites us to a dancing party in her living room, where everybody is apparently dancing to African *rumba* and *simanje-manje*. One of her guests, who is obviously dead drunk, takes me back to the kitchen to show me where 'real fun is', as he says. I see a huge deep freezer full of fresh fish – Malawi's delicious species of tilapia called *chambo* – and a high fridge-freezer jam-packed with Malawi Carlsberg beer. Mrs Thatcher joins us yet again and asks me to 'choose – the fish, the beer or both'. I wake up before I make my choice.

I hear the crickets and frogs in the swamps outside the prison, singing their shrilling night tunes. I go back to sleep and dream I am in England again, but this time I am teaching a class of British boys and girls, both black and white. They seem excited about whatever I am telling them. When I ask them a question, several hands go up; but before I choose who should answer, I wake up to the commander's bunch of keys jangling. The door squeaks open. The commander and his gang shout: "Strip-search! Everybody out! Leave everything in the cell. Come out like Adam, naked!" The indignity of daily strip-searches has increased since Mbale's escape, but there's nothing we can do about them, we simply have to persevere. About my disjointed dreams, Disi praises Allah first and, like a professional interpreter of dreams, asserts: "Mrs Thatcher's people are winning the struggle for your freedom; you will travel outside this country to work after your liberation; you may not necessarily end up working in her country; think of the swallows as they fly from place to place:

that'll be your life after this." Kadango adds: "Dreaming you are selling, buying or seeing fresh fish anywhere is a good omen. If you'd got drunk on the Carlsberg beer, you'd have suffered from a serious illness that would've caused your death in prison."

45
Chief of Detainees

26 December 1988, Monday. We hear the sound of a vehicle at the main gate outside the prison and TS, Pingeni, Chunga and Rodney quickly jump on each other's shoulders and peep through the little windows near the ceiling to find out who is arriving, but as the vehicle has already gone through the gate, they do not know who has come. We wait, huddled together in the corner of the courtyard, trying to grab the last rays of the sun – the morning is unusually chilly. Commander BK opens the courtyard gate and shouts: "The professor has visitors!" My heart jumps with expectation and hope at first, but as no visitor is allowed around Christmas, my legs falter; it cannot be the visitors I want. I stand up and follow BK who opens the gate to the office block with a whisper: "It's two Special Branch officers who've come for you." I whisper back my thanks and prepare for the encounter. I recognise the younger fellow instantly. It is he who brought Banda's detention order for me to sign months ago. And at my prompting, which was unknown to him, he came to ask me to sign my own blank cheques for my wife. This is what happened. Mercy did not believe that the surreptitious letters that I wrote her on Sunlight and Lifebuoy soap wrappers actually came from me. Indeed, anyone could have written them. The Special Branch often wrote such letters to spouses of the prisoners they abducted; sometimes they even wrote them on behalf of political prisoners they had murdered – their cynicism was inhuman. So to put Mercy's mind at peace and to prove that it was me who was writing the letters to her from Mikuyu, I asked her to take my

cheque book to the eastern division police headquarters in Zomba, tell the police that the family was starving; ask them to take the cheque book wherever I am for me to sign; she can then deposit the cheques into her bank account and pay the water and electricity bills, or buy the food she needed for the family. The police fell for my trick and sent this fellow to get me to sign several of my own cheques. My wife did not only sort out the family finances but she had substantive proof that our correspondence was genuine: I was alive and lodged at Mikuyu. Today this fellow has brought an older and obviously more senior man who looks so puffed up that the visitors' room seems too small for him. You can tell at once that the bullfrog wants the world to know where power lies on earth. And breathing through the mouth, his thick neck and the fat lips, he begins:

"Dr Mapanje, I am the chief of detainees for the entire country. My name is Mr Kapachika. I've been sent by the inspector general to find out how you are. The I.G. has reason to believe that you have problems in this prison; I've come to hear them."

Just like that. No greetings. No preambles. Pure authority. Doesn't even allow his junior to introduce him to me. And he has the temerity of referring to himself as 'Mr' as if he were a medical specialist or consultant – how sick can authority get? (His name translates as 'he who hangs or betrays something, somebody or other'). He looks at me, unambiguously radiating power and arrogance. This man must have a hidden agenda, I decide, he probably wants me to apologise about something. I have written several letters of clemency for the cellmates who cannot read or write in D4 and now in B-Wing. I've not written one seeking presidential clemency for myself. And where was this man when I walked into these stinking walls? How do they know I have problems? I must be on my guard lest they have discovered our correspondence with the outside world. But what does he expect me to do or say? Apologise? For what? And this choking brashness, is it part of their ploy to get me to apologise for the crimes I've not committed? What do I do? A voice suggests: play their game.

"*Bwana*," I begin, giving him the benefit of his pomposity, "thank you for thinking of me when you are preoccupied with more important national matters during Christmas festivities. If you or the inspector general have heard that I have problems, it is true. Problem number one. It's more than a year since I was dumped in this prison. Nobody has told me what wrong I have done or for how long I will stay here. And here is the more serious problem. Most political prisoners are writing letters, seeking presidential clemency for the crimes they are thought to have committed. As I don't know the crime that I committed, I do not know how to apologise so that his excellency the life president, the father and founder of the Malawi nation, the Ngwazi Dr H. Kamuzu Banda, can forgive me, release me and let me go back to what I know best – teaching."

They glance at each other, perplexed and I think I may have got them under the belt, that I've won whatever battle is being fought, wherever:

"Problem number two. I do not understand why you refuse to give my wife and children, relatives and friends visiting permits. Most cellmates here have families, relatives and friends who visit them. Why not me? What crime have I committed to deserve this? Problem number three. This prison is horrid, the food is poisonous, we are not allowed books, newspapers or anything to read; doctors are not allowed; priests and other religious leaders who might minister to our spiritual needs are out of bounds. Do you really want us physically, mentally and spiritually dead when we come out of this prison? Don't you see, we too are human beings like you and deserve to live in this country of our birth like everybody else? Have the higher authorities got no conscience at all? *Bwana*, is this what his excellency the life president himself actually wants? Problem number four. I am tired of looking at the blank walls of this prison. I am tired of crushing cockroaches, mosquitoes and scorpions; I am tired of chasing geckos, rats and bats at night. Don't you think two Christmases of my doing nothing is long enough punishment, *Bwana,* whatever it is I am supposed to have done against whoever? I want to go back to my job and teach. *Bwana,* if you came to hear my problems, those are my problems; how are you going to help me?"

The chief answers back by asking BK to give me a pen and a ream of paper, and looking at his watch first, he announces:

"Right, I came here at about 11.30 a.m.; I will wait up to 1 p.m. Take this pen and paper and write what you've just told me. Address your apology to the I.G. and write your letter as clearly as you can for the I.G. to see that you have truly repented. Take your time. I came here especially for you. I'll take your apology straight to I.G. myself, today not tomorrow – that's how I can help you."

My original hunch was right. After fifteen months the biro feels strange to my fingers. The fresh-smelling paper throws me. This mission must be motivated by the embarrassment that Banda and his minions are getting from human rights campaigns for my liberation. These fellows are expecting an apology from me so that they can find good reason to release me. If that is a dream from a mad poet, I must still be careful how I write my apology, as that is where I will expose what I am guilty of. To be honest, I have no clue as to what I'd be seeking presidential clemency for, but after about twenty minutes of drafting and shredding the drafts apart, I pass on the final version of my letter to the chief of political detainees, who quickly shoves it in the inner pocket of his jacket. Then, taking the shredded drafts from the wastepaper basket with him, the chief of political detainees says goodbye. I am surprised that he found it necessary to take with him the drafts I shredded and threw into the wastepaper basket, but what the hell! I return to B-Wing rather pleased that I've merely apologised for the embarrassment that the authorities in the university, the government and the Malawi Congress Party headquarters might have when human rights activists hear of my imprisonment. It's daft to apologise for being detained, but who cares? After lock-up, *Gossip International* has another hot post-mortem on Kapachika's visit. Pingeni's suggestion is wild:

> "Doc, thank the God of your ancestors. That man was sent to release you, as they did to Gadama, Matenje, Sangala and Chiwanga in this very prison. After that he'd have murdered you. Thank God for giving you the words that persuaded them against it."

Mkwanda disagrees:

> "*Baba,* Pingeni's lost his head again, don't listen to him. The truth is Banda's people are in shit! They don't know what to do with you. You shouldn't have used the word 'apology' in your letter. That bastard's visit is good news for us all. The campaign for your release is having its desired effect."

For once Disi disagrees with Mkwanda:

> "*Ambuje,*" he says, "you did well to write something that sounded like an apology; these '*athakati*' [witches and murderers] need a face-saving device, anything tangible that they can show Banda and his cronies that the prisoners they intend to release have repented is good for them."

That was my original hunch too. When Chunga picks another quarrel with Pingeni about how best to interpret Kapachika's visit, it is quickly defused before it turns into another fight. For weeks Kapachika's visit gives us hope and another subject to mull over. In my bulletins to David and Fr Pat, I suggest yet again that they should slow down the protests in case release is imminent. I know, however, that this is unrealistic: often campaigns and appeals by human rights activists and others do not need much prompting. They are like a rock rolled from the top of a cliff: the initial push is enough to gather what becomes an uncontrollable velocity of its own – a few lines begin to lurk about:

The other man, double chinned, cheeks
Still puffed from yesterday's Christmas
Carlsbergs, has hands stinking of tomato-
boiled sun-dried fish he had for Christmas.
Why do they choose unlikely salamanders
To taunt us with death, further charges
Or freedom? Why don't they just minister
To their migraines at home after the hectic
Christmas chase of their vaporous rebels?

Kapachika's visit triggers another strange visit. One Saturday morning, I am casually invited to the office. And lo and behold! My nephew, Fredrick Ziyabu, who works at the Forestry Department in Zomba, has come. "What happened?" I peremptorily ask. "The great granddad's traditional roots at Mpokonyola Village have done it," he says. We laugh as Fred gives me a hug and asks. "How are you, uncle? We were told we should forget about you, you were dead!" He offers me no time to answer, but continues. "Your grandchildren are missing you. How are you?" "I feel fine," I answer. But my mouth is unexpectedly dry after saying that. I try to utter another word, the words won't come out. Fred comes to my rescue and tells me his cousin Marshal Msonga is being asked to return to the south from the central region, where he was teaching at a primary school. Have I heard that the life president has declared that teachers should now be sent to teach in the regions of their birth? Apparently his creeps have told him that teachers from the north are sabotaging the education of children in the south and the centre. I interrupt: "Does that include university teachers?" "Not for now," he answers, "but I suppose they would do that if they had enough teachers to go round in institutions of higher learning." I tell Fred that the chief of political detainees came to see me recently. He listens intently then sighs a sigh of recognition, as if a puzzle he had been trying to solve has finally clicked into place. Then he says: "I've been given permission to visit you because a friend who is a driver of one of your recent visitors

287

suggested that I try to apply for a visiting permit now; he had overheard the 'higher authorities' talking favourably about your case. So I went to the eastern division police headquarters immediately, made my application, and here I am." Fred continues: "My family has not moved from the Forestry Department house beside the Zomba Plateau; should you suddenly find yourself in town at any time, do not forget to visit your grandchildren first." "I repeat," he says, "when you leave these premises, do not hesitate to contact us first. After this visit, I am going to tell aunt and the children, as well as your other nephews James and Marshal and your brother-in-law Barnaba Cuthbert that this seems to be the best time for everybody to begin applying for visiting permits." But time is up. Fred quickly offers me the bread, oranges and bananas he has brought. After the final hug, I return to the brick walls of my cell, his words still ringing in my ears like sweet music. After lock-up Brown, TS and I take stock of Fred's visit: our hope is rekindled yet again, but we decide to keep a low profile about the other implications of the visit. In gratitude to God I read David's Psalms of praise.

46

After Twenty-Two Months

We hear the sound of a vehicle approaching the prison's main gate outside B-Wing. TS, Brown, Pingeni, Chunga and Rodney jump on each other's shoulders to find out who is arriving – this has become our favourite ritual, recently graduated to an obsession, but the vehicle has already entered the prison. We are disappointed, but still hope that one of us will be invited to the office to see whoever has come. After about twenty minutes the sound of the vehicle leaving the prison comes again. TS and Rodney quickly jump on each other's shoulders to see what kind of vehicle it was. "Damn," they shout in disgust, "just another ordinary prison vehicle!" I decide to join the cellmates in the courtyard, but after a short while TS beckons me back into the cell. "There's a family sitting under an acacia tree outside – a mother with three children: two girls and a boy," he says. My heart skips a beat. That will be my family, I think. Then Rodney jumps on to TS's shoulder to see for himself; he climbs down and reports that the boy is wearing a T-shirt with a 'Tough Guy' label on it. I recall my son's T-shirt had that label. I bought it in Harare with a 'made in Italy' boy's bicycle when I was external examiner at the university. My heart pumps faster and faster. Pingeni and Chunga offer to take their turn. They climb down and report that the family appears to have arrived in a green car, which is parked near the little church at the prison's housing estate. TS has another go with Brown and Pingeni pushing him up the little window sill. After hanging up there longer than most, he climbs down with a message for me. The car seems to have been driven by a white man, and the family is preparing to move towards the main gate; my heart thumps faster and faster. TS appeals to me:

"Look Doc, I know you don't like to participate in these peeping games, but no white man has come with visitors to this prison in the thirteen years I've been here; this could be your wife and children brought in by one of your white friends from the university. Why don't you have a peep? Come on, get on my shoulders; you will not fall, we are all here to catch you: Rodney, Pingeni, Chunga, Brown and myself. Come on man! Don't be a coward! These could be the visitors you've been longing for, damn it!"

My heart continues to thump as I reluctantly jump on TS's shoulders with Brown, Pingeni and Rodney helping to push my feet towards the window sill. I stretch out my hands, take a firm grip of the little window sill, and urging myself forward, hang in there for a long while. I see acacia trees in yellow bloom, chickens pecking at one of the guards' houses, and when I turn to the right I see what looks like my wife and our three children.

"Can you see the white man in the green car?" TS asks.

At that instant a white man comes out of the green car and begins to walk about, probably intending to stretch his legs. I recognise him instantly. It's Fr Pat!

"Yes, it's Fr Pat in his white collar! My God! It is my wife and children coming towards the gate. After about twenty-two months!"

"Don't shout, man, every prison wall is listening!" Brown tries to shut me up.

I focus my eyes on them again. And know I am right. But wonder why *Noriega* did not bring a note from them to warn me that they had at long last got a visiting permit? My heart continues to pump fast. My hands and feet begin to sweat. I begin to lose grip of the window sill, my feet start slipping from TS's shoulders and those holding my feet and legs. I feel dizzy but Brown, TS and the others are ready to catch me before I crack my head on the cement floor.

My heart continues to beat faster and faster. I realise that jumping on other people's shoulders can be a hair-raising experience, but I'm proud I've done it and begin to wonder why I was afraid. I want to scream: I have seen the world! But I just smile to myself and thank God I didn't crack my head. I have no doubt that it is my wife and children that I have seen. As I change into cleaner *foya* and prepare to be invited to the office, I remember nephew Fred Ziyabu's sudden visit, which I had temporarily forgotten about; I recall his promise to tell my family and relatives to apply for visiting permits because the time was ripe. All the while I am thinking I could have cracked my head.

The wait is agony. Tears begin to form. I begin to worry. What will I say when I see them, after more than twenty-two months? When commander BK opens the gate and calls out my name, I bellow: "Coming, *Bwana!*" Everybody laughs at my sudden animation, wishing me well, while others hope that I do not return. BK does not need to remind me who the visitors are. He knows we've already seen them through the little windows. The visitors' bench squeaks. I offer my hand first to Mercy my wife, then Judith our first born, Lunda our second born; and as for our son, Likambale, I grab hold of him and put him on my lap. We are nervous. An outburst of tears runs down our cheeks. We do not know what to say to one another. It has taken almost two years for us to meet after my arrest. Mercy starts. I hear officially what I've heard through bulletins hitherto: that Judith is going to Limbe Convent Secondary School with the financial help of Fr Pat and Fr Lawrence Littlefair, who get donations from their friends and well-wishers in the Republic of Ireland and the UK. Lunda writes her secondary school entry examinations this year; her target is to enter Stella Marris Secondary School in Blantyre next year.

Mother is well, though she remains shocked. For months she went through spells of glumness and refused to eat. She has had to move to Mpokonyola Village in Chikwawa district, where she is staying with my late uncle's first daughter and her children. She could not stay with them at Ntcheu district hospital because the nurses' houses have a small living room and two tiny bedrooms –

barely adequate for a family of four, Mother and one help. But they do not want to complain, as they often get financial assistance from abroad co-ordinated by Landeg White in York. I try to look as cheerful and normal as I can possibly be. In truth, I am devastated to hear how my family are barely surviving under the difficult times I have left them in. Mercy explains how they left the university house, how my former friends and colleagues there pressured the vice-chancellor to stop my salary being paid and appealed to the university housing committee to throw my family out of the university house so they could move in themselves. But the families of Justus Mlia, David Munthali, James Seyani, Gerry Patterson, Steve Chimombo and Anthony Nazombe visited them regularly. Mrs Kadzombe, Mrs Mlia and Mrs Chimombo and their children always came to our house to visit them, without fear of the stigma associated with my now 'rebel family'. Only the Munthalis and the Seyanis still visit them at Ntcheu district hospital, bringing them the much-needed bags of maize and rice. She claims that people at Ncheu district hospital have been very friendly to them. I can only praise the Lord for my family's continued good health.

Still wiping her tears, Judith picks up courage and asks how I actually am and what kind of food I eat in prison. I mumble something incomprehensible. On their first visit, saying as little as possible is the best policy in case the guards report our discussion to the security authorities. Lunda does not utter a single word throughout the entire visit. Her cheeks are covered in tears that started pouring down the minute she saw me in the *foya*. I try to cheer her up by talking about her hope to enter Stella Marris Secondary School, where one of my students teaches English, but she answers me with more tears. I suggest the obvious to Mercy, that she writes to Landeg to explain that they've been to visit me. I exaggerate how healthy I am so that they can be encouraged not to worry about me. Undeterred by the strange environment Likambale asks:

"Daa, is it true you are here because you stole something in the university?"

Judith and Lunda look away, more tears pouring down their cheeks:

"And who gave you that funny idea, my son?"

"Boys at our school mock me so when we play."

"No, my son," I answer, "I didn't steal anything from the university; there isn't much that one can steal there, and anyway I don't steal, as you know."

"So why are you here?"

"I don't know why, nobody told me why; but don't worry, son, I'll be back home soon."

"Oh, when?" he says, his face beaming with hope and joy.

"Very soon, my son. Don't you worry about Daa, OK? If you pray for your daddy, work hard at school and look after Mother, your *agogo* well, you will see daddy at the door, OK?"

"But *agogo* was always singing to herself and crying after they took you away."

"Now that you've seen me, you can tell Mother to stop crying. When you visit her next, tell her you've seen daddy; he is well and healthy, he will come back only when she has stopped crying, OK?"

"OK then," he says, as he starts pulling at my unshaven beard. I feel ravaged by the questions about why I am imprisoned and when I am going back home. It hurts to be forced to tell a child lies. But that's the point about Banda's political detentions; they are meant to rough you up and disorientate you at your arrest, and undermine your confidence as to the exact details of your case and when you will be released, if at all. We've overrun the fifteen minutes allowed. Mercy takes out the medicines for our daily ailments from her handbag and the food she has brought – three kilos of rice, three of sugar, tins of beef, deep fried fish – the *chambo* – vegetables, fruit and two loaves of bread. The guard watching over the visit grabs the loaves and breaks them length-wise and across. Mercy and the children are horrified, but remain quiet, confused by the guard's action. I have no time to explain that the guards break the loaves of bread to ensure that no guns, knives or any other proscribed materials have been hidden in them. Apparently, visitors of the condemned prisoners hide dangerous objects in the loaves of bread they bring. In B-Wing that evening, my family's visit is a huge event for *Gossip International*; they are noisy with speculations about why the visit came at this time.

"*Baba*," Mkwanda declares gleefully, "so after two years the police have finally climbed down and allowed your wife and children to visit you? *Baba,* there's more to come."

Pingeni, Ndovi and Chunga do not fight over how to interpret the visit. TS and Brown are satisfied by the victory that the visit entails – the campaign for our freedom is not being wasted. Even Disi and Kadango, who had lost all hope that they would ever be considered for release, begin to feel positive about how events are developing. That a white man brought the family of a detained political prisoner to Mikuyu becomes another point of contentious speculation, though no fight breaks out amongst the lads over the matter.

"Banda's regime is cracking at the base," asserts Disi, "his cronies must be tired of the appeals, petitions and protests they are receiving about your family not being allowed visiting permits."

When I repeat my son's question – Did they arrest you because you stole something in the university? As my mates mock me at school – peals of laughter and cries of disbelief echo within the cell. For weeks 'what I've stolen in the university' becomes another joke that sustains our dull life – our hope for liberation is rekindled further.

Swallows for my son at seven

When you pulled at my scruffy
Beard, son, buoyant on my lap,
after twenty-two months of my
abduction, then asked when daddy
would come back home, it was
the visitors' bench that squeaked
before I could retort: *not to worry, son,*

I'd be back home soon, and grinning
you yelled *oh, when?* But I must
confess, son, I merely wanted to
see the milk-white teeth on your
beaming face again. And when
you asked did I truly steal from
the university to be jailed, as your
mates at school mocked and I said:
*nothing there worth stealing, son, and
I don't steal, anyway,* I must admit
I hoped you'd not notice the tears
on your mum's and sisters' cheeks
on your first visit.

           But when you had to go,
after their fifteen minutes, stunned
why prison guards viciously break
the loaves of bread people bring,
you should have seen my mates
rapture at what I lifted on their
imaginary security grounds; and
I must say, even I smiled at their
Post-mortem of your visit, son. It
was only after their whimper about
what I'd nicked that I remembered
I should've told you how swallows
of Mozambique drift with the coastal
winds each season, to nest and breed
in A-Wing, and how we often fight
when their chicks fall to ground –
the condemned desiring to fry and
crack their brittle bones to brighten
their meal, the 'politicals' wishing
the chicks could just fly away, free.

47

The Spy I Engaged

We are just recovering from the horror of the abduction of another six terminal friends, who were hanged at Zomba Central last week. This is the third abduction I have experienced, and the ritual is becoming impossible to get used to. I have been in Mikuyu for two years and six months, and I still do not know what crime I have committed against my country, my president or whoever suggested that I be dumped here. My frustration for not being taken to court is obviously immense. I have speculated and speculated as to why I am being incarcerated, or which events might have brought me here to no avail. I have managed only to try and charge myself with the crimes that I could not possibly have committed, which is precisely as president Banda and his ferocious crew would want us to do. In the time, while I have been here, I have subverted every prison rule and treated every aspect of my prison with the contempt it deserves. I have been lucky to remain intact throughout; though as for that, thanks to *Gossip International*, who have been instrumental in my remaining sane. I have learned how to be here without being here; how to feel the pain of incarceration without feeling it; effectively, how to ignore suffering and embrace survival, life. I have refused to admit the rumours I hear as reasons for my detention. I am now tired of hearing the lies people are inventing; I want to do something extraordinary; I want to see if people outside this prison still remember my case and what they are giving as reasons for my continued incarceration. If I hit another brick wall, at least I will have tried. I can then submit to whatever fate is in store for me. I have already joined the many people who are suffering from protest fatigue out there.

I want to exploit one well-known principle: If you are in authority under Banda's patronage you learn quickly that you must create your own spies, agents and informers to keep you updated of the events that matter for your survival. My college principal, his registrar and senior government officers thrive on such intelligence. I dare say Banda's political career, his Malawi Congress Party, and his government would collapse if they did not utilise such intelligence, as well as the other despotic structures they have set up. In other words, under Banda's patronage everyone tries to perfect whatever they have learned from the philosophy of divide and rule upon which Banda's policies are rooted. So, if Banda and his henchpeople have spies, agents or informers who do jobs for them, why couldn't I do the same from the stench of this prison? Why can't I make the last leap, as it were, towards the finishing line in this tedious race for my freedom? Of course, I have no authority and no power to do what I want in prison. That's a fact. And it would be daft to expect Banda's prison conditions to be any better; but I still have the change from the money that David and Fr Pat sent for us to buy fresh fish or goat meat outside prison when the opportunity arises. Therefore, I am going to dispatch a spy to the public houses, bars and bottle stores in and around Zomba town. This time I will spare *Noriega* and find a Zomba-born reliable commander who knows his way around the public houses. I want my spy to investigate whether anyone has new leads into the reasons for my continued imprisonment.

One day, after about two months, my man returns. We have just had another notorious strip-search and everyone in C-Wing is shouting their heads off about how unbearable these searches are becoming; we want the morning shift commander, my messenger, to take our complaints to the officer-in-charge for the umpteenth time. I exploit the moment and shout at my spy: "*Bwana*, don't you hear the people's complaints?" The shrewd spy does not answer; instead he grabs hold of me, and pulls me

297

with him towards the gate and starts scolding me: "You must be mad to expect me to tell the officer-in-charge to stop these strip-searches. Who are you anyway? How long have you been in this prison?" He holds his truncheon high ready to strike me; I protect my head with both hands; everyone moves away, afraid to be involved, some pleading with him not to harm me. Then he whispers for only the two of us to hear:

"I started from Chirunga campus, then St Mary's Township bottle stores, Three Miles bars, Chipande's Joint and Bottle Store, and the public houses in and around Domasi and Malosa on the way to Lake Malawi. There were two stories that every-one I asked about you told me. The first is that you were so drunk in your staffroom that you began boasting that only you travelled on British Airways first-class, and that Banda does not! Where did you get the nerve to say such a thing publicly in this country? How mad, how very stupid is that!" But I protest quietly, rattled and seething inside: "Look, man, everybody knows that Banda does not just go first class on any airline he chooses, he charters the damn aeroplane! Ask South African Airways. You yourself must know that there can't be any shred of truth in that story."

But ignoring my protest, he continues: "Second, when Prince Charles of England stayed at Ku Chawe Inn on Zomba plateau during one of his famous visits to this country, why did you talk to journalists from the BBC World Service for Africa about CCAM? Why did you tell them that Cecilia Kadzamira is waiting for Banda to die so that she could rule the country officially, competing with her ambitious uncle, whom Banda does not think highly of as a future leader of this country? Why did you tell them that CCAM, which she heads, is a political party disguised as an organisation to help Malawian women in development? And did you have to say the woman, her brothers and sisters grew up in Zimbabwe, and they are unpopular with the ordinary people in Malawi because they do not try to understand them? Man, these stories are for the consumption of the public houses: Mkwapatira Mhango is reporting some of them in the Zambian papers; why did you involve yourself in propagating these tales? Listen, after the strip-search tomorrow, I want my promised K100.00 fee," he concludes, and pushes me back into the courtyard, banging the gate behind me and disappearing to the offices. I stand alone stupefied and boiling with rage.

Nyapala Disi, who must have been straining his ears to hear our discussion but got nothing, approaches me from behind and says: "*Ambuje*, that man will not let you see the officer-in-charge about these ruthless strip-searches. These people are all the same; if I were you, I would not trust them; it's Allah who will liberate us from this brutality." I shake my head in agreement, utterly taken aback, and partly bemused by the bizarre origin of the two stories.

Take the story of my flying first class on British Airways. I was chairperson for the Africa region of the 1986 British Airways Commonwealth Poetry Prizes. And our Africa region entry for the competition, a book of poems by the Nigerian poet Niyi Osundare, tied with the Asia region entry, a novel in verse by Vikram Seth. The two poets eventually shared the increased top prize, but the sponsors of the poetry prize always rewarded the chairpersons of the winning entry with a first class air ticket on their return from London, where the chairpersons for the five regions of the Commonwealth met to choose the overall winner. So when I checked in at the British Airways desk at Heathrow Airport on my way home, I was surprised to be told I was return-ing home on a first class ticket. Which competition had I won? And how many fridges had I bought? So she could check them all in free, the lady at the check-in desk joked. "I have none," I said, "but I will welcome with pleasure the first class air ticket you offer me." And when colleagues in the senior common room asked me about the results of the Commonwealth Poetry Compe-tition, I foolishly showed off my winning African entry and told them that the chairperson for the Asia region and I had come back on first class air tickets because our entries had jointly won and shared the top prize. I did not say Banda never went first class on British Airways. Nobody would dare. However drunk they might be.

What I am supposed to have said to the BBC reporter when Prince Charles visited Malawi is another bizarre tale. The Ghanaian journalist and broadcaster Kwabena Mensa of the BBC World Service for Africa came to Malawi with the Prince when journalists were out of bounds here. Malawi had a crisis of political leadership because Banda was too senile and had not appointed anyone who could rule the country after him. Mensa must have discovered that Banda's permanent mistress was contender to the throne, obviously after talking to several people about the ailing president and the vacuum in the country's political leadership. He must have heard the rumours that the CCAM meetings she was holding in Blantyre, Lilongwe, Zomba, Mzuzu and Nkata Bay were meant to prepare her for leadership in the event of Banda's sudden death.

So when Cecilia Kadzamira heard Kwabena Mensa's BBC report on the activities of her CCAM and discovered that her secret programme had been exposed, she had every reason to be outraged. It was obvious that she would threaten Rodwell Munyenyembe, the Administrative Secretary of the Malawi Congress Party, to ring up the BBC to find out where Mensa had got the story. As Banda's cabal always did, she must have claimed that Banda wanted this matter clarified or heads would roll. And when Mensa told Munyenyembe that he'd heard the story from people in Malawi's public houses, streets, markets and institutions of higher learning, including the University of Malawi, he could not have known that there would be a witch hunt. It was natural for Munyenyembe and his cohorts to direct his investigation on whoever had contacts with the BBC in the university or outside it.

When I was a student at University College London I had contact with the BBC. After discovering this link the security officers did not need any other proof. Despite Mkwapatira Mhango's reports in Zambian papers, I must have been their natural culprit from the university. Why the authorities did not ask me how much I knew about these matters, and how such ordinary facts are distorted to justify their action, is not just irritating but frightening. I remember being told by drivers, messengers and others that my colleague and historian Isaac Lamba had told Zimani Kadzamira that I might not return home because of the contacts I had with the BBC through the poetry competition. I did not realise that that he too might have been spying on us. So after his doctorate degree from Edinburgh University, Mercy invited him to a lovely meal in North Finchley, London, as he was on his way home. Were we perhaps too naïve? Yet however plausible these stories might be, I refuse to accept them as the true reasons for my continued incarceration. If they had taken me to court, I would have told them what I knew about these and other matters.

Book Eight
The Mandela Effect

48

Another Batch of Northerners

After lock-up, Ndovi brings a belated radio Mikuyu newsflash: 'Months ago Mrs Marango Banda, a retired famous radio announcer from the north, was arrested for the usual security reasons. She was dumped in Zomba Central. That's the end of the newsflash.' There is dead silence. This must explain why no political prisoner was released at the anniversary of our independence in July or at Christmas 1988 as we had expected, *Gossip International* suggests. But why did we not hear about this story? We try to find out from our contacts. After some time David and Fr Pat confirm Marango's arrest; they thought they had already informed us. Early in 1988, Marango was attending a conference of the Church of England World Congress for Women in Birmingham, England – she is the chairperson of the organisation for the southern African region. When news of her brilliant performance at the conference reached Banda's permanent mistress who is said to be 'pathologically jealous' of Malawian women who make a name for themselves, she was displeased that Marango had chosen to attend the international conference instead of her CCAM seminar, which was taking place in Nkhata Bay – her home district. Marango had, therefore, been unpatriotic and disloyal to the country's authorities – and everyone knew which authorities were meant. The news ravages us for months.

But another story has been giving Banda headaches. It was nephew Fred Ziyabu who first told me about it on his first snap visit to Mikuyu. A report has reached president Banda's desk to the effect that education standards in the central and the southern regions of the country are very poor. Banda's cabal has told the president that teachers from the north are to blame for this: the northerners are deliberately sabotaging the education of children in the centre and the south, they say. Of course, the story of the subterfuge of the northerners is not true, but Banda has been advised to decree with immediate effect that every teacher must work in the region of his or her origin. *Gossip International* is enraged; we call Banda's pronouncements misguided, absurd and myopic. The truth is, teachers from the south have always worked with and often married men and women from the north and the centre; teachers from the centre have always worked with and often married men and women from the north and the south; and teachers from the north have always worked with and often married men and women from the centre and south. That fact is indisputable.

Banda's decree, which is neither based on credible educational theory nor on pragmatic principles, will disrupt and restrict the movement, work and marriage of Malawians between regions. It is based on Banda's and his coterie's hatred of northerners. Banda's policy of exclusion is becoming extreme and will soon wreck jobs, marriages and families across regions, as well as destroy the country's educational system – only Banda and his minions refuse to understand this. Most people suspect that this is a ploy by the Kadzamira-Tembo faction, for them to get the political support of the southern region in their search for power and fight against the north. Almost everyone knows that Banda's coven has been doing everything in their power to discredit southerners and northerners, demoting some or sacking others from jobs, retiring them early and excluding or eliminating them from Malawi society by detentions, exiles and deaths. These facts are incontrovertible.

One night, as *Gossip International* is still apportioning blame for Banda's decree on education, the gate to B-Wing courtyard squeaks open. *Nyapala* Disi trots to the spy-hole to check who is coming; he comes back horrified: "Allah, protect us," he

306

whispers, "the bastards are bringing a battalion of political prisoners; we must be destined to die here!" The door is thrown wide open and Disi is urged to deal with the newcomers – more than ten in number. The commander disappears into the night and promises to come back after an hour to put out the light. On being asked what crime they might have committed, Khonje, Maseko, Msuku, Mumba, Banda and others, have one answer: they are all northerners who have been working in the southern and the central regions. Their crime was to comment on Banda's recent decree that everyone should work in the region of their birth. One talked back at Banda's radio message: "If you want all northerners back in the north, Mr President, send them vehicles to take them home," he said. Another expressed his frustration by shouting at the radio as Banda made the announcement. And yet another got drunk and began declaring something he cannot remember. The crime committed by Thoza Khonje is astonishing: having come from the north, he should not have worked hard to become one of the managers of the Lower Shire Valley sugar estate in the south; people thought he was too proud as a manager. But the most shocking case is that of primary school boy Bright Nyasulu, who has been sent to A-Wing to stay with Macduff Mtawila Msungama, Blaise Machila and Martin Machipisa Munthali. Nyasulu is about 14 years old; he was telling one of his schoolmates that his relative, who was teaching in the south, has been ordered to return home in the north. Nyasulu's friend innocently relayed the story to his father at home; and being a member of Banda's Special Branch, his father instantly went to arrest Bright bringing him straight to Mikuyu prison, without trial and without charge. We are flabbergasted.

The following day we move to C-Wing and the terminals there transfer to D-Wing. The majority of the recent cellmates share cell C-Wing1 near A-Wing, while those who moved from D4 share the cell C-Wing 2 near B-Wing – both cells share one courtyard. Brown sends the names of the new arrivals to David and Fr Pat, who will know where to send them as part of the struggle. In their bulletins David and Fr Pat confirm that the mass detention of the northerners was motivated, in part, by reports from education experts at the United Nations, which were independently corroborated by the research conducted by Lewis Msukwa and his colleagues at the Centre for Social Research of the university. The standards of education have been deteriorating for the past fifteen years; they are currently worse than during the colonial period. The number of people who cannot read or write is particularly high in the president's own central region. According to the cabal who advise the president, it can only be the northerners who are to blame for these events. Banda's version of tribal cleansing is vindicated. But what is more sickening is the authorities' belief that whatever happens in this country is caused either by witchcraft or people from other districts or regions. Neither Banda nor his henchpeople see themselves as the cause of the problems they create for the people they rule. These are the lies that *Gossip International* finds too painful to confront in prison; if there's any hope for political change in this country, accountability for what people in power do should be top of the agenda; no tribalism; no advancement of one ethnic community over others; whether that community is the largest or the smallest in number.

49
Transfers, Arrivals & Deaths

Another batch of political prisoners joins us in C-Wing. The first is Blaise Machila, who is transferred from A-Wing. For some time our team has been pleading with the officer-in-charge to move Blaise to C-Wing where we can suffer together. The second is Frackson Zgambo, one of the first Malawian airline pilots, and his cousin Mkandawire. They have been transferred from Maula prison and seem to have been intricately involved in the crime and death of Fred Sikwese, another northerner, senior economist and chief protocol in the ministry of external affairs. Fred was presumed to have been sending sensitive material about the Malawi government's relationship with apartheid South Africa to exiled dissidents and others outside the country, apparently using diplomatic bags and with the help of Zgambo who had been making frequent visits to Zimbabwe, Zambia, Tanzania and the UK. The involvement of Zgambo's cousin is not clear: one source claims that he was the messenger or referee between Sikwese and Zgambo; the other says that Zgambo and he were tortured by the Malawi security, broken, and betrayed Sikwese; yet another alleges that they murdered him at Maula prison. In any case, Sikwese was arrested in February 1989; after a short while Zgambo and his cousin were arrested too; obviously the three vehemently protested their innocence; and although they were not taken to court, they were dumped in Maula. After about a month of his being starved and tortured at Maula, Fred died on 10 March 1989. His wife and his sister asked for his body to be buried at home, the authorities refused; instead they buried him within the precincts of Maula prison on 11 March. Zgambo and his cousin were immediately transferred to Mikuyu. Whether they were co-conspirators in Fred's crime or his assassins will probably never be known, though their transfer coinciding with his death, as it did, is rather suspicious.

Nonetheless, Frackson becomes a prominent member of *Gossip International* and as an ex-airline pilot provides what we did not know about the death of president Samora Machel of Mozambique. He explains in minute detail how the West and the apartheid regime in South Africa conspired to kill the Mozambican leader. Although his story is cloaked in pilot jargon, its essence is clear. The West and the apartheid regime did not want Samora Machel to live because the president was becoming too independent; he was organising the frontline states of Southern Africa around himself and urging the other leaders to stand firm, fight apartheid and survive without bowing down to the white-ruled regime. When they discovered where Machel's aeroplane was flying past, those who plotted his death lined beams of light as a decoy to give Machel's pilot the impression that he had reached the runway; the pilot realised too late when he was crashing into trees that he was in effect not landing on a runway. We are disappointed by these Western manoeuvres to force African countries to remain dependent on them, which Machel's tragic death implied.

The other northerner who joins us is Daniel Mhango, the stepbrother of the famous Malawian journalist Mkwapatira Mhango exiled in Lusaka, Zambia. Dan's arrival is mysterious, his story incredible. He claims to have been employed by the Malawi secret security services. The exiled journalist is 'a wanted man' in Malawi because he is on the executive committee of the Malawi Freedom Movement (MAFREMO), the exiled opposition political party led by Orton Chirwa and based in Lusaka, Zambia. But Mkwapatira is also alleged to have been divulging sensitive information on the relationship with the apartheid regime which Banda and his inner circle enjoy. Banda's cronies were also incensed by the stories Mkwapatira was publishing in the Zambian papers, particularly about how the Kadzamira-

Tembo family were desperate to rule Malawi after Banda, at whatever cost.

Clearly the journalist's life was in danger: the Malawi security authorities, who knew that Dan was Mkwapatira's stepbrother, asked Dan to kill his stepbrother for them; they offered him some K5000 to do the job. Dan accepted the money, told his stepbrother about his mission, and ran away to South Africa where he hoped to live forever with his South African mother and her relatives. He began working undercover for the African National Congress (ANC) in Alexandra township; but after several years the Malawi secret police caught up with him; they forcefully drugged him and flew him into Kamuzu International Airport, Malawi, where he came round to discover he was being taken straight to Mikuyu. When we realise that Dan is distantly related to Brown's partner at the Centre for Social Research in the university, we invite him to join our team.

One day, several weeks after Dan's arrival, the morning shift commander orders us to pack our belongings and move to D-Wing. The condemned prisoners in D-Wing intended to dig a tunnel under the three cells in order to escape from prison, but their plan has been discovered just in time. A member of *Gossip International* chokes with laughter shouting: "Someone has been watching too many black and white World War films!" We reluctantly move to cells D1, D2 and D3 that share one courtyard. Our terminal friends move back to C-Wing in block one, where their chances of escape will be naught.

Our move is punctuated by four events. The first is the arrival of new prisoners including my Mtendere Secondary School ex-student and a southerner, Richard Matikanya. He had been running a successful business between the cities of Blantyre and Harare. But somebody reported to the security officers that he had been passing sensitive government information to dissidents in Zimbabwe. We are appalled and note with shame and unease how jealousies still inform Banda's government. The second is the arrival of what we call Sanjika Palace political prisoners, Chikondi and Taimu, both from the south. Chikondi had been

311

Banda's bodyguard for over twenty-five years. In recent years he had been doing well as chief superintendent of Banda's thirteen state houses. His crime is to have alerted Banda's permanent mistress about the International Monetary Fund's latest manoeuvres with the economies of African countries. As part of the IMF's structural adjustment scheme, the permanent secretary to the ministry of finance came to Sanjika Palace to inform them about the latest IMF directives with regard to funding for the president's state houses. With immediate effect, the budget for the state houses was to be reflected in the national budget without necessarily spelling them out item by item.

Chikondi passed the message on to Banda's permanent mistress, who oversees all the state houses. Cecilia Kadzamira, who allegedly has wanted to see a state house superintendent of her choice, is furious; she sacks Chikondi claiming that he should have argued that the budget for state houses should be exempted from the IMF's restrictions. Taimu's crime is in a similar incomprehensible vein. And in their separate ways both servants of Banda's state houses are accused of mismanaging state house property by stealing office fans and other equipment for use at home. They are not allowed court hearings to prove their innocence; the inner circle's security intelligence is merely directed to take them straight to Mikuyu as political prisoners.

The third event is a natural disaster. Massive floods hit Malawi's entire southern region from the Mozambique plains near Mulanje Mountain to the mountain ranges of Zomba, down to the Lower Shire Valley. For several days the rains pour down on Mikuyu without mercy. We are soaked to the skin; for several nights we sleep standing like wagtails on the prison's wire gauze. When we see a helicopter flying over the prison on its way to the Phalombe plains and Mulanje Mountain ranges, we hear that the downpour has been so serious that South African helicopters are on a mission to rescue people from Malawian villages that are badly affected by the floods.

The fourth event is the sudden death in Lusaka of Mkwapatira Mhango. His house is firebombed and the journalist perishes with his extended family of nine. *Gossip International* suspects the cabal's hit squad has done the job. And although we feared that this would happen, given Dan's story of his flight to South Africa, we are distressed to note that Banda continues to assassinate his political opponents living in neighbouring countries. Dr Attati Mpakati, the leader of the Socialist League of Malawi (LESOMA), was assassinated at Stanley Hotel in Harare. Augustine Bwanausi was involved in a mysterious car accident in Lusaka. Now this. Banda's official defence after these deaths, including Mkwapatira's, is that these assassinations were caused by internal feuding within the exiled opposition parties. He denies that it is his spies who infiltrated the exiled political parties and instigated the feuding. For days we mourn Mkwapatira's death with prayers and hymns. Dan spends the rest of his time blaming himself for the death of his stepbrother; our team does whatever it can to cheer him up.

Then one morning we have an even bigger shock. We hear that Macduff Mthawila Msungama has died in A-Wing. It is the saddest day in Mikuyu. Msungama was one of the hardest working businessmen that Lilongwe city boasted. He owned many successful businesses, including tobacco farms that were a cause of envy for competitors in the trade. Most cellmates believe it was his success that got him into prison. But Msungama has died of asthma: he had an attack in the middle of the night; he shouted to the night shift commander and his guards to give him the inhalers they kept at the office for him. The prison regime refused to give them to him, saying once prison cells are locked up no commander or guard is allowed to open them. So they let him die, just like that. Msungama worries because it is too close to home. Most of us knew the man. When I taught at Bunda College of Agriculture, colleagues and I used to visit Msungama's and Kadango's bottle stores on Devil Street near the old Lilongwe city market.

Impotence, anger, speculations and suspicions of foul play abound. Why were we trusted to keep our medicines in our cell and he in A-Wing was not? No-one has an answer. The whole thing was nauseating. He will probably be buried at St Mary's

313

cemetery. And his family and relatives will not be allowed to see his body. What a cruel world Banda and his thugs are creating for us. On Sunday we have a special service for the repose of the souls of Msungama and others. Deaths in prison become grim realities we can do without.

50

Beads for My Children

'My dear children, thank you for the deep-fried *chambo*, the soap and sugar you sent through *Noriega*; tell *agogo* and mum that I am fine and kicking hard to get out of here. In your notes you ask about how it feels to be in a place which has no grass, flowers, birds and animals. Today I thought I should gather a few tales about what we call God's objects of wonder in Mikuyu that you might find amusing. I will loop them together for your easy enjoyment.

'I don't mean the strange flies, cockroaches or mosquitoes that suck our blood at night giving us malaria and other illnesses, or the scorpions, maggots, fleas and bugs hidden in the gaps of walls and cracks of fractured courtyard floors, poisoning our blood, though there are many of those too. There is this bean-plant I must tell you about. During the rainy season it grows in the corner of A-Wing courtyard, opposite the communal showers. Almost everyone who goes there for morning ablution forgets the stench of the place and adores the plant. Some cellmates love watering it; others pruning it; yet others, merely touching its tender leaves before entering the shower-room or returning to their cells. Often passionate quarrels erupt too. Whose bean-plant is it? Who has the right to look after it? Does it belong to the condemned prisoners, the political prisoners, or Old Man Machipisa who stays in A-Wing with your uncle Blaise Machila? When the guards hear us arguing, they always butcher the plant, taking it to the office with them to throw away, claiming they want to avoid fights amongst political prisoners, though in truth the guards will always destroy whatever might brighten our dull lives.

'Of course *Nyapala* Disi protests on our behalf: as our prison prefect, that's his job; he argues that plants and grasses that stubbornly peep through gaps of walls and cracks of courtyard floors must be protected; they symbolise the children and friends we have left behind and whom we need to be reminded of every so often. The guards invariably laugh and mock Disi when he finds other shrubs for us to water and prune. It's strange how the guards want to destroy anything that might remind us of the plants or crops or people we once knew outside. I hear they are instructed not to encourage us to think of our children, homes, plants or the grass we left behind. But we won't let them bulldoze their way into our lives: with or without the bean-plant, we think of you and blow you our love always.

'As for animals, there is this black female cat that strays into our dustbins at least twice a year. We do not quite understand why she always comes in pregnant, but the cellmates mercilessly hunt the poor animal out of prison when it comes. Kadango justifies his action by claiming that it gives us bad luck: for, every time we hear reliable rumours of the possible release of our numbers, the pregnant cat comes in and begins to rummage through the dustbins for food. When Kadango and others throw it out, the next thing we hear is that the black cat has given birth but eaten its young, and the expected release of some of our numbers does not happen. The other day I tried to argue that there is no link and perhaps we should offer the poor beast the best meal we can afford for it not to eat its young; that way God will release us from this dungeon. Kadango insists that I am mistaken, for like bats, cats belong to the world of darkness. And the bats themselves are in their thousands here, and as always, they do not seem to want people; not only because they come into the world when we are supposed to be going to sleep and they sleep when we are up and about, but the way hundreds and hundreds of them carelessly shower their droppings into the mouths of snoring prisoners as they fly away at night and fly in at dawn – this shows clearly that they do not intend to develop natural relationships with us humans.

'And the birds of Mikuyu are funny. Do you remember the wagtails that always came to pick worms in the garden around our house? Well, we have a version of our own wagtails that sleep on the wire mesh above the prison's courtyards. Immediately after lock-up, when the huge beams of light are on to ensure that nobody escapes from prison, thousands of wagtails fly in from every direction and land on the wire mesh above the courtyards, where they chatter, chatter and chatter endlessly. The noise they make before they go to sleep is deafening. We like watching them through the spy-hole on the door of our cell. And have you ever seen birds sleeping on one leg? That's precisely what some of these do! I have never seen creatures look so hilarious in their sleep. When the morning shift gang takes over its duties, the wagtails disperse to their respective homes until lock-up time, when the cycle repeats itself.

'We also have swallows, which fly in with the coastal winds of Mozambique, as one of our mates claims. And these prefer to settle in the communal toilets of A-Wing, where they nest and breed. Do not ask me why they prefer to nest in communal toilets, which stink beyond comparison. What is intriguing is when their chicks fall to the ground. The prisoners who live in the other block always want to catch the chicks and roast them to improve their poor meal, while the political prisoners wish they could let them fly away free.

'And I must tell you about what happened the other week. One sparrow attempted to build a nest under the louvres of D4, but the twigs between her little beak kept falling down. Pingeni picked them up, placed them near the ration store, and tried to entice the bird to come and get them. But she flew away and brought new twigs and continued to assemble another nest. When these too fell to the ground, she gave up and flew away, never to show up again; I felt sad that she could not even start to build the nest that she clearly needed.

'What I particularly like about the birds of prison though, and I am sure you would like to hear this, is what they teach us about the things we should know about birds but do not. As a lad I loved killing birds with string-traps, basket-traps, birdlime and catapults. But as I read for my diploma in education at Soche Hill College in order to become a secondary school teacher, I joined the group that watched and protected birds – the bird preservation society. I remember the thrill I had when we went on bird-watching trips and studied colonies of bee-eaters in their natural habitat in the Lower Shire Valley. We saw hundreds and hundreds of them that looked very beautiful, with their silver green bodies and brown beaks.

'But all that time I did not know what I now know about birds. Did you know, for instance, that some birds actually walk like humans, left-right, left-right, left-right; while others hop on both feet; hop, hop, hop! And yet others both hop and walk, hop and walk; while yet others sort of limp about? I must confess at your age I did not know this; so I was enormously thrilled when I discovered it. And now I always persuade the friends I have not to kill or chase away any birds that stray into prison until I have classified them. I feel great satisfaction when I group birds according to whether they walk, hop, limp or all three; classifying birds has become my passion and obsession, you might say.

'About the insects of Mikuyu, I was advised to look out for black ants with white spots on their bottoms, particularly as we cleaned the cells and the courtyards after strip-searches. At first I did not understand why; later, after I saw what Mbale did with one white-spotted black ant, I saw the point. After catching it, Mbale balanced it delicately between his forefinger and his thumb and pointed the black ant's sharp end at himself, which proceded to sting his forehead. When it stung him, he went into this state of frenzy, which I had never seen anyone do before, then he danced a strange dance; he then carefully took the ant and hid it in a gap in the wall so nobody could see it. When I asked what it all meant, Mbale claimed that just to see the white-spotted black ant was a good omen for political prisoners – it meant they would be released from prison; being stung by one was an even better omen because their chances for being released from prison were greater. 'But when I asked Mbale what forcing the ant to sting his forehead meant, he said it speeded up the process of being released from prison. You can imagine my laughter and disbelief. When I told him I was waiting for his quick release from prison, he laughed and challenged me to wait and see. So after strip-searches we all begin looking for white-spotted black ants; perhaps when I see one, you will see me coming home!

'My dear children, you too might laugh at these objects of God's wonder. But you must understand that where there is no book, no newspaper, no magazine to read; and where there is no radio to listen to stories; watching what grasses, shrubs, mosses, lichens, birds and insects do or look like is as satisfying as counting layers of bricks on each prison wall many times over, or fighting to see a bit of the moon at the door spy-hole after lock-up; these matters are neither trivial nor incredible. Tell Mum and Mother I am well; they should stop worrying about me. Missing you all. Lots of love. Daa.'

51
Feeling Totally Rotten

Today I got up feeling demoralised. Absolutely and totally demoralised. Not only because of journalist Mkwapatira Mhango's brutal death by Banda's death squads in Zambia. There is that too. I feel mostly impotent and worried about my friend and colleague Blaise Machila. He needs help but I do not know what to do. After moving to D-Wing, I had been bothered by his state of mind and health. First, I have not got over the fact that his incarceration was indirectly caused by me. Secondly, Blaise suffers from mental illness, which is becoming more serious every day he spends his time without medication. Since he was dumped here, Blaise has not been taking the medication that stabilises his mental state. He does not trust anybody who suggests that he should. In the university I often had literally to drag him into my car and drive him to Zomba Mental Hospital for his medication as recommended by the health experts at the Australian National University, where his mental illness started as he did research for the doctorate degree he could not complete. Since he entered Mikuyu, Blaise has had problems with almost everyone. Even after persuading the prison authorities to transfer him from A-Wing to join our team in C-Wing and then D-Wing, Blaise has been restless. If my resources of persuasion were often stretched to the limits at the university, in Mikuyu they have been exhausted. After discovering how we correspond with the outside world, and despite our telling him about the campaigns that are being mounted by writers, linguists, journalists, literary critics, churchmen, churchwomen and human rights organisations on our behalf outside prison, Blaise's reaction has been ambiguous. He admires how we struggle to communicate with our families, relatives, friends and human rights activists on the one hand; and despises the prison regime for allowing political prisoners like us to do pretty much what we like, on the other. What bothers him most of all is what bothers us all.

Life in Malawi prisons need not be as harsh as it is: prisoners could feed themselves without relying on non-existent government subventions. The land where these prisons are built is so fertile that we could grow maize, rice, cassava and vegetables of every kind to feed ourselves. We could raise domestic animals like cattle, goats, pigs and birds like chicken too. The other week Blaise was so incensed by the rotten food we ate that he made an appointment to see the officer-in-charge about it. Unfortunately, he lost his temper in the discussion that ensued: he apparently called the prison officers and guards incompetent and corrupt, which is true, but he was sent to the punishment cell for being so blunt. After three days and three nights without food and water he returned with dark scars from handcuff and leg irons on his wrists, legs and ankles. *Gossip International* has made numerous representations on Blaise's behalf to ask prison officers to invite doctors to see him, in the hope that they can recommend his release on humanitarian grounds. But the prison regime does not believe that Blaise is mentally ill. According to them, the protests he made in the university to find out where I was dumped and the anger he has over the rotten food are deliberate acts meant to dupe authority. They have known clever prisoners who have faked madness before. When I smuggle out notes to Fr Pat and David to explain Blaise's state of mind, they persuade the vice-chancellor to come and see him. The vice-chancellor, John Dubbey, is allowed to see Blaise. We are surprised, as no white man has entered Mikuyu prison office before. Yet when he is invited to see the vice-chancellor in the visiting room, Blaise throws John Dubbey out. The vice-chancellor is part of Banda's apparatus for patronage and corruption in Malawi; he is part of the problem and not the solution, he declares. I am not only disappointed but I am convinced that my friend is becoming irredeemably ill.

After moving to D-Wing with us Blaise has become even more unmanageable. He refuses to eat with us or share our news. He has stopped talking to anyone, even to me, whom he once considered his only friend. And more recently he threw away the *foya* he has been wearing since his arrival in Mikuyu, preferring to wear the rags of blanket he uses at night. Now he refuses to wash and decides to remain stark naked instead. I do not know what to do; no cellmate knows what to do. In the university I persistently asked our employers to send him for treatment in Zambia, Zimbabwe or South Africa, but they were not bothered. The prison authorities have the same attitude: they think he is faking madness; they produce a list of political prisoners who have duped the prison regime before. I cry, pray and feel thoroughly rotten every night I think of my colleague and friend.

The cost of impotence
(For Blaise Machila)

How do you thank a colleague who
sets himself the task of finding out
on behalf of your distraught family
where security officers have dumped
you after ferociously abducting you
leaving hearts throbbing with fear?

How do you treat the brother's scars
after months of torture in police cells,
when one day the security officers
should drag him into your prison,
leg-irons, hand-cuffs and all – to stay
caged throughout his incarceration
as instructed by his college principal?

And when his mental state worsens,
what do you do when your mate casts
off the *foya* he was forced to wear on

322

arrival, the blanket rags he preferred
and, to everybody's horror, decides
to do his time totally naked – refusing
to speak even to you, his only friend?

What do you do after your appeal
for vice-chancellor to come and see
the state of mind of his scholar, before
he makes his final approach for His
Excellency the Life President to have
compassion on your friend; how do

you face your comrade when, utterly
mad, he should chuck out the very
VC intending to rescue him, of course,
hoping against hope that he'd visit
you too, surreptitiously – though as
for that, what a nightmare botched!

No, Chancellor College principal, no,
your uncle and chairman of university
council, no, your sister, life president's
permanent mistress and official hostess,
the Mama – how could you unleash
your power on these culpable people?

And what homes, what families, what
lives – indeed what husbands, wives,
children, what lives, dislodged, disrupted,
scattered, what pain inflicted forever!
When will you learn there's no need
to assault the people you want to rule.

52

The Mandela Effect

We are planning another way of responding to the humiliation of the strip-searches that we are enduring every day, when *Noriega* approaches me from behind and whispers: "President F.W. de Klerk of apartheid South Africa is holding secret talks with Nelson Mandela." He vanishes. My heart jumps and begins to thump fast, which always means that I should take the rumour seriously. This is the most uplifting and soul-cheering rumour I have heard yet. Indeed, rumours play a critical, and therapeutic, role in Mikuyu; we trust them more than the stories from newspapers cuttings that are smuggled into prison. This rumour is particularly hopeful, as it entails the eventual release of Nelson Mandela and his fellow political prisoners on Robben Island, which in turn presages the official end of apartheid in South Africa; and that will have untold reverberations to other African prisons, and the political landscape of Africa as a whole. Mandela's resilience, integrity and sense of purpose have inspired the independent countries of the African Great Rift Valley. He has not only become the champion of the struggle for African political liberation, but Tanzania, Zambia and Mozambique, countries which surround us, officially support the movements for the liberation of South Africa from the white-dominated regime. And in Mikuyu we have adopted Mandela as our hero and icon; the rumour therefore rekindles our hope for liberation.

Furthermore, Banda, who is a staunch supporter of apartheid, will be embarrassed by Mandela's release; he will want to find an excuse for doing something good to his own people – our being freed is only one deed. Machipisa Munthali is delighted; he has no doubt about the relevance of the imminent release of political prisoners in South Africa to political prisoners in Malawi. When we take our showers and do our ablutions in A-Wing we find him so animated and vocal about the prospect of Nelson Mandela's release that he declares: "The time has come for me to take Banda to court!" And when F.W. de Klerk actually releases Nelson Mandela on 11 February 1990, we gather in the courtyard to thank God and sing praises to Him, all the while sincerely hoping that his liberation will rub off onto us and bring freedom to all political prisoners in Malawi prisons and detention camps. And predictably the Mandela effect begins to take root: the food in Mikuyu starts to improve, the strip-searches become irregular and living conditions in general start to change for the better.

As if to underline our speculations, one night we are surprised when *Nyapala* Disi is asked to deal with what the prison regime calls hard-core political prisoners who have been transferred from the New Building Wing to join us in D-Wing. The first is Alex Mataka. "Welcome to my kingdom, Alex," I joke; we laugh, recalling the kind of goodbye he gave me when I transferred to D4 about three years ago. The other three are Sylvester Phiri from Mchinji district in the central region, who was working for the insurance section of Old Mutual Company and was presumed to have been sending sensitive government information to Malawi's political dissidents in Harare, where he frequently flew on duty. CheJumo Owen from Machinga/Mangochi district was one of the drivers for Albert Muwalo. Lester Muwamba, who was working at the MCP branch in Blantyre and was thought to have embezzled party funds; we can only speculate that it's the Mandela effect that has caused their transfer to D-Wing at this point.

But 1990 brings news of what *Gossip International* calls 'eminent visitations' that might lead to our eventual liberation. The British Prime Minister Mrs Margaret Thatcher is scheduled to visit Malawi, so are the Archbishop of Canterbury, the Secretary General of the Scottish Presbyterian Church, and above all the Pope; even Muslim leaders from Saudi Arabia visit the

Muslim Association of Malawi. We wonder why such important leaders want to visit this tiny country in one year. Does it forebode Banda's imminent departure from the political scene? Are they coming to pay their last respects to the ailing dictator who has supported their policies throughout the Cold War? Do they know something we do not know about his health? And more poignantly for political prisoners, are these leaders bringing Banda any messages from human rights activists in their countries for Malawi to stop its blatant violation of human rights? Do these leaders even care that they will be shaking hands with a notorious dictator? *Gossip International* hopes that the global campaigns being mounted in their countries for us will sting the conscience of one or two of them; perhaps our plight will be brought to Banda's attention at their extravagant banquets. One afternoon *Noriega* brings a rather desperate but amusing bulletin from David, who claims that Fr Pat and the Catholic community of staff and students at Chirunga campus are planning to protest to the Pope on our behalf. He asks for our prayers that his mission should succeed. The protesters will target the Pope's representative to Central Africa, who is based in Lusaka. Apparently, one of the students will be carrying a large placard with the words: 'Shackled Catholic poet denied sacraments while the Pope shakes hands with his jailors!' written on it. We have a massive laugh, but doubt if the authorities will let them get anywhere near the Pope or his cardinal, though there is no harm in them trying. We discover from Fr Pat later that the Minister of Youth and Culture threatened the protesters and blocked their attempts to meet any of the dignitaries who visited Malawi in 1990.

I have yet another dream. All the political prisoners in Malawi prisons have been released. They have been invited to a national conference, which is being held in one of the biggest conference centres in Blantyre. The conference room is huge and looks like one of those cathedrals one sees in Europe. The floor and seats are all adorned in a red carpet. The platform and podium are draped in red too. The country's important personalities and dignitaries are here: Catholic bishops and their clergy; the Central African

Anglican bishop and his clergy; the leaders of the Scottish Presbyterian Church, Methodist Church leaders; Malamulo Seventh Day Adventist leaders; leaders of the Muslim Association of Malawi; Malawi Congress Party leaders; representatives of diplomatic missions; paramount chiefs and other traditional authorities are all colourfully robed for the occasion. University academics too wearing their robes crown the conference hall as if degrees were going to be presented. Members of the Malawi Congress Party's Women's League, the Malawi Youth League and the Malawi Young Pioneers, each wearing party uniforms or *chitenje* wrappers with Banda's face on them have gathered here. The hall is full; everyone is quiet, waiting only for an event.

The political prisoners who have just been released from Malawi's prisons are milling about the conference hall entrance. And these are a vociferous lot; they are laughing and shouting in expectation of the event. Among them I recognise an old friend, the Revd Dr Saindi Chiphangwi, who says he has come to represent the Blantyre Synod of the Scottish Presbyterian Church. The gathering is similar to the interdenominational assembly that Banda invites once a year to celebrate the anniversary of Malawi's martyrs, which is often presided over by Revd Chiphangwi himself, though today he is just a spectator like all of us. Then an announcement comes through the microphones: "Ladies and gentlemen, today's gathering is different from most. Today his excellency, the life president, the Ngwazi Dr H. Kamuzu Banda, the Messiah, the father and founder of the Malawi nation, has decided to pass on the keys of power to rule this country to his permanent companion, official hostess the Mama, Cecilia Kadzamira. This gathering of the general public, the church, political and diplomatic dignitaries has been called to witness and bless our new leader who is due to arrive any time."

Silence. Everyone is surprised. People start mumbling. The political detainees just released from Malawi's prisons are shocked and begin asking questions. Why should Banda's permanent companion walk into leadership without challenge? They ask. The Malawi constitution demands that when the president retires, or dies, or somehow needs to be replaced, general elections be held to choose a new president. "Why is this not happening in this case? This is undemocratic!" They shout. The people in the conference hall also begin fidgeting about why they have been brought here if the matter has already been decided upon. People begin to shout that the installation of Banda's companion as president is unacceptable. Some declare that if Banda had married the woman during his political career, they'd have understood his anxiety and probably accepted his wife as president; but he refused to marry the woman when church elders suggested the idea to him! A famous Scottish Presbyterian church minister died mysteriously for suggesting that Banda should marry her. At the conference hall entrance the ex-political prisoners continue to agitate more and more. How can Banda do this to us? They ask. Why should we be given a leader instead of being allowed to choose one for ourselves? Yet others inquire: "Are we so stupid? Why does Banda treat us like we are still babies?" The distinguished delegates on the platform, the bishops, church leaders and diplomatic representatives begin walking up and down the platform as if they were praying for God to bring down the miracle they have been praying for these years. There are shouts and protests everywhere.

Then an old village woman suddenly appears on the scene. Nobody seems to know where she has come from. She is wearing a colourfully printed *chitenje* with Banda's face on it. She brings along her daughter, who is in a colourful dress of blue and yellow spots on a white background. The old woman draws near the crowd at the conference hall entrance, grabs the microphone and begins protesting loudly. "No," she says, "I will not accept this. We should not accept this. None of us should accept being given that evil woman as our president without a competitor. If all of you men are afraid of challenging Banda's witch, I have brought my daughter here. I know she has not been in politics for long. But she is more educated in our ways of life than Banda's concubine! I want my daughter here to contest the seat that woman is being offered. She knows our ways and our political desires. The Mama does not. I demand a contest. I say, let's have a contest. I offer you my daughter. You can then choose between her and Banda's undeclared wife!"

Almost everyone inside and outside the conference hall agrees. Some people laugh. The ex-prisoners support the old woman's cry more vociferously. "Yes, let's have a contest," they shout. Chiphangwi and I watch on, pleasantly shocked by these new developments; inwardly, I thank God for answering the people's prayers; He will give us a new leader, I think. We begin to wonder which village the old woman has come from. Her daughter looks respectable and dignified in her plain dress. Arguably, she has the image and personality necessary for a presidential candidate. The distinguished delegates begin to leave the platform one by one, joining the agitators at the conference hall entrance. Everyone in the conference hall comes out. They want to see the brave old woman who is offering her daughter as a presidential candidate. Banda and his entourage appear in the distance; they do not know what awaits them. Everyone is walking on the red carpet meant only for Banda and his entourage. The old woman stands, arms akimbo, ready to challenge Banda and his courtiers as they approach the conference hall. I wake up suddenly. The commander's bunch of keys is jangling at the door. "There is no strip-search today," he declares. I thank God, but I am forced to ask: Lord, why didn't you let me see Banda and his companion confront the old woman and her daughter in the dream?

53
The Miracle Cure

9 January 1991, Wednesday. Disi was right the other night. The most terrifying aspect of our incarceration is that Banda and his inner circle are forcing people with diverse interests, beliefs, ambitions, desires, education and character to live together under despotic conditions. For more than three years now, we have been quarrelling and fighting almost daily, but we have not been reporting these feuds to the prison regime in order to protect ourselves. Today is typical. The Seventh Day Adventist church in prison, who are very active and want to convert every political prisoner, have summoned me to a local court created in cell D1. My crime is that I refused to become a member of the Seventh Day Adventists from the time I transferred to D4. Since then, my undeclared war with the SDAs has been gathering momentum until now, when it is coming to a head. In the past two years George Mtafu, the chairperson of the Saturday church-going Christians and I, chairperson of the Sunday church-going Christians, have been strange bedfellows. This is the most painful time of my incarceration. In our team Brown, Rodney and George are SDAs; TS, Dan and I are not; but we have remained good friends, sharing news, medicines, food and jokes together. We smuggle out notes and letters to family, friends and human rights organisations together. The fight for the campaign for our liberation has been conducted as a team. The fact that George is the chairperson for Saturday church-going Christians and I am chairperson of Sunday church-going Christians has not affected our relations as a team.

But for some time now, George's congregation has not been happy with me and this arrangement. They have been urging George to bring charges against me for making life tough for SDAs, essentially because I have been refusing to convert to SDA and discouraging my Sunday church-going Christians to convert. Some SDAs want George to break away from our team altogether. The court case I am coming to is not about the animosities that have developed between the chairman of the Sunday church-going Christians and the chairman of the Saturday church-going Christians *per se*. If George left our team and Brown (who converted to SDA in prison) followed, the two would be forced to share what they receive from their relatives and visitors with their church members only. In our team, Brown and George have the largest number of relatives and visitors who bring in the news, medicines and food that we share with all cellmates, including the SDAs. This court case is about news, medicines and food and survival. To be honest, I would not mind if the break-up of our team happened from within and was not imposed by outsiders. At the moment how we relate to each other depends on the team to which we belong – if the attempt to break up our team succeeds, the relationship amongst political prisoners in the entire prison will be permanently wrecked, making the smooth running relationships we have enjoyed unsustainable.

Today D1 has been turned into a court. Everyone has been asked to leave the cell to let us hold our court case. TS is ready as my main witness; George has Brown on his side. *Nyapala* Disi is preparing to set the scene as the presiding judge. George is about to begin presenting his case and charging me with the offence I have committed, when there is sudden intervention. The morning shift commander in the courtyard demands that Blaise Machila and George Mtafu come out immediately to see the officer-in-charge. Therefore our court proceedings must stop to let George attend to the call first. Suddenly Pingeni barges into D1, excuses himself, and asks TS if he could jump on his shoulders to see if there is a vehicle outside prison. Disi, TS and Brown immediately help Pingeni up the little window sill to check the kind of vehicle that's parked outside the office. He climbs down with news that the famous grey Land Rover, which belongs to the Special Branch, is parked outside. Chunga, TS, Brown, Rodney and others jump on each other's shoulders too and climb down to confirm Pingeni's hunch. Speculations on the arrival of the grey Land Rover begin.

They are interrupted by Blaise and George who return from the office. With discernible bitterness George shouts: "*A Nyapala,* someone from the Special Branch has come to take Blaise and me to the higher authorities at the southern region police head-quarters in Blantyre; we must stop the court case, we'll resume when I return; I want this thing sorted out once and for all," he says, gathering his property to go. *Nyapala* Disi praises God: "*Allah jwamkulungwa!* (God is great!). The fool does not realise that he is going to be freed! Those of you who have not seen how people are released from here, this is how it happens. Abruptly!" Then he goes into a kind of ecstatic state, effectively talking to himself: "My dreams were right," he says, "but I thought it would be the two people from the university who would be released." Nobody asks Disi about his dreams; they are too busy shouting their goodbyes and best wishes to Blaise and George in the courtyard, all the while praying that this might lead to their liberation.

At lock-up time the guards declare that George and Blaise have been released with Marango Banda from Zomba Central and the well-known central region businessman Mr W. Masiku from Chichiri prison. "This is the first release of political prisoners in a long time," declares Mkwanda. Mikuyu buzzes with hope and further speculations for more releases to come. No fight erupts among the cellmates for the different interpretations of the event – four political prisoners have been released and that's a fact. That evening Brown and TS gather around my bed to take stock of the events, decide on what to tell Fr Pat and David and to cheer ourselves. Brown and I are upset and feel totally dejected. I thank God when I realise how the case against me was immediately dropped. My confrontation with George would have wrecked the

332

relationships amongst cellmates in Mikuyu. God has prevented that by getting George released. Blaise, whom I was so worried about, is also released. I pray that his relatives understand the nature of his mental state, which has deteriorated while in prison. I hope the university can see the point of sending this fine academic to a proper psychiatric institution in Zimbabwe, Zambia or South Africa.

When my wife and children visit after a week, she tells me George specifically asked her to go by their house to get a chicken and some medicines to add to what she's already bringing us. I am surprised, but Disi reminds me that releases have incredible powers to resolve petty prison scores that people have against each other. I respect his wisdom. After a few days *Noriega* brings us David's bulletin to Landeg on the miracle release we experienced.

24 Jan 1991
Dear Lan,

Jack has asked me to write to you to try reviving the protest about him and Brown. Dr George Mtafu, Blaise Machila and Marango Banda were released on 9 January. Jack is quite convinced (& I think he's probably right) that the reason for the release is the very heavy pressure which the West (sorry, force of habit, forget "West") the German Government & donor organisations have had, to the extent of refusing to help finance the medical school which is to be built in Blantyre. They are even supposed to have sent a threatening delegation to see JT in person. Mtafu's release, therefore, is the crucial one, and that of Blaise & Marango Banda is a smokescreen to avoid the appearance of giving in to pressure over a specific case.

The effect of the release has been pretty shattering for Jack & Brown. Of course, it's a good sign that the grand inquisitors are able to give in to pressure, but there is still the bitter disappointment of being left behind (Remember the bit in The Island *where Winston tells John, "You stink of freedom"). The problem is that the rumours circulating among the prison warders were that Jack's and Brown's names were top of the Inspector General's list for release. So they feel that Mtafu has 'jumped the queue' because of the better organised support which the Germans provided, compared with the British. I've tried to explain the perfidious casuistry, which operates within Whitehall, which tends to dilute any linkage between human rights issues and aid (despite Douglas Hurd's announcements back in September). However, they feel very strongly that the iron is still hot, so it is necessary to try a lot of hammering.*

Specifically, they ask for a revival campaign from Amnesty & Africa Watch; publicity about their plight with the Beeb, and any quality papers like The Independent, The Guardian etc which might be interested. I suspect that to get the media interested, (especially now that they are obsessed with the Gulf War, a problem I've already warned Jack & Brown about), it may be better to get Amnesty & Africa Watch to do the press/news releases. One point that Jack specifically made is that he feels they are in a sense being held 'hostage' until the old man dies. The idea being that JT wants to get the credit for their release himself when he takes over (like Moi did with Ngũgĩ after Kenyatta's death). Jack feels that if this ruse could be exposed over the media, it would panic JT into releasing them. I'm not quite so sanguine myself, but I am convinced that it is JT who holds the key. I previously thought that Zimani held it. But there is evidence of a rift between JT and the Kadzamira brothers recently (JT, as chairman of the University Council, has shuffled round the college principals, sending Chimphamba to the Polytechnic, Chikhula to Chancellor College, and Zimani to the apparently punitive position at Bunda College of Agriculture – all this is supposedly because Zimani took too liberal a line over last year's student demos, and has urged giving in to international pressure over Jack's . . .).

I am still not sure what's happening to Mtafu, but I imagine he'll get his job back with the Ministry of Health (being the country's only neurosurgeon!). I admire his attitude very much. He's been sending medicine on to Jack and Brown plus messages of solidarity, and promised to ask his German contacts to keep up the pressure on their behalf. After his ordeal that's quite a risk to take. Blaise is still sick, obviously not helped by having been chained for much of his imprisonment, "as if he was a rabid dog". He's gone to stay with his relatives in Blantyre. He's lost a lot of weight. Mrs Marango Banda has even more dramatically lost weight (from 210 down to 140 pounds). Amnesty and Africa Watch may be interested to know that she met Vera Chirwa in Zomba Central Prison. They had adjoining plots of vegetables to cultivate, as part of their special privilege. Vera was reasonably well, though she has also been chained up for considerable periods (and still is). She also complains that she'd received only one letter from one of her children (Fumbani), though many more must have been written. Her spirit was still fiery, and she frequently shouted imperiously at the warders. Please ensure that the information in this paragraph is just for Amnesty & Africa Watch – not for the media. If this got out it could lead to re-arrest for Blaise, Mtafu and Mrs Banda.

Jack & Brown are fairly chirpy after recovering from the shock of not being released on 9 January 1991. Their food has improved, but they still sometimes ask for extra ndiwo (fish, meat, vegetable to go with maize meal). I'm able to correspond with them fairly easily and send money, medicine, and food. If I hear that there's a good chance that Jack & / or Brown may be released, I'll just phone saying "please cancel the arrangements". That'll mean cancel or postpone the media high profile until you hear otherwise. I do believe that Jack will be released soon. The JTs have been badly hit by the mauling they got from the Africa Watch report & the pressure from donors (including IMF); it's just a question of ensuring that the pressure is maintained. If you think you have any pull with the Foreign Office, of course that could help . . .

I may add to this while waiting for a courier (I don't know of any yet). Best wishes to Alice, Martin & John.
Sincerely,
David

54

A Score of Geese Ago

22 February 1991, Friday. After peeping through the spy-hole in the gate to our courtyard Pingeni whispers for all to hear: "The guards are pouring into the quadrangle behind us ready to come in here, I think; something is definitely going to happen; it can't be another strip-search; we've had that this morning!" The gate opens violently. The afternoon gang of commander, sergeants and guards led by officer-in-charge Sitima marches into the courtyard for cells D1, D2 and D3. They have with them a thin man not wearing prison uniform, who is carrying a piece of paper in his hand. The commander shouts for those in the cells and at the far end of the courtyard to hear clearly: "Everyone, gather around the courtyard gate now!" We leave our beds and tittle-tattle, shuffle into the courtyard and squat around the gate. Sitima raises his hand for peace and quiet and speaks: "Anyone who hears his name stand up, get out through this gate and assemble in the quadrangle behind us, you hear?" "Yes, *Bwana*," we chorus, most of us not sure what's going on. The names on the list brought by the man in plain clothes are called out: one, two, three, four, five, six, seven . . . all the way to twenty-two. Sitima stops and taking his staff with him he closes the gate; leaving behind the afternoon shift commander, who pushes us back into cells D1, D2 and D3, locks up each cell one by one, shuts the courtyard gate and locks it from outside.

Back in D1 *Nyapala* Disi courageously declares: "Those of you who do not know how political prisoners are released from Mikuyu, have just witnessed one. Those of us who have stayed long in this prison have watched these events many times over. And I

337

have a suggestion for some of you. Should you experience a sudden hollowness of heart and spirit, otherwise called despair, from now on, imagine what we have felt each time people were released in this manner these seventeen or so years." The hymn 'The Lord is My Shepherd' suddenly interrupts him from the New Building Wing. "There you are: that's what I meant," Disi continues, "our friends have been released; they are now singing songs of praise and thanksgiving to God; this will go on right into the night; may Allah be praised and have mercy on us who remain behind!"

A lump lodges in my throat. What was predicted a score of geese ago has happened. It suddenly dawns on me that I have actually been left behind; I have not been released with the others. Why? What wrong have I done anybody? My hands begin to sweat, my legs tremble. The shock is unbearable. I feel dejected. Thoroughly. Tears begin to glaze my eyes. The number of those gone is twenty-two. I recall the geese that we saw criss-crossing the blue sky more than two years ago. Pingeni claimed there were twenty-two; he was first to see them; he was one of the first to be called out: he's gone. From our team only TS, Dan and I are left behind. In January George and Blaise were released. Now it's Brown and Rodney. I am particularly happy that those who wanted George and me to be enemies are gone. I thank God for this. We know that Brown will contact Fr Pat, David and others and talk to them about what's to be done for us. He has always created something out of nothing, the philosophy which has been critical for our survival this far. Fr Pat, David and Brown will make a formidable triumvirate in the fight for our liberation. I now take firm control of our surreptitious communication with the outside world and suggest that Fr Pat and David in Malawi and Landeg in the UK again intensify the campaign for our freedom, if they can. After several weeks, word trickles down to us that Ian Mbale and several political prisoners at Zomba Central were released on the day our numbers were freed. We praise the Lord.

Despite the shock of being left behind, TS and I particularly thank God for Laurenti Mtemwende Phiri's liberation. Although his epileptic attacks had reduced considerably, given the various combinations of tablets that Mtafu creatively suggested, it was becoming difficult for us to help him after Mtafu's release. And it is after he is gone that we feel the full force of the risk that we took regarding Mtemwende. When he settled down to the boredom of life in Mikuyu and saw most of us reading the Bible and writing surreptitious notes on toilet paper, Lifebuoy and Sunlight soap wrappers and other unlikely objects; when he saw us smuggling these out to our families, friends and human rights organisations; Mtemwende felt the urge to engage in what we were doing. Although he could not join the larger revolution conducted in English, he was determined to learn how to read and write; he did not want us to continue to write letters to his wife for him. He told me that his wife managed the books for his tobacco farms very well. But he still felt terribly stupid that he cannot read or write properly: could we therefore help him learn reading and writing in any way? He asked. The literate cellmates assembled and chose how best to do this without stirring the wrath of the prison authorities. We were agreed on two matters: we had loads of time, and the exercises would help Mtemwende to worry less about his epileptic attacks.

We chose Frackson Zgambo who has been left behind and Stephen Pingeni who has now been released as 'leaders' and decided that the teaching would have to be conducted in secret. As chalk was not allowed, we used chloroquine tablets stolen from our own stocks after we'd recovered from malaria. We started by scratching letters of the alphabet on the prison walls and floors, starting with vowels, most of which Laurenti easily recognised; we discovered that he had attended school briefly in his village, and he could not continue because of shortage of fees. We got him to write these out and read them aloud as many times as he could. Sometimes he liked to chant them aloud, but we ensured that the 'blackboards' were rubbed out after use. After a few weeks we moved to a combination of consonants and vowels; soon he was able to recognise and write out simple words in the national language; we got him to write and learn about one hundred commonest words that we dictated to him.

The gamble we were taking was enormous. If the officers had found us teaching Mtemwende, we would have been mercilessly punished, summarily thrown into punishment cells, and lost the right to medical treatment for 'abusing the use of chloroquine tablets'. We were aware that we were engaged in a risky business, but life without risks, particularly in this prison, is meaningless. And anyway, some of us got a certain thrill in challenging the prison regime in this manner. Of course, after several months Mtemwende was able to write and read simple words, short sentences and small paragraphs in chiChewa. And before the year was out he was able to write on paper, using the pencil lead we had smuggled in for him. Soon he was able to read the simple stories of the chiChewa Bible we were allowed to keep.

The greatest day in Mtemwende's life must have been the time he wrote a letter to his wife under the supervision of prison guards, who had by then forgotten that he had walked into Mikuyu using ink on thumb as his signature on the pages of the prison's gate book. For after writing his letter he asked the guards if I could read what he had written to his wife. I refused, claiming it was a private matter; he insisted that I read it nonetheless. I recanted and was moved to tears at the impact of his delicate sentiments to his wife. When I endorsed and passed his letter as perfect, he shouted with delight: "I am unchained, liberated, freed; my wife won't believe it!" After his letter was taken to the offices, he thanked us 'from the bottom of my heart!' for the help we had given him.

I warned him not to expect the letter to reach his wife immediately. It would have to be vetted by the officer-in-charge here and the chief commissioner of prisons at the headquarters; it might take ages before his wife got it. This did not bother him now that the burden of ignorance had been lifted. We considered teaching Mtemwende to have been the most productive contribution we could have made to his life in prison. Helping him out during his epileptic attacks counted for nothing in comparison. The greatest achievement for *Gossip International* was to see Mtemwende write more notes to his wife, some of which we offered to send surreptitiously for him. I cannot imagine how happy she will be when her liberated husband offers to help in her bookkeeping on their tobacco farms.

The geese that left us gasping

You came in the middle of the night,
dazzled, skeletal, hungry, apologising
for what we would have to endure
when the epileptic fits you suffered
every month came on; indeed, each
time you began gasping for fresh air,
grunting like a dying beast, your legs
kicking, chest heaving – *feeling tight*,
you struggled to say, as we gathered
around, frantically fanning you with
rags, *foyas*, prayers, tears, fearing how
your ordeal might end each time. And
when you came round, we comforted
you with honeyed words, mere words:
don't worry about the pain you suffer,
it'll be just another memory one day,
we'll tell these jailors how we secretly
taught you how to read and write, with
chloroquine tablets stolen from our own
supplies, after recovering from bouts
of cholera, malaria, diarrhoea – until
you too learnt how to smuggle letters
to your wife. Now that you are one of
the twenty-two geese that criss-crossed
our blue sky three years ago, presaging
the release that's happened today, I say
forget the gaps and cracks in the bricks
or the cement floors where the scorpions
and other creeping crawlies poured out
to suck our blood at night and where we

hid our subversive bulletins to family,
friends and fighters for our liberation;
forget that embezzler of life president's
tobacco the security officers lied about;
for you are a noble bloke, relax, smirking
at the notes we smuggled out to be free.

Book Nine
Getting My Job Back

55
Mother's Smile

3 March 1991, Sunday. Martyrs' Day. Today this country celebrates the life of the nationalists who died to set us free from British colonial rule, although we are languishing in prison for unknown political reasons long after independence. Our Martyrs' Day begins with the antics of Mother wagtail. She is standing on the roof above the Ration Store, bobbing her head up and down, and stretching her fluffy wings, twirling around, chattering and dancing for the whole world to see. For Pingeni, Old Man Mkwanda and the others, Mother wagtail's tricks signal the arrival of visitors for those who are allowed visitors. For the others, Pingeni claims, the only visitors they can expect are political prisoners who will join us after breaking the unwritten laws of the land about what they should do or not do on Martyrs' Day. The drunks celebrating this special day by shouting their heads off; those who will be singing about what still remains to be achieved after independence; and the others who, for reasons best know to themselves, will refuse to keep quiet. These will be arrested or beaten up by the Party's youth league and young pioneers; and some will be brought to prisons for their disobedience. When Martyrs' Day comes around in this manner we often discuss, argue, even fight over who the true martyrs these days are; but today nobody in Mikuyu is in the mood to discuss the subject.

Apart from the prisoners that Mother wagtail's song and dance predicted today what baffles me is the meaning of the dream I had last night. I dreamt that Mother was smiling at me; she did not

345

utter a single word; she merely stared at me looking exceedingly happy, then suddenly disappeared; and I woke. On previous occasions when Mother smiled at me in dreams, it meant that she was wishing me well in the endeavours I was going to be engaged in. I recall two occasions when this happened: the first when I was waiting for my doctoral degree's viva voce at University College London; the second when I was going to read from my first book of poems at 'the first third world radical black international book fair' organised by John La Rose, chairman of race relations in London at the time. On both occasions I had been apprehensive of my performance, and seeing Mother smiling at me in a dream gave me hope and reassurance – and indeed in the end everything worked out fine for me, I performed very well. But today a part of me fears that her smile might not bring the assurance I need. And I miss Mother. I love her dearly. I do not know how she is coping in Mpokonyola village without her grandchildren, my wife and me. I have always marvelled at her resilience: how she managed to feed and clothe us, three children, in the absence of her husband; how she often brewed sweet beer and sold it around Kadango village in order to provide school fees for my sister, my brother and me. I treasure the stories she told us at the fireside too. Even now, when I write verses in my head, I recall how Mother strung together the various strands of events into her narratives – always concluding her tales on one final proverbial crunch. By recalling and re-examining the oral narratives she once created at the fireside, I can see how I should loop together my lines and ideas when crafting my verse.

Today I also recall how Mother choked with anger when the Special Branch brought me home shackled; how she challenged and embarrassed them to arrest and kill her instead of me. I was proud of Mother's gallant temper; I am still proud to be her son. I suppose that is why I was reluctant to go into exile, to follow the brave people who were frustrated by Banda's autocratic regime. I am a mother's kid and will remain so forever. I have always wanted to stay with Mother, to thank her for what she has done for her children. I still entertain the thought that when her time for passing comes around, I will buy her the best coffin in the world and take her to the grave myself – that's the least gesture I hope to make to pay for what she has done for us. And I have often wondered what I will bring Mother if I return home alive from here. I know she will appreciate a story. Although a story cannot adequately make up for the pain that my absence is causing her, I have always thought of bringing Mother a story, perhaps the best story of my prison experience so far – how TS tamed frogs in Mikuyu.

When I first arrived in Mikuyu I found Pingeni and other cellmates swearing by the frogs that TS had tamed to support their arguments or justify their statements. I did not understand what they saw in the story for them to adopt it as their language. And as everyone had their own version of the story, I was not certain which aspect was true, which was mere fantasy and whether the difference between the two mattered. I had seen frogs, toads, tadpoles in people's ponds around their houses. I had not heard of anyone who actually tamed them in the villages I knew intimately. I simply could not imagine anyone taming frogs, except perhaps in schools or colleges under laboratory conditions. The idea of taming frogs in the kitchen of his excellency's maximum detention prison sounded absurd for two reasons. If humans were uncomfortable living with fellow humans within these walls, and I dare say outside prison, what of living with frogs? And why would the relationship between man and frog choose to establish itself in the kitchen, a hostile environment for fragile creatures like frogs? Yet 'I swear by TS's frogs!' was the expression I frequently heard. When I asked TS whether he indeed tamed the creatures or if this was just another way of talking, he agreed that he did tame the creatures in Mikuyu but refused to dwell on the tale. It was as if the encounter was too painful for him, too traumatic to recount, and he did not understand how the story seemed to symbolise 'rebellious spirit' for some cellmates.

"It's simple, really," TS begins. "D'you remember the drainage running along the kitchen floor through the wall in the corner going out, which I showed you when you transferred to D4?"

"I do."

"Well, the water we pour down the drainage when we clean saucepans, mugs, buckets and plates has ostensibly formed a swamp outside the kitchen and frogs have made a home there. One day I saw a frog peeping into the kitchen from the drainage. I gestured to it, snapping my fingers as we do when we want to entice cats or dogs to come to us. The frog leapt forward. I smiled to myself. I couldn't believe what I saw. I pushed some termites, ants and leftovers of *nsima* in its direction and saw that it touched them. I wouldn't call it eating really, but some bits and pieces of the food I offered it disappeared down the drainage with it. I was amazed. I was not sure what frogs ate. When he came back several days later I recognised him. I snapped my fingers at him as I had done before. In he came – I assumed it was male though I know it could have been female – and I gave him whatever I had been gathering, some of which he took down the hole."

"How long did this go on for?" I interrupt.

"How long? Months I think. But it peeped through the drainage first, as if to ensure that I was around. Then one day three frogs peeped. I enticed them in. I fed them. Well, what seemed like feeding them!"

"TS, you are pulling my leg, right?" I ask.

"What does that mean?" He answers.

"Are you lying?" I clarify.

"I see, but man, why would I want to pull your leg?" he answers. "You haven't got much leg there to pull anyway, after losing so much weight in so short a time, wallowing in these stinking walls!" We laugh and laugh until tears begin to come.

"But I've not seen you feeding any frogs since I came here, so who divorced who?" I inquire. He is pensive at first, then continues:

"D'you recall the prison rule that says there shall be no fighting in prison or else?"

"I do."

"Well, I quarrelled with this fellow who comes from my home district and who had stayed here longer than me. It was about what you can or cannot reveal about the secret rituals of mask dances, I think. And we quarrelled so violently that it was as good as a fight. People had to intervene and separate us. Obviously, I won the verbal fight but my friend was so angry that the matter reached the officers. If it had not been for the intervention of the *Nyapalas* at the time we would have been transferred to another prison. We never forgave each other; you should have seen the tension that ruled D4. One day the fellow decided to hit back definitively; he must have been thinking about it for some time." TS falls into another trance.

"And what did he do?" I disrupt his meditative mood.

"Oh, I was quietly feeding my frog with his visitors when my countryman came along menacingly, clearly smarting for a fight. I ignored him and went back into the cell leaving my frogs feeding. When I returned, he was walking out of the kitchen gleaming with satisfaction. I instantly knew what he had done. He had picked up a bucket, dipped it into a huge pot where the water was boiling and simply poured the boiling water onto my visiting frogs, pushing the lot down the hole into the swamp outside. No frog has peeped through the drainage since. A few weeks after this, the bugger walked out of these stinking walls, free." TS stops. I see his eyes glazing with tears, pat him on the shoulder and invite him to a game of Ludo in the courtyard, all the while wondering at how deeply he felt about the story. That's the story I thought I would take home to Mother.

But when I am told that I have visitors at the office on Martyrs' Day, my first reaction is to recall Mother wagtail's song and dance above the Ration Store this morning. When I enter the visitors' room and see Mercy on the bench without the children; and when she greets me with tears trickling down her cheeks; I suddenly remember Mother's smile and begin to think that what I had feared might have happened. My heart starts to pound. I remember that when my family first visited me in prison, I had told my son to tell Mother that I would return home only after she had stopped crying. I now fear that she might have stopped crying forever. When I try to comfort Mercy, all she says between sobs is: "I do not know how it happened; Mother was fragile; but she did not appear to have been

349

suffering from any illness. And she was apparently joking with your cousin's daughter when she was going to school that day. Mother told the child that she would not find her at home when she returned from school. 'Who is coming to take you away?' The child asked. 'Nobody, I will be right here, but you will not find me!' Mother answered smiling. What upset me most is how the higher authorities refused to let me tell you earlier about her death. What crime have you committed not to be allowed to bury your own mother?" I touch her shoulders to comfort her, as I try to hide my own tears. And feeling totally crushed I tell her: "Let's pray for the peaceful repose of her soul; we'll meet her one day, where all good people are waiting for us."

Fr Pat's bulletin, which follows Mercy's visit, fills out the details of Mother's burial ceremony and what happened at Chirunga campus. Apparently Fr Pat courageously put up a notice at Chirunga campus to invite staff and students who wanted to attend Mother's funeral in Chikwawa district to sign up; they had hired the college vehicle to get them there. The list of names grew and grew until the page was full. Another sheet was hung. That too filled up in no time. "Soon the huge support we got embarrassed the college regime." Fr Pat said. "And for fear that the authorities in government, the Congress Party or other high places would hear about the support you were getting because of your mother's death, University Registrar Geoff Chipungu directed Chancellor College administration that the sheets be pulled down and the trip to Mother's funeral cancelled." In the end only Fr Pat braved it and went to Chikwawa district to bury Mother.

Your Tears Still Burn at My Handcuffs[*]

After that millet beer you brewed, Mother,
(In case Kadango Mission made something of
Another lake-son for the village to strut

---

[*] First appeared in *The Chattering Wagtails of Mikuyu Prison*, HEB, 1992.

About); and after that fury with the Special
Branch when I was brought home handcuffed –
How dare you scatter this peaceful house?

What has my son done? Take me instead, you
Insensitive men! You challenged their threat
To imprison you too as you did not *stop*

Your gibberish! – after that constant care,
Mother, I expected you to show me the rites
Of homing in of this political prisoner,

Perhaps with ground herbal roots dug by
Your hand and hoe, poured in some clay pot
Of warm water for me to suffuse, perhaps

With your usual wry smile about the herbs
You wished your mother had told you about.
Today, as I invent my own cleansing rites

At this return of another fugitive, without
Even dead roots to lean on, promise to bless
These lit candles I place on your head and

Your feet, accept these bended knees, this
Lone prayer offered among these tall unknown
Graveyard trees, this strange requiem mustered

From the tattered Catholic Choir of Dembo
Village. You gave up too early Mother: two
More months, and I'd have told you the story

Of some Nchinji upstart who tamed a frog at
Mikuyu prison, how he gave it liberty to invite
Fellow frogs to its wet niche, dearly feeding

Them insects and things; but how one day,
After demon bruises, his petulant cellmate
Threw boiling water at the niche, killing

Frog and visitor. And I'd hoped you'd gather
Some tale for me too, one better than your
Grand-daughter's about how you told her she

Would not find you on her return from school
That day. But we understand, after so many
Pointless sighs about your son's expected

Release, after the village ridicule of your
Rebellious breasts and sure fatigue of your
Fragile bones, your own minders, then your

Fear for us when the release did finally come –
You'd propose yet another exile, without you –
We understand you had to go, to leave us space

To move. Though now I wonder why I still
Glare at your tears burning at my handcuffs.

56

The Telephone Call

10 May 1991, Friday. I have been hurriedly invited to see officer-in-charge Sitima whom I find in an unusually animated mood. Instead of letting me squat before him on the cement floor, as he expects all political prisoners to do, he offers me a chair to sit on and before I begin to speculate why, he goes straight to the point: "Dr Mapanje, I've just received a telephone call from the southern region police headquarters in Blantyre. They are sending a driver at 1 p.m. to take you to see the higher authorities there. Could you go back to your cell, therefore, get something to eat and prepare to travel?" He stops. I am speechless. My heart, which missed a beat at the mention of the southern region police head-quarters, continues to throb faster and faster. I catch myself trembling though I am still glued to the chair like a trapped bird. When I followed commander BK to the office block, I was not feeling particularly buoyant about the outcome of this visit. I had heard my name reverberate within the prison walls that BK was calling at the gate, but it did not register that it would come to this. In January, two of our mates were invited to this office and in February twenty-two, making a total of twenty-four altogether. These having been eventually released from prison, nobody invited here after that had the luck of being released; despair is on the face of every prisoner. Must I now go back to the cells to prepare to travel as Sitima suggests? It's dangerous to ask about these matters, I know, but shouldn't I ask what's going on? I will ask... "I am sorry sir, but what, in your considered opinion, might this be about?" The words come out cautiously.

"To be honest with you, I don't know," he answers boldly and continues, "As you know, when the Special Branch arrest people, they bring them here; often they take them back to their offices as they please. But things are changing drastically; these days we are not even consulted about the state of health of our prisoners. So this could be anything." Sitima stops, breathes hard and watches me watching a gecko scuttling on the ceiling rafters above the president's portrait. He continues:

"Perhaps after your three-and-a-half years here, the security officers have now discovered what crime you committed and they are now inviting you for further charges in which case we'll welcome you back to this prison, which is meant for prisoners of that category. Perhaps they want to transfer you to Chichiri prison in Blantyre; in that case I suggest you take your tooth-brush, soap and sugar, as you may not find these easily there. This could also be your release, and if it is, remember you'll be leaving your friends behind; do not shout too loudly against government or your friends will never be released. And if the higher authorities are inviting you for something else . . . " he pauses and continues contemplatively, "Well, we'll all know where they'll have sent you as our man will come with you. We'll tell your wife and children that you were alive when you left Mikuyu; in that case, have courage and pray for yourself, for your friends here, for us and for the rest of this country. It's about 11 a.m. now, go back to your cell, eat and get ready to travel."

I could not have expected a more honest answer. Sitima's last point about leaving prison alive is particularly poignant. In this country political prisoners are often 'invited' to the police headquarters only to meet hit squads. That is what happened to the famous 'gang of four', who left this prison in May 1983 only to be mercilessly clubbed to death afterwards. I find the officer's last words hard to take, coming from a man in his position; but I am pleased that he trusts me with what he has just told me about what goes on in this country; I can only admire his candour in warning me in advance about this final possibility. Back in D-block, I tell the twenty-five or so cellmates scattered in cells D2,

D3 and the courtyard to follow me into D1, if they want to hear my story, which I repeat to them and conclude gallantly: "So, if this should turn out to be my release, dear friends, I promise to fight for your liberation with all my energy and might. I don't know how, but I'll do it. If I'm going to be murdered, well, tough luck, but you'll eventually know, and please pray for me. Yet whether this is about my release, transfer or death, I suggest that you continue to pray: God is listening to our prayers; we've all witnessed the two releases that have happened when we least expected them; there will be more where those have come from, and don't ask me how I know. I repeat, in times like these, go on with the choirs, the prayers, and the struggle for our freedom, God is listening."

Frackson Zgambo suddenly intervenes: *"Let us all kneel down, bow our heads and pray: God of our fathers, you who created the heavens and the universe, listen to us your troubled sinners. Almighty Father, we fall on our knees to implore you; that the journey our friend is about to make should be productive; it should lead to his release not to his death. We know, Father, that if you release our friend, we too will be released. And give us courage, Almighty Father, help us to contain the emptiness we will suffer when our friend is gone. Through Jesus Christ, your son, we pray. Amen."* The general 'amen' that follows is so deep, touching and genuine that I feel God has heard our prayer. Mkwanda wishes me good times abroad – as far as he is concerned I am not going to my death, and I would be foolish to hang around having experienced Banda's brutality and that of his toadies. Disi and Kadango wish me well too – I should not think of death, they say. Alex Mataka, Sylvester Phiri and the other cellmates wish me well and disperse, each to his own speculations as to what might happen to me in Blantyre. And taking me aside, TS says he wants to give me the last rites according to the Catholic Church, before I meet the Kadzamira-Tembo death squads, to which everybody laughs with discomfort. But I know that TS merely wants to remind me of the route I should follow to get to his family in Mtchinji district, where they will show me

355

the way into Zambia across the long Malawi-Zambia border, should I need to fly away – TS and I have rehearsed these routes *ad nauseum* in the three-and-a-half years I have been with him. And Dan Mhango, the only other member of our team remaining, reminds me of the importance of controlling my anger at police station interviews, if I want to be released. I tell them what they have stressed to me for my survival these years; I urge them to continue the struggle to survive in order to beat Banda's autocratic regime. There simply is no other way. With disquiet I remind them about how the 'gang of four' died; but TS quickly dismisses my point, and with tears glazing his eyes, prays that this journey should not lead to another unnecessary death. Frackson joins us and declares:

"*Imwe ba*, Doc, be rest assured that what is left of *Gossip International* will continue to speculate about the campaigns for our liberation you are going to be involved in and what prospects there will be for the eventual liberation of all political prisoners in Malawi." The sound of a vehicle entering the prison comes faster than we had anticipated. TS, Kadango and Disi quickly climb on one another's shoulders to peep through the little window near the ceiling. They confirm that the famous grey Land Rover has arrived and is parked in the little roundabout outside the prison's office. Soon commander BK comes to Block-D courtyard gate and calls out my name; I give my mates one sweeping glance, as they wave me goodbye, wishing me well. My clothes feel strange and stuffy after three years, seven months, sixteen days and more than twelve hours today. The police officer signs me out in the prison's gate book. Officer-in-charge Sitima offers me my two postcards from The Hague and London respectively, shakes my hand firmly and wishes me well as would a father to his son going out on a long mission. The police officer gently touches my shoulder and leads me to the vehicle standing outside. The driver's face beams with recognition – something tells me this must be my nephew's friend. The officer, his driver and I take the Land Rover's front seats. The prison's commander takes the back seat; the engine starts; we're off.

The smell of petrol and of the fresh dust on the dirt road immediately hit my nose. I feel dazed by the bright mix of colours of the landscape before me, and doped by the various smells of earth and vegetation. The flames of the forests, the purpling jacarandas, the mango trees, the yellow paw-paws hanging delicately, the acacias, the tall grass on garden patches and the dirty wooden bridge as we head for The Turf Club – everything looks and feels weird, as confusing thoughts about the true nature of my destination begin to concern me. I have not seen this landscape for three-and-a-half years; I can see it now and wonder if they are really going to release me, transfer me to another prison or to kill me. The landscape, which looks familiar and strange at once as crowds of people on foot, bicycles and trucks whizz past, provides no clue where I am headed. I find myself constantly rubbing my eyes to give the objects I see proper focus – I would have gone blind if I had stayed in that dungeon another month, I tell myself. The Turf Club has not moved from where I left it, Kamoto's Home Garage is no more, and Matawale Night Club looks derelict. As we approach Zomba plateau, the massive range of mountains to my right still looks awe-inspiring and colourful, spotted in brown and green patches of vegetation. Silver brooks still trickle down the plateau's grey rocks as they have done from time immemorial to become the rivers we know below. We join the main highway to Blantyre, turn left opposite Zomba Inn, and soon we cross Mulungusi then Mponda bridges. The narrow colonial streets of Zomba town are still draped in purple jacarandas and flames of the forest – I remember the woman at Zomba market whose vegetables and fruit I never paid for – I decide to check her out and pay what I owe her at the earliest opportunity should I live through this ordeal. We cross the nondescript Bwaila bridge, past Zomba Memorial Tower and the barbed wire redbrick wall of Zomba Central both on my right; the ugly buildings of crumbling Zomba General Hospital are on my left; we cross Likangala bridge, St Peter's Seminary on the left, Zomba Catholic Secondary School on the right, and we are on the open road to Blantyre.

The huts of Three-Miles village in their mix of mud, brick, rusty iron roofing and grass-thatch look stunted after three-and-a-half years. We speed past rattling and booming African rhythms of *rumba* and *simanje-manje* in the bars and bottle stores of the township slums; the hustle and bustle of people from the roadside markets; men with heavy sacks of cassava, sugarcane or charcoal on their bicycles, women with bundles of firewood on their heads and babies on their backs. Major Anderson's blue gum trees at Seven Miles village look taller than I had known them; I wonder if the major is still alive; I should have interviewed him to tell us how Nyasaland soldiers rescued him during the world war, causing him to decide to die here in gratitude. I missed these roadside markets. How can they go on selling their sugarcane, tomatoes, sweet potatoes, vegetables, paw-paws, cassava, fresh maize cobs, cucumber, pumpkins, clay pots and wooden curios as if the world never changes? Is this the world that Banda and his vicious cabal did not want me to see again? How evil is that! After crossing Thondwe and Namadzi bridges our vehicle squeals to a stop beside Mbulumbuzi market, near Chiradzulu Mountain, where we nearly killed somebody's goats crossing the road as we drove at break-neck speed to the southern region police head-quarters for my interrogation about four years ago. Today the Special Branch officer turns to me: "Do you mind if the driver buys boiled groundnuts for us – I am starving!" "I don't mind," I answer, and begin to wonder why he is asking me, the prisoner. Suddenly the driver's name rings a bell: that's the name nephew Fred Ziyabu mentioned when he came to visit me in prison; we both look at each other and quickly look away as if suddenly caught in the act of recognition.

I am sure that he knows that I know that he is my nephew's friend. I am sure that he remembers that he told my nephew about what he had overheard from his masters about my imprisonment, suggesting that it was time for my nephew to apply for a permit to visit me in prison. After bringing the boiled groundnuts, my nephew's friend tempts me with some. I turn down the offer and justify myself thus: I do not know where I am going; the nuts could have been poisoned beforehand; I want to die properly – in truth I am so scared by the officer's casualness and the driver's ease that I feel enormous unease myself.

57

My Second Birthday

MacWilliam Lunguzi was chief of security and intelligence services when I was arrested more than three years ago. I knew there was something unusual about the way he used his power. It was as if he were trying to impress me to accept him as a possible future leader when everyone was hoping to rule the country after the dictator's departure from the political scene. Whether the Kadzamira-Tembo faction of Banda's inner circle would let him fulfill his political ambition, I was not sure. But something told me to fear for his life: he was the staunchest supporter of Banda's presidency; he was not in the Kadzamira-Tembo camp of the country's security and intelligence service. This was clear even when he claimed he did not know why I was arrested and promised to find out and fight for me as he had direct access to the life president himself; he did not need to prove anything to justify his action; he almost felt guilty for letting me enter prison without proper reason. Lunguzi radiated power; the stories I had heard about him from the political prisoners who knew him helped to change my mind about his brutality. It is then that I realise he was serious when he suggested that I say three Hail Marys every day for the life president not to forget about me in prison. And I had never prayed so hard in my life, though often I skipped days and weeks without praying when I thought about my family and the hopelessness of my state.

Anyway, having been recently promoted as head of the country's entire police force, Lunguzi has found it necessary to invite me to see him today. What's up his sleeve this time around,

I have no idea. As I step into his office he smiles broadly at me, extends his hand, offers me a solid handshake, tells me to sit down in the chair opposite his huge desk, then gestures the police officer and the prison guard, who brought me here, to leave us alone. My armpits begin to pour out sweat as they had done when he dragged me into his office immediately after my interrogation, more than three-and-a-half years ago. I do not know what to say. His telephone suddenly rings, he picks up the receiver and talks. Some bank manager is trying to persuade him to take a loan for one of his tobacco farms. He firmly declines the offer, repeating that he does not really need a loan for his farm; he had a wonderful crop without a loan last year. After putting the receiver down, he apologies for the interruption. I begin by congratulating him warmly on his promotion – intending essentially to shake off my nervousness and fear – but he gratefully accepts my felicitations and welcomes me to his office with a question:

"Dr Mapanje, how are you?"

"As healthy as a prisoner can be, sir," I answer carefully.

"I understand," he says, with some concern and continues, "Well, Dr Mapanje, it may have taken me long but if you remember the last time we met I made a pledge that I'd bring your case to his excellency's attention myself as I had direct access to him. I want to report that from the time I promised you I've been trying hard to persuade his excellency to have you released. But every time I put your name up for consideration, the H.E. himself either refused to sign my memo or he sent me out of his office empty-handed. Very frustrating indeed. Do you remember Blaise Machila and George Mtafu released from your prison in January this year?"

"I do, sir."

"Well, initially I proposed five names, including yours, for the life president to consider releasing in January." He pulls out his drawer and says: "Here, read this."

He offers me the memo he wrote to the president on the matter; I see clearly the five names he had recommended. The first is that of Mr Willy Lyton Masiku, the popular central region chief of the agriculture board, ADMARC, allegedly imprisoned for being John Tembo's business rival. The second is Marango Banda's, the famous broadcaster who was imprisoned for choosing to attend an Anglican women's international conference in Birmingham, UK, instead of attending Cecilia Kadzamira's CCAM seminar in her home district of Nkhata Bay. The third is Blaise Machila, who was imprisoned for harassing Zimani Kadzamira about my whereabouts. The fourth is George Mtafu, the neurosurgeon who was imprisoned after attending Banda's meeting of senior government bureaucrats at Sanjika Palace. The last is my name. Lunguzi inquires:

"Dr Mapanje, what do you see in the margin against each of the first four names I recommended to his excellency?"

"I see the word 'approved' against each name, followed by his excellency's initials and date, sir."

"And what do you see against your name?"

After checking his memo again I answer: "I see the word 'never', sir, followed by the president's initials and date."

"Thank you, Dr Mapanje, but I am sorry to tell you that at the January release, and at other times before that, you were a political prisoner 'never' to be released from prison according to the higher authorities in this country – and to date I do not understand why. And in February when I released about twenty-two of your friends at Mikuyu, if you recall, and more than one hundred political prisoners from other prisons, I did not bother to put forward your name. But this morning" – my heart leaps at the implication of his use of the word *but* – "today, May 10 1991, I confronted his excellency the life president again."

He pulls out another memo from his drawer and decides to read it aloud to me: "As his excellency's official birthday is about to be celebrated on 14 May, and as it is the custom for heads of state throughout the world to release a selected number of political prisoners on their official birthdays, we, your excellency's trusted police service, propose that in your wisdom, your excellency might like to consider releasing, at your forth-coming birthday, the following political prisoners, whom we believe to have repented of the wrongs they were believed to have committed against your person and the state. We are sorry to have to say, however, that the list we provide has only one name, Dr Jack Mapanje. If your excellency the life president, the father and founder of this nation, should feel pleased to release Dr Jack Mapanje, we, your most trusted police force will ensure that Dr Mapanje is under your excellency's most dependable and strict surveillance at all times." Lunguzi passes the memo to me to confirm for myself what he's been reading to me. I see my name right in the middle of the memo. After a short while he asks again:

"Dr Mapanje, what do you see in the margin of my most recent memo to his excellency?"

Ha! My heart jumps in disbelief.

"I see the word 'approved' sir; and it's followed by the president's initials and today's date. I also see a big full stop, sir."

"Thank you for your sharp observation, Dr Mapanje. As for the big full stop, his excellency's pen paused there today, as it has always done on similar occasions. At that point he must have been considering whether to cancel his signature, give me back my memo and throw me out of his office, which he has done on other occasions before, or to go ahead and sign my memo. But after a minute of pondering, the H.E finally lifted his pen, put it back into its inkpot, and gave me back my memo signed and dated. Dr Mapanje, may I take this opportunity to declare that it has pleased his excellency the life president of the Republic of Malawi, the Ngwazi, Dr H. Kamuzu Banda to have you released from Mikuyu prison forthwith and without preconditions. And this, I think, is a miracle. I repeat, Dr Mapanje, this is a miracle. Therefore, go home to your wife and children at Ntcheu district hospital before his excellency changes his mind. And let me categorically assure you that you will not be under our surveillance. What I promised his excellency is our way of talking to him as civil servants. Let me repeat, therefore, you are being released without preconditions, Dr Mapanje. Please accept my congratulations and that of my police service. But before I let you go, I want to ask you one or two questions: if you don't mind, Dr Mapanje, who are you?"

I am totally thrown. I remember this to be the question his boss asked at my interrogation three-and-a-half years ago. Why are they obsessed with this question? What precisely do they want to know about me that they do not already know?

"Do you mean you do not know who I am, sir?" I ask, visibly embarrassed.

"No, Dr Mapanje, what I mean is we've imprisoned tens of thousands of people in this country, some more distinguished than yourself, but we've never had the same amount of trouble as we've had over your case. People who supported you came from unexpected corners of the globe. That's why I ask who you are. And your answer will not change the position of your release: I am only enquiring for my own information, to enlighten my police force and myself. You see, Dr Mapanje, there were so many versions of the causes of your imprisonment, in the university and outside it, that my staff were surprised and often confused. We still do not know what happened to you in the university or who reported what to the H.E. So, tell me, who are you?"

"Look, sir, I do not know who I really am myself, but I suppose you could say, I am only a linguist who happened to write poetry; in truth, I am an ordinary university teacher; that's who I think I am, sir."

"Thank you for your co-operation, Dr Mapanje, and let me take this opportunity to inform you that at this point in time, only three people in the whole wide world know that you are being freed – his excellency the life president, myself and yourself. Nobody else knows that you are leaving prison today. I repeat Dr Mapanje, people will hear about your release only after I've told our embassies, high commissions and representatives throughout the world that you've been released. So, go back to Mikuyu now; collect your property; stay in Zomba town at the rest house or with a friend tonight. And tomorrow, get bus warrants from Zomba eastern division police headquarters to take you home to your wife and children at Ntcheu district hospital."

"But if you don't mind, sir, I've already taken my property."

"What? Did you know that you were coming here to be released?"

"Oh no, sir, of course not. You see, sir, when you invite us to see you this far, prison officers always recommend that we take our property with us, in case you want us transferred to other prisons. In fact, what I am wearing and the little bag I am carrying is all the property I possessed in prison, sir."

"I understand," he says in a meditative mood as I continue:

"And I have a friend in Zomba town, sir, where I can spend the night. He'll take me to the eastern division police headquarters tomorrow morning to get the travel warrants that you suggest, sir."

"Good! And finally, Dr Mapanje, let me take this opportunity to tell you that his excellency the life president has given you permission to go back to your job in the university with immediate effect. If the university authorities are not sure about your official clearance, ask them to ring or write to me. I'll give them the life president's official clearance. And if, for some reason, they do not want to re-employ you, his excellency has given you clearance to work anywhere in this country or anywhere abroad. Go home now. And please accept our congratulations."

"Thank you very much, for releasing me, sir."

"There is only one other matter that I need to clarify with you, Dr Mapanje, and I hope you'll appreciate my intention in this. Because my police force did not know the precise nature of the crime you committed in the university, from now on you should send me a copy of every job application you make. Do not consider this part of our surveillance on your activities, Dr Mapanje, I only want to ensure that my service and I can defend you better in future. As for your employment outside this country, I have only one very final suggestion to make. I suggest that you do not rush into joining human rights organisations such as PEN International, Amnesty International, Africa Watch, Human Rights Watch and others. By and by you will understand the reasons for this; otherwise, once again, please accept our congratulations on your being free."

When Release Began Like a Biblical Parable[*]

When the prison gates opened for apostle Simon
Peter who was sleeping, chained double, guarded
By four squads of four Roman soldiers each; when
The angel's blinding flash tapped his quiescent side
The decisive chains on his blistered wrists suddenly
Dropping; when he belted up, the soundless sandals
Springing as he gathered his cloak around him on his
Way out; why, why did Peter not believe the vision
Until the last solid bar gave way on the Lord's own
Terms, the angel abandoning him unfettered outside,
Alone, as the Rock, liberated from Herod's clutches
Returned to his praying Antioch Church, stunned?

And why should this firefly at the back of another Land
Rover whose bleached canvas stutters in the whining
Wind speeding nowhere, believe; why must I believe
Minded by these nervous guards as my Special Branch
Driver ravages his boiled groundnuts without a wink;
Why should my crumb of Lifebuoy, my toothbrush with-
out its teeth, my toothpaste flattened clean, this partner
Of hole Levi's shoes, this polythene kilo of sugar (for
Porridge wherever I am going said officer-in-charge) –
Can this be the reprieve of this flustered Peter, the clod,
Your late disciple, Lord, without the staff to lean on?
Let the dazzling dust of distant familiar mountains,
Let these eternally dry maize fields, the truncated leaf-
less mango trees that feel taller than blue gums (Your
'Ephpheta', Lord, brings such clash of memories I did
Not dream I would ever see again!), let peculiar colours
Soak up then, let the Land Rover's rails rattle as I blink
At my officer-in-charge: We do not know what it is,
As you know, nobody tells us anything; but if it's transfer

---

[*] First appeared in *Skipping Without Ropes*, Bloodaxe Books, 1998.

To another prison, take your sugar; if further questing,
Further charges, we'll welcome you back; if release, best
Wishes, remember the friends you leave behind; other-
wise, we'll note the Gate Book names of your assailants
For your wife and children or, for posterity, good luck!

58

Mercy's Little House

When I knock on David Kerr's door late that Friday afternoon, it is Tamya his daughter who explodes with disbelief, shock and delight all at once.

"Uncle, is this you or a ghost of you I see?"

"Both!"

We laugh and laugh at this extraordinary meeting. She offers me the sofa to sit down on, dashes to the fridge to get a bottle of orange juice, pours me a glass, herself a glass and sits on the other sofa, then she suddenly wonders:

"Uncle, you must be hungry; should I perhaps warm you a shepherd's pie?"

"Yes, please, Tamya," I eagerly answer.

The thought of a warm shepherd's pie reminds me of TS, Dan Mhango and the other twenty or so cellmates I have left at Mikuyu. Standing up, looking through the window and casting my eyes past the woods of Zomba plateau to the distant valley, I spot the beams of light around Mikuyu, about seven miles away – the prison is already alight. I imagine what's left of *Gossip International* taking stock of the events that have led to my release. I hear them quarrelling, even fighting over the most plausible interpretation of my release. I want to laugh but my eyes have tears instead. We suffered together; we were bonded; I feel guilty for being freed alone. I console myself with the promise that I'd fight for their liberation, although I still do not know how. As I begin to recover from the shock of the moment, I ask Tamya if I could phone up her auntie at Ntcheu district hospital. Mercy does not believe what she hears: she does not believe it's me, though she lives in hope it will be true one day and rings off. Before it gets completely dark, I take a brief stroll around the house to remind myself of the little brook that used to run beside the house, the bridge I knew down the road, the surrounding rocks, plants and flowers that Tamya's mum loved to tend, and Berlings Kaunda's house further down, surrounded by his wood carvings and marvellous stone artwork.

When David Kerr walks into his house, and sees the political prisoner to whom he has been smuggling food, medicines and bulletins for more than three-and-a-half years sitting on his sofa, enjoying his shepherd's pie and sipping his orange juice, he is stunned. Our handshake is firm, the hug long, followed by a sudden outburst of laughter and tears. What have we done to get ourselves liberated? We ask in our different ways looking into each other's eyes in disbelief. Another hug, followed by another outburst of laughter and tears. David rushes for the telephone receiver to ring Fr Pat who is officially on holiday in the Republic of Ireland, he says, but he does not get through. Fr Pat could be anywhere by now – Harare, Dublin or Rome. He tries phoning Landeg White in York and fails to get through. Frustrated, he declares he will try again at night when the lines are clearer and those who listen in have gone to bed. I ask him not to panic but to sit down and hear my story of liberation. We are both too excited to know where to begin. An idea hits David. We should not bother about the eastern division police headquarters travel warrants that inspector general Lunguzi suggested I get tomorrow. If we can dash to the petrol station before it closes, the car will have enough petrol to take us to Ntcheu district hospital and back today. "Let's do it now!" he says. I can't wait.

On our way to Ntcheu I find myself wondering. Am I really free, truly liberated, indeed unchained, emancipated, discharged, whatever, from the notorious Mikuyu maximum detention prison? I praise the Lord but still do not believe it. No wonder the inspector general thought this a miracle. When I tell David about Lunguzi's warning that I must take my time to join human rights organisations, we laugh and laugh until I rub tears from my eyes. The inspector general would probably have gone berserk if he had discovered that it was David who sent the first note about my arrest to Amnesty International in London. Soon we begin to joke about the motels, bars and bottle stores we once frequented on both sides of the road from Zomba to Ntcheu, noting the obvious fortunes of some and demise of others. I resist the temptation to stop at any of them. After Balaka township, I put my head through the window; lo and behold the glory of God through the shining moon and glittering stars! I involuntarily shout: "Look! The Moon! I'd forgotten the moon existed!" When I tell David about the fights we used to have at prison spy-holes after lock-up as we sought a glimpse of the moon, he falls apart with more laughter and says: "This time you'll have the whole moon to yourself; you'll watch it all the time!" I wonder whether I should stop the car, get out and see the moon properly, or am I getting too carried away for nothing? Who first coined the expression 'over the moon'? That definitely seems the most appropriate expression to describe my state of mind right now – the event is later to become the subject of one of David's finest poems.

When my son Lika recognises Uncle David's car outside the house, he ignores the darkness and rushes at us with excitement and overflowing joy, grabs my hand firmly and immediately asks why I have taken so long to come back home: "You promised to come early when we visited you in prison," he says. "Never mind why," I reply, "I am here as I promised I would be, aren't I?" "But you should have been here last month when I celebrated my ninth birthday," he says. Mercy welcomes us to her Ntcheu district nurses' house with an unbelieving grin and a deep sigh of relief, her eyes swiftly blinking and tears streaming down her cheeks. She runs to her little kitchen to check if there's enough firewood on the brazier – but I know she doesn't want me to see her tears. The three of us huddle together at the little entrance to the kitchen, as if we were basketball players, whispering to one another about our next move. David looks away, leaving us to ourselves; then he says he cannot wait for tea; he must get back home to phone up our friends, compatriots, colleagues and human rights organisations about my release. He solemnly declares his private mission finally and dutifully accomplished. "Amen", I answer, thanking him enormously. And as he drives off we feel we'll never thank him enough, nor Fr Pat, Landeg and those they have involved in my liberation.

When aMbewe walks into the kitchen with a bundle of chopped wood, he is shocked to see me. "Have you really come back, Dad?" he exclaims with delight and wonder, not knowing what to ask. "I have," I reply, "and thank you very much for looking after my family during the ordeal I put you all through." He says I should thank Mai Mercy instead, for taking him in as one of the family. For many years, this young man cooked for us in Zomba, and when I was arrested he offered to leave his family there and come here to stay with Mercy and the children without payment, and regardless of the danger of being associated with whatever political crimes had led to my imprisonment – he is another of the many unsung heroes of my liberation. Mercy asks Lika to run to Agnes Kaposa, her friend and neighbour several houses away, and to tell her that Dad's back; he gladly sprints away.

"So, you're home permanently?" Mercy begins her proper greeting and, without waiting for a reply, she walks to her tiny kitchen again, stokes the brazier with aMbewe's wood, and blows her breath into the fire to start the flames. aMbewe takes over and proposes that he cook the evening meal as Mercy tells me how they survived while I was away. Her house is humble. The living room is graced by a set of chairs locally made when she moved here. The shower, the toilet and the tap of cold water are outside. No hot water tap. She has to boil the water on the charcoal brazier and pour it in a big tin basin where we take our baths. We are back to the beginnings of time. The first main bedroom is about three paces by three, the second about two-and-a-half paces by two. Dasiyano, my late brother's son, and Chilungamo, Mercy's brother's son, who stay with her, are temporarily away in Mangochi and Salima districts respectively. Normally they would sleep in the bigger bedroom with aMbewe, while Mercy and Lika slept in the smaller bedroom. Obviously, when Dasiyano and Chilungamo are around and our two daughters, Judith and Lunda return 'home' from their boarding schools, the house gets crowded. I recall the single cells of the New Building Wing of Mikuyu, and understand why Mother could not have stayed with them. Lika returns and switches on the radio: "To celebrate Dad's return," he declares. We instantly recognise the croaking disjointed voice of the man reading the English eight o'clock evening news – the batteries are going – it's John Asani's voice. And this leads to a discussion of the whereabouts of the family of his dad – my cousin. We are getting back to reality. Mercy's mother and uncle at Chipoka and her sister, brothers and their families are well. Otherwise, she is anxious to provide the details of Mother's death. I tell her to hang on; we'd discuss that later.

A knock on the door. Agnes Kaposa walks in radiating warmth. Greetings of tenderness are exchanged all round. She tells me Mercy has been wonderful. She has many friends around Ntcheu district hospital, some of whom have formed a prayer group, which fasts, discusses the Bible, sings and prays particularly for my release. Agnes enthuses: "Last week, Mercy and I began our own programme of extra fasting and extra prayer, meeting in my living room. Now we know God has answered our prayers," she concludes jubilantly. I feel humbled to realise that while compatriots, colleagues, friends and the world's human rights organisations have been fighting for my liberation, these ordinary people have been fasting and praying for me too. I am convinced about what I have all along believed, that there's a listening God out there. Then Agnes invites us all to come and sit with her on the mat surrounded by the chairs. She tells us to close our eyes as she says a simple prayer, thanking and praising God for my release. She opens the Bible at Psalm 126, and begins to read aloud:

> *When the Lord brought us back*
> *to Jerusalem,*
> *it was like a dream!*
> *How we laughed, how we sang for joy!*

Then the other nations said about us,
"The Lord did great things for them"
Indeed, he did great things for us;
how happy we were!
Lord, make us prosperous again,
just as the rain brings water back to
dry river–beds.
Let those who wept as they sowed their
seed,
gather the harvest with joy!
Those who wept as they went out
carrying the seed
will come back singing for joy,
as they bring in the harvest.

Tears run down my cheeks as she links the story of the liberation of the Israelites to mine. It is as if her thanksgiving prayer has been offered for the return of all those imprisoned or forced into exile since independence. I feel deeply moved. I thank Agnes for her solidarity in prayer and deed with Mercy throughout my incarceration. The evening meal of delicious *chambo* and *nsima* is punctuated by stories of pain, tears, joy and laughter.I promise Agnes I will not be a naughty boy again. We laugh with all our hearts. With tears of delight, Mercy explains the desperate visits she made to my friend Revd Dr Saindi Chiphangwi of Zomba Scottish Presbyterian Church immediately after my arrest, then she records her restless encounters with my principal, the university office and the eastern division police headquarters. When she went to ask Kadzamira why I was arrested and where I had been dumped, he told her he had nothing to do with my arrest, she should ask the police who arrested me; when she went to the eastern division police headquarters with the principal's reply, they told her they did not know what crime I had committed: they were only directed to arrest me; the truth was with my principal and university office authorities. Mercy paced in vain from Chancellor College to the university office to eastern division police headquarters and back.

Each 'higher authority' she met claimed it was the other 'higher authority' who knew what was going on and where I was. Mercy concludes: "I was very frustrated; I did not know who to turn to, who to believe and what to do; only God saved us from our trouble."

I soon realise that my absence brought the kind of nightmares I had not anticipated for my family, relatives, friends and other unlikely people who fought silent wars, often using unconventional methods. My nephews James Nyilenda, Fred Ziyabu and Marshal Nsonga and their families; Mercy's brothers, especially Cuthbert and Bernard Chandiyamba and their families; friends like Joe Masinga, Martin and Thomas Kanyuka, Justus Mlia, James Seyani, David Munthali, Gerry Patterson, Steve Chimombo and their families – these and many others prayed for me, felt helpless, betrayed, upset and often totally impotent. Some of the most heart-rending tales come several days later when members of Mercy's prayer group visit us. I learn to my horror the frustration that my family, relatives and friends suffered at the hands of the Kadzamira-Tembo clan, who told the Special Branch who was to get permits to visit me and when, and who was not. In order to get me freed some of my relatives and close friends resorted to visiting traditional healers, medicine men and medicine women, herbalists and other practitioners in these trades found in Zomba, Blantyre, Mulanje, Thyolo, Chiradzulu, Ntcheu, Mangochi, Lilongwe, Mchinji and Salima. Mercy and some close relatives and friends were made to drink weird herbal concoctions on my behalf, and to dance in the glaring moonlight, naked, shouting at Banda, Tembo and the Kadzamiras to leave me alone in body and spirit. Others had tattoos cut on their thighs, buttocks, foreheads, shoulders, arms and between their breasts by the medicine people they visited, forcing them to dance facing the luminous Milky Way.

Other medicine men told Mercy, my nephews and their friends to throw their precious coins and paper money in running mountain brooks after bathing in medicinal waters, at dawn, chanting their wishes that I should be unchained, and soon. When one medicine man, living between Zomba and Blantyre, discovered that it was president Banda and his cabal whom I was presumed to have wronged, he demanded that the medicine-seekers leave his premises immediately. He claimed that his medicines were too weak to fight the Mozambique snakes, charms and other poisons, which protected Banda and his self-styled 'royal family'. Today, when my family, relatives, friends and colleagues recount the encounters and horrors, the anxieties, humiliation and shame that they suffered to get me out of Banda's prison, they seem so farfetched.

Tamya's Shepherd's Pie (10 May 1991)*

Child, this shepherd's pie you offer this starved
stomach this late Friday afternoon, this china and

stainless knife and fork you place in his hands, this
glass of orange, your civil genuflection, your voice

so delicate and your wonder at the return of another
denuded memory witnessing the purple Jacarandas

strewn on the rocks and avenues of Zomba Plateau;
my dear child, do not ask where this bundle of blunt

tissue before you comes from nor where it proceeds;
having left behind other unsullied souls fumbling for

breath and gnashing clods of rubbery weevil-ridden
pigeon peas from crumpled enamel mugs and maggot-

riddled maize *nsima* on holed rusty plates, besides,
denied the luxury of cutlery in those flaming beacons

---

* First appeared in *Skipping Without Ropes*, Bloodaxe Books, 1998.

of prison visible at night from where you stand, this
bundle of memories is not your Peter knocking on his

disciples' church door nor Lazarus resurrected, this is
your Mlungusi Avenue rebel uncle returning from

that eternal abomination to which they slung him –
Could I give your auntie the fright of a lifetime call?

59

Getting My Job Back

13 May 1991, Monday. I have decided to visit the university office to report for duties. I want my job back. I am nervous and do not know what to expect now that I have acquired the stigma of a political prisoner. I praise the Lord, therefore, when I discover it is Angela Nazombe, my colleague's wife, who is my first point of contact. She is the university registrar's secretary. I am excited to see her. She is delighted to see me. And after offering her my belated congratulations on their wedding, and sharing a joke or two about the number of children they now have, I confirm that it's to Geoff Chipungu that I must report. Angela informs her boss about the 'special visitor' who would like to see him without proper appointment. He says, fine. She opens his office door and let's me in; Chipungu opens his mouth wide open, obviously surprised, perhaps even shocked:

"Jack, is this really you I see? What are you doing here? Where have you come from? When were you released from prison? Who released you? Is this the previous head of English who stands before me?"

"Geoff, you ask too many questions, how do you expect me to answer them all at once? It's me that you see before you, my friend, and I have only one question in return: Geoff, when did you become the UR, the university registrar?"

"After you were gone, of course."

"Really? Imagine that! But congratulations."

"Thank you."

"And Geoff, may I ask again?"

"Do."

"Is this promotion from the university finance officer that you were when I was arrested?"

"Jack, don't you start; some people never change, do they?"

"OK, OK, OK, I am sorry; I won't ask another question."

"Anyway, what d'you take? Coffee or tea? No? Tea? Coffee? No? Nothing at all? Come on! Don't be shy! We won't poison you," he says, and I wonder where the thought of poison came from. He shouts to his secretary for one coffee and continues:

"But seriously Jack, sit down and tell me how you are and why you are here."

"I'm fine. I'm here because it pleased his excellency the life president, the Ngwazi Dr H. Kamuzu Banda, father and founder of the Malawi nation..."

"Yes, yes, yes, we know about all that."

"...to have me released from Mikuyu prison. Inspector general Lunguzi tells me his excellency is delighted for me to come back to teach in his university if the university still requires my services. I've come, therefore, to get my job back."

"You are joking."

"Geoff, who would want to joke about that after imprisonment? Everyone knows how dangerous joking is around here."

"But why were *we* not warned about your release and your coming?"

"Don't ask me about that, my friend; if the chancellor of this university and head of state of this country has released me and allowed me to report here, who am I to dispute his decision? Ask I.G. Lunguzi who has given me the H.E.'s official clearance to return to work, if you need to confirm my story."

"But neither the chairman of university council nor his members are aware that you've been released, as far as I know. I mean, you know that I cannot act on my own, Jack, I have no power to give you back your job; I will have to get instructions from above, from the powers that be."

"Geoff, I did not, for a moment, expect you to act alone unless things have changed drastically since I was here last."

378

"Thank you for your understanding. So, Jack, you've really been released, eh?"

"Yes, Geoff, the chancellor and head of state, the H.E. himself has had me released."

"Well, well, well; welcome back – but as I say, I will have to tell the authorities about your wish to return to your job; come back in two or three days' time."

He shows me the door. I thank Angela and leave for Ntcheu hospital nurses' quarters. Mercy is puzzled and rather disturbed that the chairman of the university council did not know that I had been released. I begin to understand why Lunguzi repeated that there were only three people who knew about my release. Banda and his chief of police had not told anyone else in the university about my being released in order to protect me – these two must have known, therefore, that the Kadzamira-Tembo faction of his henchpeople were responsible for my imprisonment – Banda could not say or do anything directly to confront his inner circle which he knew to be ruthless. I begin to understand. If the chairman of the university council has not been told, as Chipungu claims, he will use every trick available to block my return to the university. He has done this for other local academics before. My own teacher, Felix Mnthali and my colleague Mupa Shumba, were his victims.

When I visit Chipungu again after two days, I find his tone somewhat subdued. He tells me the chairman of the university council, acting on behalf of the entire council, has directed him to tell me that I should reapply for my job.

"Geoff, did the university sack me when I was imprisoned?" I ask.

"Not to my knowledge," he replies.

"So, how am I going to write such a letter? What should I say – I am reapplying for my job as head of the English department and senior lecturer in English, which is what I was before my arrest? Look, my friend, this is getting serious. You know how delicate these matters can be; I am truly seeking your advice on this. How should I write the letter of reapplication for my job?"

"I don't know what advice to give you, but I suppose if I were you, I'd talk about how you'd like your job back because the education of your children has suffered when you were imprisoned."

I thank him and return home. Mercy and I know that this does not augur well for my return to the university – we are worried, very worried. Anyone who has lived in Malawi under Banda knows that what Chipungu has been directed to tell me is tantamount to saying that the chairman, acting on behalf of the entire council, does not require my services. But our employers in this country never put matters like these so directly. They never tell us explicitly that they do not require our services: they provide the necessary facts and create all the contexts for us to deduce this for ourselves – these people are a subtle and 'pragmatic' bunch; they still want us to accuse ourselves of the crimes we have not committed against them. Mercy insists that I do as Chipungu has suggested. I argue that I have suffered enough shame and humiliation. After cheerfully quarrelling with my wife, I submit, write the letter of reapplication for my job and, on 22 May 1991, take it in person to the university registrar's office. I copy it to inspector general Lunguzi and ask David Kerr at the university to deliver for me Lunguzi's copy through Zomba eastern division police headquarters. May ends. No letter acknowledging the receipt of my reapplication arrives from the university office.

Meanwhile, Brown Mpinganjira, who had taken employment with the British Council office in Lilongwe after his release from Mikuyu, visits me at Ntcheu nurses' quarters, and suggests that I should not force the university authorities to give me back my job if they appear reluctant to do so. When I visit Lilongwe he introduces me to the British Council director, Stuart Newton, who takes me to see the British High Commissioner, Nigel Wenban-Smith. Later Brown and I visit the German and US embassies. The German Ambassador Dr Wilfred Rupretch has a special story for me. He had decided that he would pay for the education of my son if I had stayed in prison longer. I thank him for his generocity and note with gratitude that the three missions have agreed a rescue plan for me. The US will offer me security in and around the nurses' living quarters at Ntcheu hospital. The British High Commission and the British Council will revive the visiting scholarship I was offered at the University of York. The German embassy will offer me a stipend every month until I get a job. I get enough indication from the three representatives that it is dangerous to hang around too long. I thank the Lord. I am convinced that Banda's cabal are unhappy that I have been released from prison. June begins. Still there's no letter from the university office acknowledging the receipt of my reapplication.

My car, which Fr Pat had kept at the Montfort Press garage in Limbe when I was imprisoned, is made roadworthy, and I am mobile again.I visit our second daughter, Lunda, at Stella Maris Secondary School, my brother-in-law Barnaba Cuthbert Chandiyamba at ESCOM in Blantyre, my nephew, James Nyilenda at The Grain & Milling Company in Limbe, as well as my friend, Joe Masinga at Manica Travel Headquarters in Blantyre. Our mutual friend Alice Nyirenda Jere pays me a visit at Joe's house. I tell her about the dream I had in prison when she rebuked me for not accepting Banda's offer of food and drinks. She calls dreams, 'dreams', as she welcomes me back to the real world and suggests boldly that I leave the country with my family when the opportunity arises – which looks like the interpretation of my prison dream. A visit to nephews Fred Ziyabu and Marshal Msonga and their families, my niece Lizzie and her husband, all in Zomba town follows. Then come visits to my mother-in-law in Salima District and brother-in-law Bernard Chandiyamba in Lilongwe. We end with a visit to our first daughter, Judith, who is at St Michael's Secondary School, Malindi, Mangochi district. As we drop off Judith's friend at MADECO fishing centre, where her parents live and where we want to buy a crate of fish, there is an incident. While I am standing in the queue for the fish, my Chancellor College colleague who teaches economics, Benson Kandoole, arrives. I recognise him instantly and with a broad smile extend my hand to greet him, but he ignores my hand, and walks past leaving my hand hanging in the air; humiliated and embarrassed I withdraw my hand. Mercy cynically asks: "What happened?" We laugh and laugh at the meaning of the event. "I thought that man is the husband of your so-called distant cousin?" I ask her. "I was coming to greet him too," she replies. The men and women in the queue who saw the incident were amused. It them dawns on me that the story that *Noriega* had told me in prison, about the wife of my economics friend taking an article about my poems to her husband who took it to the principal, might be true. Why did Benson refuse to shake my hand? We had never crossed words before. As we drive home we discuss the matter; I remind Mercy of the belief that you should not shake hands with the person you have bewitched or you want to have bewitched because the ill you want to happen to them will be neutralised. We continue to laugh and discuss the incident, puzzled by the nature of witchcraft until we reach home. June ends. Still no letter to acknowledge the reapplication for my job appears from the university office. I wonder why it should take more than a month for university council to indicate whether or not they have received the letter of reapplication for my job.

Before long the horrors I had not anticipated begin to come in the form of advice from unlikely people. I am having a tyre changed at the local garage near Ntcheu district hospital when a man takes me aside and inquires: "Are you the person who was being talked about on the BBC World Service for Africa recently? If you are, I suggest that you should be careful; you should always drive with another person in your car; you should avoid driving at night; you should not frequent local bars to drink beer. In fact, it might be advisable to stop drinking alcohol in local bars around Ntcheu township altogether. I am just a friend," he says, and leaves the garage. Later, at the shops in Ntcheu town, another man takes me aside and warns me to watch my movements: "Hit squads for Banda's cabal have been unleashed to bump you off," he says and disappears. July begins. No invitation to return to my post arrives. I begin to panic. I visit James Nyilenda and Joe Masinga again, this time to discuss prospects for jobs in Blantyre, but every cockroach, every gecko, every rat, every scorpion and every bat I meet offers me more advice about how unsafe it is to hang around. One fellow rudely reminds me of the death suffered by Mkwapatira Mhango in Lusaka and leaves it to me to draw my own conclusions as to my continued stay in Malawi. Soon it seems I cannot pee without some mosquito zinging past first, telling me how dangerous it is to pee in my country of birth! In truth, I am not free at all; I am too preoccupied with my safety and that of my family even to consider what I can do to help my friends at Mikuyu. At the end of July *Noriega* arrives with an urgent note from TS; they are desperate for food and medicines; we send whatever we can from our resources. But both *Noriega* and TS's note warn me that according to their grapevine, which I grew to respect throughout my imprisonment, some higher authorities have let loose on us their vicious hit squad. TS's note has other unwelcome news. On 28 July 1991 Aliki Kadango died in the cell that we shared; TS and the others are devastated; they have reason to believe that his death was not natural; they are urging me not to hang around for too long.For days I remain shocked. The only consolation I have is from the German Embassy in Lilongwe, who offer me the month's salary because the university is still reluctant to re-employ me.

I remember one of Landeg's 'bulletins' offering me a place as visiting scholar at the University of York. I remind Stuart Newton at the British Council about it, and he in turn reminds Nigel Wenban-Smith at the British High Commission. They offer to contact Landeg, who tells them my visiting scholarship is still available. The Poetry Society and Irina Trust, both in London, have offered to buy my family and me one-way air tickets. The Society for the Protection of Science and Learning in London, (an organisation which is now called the Council for the Assistance of Academic Refugees – CAAR), has offered to pay for our upkeep for one year while we are in York. All I need is to negotiate for a visa for entry into the UK trouble free. August begins. Still no acknowledgement of my letter of reapplication shows up from the university office.

I am convinced that the university council will not re-employ me; two months is more than enough time to call for a snap meeting of council to decide whether they want my services or not, especially as I have already got official clearance. I know that John Tembo wants me to fall down on my knees in total desperation before he gives me back my job. He has done this to others before. Of the dozen or so local academics who were imprisoned for nothing in the 1970s, only one or two were cleared by Tembo to return to the university.Most people suspected that he might have been the cause of their imprisonment; otherwise why did he not allow them to return to the university? The answer is simple. They would compete with Kadzamira for the position of vice-chancellor of the university, for which he was being groomed, despite his not qualifying for the post. But what wrong have I done Tembo or the Kadzamiras? What unpardonable crime have I committed against them? I do not want to become principal or vice-chancellor; I loathe administrative jobs.

For the first two weeks in August I shuffle from Ntcheu district hospital nurses' quarters, the British High Commission, the German Embassy and the police headquarters in Lilongwe. The British are trying to help us enter the UK trouble free; the Germans are still helping me with a stipend for my family's upkeep. Inspector general Lunguzi and secretary to the president and cabinet Justin Malewezi are ensuring that our passage abroad is not blocked by some other higher authorities. Lunguzi actually instructs deputy inspector general Chikuta in my presence: he wants our passports, which had not been returned to us after my release, to be brought to me in Ntcheu. The following day he brings them himself to our house in Ntcheu, duly renewed. Meanwhile, my nephews, relatives and friends are giving us every moral support imaginable. Mercy's friends around Ntcheu continue to fast and pray for our safety. I have the pleasure of joining them in some of their prayer and discussion groups. And the warnings for our safety continue.

Book Ten

Goodbye the Jacarandas of Home

60
The Sentence

After about three months of frustration, I decide we must leave before the situation gets too dangerous. My university will not re-employ me. That's a fact. And it will not be the first time that this has happened. My teachers have suffered a similar fate before. I persuade Mercy to apply for leave of absence, which she does reluctantly, knowing there's another Kadzamira at the ministry of health headquarters who decides on the clearance of wives of political prisoners and that her request will not be granted easily. The threats for our safety in Ntcheu district multiply. I write a research proposal in linguistics on 'The semantics and pragmatics of temporal distance' on which I was writing a paper before I was arrested; I send it with our plans to leave the country to Landeg White at the University of York. I write a second letter to Chipungu informing him that I am going on sabbatical leave, that I need to recuperate from my prison experience and catch up on theoretical linguistics before I return to the lecture rooms; that I have already got a scholarship and a place for one full year in the UK; and that I will be going with my family. I tell him I hope that the authorities will appreciate that I cannot possibly walk into lecture rooms straight from prison walls. I send a copy of the letter and the research proposal to inspector general Lunguzi by registered mail. When I visit Lunguzi the following week, I discover that the copy of my letter of reapplication for my job, sent to him at Zomba eastern division police headquarters through David Kerr, has not arrived. It is the registered letter that has reached him. The moral of the discovery is that Lunguzi too is being spied on within his own police service; otherwise, where did the copy of my letter go? Within two days of the delivery of my second letter, Chipungu sends his driver to Ntcheu district hospital nurses' quarters, to deliver in person his reply to my first letter. His letter says he has been directed by the chairman of the university council to ask me to report for duties at Chancellor College immediately, so that I may be put on the pay roll. The offer does not indicate the level at which I would re-enter the profession – he knows that some of my colleagues have now been promoted as professors and readers while I was away. It does not indicate what my salary will be. It is also silent about what has happened to my salary while I was imprisoned, and whether the university will compensate me for wrongful imprisonment. I wonder if I should take his letter seriously as it is obvious that I am expected to argue for these conditions of service when I start work; it is patent that my employers will say I have not learned how to respect them even after being imprisoned; it is clear that they will claim I am still the same ungrateful fellow. The stage is set for a second cycle of disagreements and a new form of witch-hunt. It is obvious that they do not want me to leave Malawi – they probably still fear that I'll tell too many stories about them. They stopped me getting the writer's residency in the University of Zimbabwe four years ago; now they want to stop me going abroad. This time around, however, I have the support of Banda himself, his inspector general, his secretary to the president and cabinet, some of the donor community and human rights organisations abroad.

Mercy insists that I report to Chancellor College according to Chipungu's letter. I am persuaded. After introducing myself to the college registrar and showing him my letter of re-employment from Chipungu, he asks why I have come alone; where my head of department, who should introduce me to him, is. Wasn't I the head of department once? Have I already forgotten the rules that used to operate? I am taken aback and do not remember the rules he is talking about. And the registrar who claims he does not know me was a student I had known throughout his studies at the college. Besides, I had good reason for not contacting the head of English, Brighton Uledi-Kamanga, after my release. The first point of call for any academic who has acquired the stigma of 'political prisoner' has always been the office of the university registrar. Nor did I want to involve Brighton in the politics of my re-employment. In times like these it is prudent to protect one's colleagues from accusations of complicity with the 'political rebel'. The college registrar also tells me he has nothing to do with putting me back on the pay-roll; and that I should go to the university office where my letter of appointment originated, which I find to be fair enough. Nor does he find it necessary to introduce me to the new principal of the college. Apparently the chairman of the university council had sent his nephew to Japan as ambassador after my arrest, after he had bungled his job as principal at Chancellor College and later at Bunda College of Agriculture. In the end I find myself yet again crawling back to Chipungu's office to face further accusations of my being the same troublesome person the university has known. To exemplify his point Chipungu holds up my second letter and the research proposal I had sent him and asks me:

"Jack, how can you do *this* to *us*?"
"Do what to you, Geoff?" I reply.
"How can you want to go on sabbatical leave after we've just re-employed you?"
"But Geoff, I am still unemployed."
"Haven't you received my letter giving you back your job?"
"I have; and I am coming from Chancellor College, where the registrar says he does not know me; that I should get my head of department to introduce me to him; and that I must report to you about the rest. Look, my friend, I've only just been released from prison; how am I supposed to know what the rules of re-employment are when I've never been re-employed before? Besides, your letter simply says I should report at Chancellor College in order to be put on the pay roll, it is silent about salary scales and conditions of re-employment et cetera et cetera. Listen, my friend, if the university does not want to re-employ me, why don't you say so in plain English?

389

You are employers; you are not obliged to re-employ me; the decision whether you employ me or not is yours. I do not want to start fighting for my conditions of service and be labelled as another ungrateful character. I know you were forced to re-employ me because my second letter – to which you have not responded – says I am going abroad."

"Haven't you received my reply to your second letter then?" He asks.

"No," I reply, trying to control my temper.

He yells at his secretary again to bring my file, where a copy of his reply to my second letter is lodged. He reads it aloud to me. I peep at its date and notice he wrote it only yesterday; it could not have reached me. The letter essentially says that he has been directed by the chairman of the university council to inform me that if I want to go on sabbatical leave as set out in my letter, the university will have nothing to do with me. If I take up my post at Chancellor College, as indicated in his offer of re-employment, the university will consider my application for sabbatical leave in the usual manner. No mention of the need for my recuperating from my prison experience before I teach is made.

"Geoff, does this mean the university has given me permission to go on sabbatical leave or not?"

"Jack, don't you remember what going on sabbatical leave means in this country? Don't you remember that we, as your employers, must get you official clearance to travel? Have you already forgotten how long it takes us to get academics like you official clearance to travel? Why are you in such a hurry to go away, anyway?"

"But Geoff, I don't need official clearance to travel."

"What do you mean, you don't need official clearance to travel? Everyone needs official clearance to travel in this country."

"His excellency the life president, the Ngwazi Dr H. Kamuzu Banda has already given me official clearance to travel."

"What do you mean?"

"I mean, his excellency the life president, the chancellor of this university and head of state of this country."

"Jack, do you mean his excellency himself has already given you the official clearance to travel?"

"And to get employment anywhere if you do not need my services."

"I don't believe this."

"Geoff, you were not listening the day I came to your office to ask for my job back. I repeat, his excellency the life president has given me official clearance to work in this university, to travel and work anywhere in the country or outside if my services are not required here. Why don't you ask inspector general Lunguzi, if you do not believe my story?" I ask in exasperation.

Chipungu is perplexed. I am worried. When *Gossip International* took stock of our daily events after lock-up in Mikuyu, we always came to the one and only conclusion, which Chipungu has unwittingly confirmed. It is not Banda but the Kadzamira-Tembo cabal who rule this country. Banda as head of state and chancellor of the university has released me from prison and directed his police chief to let me return to my job. How dare John Tembo, mere chairperson of the university council, put every impediment for my return? Why doesn't the university council simply say my services are no longer required; then I can get a job anywhere in the country or abroad, as the president has directed? What Banda's coterie does not realise is that the president has set them a trap too. He must have been told and probably already knows that these people have been exploiting him all along. He must be aware that it is these lieutenants who are bringing his name into disrepute. That is why he did not bother to tell them about my being released. Again, I recall Lunguzi's words: only three people know that you are being released, the life president, myself and yourself. I find the attitude of my employers repugnant, unacceptable and indefensible. I understand that

Chipungu is following instructions from the chairman, but there is no need for him to be hostile about it. However much I might love my job, it would be foolhardy of me to return to an institution with such bosses as my employers.

The following morning I get a postcard from Professor Martin Banham of the University of Leeds, in the UK. He has heard that I have been released from prison, and now welcomes me to the free world and wishes me well. The School of English at Leeds always had warm thoughts for me when I was imprisoned, he says, which helps to dispel my anger, anxiety and despair. I resolve to leave Malawi. It is a huge sentence, which I have to bear. The decision is strengthened by news of other sinister events that have occurred in the four academic years I have been away. Most friends I meet remind me that five colleagues from Chancellor College alone, three of them very close friends of mine, have died in mysterious 'car accidents'. Most of them believe that the deaths suffered by Martin Kanyuka of the Department of Education, Justus Mlia of the Department of Geography and Earth Sciences and Isaac Botomani of the Department of Public Administration follow the grim pattern of 'accidentalisation' that we have come to know. And given the scary warnings that I am persistently getting, who, in his right frame of mind, would want to hang around and work under such employers? Not me. But my wife's application for leave of absence has not yet been granted; the chief nursing sister who deals with such matters has not even acknowledged receipt of her application. This is as we had feared. Therefore I decide to travel to Blantyre to appeal to the secretary to the president and cabinet Justin Malewezi. He tells me that inspector general Lunguzi and he have decided to let my family leave the country; they have instructed the airport authorities not to bother us about letters of clearance and of leave of abscence. If they do, we should tell the officers to contact either one of them or both for our leaving the country without letters. I thank him and return home somewhat triumphant. As I tell Mercy I feel like Lazarus resurrected.

The risen Lazarus at very tedious last!*

I used to wonder about the details of the risen Lazarus,
Not merely how thankful he must have been to Jesus for
Raising him from the dungeon of death after four days
Nor the unbelieving bystanders, startled then stupefied,
But how Lazarus managed to get up with hands and feet
So tightly strapped by ribbons of death, his face blinkered
Like a hostage; how he must have bashfully wriggled as
They sheared the shroud after Jesus had intoned, 'Untie him!'
I dreaded his rotting body too, once catacombed always;
Even sister Mary conceded: Lord, four days, the stench!
And does the tomb stench just disappear at resurrection?
What welcome tears ran down their cheeks, what embrace?
And were Martha's hot porridge and Mary's warm bath
Water sprinkled with crushed herbal roots and leaves to
Sever Lazarus from the dead as we do when the prisoner
Is released from Mikuyu, say, after three-and-a-half years?

What bothered me above all, and I fear bothered Lazarus
As well, was the global truth that there would be no second
Time, once Lazarus died again, after Jesus Christ had really
Gone, there would be no second time for Lazarus to return
To his beloved sisters until perhaps the very final day. So
Now that this Lazarus is home and dry, the stars cellmates
Scrambled over in Mikuyu prison cells are up for grabs,
This Lazarus must watch every assembly, ritual and feast
Of the Sanhedrin for those further charges the officer-in-
charge noted at send-off; those mates Lazarus once knew,
The company he cherished, the bottle particularly – he will
Have to ruefully bolt; and though it's fear of the everlasting
Pit that baffled Lazarus, it must have calmed his nerves
To feel again that dusty clay of home at very tedious last!

---

* First appeared in *Skipping Without Ropes*, Bloodaxe Books, 1998.

61

Goodbye Jacarandas of Home

17 August 1991, Saturday. When your life is in danger in your country of birth, do not hesitate to move house, especially where the politics of elimination of presumed political opponents are the common practice, and you are somehow intricately involved. Do not wait to be ready, either; you will never be ready to leave home. Today I must say goodbye to the purpling jacarandas of home. I have loved these jacarandas enormously. All my life. I feel sad and betrayed. It's painful to abandon them, but we have decided that our country of birth is not good enough for us. The truth is the president's cabal wants to kill us without his knowledge. And we don't want to die. So we are literally running away to save our lives: my wife's, our two daughters', our son's and mine. That I would be forced out of my country in this manner never crossed my mind. I was born stubborn. I did not see the point of going into exile when braver Malawians could not stand Banda's totalitarian regime. I entertained the view, perhaps naively, that we should not all go into exile. Someone must hang around to see how things are done, pick up the pieces, and explain what was going on, after the brave ones have returned from their exiles. But stubbornness has its limitations beyond which one should not go. In normal circumstances I should be happy; it is as if we were going for greener pastures. But the times are out of joint. And how dare I take my family to a foreign country when I am broke? And with only a verbal promise of a year's scholarship? We do not even know what to expect where we are going. We carry passports and no other documents; we have no letters of official clearance to travel,

394

without which no-one is allowed to leave the airport. This is daft. Madness. Of course, both Justin Malewezi and MacWilliam Lunguzi have assured me that there will be no trouble at the airport. The immigration and customs authorities will not bother us; I should mention their names if they do. Still I am scared. Where nobody believes anybody, I will not be surprised if immigration officers do not believe that I have the president's verbal official clearance to travel.

Yet I will admit. I am secretly delighted. I do not mind seeking greener pastures, if that turns out to be the case. Fortunately, our move has been supported by lots of people. Malewezi and Lunguzi, the two public figures who are closest to president Banda, have gone the extra mile to support our move. The British High Commissioner Nigel Wenban-Smith did not need to intervene personally with both Lunguzi and Malewezi for us to get our passports back and renewed in order to travel trouble free; still we are grateful that Nigel intervened on our behalf as he did. And Stuart Newton has made the necessary contacts with Landeg, with whom we hope to stay in the UK. And why should I complain when Dr Wilfred Rupretch, the German Ambassador and his colleagues, have been giving me financial assistance since I left prison? All these people have been remarkable; I cannot believe my luck. I will concede further. The send-off at Kamuzu International Airport has been a dull affair so far. That sudden cracking laughter, the firm handshakes, the noisy goodbyes with children crying for their departing cousins, uncles and aunts – the excitement characteristic of African send-offs – has been absent. The fearless relatives who have gathered to see us off are subdued by the sight of the many spies and informers mingling with the crowds, noting any rebel jokes from the passengers queuing for their boarding passes. A shiver of fear suddenly runs up my spine. Countless Malawians have been forced out of this country over the years. I do not know if they felt as demoralised as I do. However, the departure of our flight has just been announced; we must therefore have our last-minute hugs with relatives and friends; ignore their tears and ours; take courage, and get ready for the passport controls.

The passport officer begins with a rude reminder that no-one in this country is allowed to travel on one-way air-tickets. And where on earth are our letters of official clearance to travel? He asks. I audaciously invoke Lunguzi and Malewezi on both counts. At first the officer stiffens, casting a quizzical look at my family of five; then he attracts the attention of his colleague at the other desk by nodding and winking at him; he in turn nods and winks back in agreement. He reluctantly stamps our passports, motions us upstairs, grinning his goodbye as we wave to our relatives and friends below. A white guy in khaki shorts and a light pink T-shirt with a walkie-talkie stands near my brothers-in-law below; he also waves to us – Nigel at the British High Commission intimated that he would ensure that we did not miss the British Airways plane bound for London Heathrow. I feel humiliated by the thought that foreigners are prepared to protect us from the dangers of our own country. Shame. After ensuring that Mercy and the children have taken their seats and belted up, I take mine and belt up with a heavy heart. I am comforted only by the memory of relatives, friends, colleagues, compatriots and cellmates who have strongly recommended that we leave. It is worrying that we do not really know where we are going. All we know is that initially we are going to stay with Megan Vaughan and her daughter Anna in Oxford, then with Landeg and Alice, and their sons Martin and John in York. Both families have been instrumental in my release from prison: Landeg as the UK's effective chairperson for the campaign for my release and the liberation of other political prisoners in Malawi; Megan as one of the many couriers of news to my family. But the detailed plans for our stay remain vague. We cannot tell, for instance, how long Megan and Landeg are prepared to accept the burden of putting up a family of five. We are not sure that my wife and I are going to find jobs.

After four academic years in prison my theoretical linguistics has rusted; knowing how fast that discipline changes, perhaps I will need to get another PhD to teach linguistics. Will the children get places in British schools when we arrive? Mercy and I are apprehensive, though Nigel Wenban-Smith has given us hope. The British High Commissioner has given us a letter of introduction to John and Pauline Craven, his friends in York. We are to talk to them in case we have matters which Megan and Landeg cannot resolve. And with God, who has protected us throughout, on our side, we will not be on our own. I look through the window to see for the last time the landscape of home, with its mountain ranges and green valleys that I will deeply miss. I feel hollow.

The day I say goodbye to the jacarandas of home is like the day I heard the saddest and most deeply disturbing news in my life – when the hero and icon of my life died. It happened one Saturday afternoon in 1978. We were at the police headquarters football ground, Zomba, with thousands of people. University students, staff and the general public – altogether about ten thousand people – had been shooed there by the Party's young pioneers and youth leaguers to attend one of Banda's endless political rallies. Brother and compatriot Matthew Chilambo and I were listening intently as Banda threatened to imprison anyone who opposed him at home or abroad. Then suddenly Banda began shouting about something and praising his police service for being the most vigilant in the region. Matthew and I were troubled; we knew that sooner or later Banda's words would encourage the Party's youths and young pioneers to take the law into their own hands and beat up innocent people. Many presumed political opponents would be arrested and imprisoned for petty crimes against the president, his coterie and the state. Whatever the cause of Banda's ranting, I felt uncomfortable and asked myself two questions: Is the time perhaps ripe for me to join the brave compatriots who had wisely gone into exile? Or should I continue tolerating Banda's interminable political banter?

As I am thinking these thoughts, Banda suddenly draws everybody's attention and makes a special announcement: "Today I have a message for those of you who still believe that Henry Masauko Chipembere will come back to rule this country. Chipembere will never rule this country. Why? Because he has died in California, the United States of America. My security officers have told me this. I repeat Chipembere has died in America." He pauses. Silence suddenly grips the entire audience. I hold Matthew's hand firmly, my nerves instantaneously shattered by Banda's audacious announcement. Then, as if recovering from a momentary trance, the Party's women's league starts ululating and singing praises. It does not cross Banda's mind that they might be ululating and singing for the fallen Malawi hero. Banda's boast continues unabated. I close my ears to his rage for the rest of the meeting. When I return home I tell Mercy about Chip's death. She is shocked. Terribly. Her family knew the Chipemberes intimately. I loved him as a man from my home district of Mangochi. I remember how he came to visit Zomba Catholic Secondary School as minister of education; how the students ran to the main road; and at the gate to the school how they told his driver to stop the engine and put the gear in neutral; they would push his car the quarter of a mile from the main road to the school in respect, singing songs of joy. That's how much the students loved Chip; they loved him as an honest educator, a liberal politician, a brilliant parliamentarian and a future leader who would unite into one hardworking nation all the ethnic groups of the country. That night I got the inspiration to complete the poem I had been writing for some time, and to dedicate it to a compatriot and brother exiled in the US.

Seasoned Jacarandas*
(For Frank Chipasula)

Stiff collared, hands in pockets,
spitting out phlegm and scanning
the point of thankless patriotic
wakes and timid nights, we lied
brother, believing we would soon

---

* Appeared in *The Last of the Sweet Banannas: New & Selected Poems*, Bloodaxe Books, 2004.

arrive, someone must hang around,
knowing there would be no pieces
(the true warmth was outside). Today,
though seasoned, our metaphors
blanch. The jacarandas still deeply
purple our pavements; but for once
their pop under foot or tyre chills,
like those still fresh squads firing.
Who'll watch whose wake tomorrow,
This self-imposed siege trembles!

Oxford welcomes us with a social whirl of parties and readings organised by Megan and her friends. Bottles of champagne pop for the first time since my freedom. A particular joy is hearing first hand how Megan and others took news and gifts from the UK to Mercy in Malawi. The celebrations continue when we reach York to stay with Landeg and Alice in their Newton Terrace house within the ancient walls of the city. The warmth of welcome we get everywhere softens the pain of exile. And for the first time in the safety of our new home, we have time to reflect on the many individuals and organisations we have to thank for our freedom. Gillian Tindall, Alastair Niven and others, mostly members of PEN International's Writers in Prison Committee, organise a service of thanksgiving for us in St Bride's Church, Fleet Street, London. The host of International PEN, Amnesty International, Africa Watch and Human Rights Watch, to mention just four human rights organisations; the Linguistics Association for Great Britain, its sister organisation of applied linguistics, and the association of university teachers and others, are all delighted that their campaign has borne fruit. We are humbled by our discovery that MPs, MEPs and Lords in the UK; senators in the US and Canada; academics and writers in Africa; scholars, journalists, doctors, churchmen and churchwomen and those who fought for my liberation are pleased at our arrival in the UK. We find that our story is a source of joy to people in many capitals in African, European and North American cities. I visit friends and human rights organisations in the Netherlands, Germany, Austria, Norway, Sweden, Canada, the US and Africa.

But the parties and visits must eventually come to an end. We must face the stark reality that we are in a foreign land, without a permanent source of income – and there are five of us. The first shock is the length of the queue for a council house or flat in York. We refuse to admit that we are refugees who should get priority for accommodation; it's like admitting that we will never go home again. With the assistance of Megan, we finally find a house at 79 Seventh Avenue, Tang Hall – the first Africans the neighbours have met. Half the scholarship that I get from the society for the protection of science and learning goes to pay the house rent, fuel bills, children's clothes, food and transport. Only God knows how we survive. John Craven advises Mercy to take an adaptation course to enable her to register with the UKCC to let her work as a staff nurse; after six months she begins her course based at York district hospital. Soon she becomes the effective breadwinner of the house. Meanwhile, I am madly applying for university, college, school and prison jobs in linguistics, literature, creative writing or anything that is going, without success. Often the racism I encounter at interviews, after applying for the jobs I know I am qualified to do but I am told to look elsewhere, is astonishing; but we soldier on.

After about a year and a rigorous interview for the post of writer in residence at Durham prison (irony of ironies!), the boards of Northern Arts, Yorkshire and Humberside Arts and North Western Arts jointly put together a rescue plan. They call me the First Greater North International Writer in Residence. For ten months, the first half of which are in the cold English winter, I will be reading from my work and running writing workshops across the north of England, from County Durham to Liverpool. The programme includes running creative writing workshops in Frankland prison, Durham prison, Wakefield prison and Garth prison; and discussing African literature in public libraries, community and city centres, schools and colleges from Durham through Leeds, Manchester to Liverpool. Fighting for seats in

Trans-Pennine Express Regional Railways in the freezing winter of the north of England and getting used to the stale coffee and sandwiches on its trolleys become one of the challenges of a new life.

At home we are nonplussed by another rather embarrassing event. Crowds of Tang Hall youths mill around our house after school, throw eggs at our windows, sand and mud across the hedge into Mercy's saucepans in the kitchen. Some write filth on the rusty car that we acquired from a nearby scrapyard. Their language and message is unambiguous: we should go back where we have come from! But Fr Austin O'Neil at St Aelred's Roman Catholic Church on Fifth Avenue, Tang Hall, comes to our spiritual assistance. He welcomes us into a truly caring congregation. All we have to do now is deal with the unwelcome youths. The British way is to invite the police for a cup of tea.

After three appeals to North Yorkshire's police headquarters, PC Bailey is sent one day to interview us and assess the nature of the harassment we are encountering. Luckily, before he finishes his cup of tea, the Tang Hall youths we have been talking about appear outside the house. We spot them, and before they start throwing sand in the food cooking in the kitchen and eggs at our windows, we invite PC Bailey to come to the window and see them; he is angry and goes out to chase them to their homes, where he issues a warning; he does not return to finish his cup of tea. There is no harassment for the rest of our stay in Tang Hall – as we move house after about two years these ironies inspire a few lines:

The Delights of Moving House, Tang Hall, York, 1991 *

When we first arrived in Tang Hall
The children welcomed us by stealing
Glances at us, sniggering over the hedge
Milling about the front door after school

---

* First appeared in *Skipping Without Ropes*, Bloodaxe Books, 1998.

Spitting loudly, monkey-faking without ambiguity
Until some started throwing eggs at our windows
Sometimes writing 'FUCK OFF' on the windscreen
Of the car we bought near the scrap-yard
Judy's laughter fired,
"How dare crowds of Tang Hall kids do this to chaps
Just rescued from the jaws of African crocodiles?"
Lunda joked,
"I wish they gave us the eggs they waste on our walls!"
Lika merely sulked as he mended his bicycle,
Mercy frenetically mopped the kitchen floor
Shouting, "Hold on, children, what lies here?"
And I thumped my chest recalling my Latin:
'Mea culpa, mea culpa, mea maxima culpa!'
(I've sinned, I've sinned, I've sinned most grievously)

Jack Mapanje welcomes Aleke Banda, Patrick Mbewe and other delegates to
the Malawi Cabinet Crisis Conference at the University of York, 1992.

62

The Cabinet Crisis Conference

The politics of my country have been transformed beyond recognition. It is as if Harold Macmillan's 'winds of change' speech of the 1960s has been declared for the second time. I left home in August 1991. The stories I hear after staying in the UK for about a year are unbelievable. You will recall how Brown, TS and I were engaged in surreptitious correspondence with Fr Pat, David, Mercy and the children in Malawi, and Landeg in the UK – this is what led to my eventual release from prison. Well, as we predicted, all the political prisoners I left at Mikuyu have been released, including Banda's longest living political prisoner, Martin Machipisa Munthali. We praise the God of our ancestors. But these changes have not happened without a catalyst. Since I left home Brown, Fr Pat, David and others have rekindled the surreptitious communication we began in prison. They have started an underground political movement, which seems to have originated from the British Council offices where Brown works; Stuart Newton probably looked away as they planned their revolution. When I was a student at University College London we used to believe that nothing radical could be expected to emanate from the British Council. Yet that is precisely what seems to have happened, which goes to show the disgust that even foreigners have for our dictatorship; no person or institution of honour needs persuading to change the state of siege my country is under.

So, Brown at the British Council, Fr Pat and David at Chirunga campus have been engaged in a small revolution. They have been writing what they call underground 'open letters' and scattering them at night in public houses, markets, churches and other public areas. The letters have been exposing Banda's corrupt government, the brutality of the Malawi Congress Party and that of the Kadzamira-Tembo cabal. The open-letter revolt, as they call it, has been so devastating that Banda, his henchpeople and their security officers are mystified by open letters, penciled or stencilled and hammered on tree trunks in village or town markets, schools, public toilets and traditional courts, for all to read. The people have spoken! They are crying out for multiparty politics in Malawi. And with the Berlin Wall having crumbled, the Cold War gone, Western governments preaching good governance and demanding that African governments respect human rights and stop their corrupt practices before they get economic aid from the West; above all, with apartheid in South Africa technically gone after the release of Nelson Mandela, Banda's invincibility, and that of his Malawi Congress Party and government, has been shaken to its foundations. Bakili Muluzi, once a discredited administrative secretary of the MCP under Banda and business-men Makhumula Nkhoma and Patrick Mbewe; veteran politician Aleke Banda with more than twelve years as a political prisoner; Justin Malewezi, once Banda's secretary to the president and cabinet, and other leaders have been invited by Brown, Fr Pat and David. They have formed an underground movement they call the United Democratic Party (UDP). In the north another under-ground political movement called Alliance for Democracy (AFORD), and led by the well-known Malawi trade unionist Chakufwa Chihana, has started too. The two movements are fighting Banda independently.

The groundwork for the establishment of both underground movements has in fact been laid by Malawian exiles. As soon as they left Malawi after Banda's cabinet crisis, running away from his wrath and the brutality of his young pioneers and youth leaguers, Malawian exiles began lobbying the lords, parliamentarians and senators in the UK, Europe, the US and Canada and other countries calling for a change in the direction of Malawi politics. Even I recently joined several delegations to the British Houses of

Parliament, to urge listening British politicians to take the struggle for multiparty politics in Malawi seriously and to help establish democracy and good governance there. Encouraged by the birth of the underground political movements in Malawi, South Africa and other countries, Landeg and I, organise a conference at the University of York on the subject that is taboo to Banda – 'The Malawi Cabinet Crisis'. We invite Malawian and British civil servants, missionaries and bureaucrats who worked under Banda, on the one hand; and the ministers still alive whom Banda sacked from his cabinet causing the crisis, on the other. We also invite to the conference UK, US, Canadian and Malawian representatives of Alliance for Democracy and what they now call a front rather than a party – the United Democratic Front (UDF). We include youngish Malawian academics living mostly outside Malawi. The conference is to be oral and informal. We do not want participants to present learned academic papers: we want them to present informally their memories of Banda's wrath during the cabinet crisis. Our hope is that those secretly fighting Banda and his minions will learn from the errors of the past. It turns out to be the most innovative conference we have had to organise. It confirms what we have suspected for some time: that Banda's wrath might have been motivated by the secrecy and cover-ups that characterised his life from childhood to the time he was involved in the scandal with his receptionist nurse at his London surgery; most of what Phillip Short documented in his famous book simply called *Banda,* including the story of the abortions that he was illegally engaged in during his stay in Ghana after his experience in the UK – almost everything is corroborated. The correspondence between Banda and his friend Kwame Nkrumah of Ghana, after the two leaders had achieved independence for their countries, is brought in for participants to examine. Judging from the exchange of letters between the two leaders, it is clear that there had been a special relationship between them.

However, their views on how to punish political opponents were evidently diverse. When Henry Masauko Chipembere waged guerrilla warfare against Banda from the mountain ranges of

Mangochi district; when Chipembere's staunch lieutenants Evance Medson Silombera and Kumpwelula Kanada were captured and Banda wanted to hang them publicly, Nkrumah appealed to Banda through his ambassador not to hang his political opponents in public, as a matter of principle. Banda refused to take his friend's advice. Nkrumah withdrew his ambassador from Malawi, abruptly ending the flourishing diplomatic relations between Ghana and Malawi. The conference also confirms Banda's anxieties about the radical nature of Dunduzu Kaluli Chisiza whose views on the conduct and progress of African politics at the time are well documented. Chisiza was arguably the most articulate and perhaps the best-known economist throughout the independent states of the African Great Rift Valley. The papers that Du presented at various economics conferences, even after the publication of his seminal pamphlet called *Africa What Lies Ahead* were characterised by originality and perception and confirmed that he had an independent mind. After making his views about the future of African leadership known at the economics conferences he attended, Du's reputation grew; and his fame bothered Banda immensely. It turns out that Du's sudden death in a car crash at Thondwe Bridge, as he travelled between Blantyre and Zomba, was a brilliantly orchestrated affair. It might even have been the first recorded case of Banda's presumed political opponents being 'accidentalised', which other Malawian politicians later suffered under his despotic rule. Banda's victims of the cabinet crisis who came to the York conference effectively confirmed that Du's death might have been planned well in advance; the absence of documentary evidence to support this view was characteristic of the oral culture that Banda was to establish firmly during his political career.

We close the conference in high spirits. We hope that future political leaders from UDF, AFORD and other parties will be open about their past, creating an environment of honesty, trust and a corruption-free society: an environment not dependent on privileges for leaders and their ethnic communities, but open to all the people they will rule. Only then can we hope to establish the genuine multiparty politics, democratic and open societies that the underground movements have been seeking. On the third and final day of the conference I decide to drive three of Banda's political enemies to the English seaside of Scarborough. I want them to relax and sample the delicious Scarborough fish and chips, as we unravel the mind of Banda's dancing witches.

On driving his excellency's political enemies to Scarborough[*]
(For Kanyama Chiume, David Rubadiri & Felix Mnthali)

And if you should wish me another prison let it be
For rallying within the city of York those rebels you

Could not stomach only weeks of our independence,
Seeking not their scholarly papers, but their learned

Memories of your wrath at the first cabinet and other
Crises you'll doubtless bequeath this tender nation.

And what a conference, what revelations, what cheer!
Did you really get struck off the medical register for

Consuming another man's assets, your own receptionist
Nurse, what is it about receptionist nurses with you? And

Those abortions in Ghana, did you thank the rhinoceros
Who summoned you to liberate your homeland instead?

What treason did you see in the moustache of your
Political enemy number one? What revolt in the verse

Of your UN envoy that we read hidden in our youthful
Blankets, and how dare you jail my teacher for being

---

[*] First appeared in *Skipping Without Ropes*, Bloodaxe Books, 1998.

Just another clever northerner? If you should invent
Another prison for me, let it be for driving your three

Political enemies to Scarborough one English summer
Afternoon, letting them relax to watch Scarborough

Children surfing with the seagulls and riding the tender
Crests and splashes of the calm bay; let it be for buying

Your rebels huge portions of Scarborough fish 'n'chips,
Sitting at the wooden table to analyze the songs your

Dancing witches sang to you; let it be for good reason
Not the conjectures of your mistress about my treason!

63

Joe's Telephone Call

79 Seventh Avenue, Tang Hall, York. The telephone rings. I put down the batch of poems I am working on and dash for the receiver. I had not been anticipating a call, and when I recognise the voice at the other end of the line, my heart jumps. It's Joe Masinga, a long time friend in Malawi. My heart begins to beat faster and faster. I fear the news that everyone in exile dreads – another death in the family and I'll be unable to travel for the burial ceremony! Telephones calls from Africa to Europe are expensive to make; you don't make them without good reason. But Joe, who is calling from his office at Manica Travel Headquarters on Victoria Avenue, Blantyre, eases my fears by his reassuring tone: "Every member of the family you left behind is fine; they are wishing you all well; and advising you not to do anything stupid that would cause the security authorities to bother them," he says. Then, suddenly changing tack, he teases: "*Mchimwene**, do you know I have always wanted to be a journalist?"

"No, you never told me you had that ambition," I answer, wondering where this is leading.

"But today," he says, "I've decided to become your correspondent, and on this occasion, and this occasion only, I promise to be more reliable than the BBC World Service for Africa correspondents."

"I am all ears," I tell him, although I am uncomfortable about the wisdom of his idea as I believe people are listening in to our

---

* Brother, Comrade.

409

conversation; but Joe cheerfully and rather provokingly announces:

"Seriously, *Mchimwene*, today I want to confirm what you might have already heard about the political changes currently sweeping across our country. Do you remember the British politician's famous speech in the 1960s? Harold Macmillan's speech about the winds of change that were sweeping across the African continent, or something to that effect?"

"I do," I reply, though the sceptic in me marvels at his daring. Doesn't he expect his office telephone to have been bugged like everybody's? Or has life president's law and order, peace and calm, broken down completely? But Joe is determined:

"Listen carefully, my brother."

"Man, I am glued to the receiver," I reply impatiently.

"Right, I am on the second floor of the building at Manica; I will take the receiver in my hand past my office window; I will turn it face down towards the streets; I want you to hear for yourself what's going on in Victoria Avenue, Blantyre, Malawi. Today is a very special day in the history of our country; and I want to share this rare moment with you."

He must have done what he said he would, for, indeed, through my receiver I hear people chanting: "We want change; we want change; we want change!" And others laughing, shouting and declaring Banda and his cohorts politically finished. Then again: "We want change; we want change; we want change", which continues as the voices get louder, sharper and closer to the receiver. I decide that this cannot be the Malawi I know; I do not believe it; I am too overwhelmed by it all. I suggest that Joe put the receiver down; I'll ring him instead; but he dismisses me with:

"*Mchimwene*, don't you remember you are talking to a historian who for thirty years has not been allowed to write his country's history?"

I remember Joe and I were among the top ten best candidates in our Primary School Leaving Certificate Examinations many years ago; and we both got what was called the Timcke bursary, which enabled us to enter Zomba Catholic Secondary School for four academic years. I also recall that at Soche Hill College Joe got a better grade in his A-level History than I did, though we both passed, and he went on to major in history and geography at the university. So I let him go on:

"You are one of the few friends I still have who will appreciate the meaning of what is happening today. Enjoy this rare occasion; enjoy the chanting of the people you have written your poems about. I had decided to talk to you for about twenty minutes; I've done only ten; I'll give you ten more minutes. I'll stagger the payment of the phone bill in case you're worried about that!"

Joe must have put the receiver out by the window again. For I hear Blantyre street voices shouting again: "We want change, we want change; we want change; Banda is gone; Tembo gone; Mama gone; the MCP no more!" I honestly cannot believe what I hear; and when I ask where the country might be heading with all this, Joe replies:

"We don't know whether or not Banda and his inner circle will incite their young pioneer hit squads to kill these street people. They would be foolish if they did. There are thousands of them in the streets, and killing them all would create a massacre impossible to hide from the world. At the moment we are assured by the army's support, for, wherever army vehicles appear, the people cheer the soldiers' bravery for not intervening in Banda's demise. *Mchimwene,* do you remember Chipembere and his leading youth leaguers Chikwakwa, Phombeya and others? Do you remember them urging Blantyre street-crowds to riot during the fight for independence? That was nothing! This victory, *Mchimwene,* is sweeter than the fight for our freedom from the British; it is sweeter than the burial of the 'corpse' of the Central African Federation of Southern Rhodesia, Northern Rhodesia and Nyasaland!"

"But what happened? What's caused all this furore?" I ask.

"What sparked off these street festivities is the unexpected radio announcement that Banda has just made: he has finally conceded that there's to be a national referendum on multiparty politics in Malawi. Everybody now hopes that multiparty elections are around the corner. We are all praising the Lord, and thanking Him for answering the people's prayers at long last."

"At very, very long last indeed," I intone.

"And as you well know," Joe continues, "I may never live to write the story of this historic day. I am not well. Terminal. But I'll not dwell on my health; let me place my receiver down one final time, for you to enjoy."

After hearing the chanting voices again, I say goodbye to Joe and conclude: "Sorry about your health, my friend; may the Lord keep you tight, safe and sound. Thank you and hallelujah for the news. You have indeed beaten BBC correspondents!" I put the receiver down, overcome with relief at the news of the forthcoming referendum, followed by possible presidential and general elections; though I am more overcome with grief at the news of Joe's failing health.

64

Brown's Story

Clifton Without, Beaverdyke, York. The meal over, Brown Mpinganjira dramatically invites Mercy and me to sit down on our sofas to hear the story he has brought us. We know he is Minister of Information, Broadcasting and Telecommunications in the new democratically elected government in Malawi. What we do not know is that he has been currently heading a delegation informing Malawians abroad, among other things, about the changes in the politics of our country. "I have just been visiting Japan," he begins, "where I met the Malawian Ambassador Zimani Kadzamira – your ex-principal at Chancellor College, no less! My delegation and I invited the ambassador and his wife to dinner at our hotel. He refused and insisted that we should be his guests instead. Naturally, my delegation did not trust Banda's effective 'brother-in-law'. They told me boldly that they did not want to be poisoned. But I held my ground and told them I had already accepted the invitation on their behalf and he would be foolish to poison us during the political transition of our country.

"At dinner, the ambassador was embarrassed by the younger members of my delegation, when they enthusiastically described the results of the presidential elections of 17 May, 1994, where Dr Hastings Kamuzu Banda of the Malawi Congress Party had 444,000 votes; Chakufwa Chihana of the Alliance for Democracy, 888,000 votes; and Bakili Muluzi of United Democratic Front, 1,400,000 votes! But the ambassador manoeuvred the discussions so that three questions dominate the table: what the new government's policy would be regarding those who were sent on diplomatic missions by Banda; whether the new government would help them transfer their property home; and what would happen to the education of their children? Our reply was candid and clear: there would be no problem for anyone who accepted the democratic principles upon which the new government was voted into power. As we were about to return to our hotel after dinner, I took the ambassador aside and asked for a favour:

'Mr Ambassador, thank you for your dinner, we've all enjoyed it. You've asked me questions about what the new government is going to do about those who were sent to missions by Banda's regime. I've answered you to the best of my ability. May I now ask the question I've always wanted to ask but never had the opportunity to do so? And, could you, please, give me an honest answer?'

'I'll answer to the best of my knowledge, honourable Minister,' answers your ex-principal."

And sitting properly on our sofa and smacking his lips with glee, Brown continues:

"I asked the Malawian ambassador to Japan, Zimani Kadzamira, your principal, the question I promised you I would ask after I left prison: 'Mr Ambassador, why did you and your family get Jack Mapanje arrested and imprisoned?'"

"*Mbwiye*," Brown continues, "I've never seen a black man go suddenly blacker in the dazzling corridor of his own house! For, the diplomat twisted his lips, swallowed his consonants and vowels, sighed and gasped the most incomprehensible noises I have ever heard. He mumbled something about how powerless he had always been. How difficult his uncle and his sister were.And how he had always wanted them to change their ways. From the way the ambassador agonises over the answer, totally taken aback, I got the message, thanked him and took my delegation back to the hotel. After gladly joining us for breakfast at the hotel the following morning, the ambassador plucked me aside before he returned home and said:

'Right Honourable Minister, yesterday you asked me a question I did not expect; but I answered you to the best of my knowledge. May I also ask you a question? And could you also give me a truthful answer as far as possible?'

'I'll try,' I reply firmly.

'Honourable Minister, what does Jack think of me now?'

'Mr Ambassador,' I began, 'Jack and I used to discuss the reasons for our detention as we battled the scorpions, cockroaches, fleas, bats and the stench of Mikuyu prison. As a journalist and Jack's friend, I promised him I'd get to the truth about his detention when I get out of prison. I was convinced then, as I am now, that you got the wrong man. You got an innocent man who loved freedom and respected you as his boss probably more than you knew. As for what he thinks of you now, I am going to Jack's place in York, England, from here. He will tell me what he really thinks about you after I have told him we've met. But let me assure you of one thing. Jack is so worried about how to make ends meet for himself and his family in exile that I would be surprised if he ever thinks of you at all.' "

65

Malawian Vision 2020

25 November 1997, Tuesday. Mount Soche Hotel, Blantyre. Malawi politics have changed. That's a fact. Exiles who had been banished from home these thirty years are trickling back one by one, some to stay for good, others to visit and assess the genuineness of the changes brought about by the new political dispensation. The democratically elected government of President Bakili Muluzi has organised the Malawi Vision 2020 Conference to redraw Malawi's social, economic and cultural vision in the context of the recently achieved multiparty politics. I am amongst the few lucky exiles who have made it here. We are currently at a reception. It's one of the real pleasures of conference receptions to catch up with the gossip. I am talking to James Chipeta – a classmate at Zomba Catholic Secondary School once and now the registrar of the University of Malawi – when a ghost from the past known to both of us materialises. Sam Kakhobwe was secretary to the president and cabinet at the time I was arrested and imprisoned. A very important person indeed under Banda's totalitarian regime. Indeed, one of the untouchables in Banda's clique of higher authorities.

"Jack, could I have a word with you when you've finished here?" he asks politely.

"Sure," I reply guardedly.

He moves across the reception room and waits patiently in the corner with his glass of beer. I feel like a young priest at the confessional being waited upon by some old sinner. I wonder what he's up to now? Sam has been part of our lives, James and

I, since our days at Zomba Catholic Secondary School, where he was our senior – and protector from the occasional bully. We used to refer to him fondly as 'Uncle Sam', and he loved it. After school he went to the Roma Campus of the then University of Botswana, Lesotho and Swaziland, where he graduated with a good degree. He joined Banda's government and, having come from the central region, he rose and rose in the administrative and political hierarchy of Malawi until he became secretary to the president and cabinet (SPC) and head of the civil service. The University of Malawi's vice-chancellor, John Dubbey, in his desperate search for the reasons for my arrest and imprisonment, once approached Uncle Sam to shed light on the nature of my crime. Sam apparently told Dubbey that the only crime I had committed against Banda and his coven was that I came from the rebel district of Mangochi. This time around I wonder what he is going to say. Gossip with James over, Sam comes forward and starts: "D'you mind if I tell you what happened on the day you were arrested ten years ago?"

"Mind?" I think to myself. Dear God, for ten years I have been a victim of nightmares, trying to find out what happened and why. I'm surprised too; other relics of Banda's power cliques at the conference have not acknowledged me even with a nod or wink. Why would Sam bother to tell me about this now?

"No, I don't mind at all; whatever happened, Uncle Sam?" I ask teasingly.

"That Friday morning, 25 September 1987," he begins, "the direct telephone line on my desk rang at about 9.30 a.m. It was Mary Kadzamira. You'll remember she'd taken over her elder sister's job as Banda's private secretary after he had promoted Cecilia Kadzamira as his Official Hostess, the Mama. 'You are being summoned to Sanjika Palace instantly, his excellency the life president wants to see you at 11.30 a.m. sharp,' she threatened. Mary's tone was always harsher than her sister's, particularly when trouble was in the air. I had two hours to cover the two hundred miles. Impossible by any road, but especially the pot-holed road from Lilongwe to Blantyre.

"Afraid that this could be the end of my job, I drove as fast as I could to the police headquarters to ask for their helicopter, but neither the inspector general nor the chopper was there. I drove madly to the army headquarters; the army chief wasn't there either, but I demanded that someone in charge provide me a helicopter with a pilot. I had to get to Sanjika Palace or else. I eventually got there with minutes to spare, only to find the inspector general and the army chief already there. 'Gentlemen, why are we three gathered here?' I asked, not really thinking of Shakespeare's three witches! The army chief smiled. 'You're the head of the civil service, you tell us why we three should gather here,' they said. 'D'you think we're being sacked? Or,' lowering my voice further, 'has he finally popped off?' They smiled grimly at the thought of the president for life ever dying, but said they had no idea why they'd been sent for or why the urgency, as there was no problem about the country's security to their knowledge.

"At that point the door in front of us suddenly swung wide open and – wait for it – John Tembo – you'll remember he was Treasurer General of the Malawi Congress Party as well as chairman of your university council – and Katola Phiri, central region chairman of the MCP, appeared and walked past us without even a nod. We looked at one another. Totally surprised. All the signs were that someone big, perhaps one of us, was for the drop. But before we could speculate any further, Banda himself suddenly stood before us; we leapt to our feet, and without greeting us as he usually did, he barked his instructions at all three of us:

'I've been told there's a young man called Jack Mapanje in the department of English at Chancellor College, University of Malawi. Arrest him. Put him in prison and there let him rot, rot, rot forever. D'you hear?'

'Yes, sir,' we chorused. He immediately went back where he'd come from.

"Outside, my two colleagues wondered who Jack Mapanje was. I lied that I didn't know you. The rest of the story you know only too well. Except perhaps to share with you my experience as

Banda's SPC. When he says: 'I've been told', he means the self-styled royal family have told him. But when he just gives you orders to do this or that, then the usual security officers have told him. I didn't have the opportunity to tell you the story when you were released from prison. I thought you might like to hear it now; better late than never, goes the cliché," he concludes.

So, ten years on, I breathe heavily to myself, I am finally told, almost by accident, how, though not why, I was sent to prison, and realise with some trepidation how lucky I am it was only for three years, seven months, sixteen days and more than twelve hours that I stayed in prison. Uncle Sam gives me permission to reproduce his story in any way I see fit. I thank him effusively and sincerely mean it. Before I get into bed that night I ring up Mercy in York, to tell her about Uncle Sam's confession.

66

The Midnight Call

28 November 1997, Wednesday. The phone shocks me out of sleep and kicks my heart into my throat; I had been dreaming about goodness knows what. Definitely not about Sam Kakhobwe's confession! It's 3.30 a.m. in Mount Soche Hotel. Outside, I imagine ghosts of Banda's 'accidentilisers' still lurking about, looking for their prey downtown Kabula alleyways and street corners. With my heart thumping, I lift the receiver.

"Hello," I croak, sounding nervous even to myself.

"*Mbwiye*, why don't you tell your friends you've arrived?" I recognise the jovial voice instantly, and so I should: for three-and-a-half years I shared prison cells with the man behind the voice.

"Brown! I assumed you'd know I am here. Didn't you help organise the damned conference? I'm in town as a delegate to your Malawi Vision 2020 Conference. Officially invited by the deputy chairman of the ruling United Democratic Front and your cabinet colleague Aleke Banda. You must know about that. I was hoping we'd meet for a chat, to take stock of events as we used to once?"

"Some of us are MPs, you know, and put our constituents first," Brown answers.

"What? Brother, am I impressed! I hope your enthusiasm for the people lasts. But didn't your telephone throw me off balance at such an hour! How did you know I was here, what's the matter? You could not ring at this hour just to greet me?"

"*Mbwiye*, admit it, you are still afraid of being bumped off, aren't you? Come on admit it," Brown says.

"Well... " I begin.

"But forget the buggers," he says, "Banda's death squads are history. These times are indeed changing; do you remember that song, by Bob Dylan, I think? And in case you want to know, I got your room number from your wife in York, England. These days there's no telephone bugging."

"And do I hear noises of celebration in the background, is there a party going on in your house at this late hour? What's happening? Am I invited?"

"Of course, come on over – my new wife will be delighted to see a professor!"

"Yes, I gather you've got a new wife."

"That's right."

"Man, how do you do it?"

"Look, Man, if you want to be rude about my private life... "

"*Mbwiye*, I am sorry; I was only joking, just joking."

"Anyway, I phoned to keep my promise. Your friend is dead," Brown announces this matter-of-factly.

"Oh, no, not TS, please God! I was hoping to look out for...!"

"Nooo! TS's working at the post office, Lilongwe city."

"Which friend then? Mataka? CheJumo?" All our friends and Banda's VIP 'guests' at Mikuyu prison rise up like ghosts before me.

"No, Alex Mataka is back in Mozambique. Got himself a proper job with their Foreign Service. Years of detention at Mikuyu can be impeccable credentials, you know! And I met CheJumo Owen at Namwera Trading Centre a few weeks ago. D'you know what he said when he saw my ministerial vehicle?"

"The Mercedes Benz?"

"The very one."

"What did he say?"

"'*Mlamu**', it's me, CheJumo Owen. Don't you remember me? Mikuyu prison? I'm not mad. I never was. I was faking it. I had

---

* Brother-in-law

421

to do something to be left alone!'"

"You mean those lumps of *nsima* he shoved into his ears to stop hearing Banda's voices, as he claimed; that crying, shouting and singing, sometimes all night – all that was faking? Brown, tell me another story."

"No, it's not CheJumo, guess again."

"For God's sake, Brown, stop playing Mikuyu's riddling games. It's late in the day. Deaths are no longer funny for me these days. In the six years I've been away, I've found most of my friends dead.Which one is it now?"

"His excellency the life president, the Ngwazi Dr H. Kamuzu Banda, the father and founder..."

"Yes, yes, yes Brown, cut out the obvious rubbish, for God's sake. But hang on, you don't mean...?"

"I do."

"The H.E. himself?"

"The very him, dead!"

I'm struck dumb. Can't believe what I just heard. The world has stopped. Brown seems to sense that I am too shocked to speak.

"*Mbwiye*! Still there? Happened about half an hour ago. In South Africa." He continues,"Hello, *Mbwiye*! Not still afraid of being 'accidentalised', are we?"

I still can't find words to respond to the shock. Brown's eternal buoyancy carries on:

"We've only just heard the news ourselves. One of the perks of our being a government minister, you know."

I take his use of the royal 'we' with an inner wry smile. He deserves to use it. A damned sight more than Banda's toadies, I bet.

"Remember the promise we made, you and I?" He's talking now of the pact we made in prison about Banda's death.

"Whoever heard about Banda's death first would tell the other as soon as possible, wherever we were, whatever time. I'm keeping that promise now, *Mbwiye*, are you listening?"

"It's a fact then?" I ask, stunned.

422

"Very much so."

"No hoaxes, Brown?"

"Not this time, old friend, not this time."

"His excellency the life president, the Ngwazi?"

"The very him, dead!"

"In that case I have a story for you. D'you remember Banda shouting at one of his political rallies in 1967: 'I am too busy to die...too busy to die...I want to develop this country... those of you hanging around waiting for me to die have thirty years to wait'! Remember that? It's thirty years this year. The old bugger was right. The devil he made a contract with must have told him so."

"But *Mbwiye*, what's wrong with you?" Brown asks. "I thought you'd given up believing in superstitions. Believe me the cockroach has been well and truly squashed. And for real this time around. Started with a brain tumour operation, apparently, amongst his apartheid chums in South Africa. And as Stephen Pingeni, Mr Definitely, at Miyuku would have it: what a shame!"

That afternoon, I decide to revisit Zomba Market to check out the woman from whom I used to buy vegetables and fruit. I had not paid for the produce I had taken from her stalls at the end of the month I was arrested and imprisoned. I find her there. She is still stubbornly looking after her wobbly stall. When I remind her who I really am and what I have come to do, she ignores me, says she does not recognise me, and looks away, as she tries to remember, I think. When she recovers from her reverie, as it were, she confronts me with: "According to the information I got at the time, you had died at Mikuyu like all other political prisoners at the time. Why are you reminding me of the best customer I once had? Don't you know his bones are buried among the nameless mounds at St Mary's township cemetery? If you owe me anything, don't worry, you don't have to pay it; I can't remember you; I have forgotten about your debt; go away; I don't want to be haunted by evil spirits," she concludes. I stubbornly stand my ground, smiling at her memory of my bones that are interred at St Mary's cemetery.

Later, I reconstruct in verse the event in its entirety, if only to cheer myself up:

Guilty of nipping her pumpkin leaves[*]

I
The fear of dying without paying for those
Pumpkin leaves he pinched from her stall
Brings him here though she fiercely declares
Total innocence of the time and vegetables
She lent him seven years ago; she cannot recall
When the pigeon was 'taken' or the swallow
Wafted to those dissonant frosty habitats to
Gather twigs to nest its young after grudgingly
Revoking the blinding mirage of the sand
Beaches of the home to which he now returns;
Her vegetable hutch is still organic, though
Grown surer, but she attests vague memory
Of the pigeon and his story – Oh time, how
Could you be so callous as to sever memories
So precious when all he desires is to redress
The anguish of nipping her pumpkin leaves!

II
Her altercation becomes bolder: is he serious,
Could he have returned home to ridicule her
Nudity with his cameras as strange visitors
In the dead monster's regime once did, has he
Got no shame for asserting the resurrection
Of the best customer she once boasted about
Now presumed dead; no; she would have none
Of his alien stratagems nor would she license
Another of her own grins to enter his cameras,

---

[*] First appeared in *Skipping Without Ropes*, Bloodaxe Books, 1998.

Tourist or traveller; today the market deals
In graver business, grimaces of her children's
Tatters have fattened the albums of the likes
Of him before, they got the patches for their
Generous gestures instead, she would not offer
Any of her children as prey to another natty
Gimmick, never! 'Not today with the beast
Gone, never if he shouted decide to resurrect!'

III
'Woman, I hear your passion, I too withheld
The spite I felt for the beast to save my life
And my children but do you not remember
That son-in-law living on Mulungusi Avenue
Whom you buoyantly married your daughters
To every time he visited this stall? Do you not
Remember the groundnuts and spinach you
Lent this face that paid back each month-end?
Well, the turtle has come back home to pay
For the pumpkin leaves and okra he nibbled
From this stubborn shack those many years ago;
Here, take your money which has tormented
Me in my prison and exile these many years!'
Even his London filming crew is unmoved by
His confession under the market's Jacarandas –
It's not in the script for their tale of his return!

IV
Then rubbing her eyes to weigh the ghost she
Gibes in disbelief: They are all returning home
Those buffaloes who left these kraals many dry
Seasons ago, as for you my son, what kept you?
My daughters are too old for you now, why did
You not dispatch your uncle or some emissary
For the bride price up front? Today, the price of
The pumpkin leaf you knew has more than trebled,

It continues to climb, though with the lion-for-life
Permanently settled, the options in our vegetable
Calling are multiplying; the land is still desert
But whoever dreamt that the fiend would go for
The thundering rains to pour? Imagine no man,
No woman strips us naked for Party Cards at
The market gates any more! Then grasping his
Hand she shoves his money into her camisole
And gazes right past him to the next patron!

Afterword

Like most leaders of independent African countries in the 1960s, Dr Hastings Kamuzu Banda started well, first as prime minister then as president of Malawi. But after he had sacked six of his cabinet ministers for disagreeing with him only weeks into independence and he had got himself appointed president for life at the 1971 Malawi Congress Party Convention, political power went to his head and made him indifferent to his people's problems. Instead of serving the people who had elected him to lead the Party, government and country, he brought them to their knees to serve him and his inner circle. The last ten to fifteen years of his political career were particularly horrendous and the country's political life turbulent. The president for life was too senile to rule, a fact that was taboo to even whisper – you could be arrested and imprisoned for mentioning the point publicly. Many academics, lawyers, economists, doctors, teachers and others left the country to seek employment elsewhere; they could not bear to work under the state of siege that prevailed at the time. Malawi was being ruled covertly by a despotic triumvirate of Banda's private secretary turned permanent companion, Cecilia Kadzamira, upon whom the president had heaped honours and titles; her uncles, especially John Tembo, who appointed himself chairman of the country's institutions that mattered, including the University of Malawi; and her brothers led by Zimani Kadzamira, their advisor and principal of the university's largest college, who was being groomed for the post of vice-chancellor for which he was totally unqualified.

This trio was hostile, ruthless and pathologically jealous of anyone who appeared clever, independent minded, or close to the president's favour. To disagree with them was to put your freedom, not to say your life, in peril. And they wielded enormous power, dominated major events, mercilessly exploited the ailing president and ruled Malawi largely under the pretext of his say-so. Life became even more insufferable after Banda's security and intelligence services in the police, the army and the Young Pioneer paramilitary movement splintered into those who claimed allegiance to the president and those whose allegiance was to his inner circle. And officers from the two sites never saw eye-to-eye; they fiercely extended the philosophy of divide and rule, which Banda had learnt from the British and arbitrarily arrested, jailed or deported anyone the president or his cohort considered their real, imagined or potential political enemy.

In December 1997, Dr Fergus McPherson of Edinburgh, Scotland, writing the obituary of his friend Dr Hastings Kamuzu Banda, who had died in November that year remarked: 'Many observers have spoken of the members of Malawi's first cabinet as a bunch of very able, dedicated people. However, Banda called them his boys and would not tolerate opinions at variance with his own. Fear began almost at once to set some of those he chose for public office against each other; and perfect fear casts out love. Then inevitably the race was on for who could capture sole access to the life president's ear. Those who expressed grief at what was souring the long-cherished hopes (of freedom, debate and true independence) were then branded as "rebels" and "traitors". Banda actually ordered his Young Pioneers to act against any who were against him. "Tell the police," he said. "But if they do nothing, I put you above the police. And crocodiles are hungry at night." '

When Banda put his Young Pioneers above the police, he had effectively put them above the law and chaos was unleashed. The prisons choked with thousands of dissenters who were merely presumed to have been the regime's opponents; Banda built a new prison in every district. As the victims they jailed were neither tried nor charged with specific offences, many languished in prisons indefinitely, while others died there, or in the custody of security officers who disposed of them without the knowledge of family and relatives. The rebels who were not imprisoned were often abducted from their homes at night and driven at break-neck speeds in Malawi Congress Party Land Rovers bound for the Lower Shire Valley, where they became meat for hungry crocodiles. When I entered Mikuyu prison the number of political prisoners had reduced from seven hundred and eighty-eight to forty-seven; the prison had acquired another forty-eight condemned prisoners who were being hanged at nearby Zomba Central prison twice a year at the rate of six a time; the number of both political and condemned prisoners rose as the years rolled by. What astonished many was why a president, who was a medical doctor, found it necessary to build for his people more prisons than hospitals?

These were the indisputable facts that most politically mature Malawians had no doubts about, although no-one dared to acknowledge them publicly for fear of paying the ultimate price.

Today, fourteen years after Banda's death, we are told to forget the pain and suffering that the tyrant and his coterie inflicted on us. The deaths and misery they caused thousands of Malawians belong to the past and we must move on, they say. We do not even need the kind of truth and reconciliation that South Africa had so that those who were responsible for the atrocities could be brought to book or could at least accept and apologize. But I beg to differ. And vehemently so. Those of us who suffered under Banda and his Kadzamira-Tembo cabal cannot afford to forget the brutalities they exacted on us. Forgive perhaps we can; forget we could not possibly do; only death can erase that. First, to forget is not to be virtuous, it is to be grossly disingenuous. It is tantamount to telling further lies that Banda's so-called rebels were not murdered, exiled, imprisoned and deported without discussion, trial or charge, when thousands of them were. Second, however much we might deny, ignore or hide the injustices of the past, truth will eventually catch up with us. We must, therefore, talk frankly about the evil and injustices that were going on and try to understand the mindset of those who brought them about so that future generations are spared such calamities.

The world has witnessed the innocent blood that has been spilt in conflicts based on old, unresolved ethnic scores in Kenya, Uganda, Somalia, the Democratic Republic of Congo, Rwanda, Sudan, Nigeria, South Africa, Cote d'Ivoire and elsewhere in recent years – conflicts that are sadly still ongoing. To stop such ethnic tensions and wars happening again we need to talk candidly about the past, naming without fear those who instigated them, or were thought to have caused them. The perpetrators need to be liberated from their guilt too; they must be reconciled with themselves and their victims; their admitting that they destroyed people's lives and careers might be the beginning of the restitution of the justice and truth that we all require.

This narrative chronicles my incarceration with a batch of political prisoners under president Banda's despotic regime. We were merely 'picked up' and dumped in Mikuyu prison without trial and without charge. Together we brushed aside the pain and suffering of prison, subverted the dictator's despotic apparatus and achieved our freedom, albeit with clandestine assistance of family, relatives, friends, compatriots, colleagues, strangers and human rights organizations. But ours was no mean struggle. We had opposition even in prison where those who feared retribution, did not want us to send surreptitious messages about our subhuman living conditions to human rights organizations. For example, the prison prefect I grew to respect, Alidi Disi, often privately told me off thus: "When you leave this dungeon you had better write down, for future generations, everything you are doing, thinking and quarrelling about in this prison, so that *this* does not happen to our children's children; but you are making my job as *Nyapala* (prison prefect) unbearable!" *And crocodiles are hungry at night* tries to fulfil Disi's hope, and claims special relevance to post-dictatorship Malawi.

After taking the reigns of power, democratically elected president Bakili Muluzi began to make significant changes to the social, political, economic and cultural life of Malawi. He began with the freedoms that Malawians had not known since independence. Trade unions and professional associations of lecturers, teachers, students, nurses, civil servants and other workers, were reinstated. The agents, informers and spies who roamed our lecture rooms, classrooms, hospitals, markets, churches, buses and bus stations, court rooms, taxis, public houses and work places, began to disappear. The censorship board was disassembled and academic freedom was becoming a reality. Students and staff in the university began to do research in areas that had been effectively proscribed by Banda and his cabal. The lawyers who had been largely impotent throughout Banda's rule began to regain and assert their control on what was legal and what was not. Almost everything that had been anathema throughout the thirty-three years of Banda's dictatorial rule was being redesigned. Muluzi even surprised many by taking advice from citizens with impeccable credentials; for instance, he listened to respected religious leaders, including the Catholic bishops whose pastoral letter effectively voted him into power.

Of course, the cynics among us were aware that anyone who had lived and worked under Banda's tyrannical regime would bring the changes that the people wanted; we suspected that rampant corruption would characterise any government after Banda's dictatorship; that the country's wealth once shared by Banda and his inner circle would be distributed amongst a wider web of new cronies; furthermore, we knew that taking over from Banda or any despot could not be an easy task. For most people the burden of corruption in high places seemed to have been softened by Muluzi's personal charm and the humour, which characterised his political rallies. And he left behind one precious legacy: freedom of speech, thought, action and association – he allowed people to criticise him without fear of arrest, imprisonment, deportation or death. When I returned home after six years of exile, I could not believe how free people were in the buses I took and the public houses I visited. Obviously, the situation was not perfect; and John Tembo, his nieces, nephews and the cronies they had scattered throughout the country, were still at large, trying to influence the course of events in the new dispensation, 'looking for another leader to bewitch and destroy as they had done to Banda', people said. In one 2001 edition of the *Daily Times* newspaper, even Dr Hetherwick Ntaba, who had been Banda's physician and knew the political manoeuvres of the 'self-styled royal family' surrounding president Banda warned that "Muluzi should watch out for Tembo," who would destroy his presidency.

I am publishing this memoir after more than twenty years of my incarceration, not because I want to take my revenge on Banda and his inner circle for permanently shattering my academic career. I left vengeance to the Lord, who knows my opponents better than I do. Nor do I want to be a spoiler when most Malawians are intent on forgetting the past in order to move on. This memoir is not meant just to make my verse more accessible either, filling the gaps for readers of my poetry. I merely want to remind my compatriots that we should not allow ourselves to revert to the brutal days of Banda and his Kadzamira-Tembo cabal, when we lived in fear of everything and everybody including our own shadows, and when the only life that mattered was that of the president, his relatives and the coven around him; and more importantly, when the lives of the rest of us were considered worthless to them.

The history of the nation perhaps needs to be sketched again and again, if only to underscore the fact that the past is embedded in the present, which in turn is embedded in the future – and that the three times are inseparable. All ethnic communities in the three regions of Nyasaland Protectorate supported John Chilembwe's uprising against the British in 1915. From that uprising Nyasaland African Congress was born, principally to fight for an African voice in the Nyasaland Legislative Council – a move that was supported by the ethnic communities in the three regions. Henry Masauko Chipembere, Kanyama Chiume, Dunduzu Kaluli Chisiza and other radical members of the Nyasaland African Congress invited Dr Hastings Kamuzu Banda from abroad to help them break up the Central African Federation and gain Nyasaland Protectorate self-rule and independence. Banda arrived in 1958. The struggle for self-rule, supported by all ethnic communities in the country, began in earnest. Many Malawians fought and died for us to be free. The British declared a state of emergency in 1959. Dr Banda and other nationalists were arrested and dumped in prisons in the then Southern Rhodesia and at Kanjedza Detention Centre in Limbe Township. Before their release the Malawi Congress Party was born. Eventually, the Central African Federation broke up and Nyasaland Protectorate became Malawi. These events were possible because the ethnic communities in the country's three regions were united against the British and the Central African Federation. And when Banda's autocratic regime fell and multiparty politics introduced, it was primarily because the ethnic communities in the three regions voted unanimously for political change. No region, no district, no ethnic community, no individual can claim to have done more than others – everybody was crying out for a unified Malawi.

This narrative is, therefore, a warning that future leaders should avoid treading the despotic and corrupt paths of the past. If it reads like an alternative history of the nation seen through the lens of my prison, I make no apologies. It is my turn to tell the truth without fear. It is my human right. I hope the ideas and controversy the memoir generates will eventually bring some good to my country. We have suffered and endured so much to get here – from John Chilembe's uprising against the British in 1915 to the present – I beg our political leaders, to spare us the violence, injustices and siege mentality that characterised Banda's regime and please give us the peace and freedom we have been crying out for these years.

Jack Mapanje,
York St John University, UK
30th April 2011.

Other Books by Jack Mapanje

Beasts of Nalunga, 2007, Bloodaxe Books, UK; shortlisted for the UK's Forward Award for best poetry collection in 2007.

The Last of the Sweet Bananas – New & Selected Poems, 2004, Bloodaxe Books, UK.

Gathering Seaweed: African Prison Writing, edited with an Introduction, 2002, Heinemann Educational Books, Oxford, UK.

The African Writers' Handbook, 1999, African Books Collective, Oxford, UK (co-edited with James Gibbs).

Skipping Without Ropes, Poems, 1998, Bloodaxe Books, UK.

The Chattering Wagtails of Mikuyu Prison, Poems, 1993, Heinemann Educational Books, Oxford, UK.

Oral Poetry from Africa: An Anthology, 1983, Longman, UK (co-edited with Landweg White).

Summer Fires: New Poetry of Africa, 1983, Heinemann Educational Books, Oxford, UK (co-edited with Angus Calder & Cosmo Pieterse).

Of Chameleons and Gods, Poems, 1981, Heinemann Educational Books, Oxford, UK.